$7
FIRST
EDITION
2014

COUNTY CLASS GUIDED MISSILE DESTROYERS

County Class
Guided Missile Destroyers

by

Neil McCart

Previous Page: HMS *London* at speed (*Ken Kelly Collection*)

© Maritime Books 2014

All rights reserved. No part of this publication may be reproduced, stored in a retrieval system, or transmitted, in any form, or by any means, electronic, mechanical, photocopying, recording or otherwise, without the prior written permission of the publisher and copyright holder. This publication contains public sector information licensed under the Open Government Licence v 1.0

First published in the United Kingdom in 2014 by Maritime Books, Lodge Hill, Liskeard, Cornwall, PL14 4EL

CONTENTS

Introduction	....	i
Chapter One	HMS *Devonshire* 1962-1978..	1
Chapter Two	HMS *Hampshire* 1963-1976	35
Chapter Three	HMS *Kent* 1963-1997...	59
Chapter Four	HMS *London* 1963-1982	89
Chapter Five	HMS *Fife* 1966-1987	123
Chapter Six	HMS *Glamorgan* 1966-1986	151
Chapter Seven	HMS *Norfolk* 1970-1982	195
Chapter Eight	HMS *Antrim* 1970-1984	217

APPENDICES

Appendix One	Sea Slug and HMS *Girdle Ness*	251
Appendix Two	Sea Cat..	257
Appendix Three	Exocet MM38	259
Appendix Four	County Class Technical Data...	261
Acknowledgements	....	263
Bibliography	....	265

INTRODUCTION

Those who were serving in the Royal Navy in the early 1960s will remember clearly the dramatic and significant introduction into service of the first of the County-class destroyers. Described in the press as 'Super Destroyers' they ushered in a revolutionary type of naval warfare, for they were the first warships to join the fleet armed with guided missiles – the Sea Slug, medium-range ship-to-air missile, and the Sea Cat, a short-range ship-to-air weapon. The large Sea Slug launching ramp was mounted on the quarterdeck, while the smaller Sea Cat launchers were sited abaft the after funnel.

Not only did the County-class destroyers carry revolutionary new weapons systems, but their appearance was without precedent. Their sleek, clean and streamlined design was quintessentially of the 1950s, not marred by scuttles in the ships' sides, and with their dome-topped funnels the hulls were designed to facilitate washing down with pre-wetting systems should they be required to steam through radioactive nuclear fallout.

In 1893 the first destroyers, or torpedo boat destroyers as they were originally known, were launched with a displacement tonnage of just 280, an overall length of 185 feet and a beam of 19 feet. Some 67 years later, when the first of the County-class destroyers was launched, all of which had a full load displacement of 6,200 tons, an overall length of just over 520 feet and a beam of 54 feet, there were many who boggled at their designation as destroyers for they were almost the size of light cruisers. The answer, it seems, lay in the fact that the term was applied in order to facilitate Treasury approval, for they were later rated as DLGs, from the American term 'Destroyer Leader - Guided Missile', which was a more accurate description. Three roles were envisaged for the new vessels: 1) Escort roles with a task group, including both anti-aircraft and anti-submarine duties. 2) Operations as part of a task unit of light forces with the ability to bombard shore installations in support of land forces, and to engage enemy surface units. 3) Policing duties in any part of the world, for in the 1960s Britain still had worldwide defence responsibilities for Crown Colonies and Protectorates; these would, however, be drastically reduced during the 25 years the class remained in Royal Navy service.

The story of the County-class destroyers goes back to April 1954, when a decision had to be made as to the type of guided-weapons ship to complete. The two alternatives put forward were either new construction, or conversion, for operational use in the early 1960s, which was the earliest date considered possible given the equipment provision, the design effort and ship-fitting capabilities. The 'secret' report submitted by the Director of Gunnery at the time described the advantages and disadvantages of the two alternatives. The policy of conversion would have been cheaper, but would have proved uneconomical in the long

run given the shorter remaining life-span of such ships. One serious possibility which was investigated in depth was the conversion of the battleship *Vanguard* or one of the King George V-class battleships as guided weapons ships, with a twin Sea Slug launcher at the after end. The arguments given at the time read thus: 'Although the time required for the conversion of, say *Vanguard*, could be expected to be sensibly shorter than that required to build new ships, the effort and cost of the former would be a substantial part of that for the latter, and the short remaining life might balance any saving.' The report also went on to state: 'The expense of operating a conversion such as the *Vanguard*, and her potential as a fleet flagship, may militate against her employment for all the tactical investigations inevitably required of the first operational GW ship.'

In the event the idea of converting one of the battleships, or indeed cruisers, was dropped and the new guided weapons ships were to be built ab initio. They were described at the time as the 'small guided weapons ships' and to reduce production costs there would be a Sea Slug launcher at one end only as well as two twin-Bofors mountings, which in the event were replaced by Sea Cat. It was clear that the ships would, for their size, carry a large complement and initial estimates were that at least 500 officers and men would be required to man a ship of 28+ knots, proved to be an accurate assessment. As to the Sea Slug itself, the requirements were that: 'To make optimum use of a launcher ideally it should be served by two Directors and control systems. With such an arrangement the launcher can be switched alternately between Directors and a second salvo launched and another target engaged while the first Director is still guiding the first salvo to its target.'

The controversial Sea Slug guided missiles, designed by Armstrong Whitworth which later became part of Hawker Siddeley, had been developed at the Australian missile range at Woomera and on board the trials ship *Girdle Ness* in the Mediterranean over a period of at least seven years and were large, cumbersome weapons powered by a sustainer motor and four boosters which jettisoned after propelling the missile to supersonic speed. On board ship they were brought up from the missile magazine forward and run aft through a tunnel, with the small wings and fins being fitted and assembled within the superstructure, after which the missiles slid out through ports into the launcher. They were powered by solid fuel with wraparound launch boosters attached before the weapons arrived on the complex quarterdeck twin launcher. Guidance was provided with a radar beam from the large Type 901 'searchlight' radar aerial and the Type 965 air-search radar. Such was the size of these missiles that the ships were essentially built round the requirements of Sea Slug.

Helicopters had been assuming a role of increasing importance during the mid to late 1950s and this was immediately apparent in the County-class ships, with the large flight deck and hangar situated at the after end of the upper deck for operating a Westland Wessex HAS1 helicopter fitted out as a submarine 'hunter killer', equipped with dipping Asdic and armed with anti-submarine homing torpedoes. The facilities in the hangar, however, were limited and may possibly have been an 'afterthought', situated as it was forward of the large Type 901 radar fitting, which meant that the Wessex helicopters had to be manhandled along a narrow deck space on the port side of the ship to an awkwardly placed side door.

In addition to their guided missiles the County-class destroyers were armed with two dual 4.5-inch, radar controlled, dual-purpose, quick-firing guns in Mark 6 mountings, for defence against air attack, and for surface actions against enemy warships. This gave them the ability to bombard shore installations in support of land forces, a duty which, in the early 1980s during the campaign to liberate the Falkland Islands, two ships of the class would be called upon to perform.

The County-class destroyers were, with the Tribal-class frigates, the first large warships to incorporate combined steam and gas turbine propulsion (COSAG), with machinery plants which were exceptionally light and compact enabling the amount of fighting equipment to be increased. The main machinery instal-

lation was of a novel type with steam and gas turbines geared to the same propeller shaft. Both of the twin shafts consisted of a high-pressure English Electric (AE1) steam turbine of 15,000 SHP, plus two G6 gas turbines each of 7,500 SHP, giving a maximum speed of 32.5 knots. Steam for the main turbines was provided by two Babcock & Wilcox superheat boilers. The Metrovick G6 gas turbines provided a high concentration of power and were used to supplement the steam power for high-speed manoeuvring. Just as importantly they were also able to develop their full power from cold within a few minutes, providing an unprecedented mobility and enabling a ship lying in harbour without steam to get under way instantly in an emergency.

The living accommodation for both officers and ratings set new standards, with air-conditioning throughout and, for the first time in a Royal Navy warship, gone were hammocks and all personnel had their own bunks. Gone too were meals taken on messdecks, often after a long and precarious walk in heavy seas carrying one's pressed metal tray of food from the galley servery to the messdeck, and often having to dodge swinging hammocks while eating. For the first time in a major warship large dining halls were provided for both senior and junior rates, and these were capable of providing varied meals on the self-service cafeteria system. The facilities also included a sickbay and operating theatre, a dental surgery, a NAAFI kiosk, a 24-hour laundry service and even a small TV studio which enabled a ship to provide internally produced programmes. In the words of Admiral Sir Frank Twiss: 'At last we were getting to a state where to live on board a small ship, a destroyer compared to the old battleships, was much more pleasant than it had ever been before.'

Like light cruisers, these destroyers had a large complement of 33 officers and 407 ratings, many of whom were technicians, and the ships would make great demands on the Navy's manpower at a time, in the 1960s, 1970s and 1980s, when recruiting was difficult. The fact that the eight ships were so expensive to man and maintain, combined with the diminishing value of the Sea Slug missile, led to the withdrawal of the first four ships during the mid-1970s. With their excellent command facilities it was intended that the four later vessels would remain in Royal Navy service until the late 1980s, and indeed two ships of the class played a vital role during the campaign to recapture the Falkland Islands in 1982. However, it was not enemy action which brought about their early demise but, as so often has been the case in post-war Britain, it was the 'friendly fire' of Treasury spending cuts and the notorious Defence Spending Review of 1981 which was responsible for them being withdrawn early and sold to the Chilean Navy, where they had a successful second career.

Many ex-Royal Naval personnel and, indeed, some of those who are still serving, will remember with nostalgia and pride the time they spent in the County-class destroyers.

Neil McCart
Cheltenham, December 2014

Chapter One

HMS Devonshire
1962-1978

The launch of the first County-class destroyer, HMS *Devonshire*, at Birkenhead on 10 June 1960.
(Williamson Art Gallery & Museum, Birkenhead)

Cruisers or Destroyers? It was a question which appeared to vex the Admiralty, during the seven years between planning and commissioning, for although the County-class destroyers were very much icons of the 1960s their origins go back to the mid-1950s. They were designed specifically around the Armstrong Whitworth Sea Slug surface-to-air missile, which itself had been under development since 1949. The first hint of these new warships came in an announcement to Parliament in February 1955 and in the following year it was announced that '...a new type of cruiser is being designed with an anti-aircraft guided weapon. It has been found possible to greatly increase the fighting power of the two new fleet escorts with a guided weapon instead of anti-aircraft guns. They will also carry very modern anti-submarine equipment.' Although the announcement had mentioned only two ships, the 1955/1956 Naval Estimates provided for four 'guided weapon ships'. Following these brief and tantalising statements little more was heard of the new ships until the summer of 1957 when the First Lord of the Admiralty, who was in Birkenhead for the renaming and handing over to the Indian Navy of the cruiser HMS *Nigeria* as INS *Mysore*, announced that the order for the first 'guided missile destroyer' had been placed with Cammell Laird & Company at Birkenhead. By February 1958 trial firings of the Sea Slug from HMS *Girdle Ness* had achieved a marked degree of success and even at that stage there was speculation as to whether the missile could be developed as a ship-to-ship weapon. Amid the news of the Defence budget being reduced by

 County Class GMDs

8 July 1961 and *Devonshire* is still alongside her fitting-out berth. She is taking shape, but it would be another eight months before she would be ready for sea trials.
(Williamson Art Gallery & Museum, Birkenhead)

HMS Devonshire

some £15½ million came the announcement that four 'guided missile destroyers' had been ordered and '... to reflect their importance as "cruisers" rather than destroyers, it is proposed to revive the famous County-class names'. It seemed that in order to obtain Treasury approval the designation of cruiser had been forced to give way to destroyer.

At the time the order was placed it became known that the first ship of the new County-class would be *Devonshire*, a name which had been in use in the Royal Navy almost continuously since 1692, the first having been a third rate, 80-gun ship sunk by the French off the Lizard in 1707; the last was a 10,000-ton cruiser which, in December 1954, after a distinguished 27-year career, was sold for scrap. It was an indication of the importance attached to the new class of ships. Despite the fact that the order had been placed with Cammell Laird in the summer of 1957 it was 9 March 1959 before the first keel plates were laid on the slipway at Birkenhead and a few days later the first key naval personnel, under the command of Cdr (E) K. B. Birkett, travelled north to stand by the ship as she took shape.

Although Cammell Laird was to suffer from industrial unrest during the early 1960s, building work on *Devonshire* was not seriously interrupted and by the summer of 1960 she was ready to be launched. To emphasise the importance of the new ships to the Navy the sponsors of the first four would be members of the royal family. *Devonshire*'s was fixed for Friday 10 June 1960, with Princess Alexandra having agreed to perform the ceremony. The day itself dawned sunny and bright and at the shipyard *Devonshire*'s hull, having been given a fresh coat of grey paint, looked spick and span for the occasion. The royal party arrived at the shipyard at 1030 for an official reception and at 1200 exactly, after a religious service conducted by the Bishop of Chester, Princess Alexandra triggered the switch which broke a bottle of wine against the bow and sent the destroyer down the slipway into the River Mersey, where tugs were waiting to tow her into the fitting-out berth. In his speech following the launching ceremony the First Lord of the Admiralty Lord Carrington pointed out that although *Devonshire* and her sisters were referred to as guided missile destroyers they were '...much bigger than any destroyers we have known before.' He went on to outline their primary role, which would be to '...provide anti-aircraft defence for a task group of ships in war; but they will be equipped for the variety of tasks which the Royal Navy have to tackle in the uneasy conditions which pass as peacetime today.' Ironically, some 22 years later Carrington would be forced to resign for being unprepared for war. In his speech to the guests in the Board Room of Cammell Laird and Co, the chairman Admiral Sir Michael Denny summed up the feelings of many when he said: 'I cannot understand why *Devonshire* is classified as a destroyer. As an ex-Admiral my career happened to coincide with the Dreadnought era from the *Dreadnought* to *Vanguard* and in this era a destroyer was something of a pipsqueak. This is not what the *Devonshire* is. I suggest that the Admiralty might think of another name'. Even as Admiral Denny was speaking *Devonshire* was being secured alongside her fitting-out berth.

During the months which followed her launch the advance party of naval personnel standing by the ship grew steadily and from their offices close to the main gate of the shipyard they were able to watch the progress of work. On 8 January 1962, the ship's first commanding officer, Captain P. N. Howes DSC RN, joined and within weeks he had some 30 officers and 140 ratings standing by the ship. One member of the ship's company at Birkenhead remembers: 'On board work went on steadily, as did the forecasted dates for sea trials and commissioning. For each compartment on board meetings were held to discuss and finalise drawings, then a "lineout inspection" was carried out by the appropriate experts, when all the fittings were marked in the empty shell. How much more space there appeared to be in the empty messdecks. Next came the progress inspections when the larger fittings and electrics were installed and inevitably a few alterations were made, often at the instigation of the advance party. Eventually the final inspection was carried out. At last, in March 1962, the ship

County Class GMDs

was ready for Contractor's Sea Trials and these started with two days anchored off the Mersey before continuing for three fortnightly periods in the Clyde. Accommodation on board was limited, so only portions of the advance party could be on board at any one time. The trials themselves were most impressive - you don't often see your ship at full power astern for four hours, or see her being forcibly rolled to over 27 degrees. It was unusual, too, to see the ship being run on Merchant Service lines - but we were impressed by the food, which was rumoured to have cost four times the "pussers" victualling allowance.' The trials included test firings of the Sea Slug missile and they continued well into May, before the ship returned to Birkenhead.

Having completed her initial trials *Devonshire* returned to the fitting-out basin for the builders to complete their work. Originally it had been intended that the ship would commission in late October 1962, but in the event a painters' strike at the shipyard caused a two-week delay and it was Tuesday 13 November before the Commodore Superintendent Contract Built Ships made his final inspection. The advance party then moved on board, some of whom had watched for over two years as she took shape on the slipway and in the fitting-our berth. Next morning the main draft of the ship's company, consisting of some 250 officers and men arrived on board, having travelled from Portsmouth in two special overnight trains. As they arrived at the dockside they were guided round the destroyer by members of the advance party and soon afterwards the task of storing ship began in earnest. The climax of a very busy week came at 1045 on Thursday 15 November 1962, a cold winter's day with a bitter north-easterly wind blowing across the shipyard. Led by the Royal Marines Band, the ship's company marched onto the jetty where Admiral of the Fleet Earl Mountbatten took the salute and the Commissioning Warrant was read by Captain Howes. Finally, as the band played the national anthem the White Ensign was hoisted at the ensign staff for the first time.

Two days after commissioning, with the ship still in the hands of Cammell Laird, whose representa-

tives were aboard, *Devonshire* left Birkenhead for what should have been a short full-power trial, but with heavy seas and gale force winds it was clear that it would not be possible to carry out the evolutions in the Irish Sea and so she steamed north to the more sheltered waters of the Clyde. It was said that Cammell Laird's staff, who were squeezed into the most unlikely places, long remembered their very uncomfortable night on board during their cruise. Finally, however, at 0421 on 18 November 1962, in a position Lat 55°34'N/Long 04°57'W, off the town of Troon in the Firth of Clyde, Captain Howes officially accepted *Devonshire* from Cammell Laird and Co. Three hours later, off Greenock, the reluctant passengers were disembarked.

With the civilians safely ashore *Devonshire*'s ship's company could begin the shake down process in the Clyde area. After a weekend at anchor off Greenock she steamed south and during the forenoon of 22 November, off the south coast, she rendezvoused with a Whirlwind helicopter to begin deck landing trials, which continued for a week before she made her way along the south coast, calling briefly at Plymouth Sound and Torquay before, finally, on 1 December, she arrived at Portland. There she carried out four days of trials on a day-running basis. By 5 December the ship had arrived off the Isle of Wight to embark a trials party for a further 48 hours at sea. Finally, during the afternoon of 7 December she steamed up harbour to secure alongside Portsmouth Dockyard's Middle Slip Jetty.

The winter months of 1962/63 were bitterly cold throughout Britain and the scene in Portsmouth Harbour, with ice forming on the water, somewhat resembled the Arctic. For *Devonshire*'s ship's company there was seasonal leave and despite the weather *Devonshire* herself was a great attraction and, in the words of one officer; 'A great deal of interest was shown in our shiny new ship and every day brought some party of visitors to pry, or just to tell us that she didn't look much like the last *Devonshire*. The brass didn't leave us alone either and by the time we sailed for further trials the "Admiral Tote" which was being kept in the opera-

HMS Devonshire

HMS *Devonshire* undergoes her contractor's sea trials. This photograph, taken in the spring of 1962, gives an excellent view of her Sea Slug launcher and Type 901 radar aerial. At this stage her Sea Cat missile launchers have not been fitted. *(Williamson Art Gallery & Museum, Birkenhead)*

HMS *Devonshire* manoeuvring at speed during her sea trials. *(Syd Goodman Collection)*

tions room showed that we had been visited by 13 officers of flag rank.' As the 'first of class' *Devonshire* would undergo a further three months of trials and each phase entailed the embarkation of a different trials party, from engineers and Fleet Air Arm personnel, to scientists who were interested only in the guided weapons systems. On 16 January 1963 the ship left Portsmouth to carry out further machinery and flying trials, most of which took place in the Channel between the Isle of Wight and Portland, but in mid-February she paid a short visit to Devonport. In early March the ship entered the final phase of her trials, this time operating off the coast of Wales and the missile testing range at Aberporth in Cardigan Bay. On 7 March, in the words of one ship's company member: 'Most of us for the first time heard the noise which sounded like cloth being torn which was, in fact, the noise made by the Sea Slug being fired.' By 18 March the firings at Aberporth had been completed successfully and two days later the destroyer returned to Portsmouth to prepare for the next stage of her commission.

On Monday 1 April 1963, having replenished her stores, *Devonshire* left Portsmouth to set course for Gibraltar where she spent a weekend before steaming east through the Mediterranean to Malta. Although she had completed her acceptance trials the ship still had to undergo a long series of machinery trials, which would follow a four-day visit to Barcelona and a period of self-maintenance in Marsamxett Harbour, Malta, alongside the repair ship *Ausonia*. Once again *Devonshire* proved to be a star attraction and she received a steady stream of VIP visitors, from the C-in-C downwards. On 6 May, however, she sailed to begin her machinery trials, including a brief period operating with the fleet carrier *Ark Royal*, which was on her way to join the Far East Fleet. On 20 May *Devonshire* suffered machinery problems and next day she returned to Malta to secure alongside *Ausonia* for eight days of repairs. Then on 29 May when she put

On 22 November 1962 *Devonshire* arrived in Plymouth Sound for the first time. Here she refuels from RFA *Birchol* and as soon as this was completed she sailed for Falmouth Bay to begin trials. *(World Ship Society)*

HMS Devonshire

During the afternoon of 26 April 1963 *Devonshire* arrived at Malta for the first time to undergo maintenance alongside the depot ship *Ausonia*. This rare photograph shows her approaching *Ausonia* alongside Manoel Island.
(Michael Cassar)

to sea again it was to set course for Portsmouth to undergo a further 11-week period of dockyard-assisted maintenance and dry docking.

On 29 August 1963, with her main propulsion machinery having been thoroughly overhauled, *Devonshire* put to sea for a busy programme of main machinery trials, anti-submarine exercises with *Talent* and more missile firings at the Aberporth ranges. Finally, on 24 September, having collected a Royal Marines Band at Portsmouth and replenished a full outfit of missiles at Devonport, the destroyer left Plymouth Sound to set course westwards into the Atlantic Ocean, bound for Bermuda and the United States. *Devonshire* had been chosen to make an official visit to Philadelphia as part of 'Exposition Britannia', a large trade fair which lasted for three weeks and was intended to encourage American interest in Britain and the sale of British goods by highlighting various aspects and achievements of British life. Also on the ship's itinerary was a visit to Washington DC, where she would manoeuvre up the Potomac River to the US Naval Base just outside the city.

After an uneventful but busy ten days at sea, during which the opportunity was taken to exercise with RFA *Wave Ruler*, which was accompanying her during the deployment, *Devonshire* arrived at Bermuda where she secured alongside the jetty on Hamilton seafront; during the four-day visit the ship's paintwork was touched up before she sailed for Philadelphia. Two days after leaving Bermuda *Devonshire* anchored in Delaware Bay and during the morning of 11 October she began the four-hour passage up the Delaware River to secure alongside Philadelphia's No 4 jetty. During her five days in the city the ship was opened to the public as well as taking a major role in the ceremonies connected with the British trade fare. The ship's company marched through the city centre, first to the City Hall where there was a welcoming address, before the Freedom of the City was granted. From City Hall, with the Royal Marines Band leading the way, the ship's company marched past enthusiastic crowds to Wanamaker's Department Store, whose windows and counters featured a wide range of British goods and where the British Ambassador to the USA officially opened the exhibition. For the ship's company it was a very busy few days, with over 15,000 invitations to social and sporting functions, which even included cricket matches with local sides.

During the afternoon of 16 October *Devonshire* left Philadelphia to steam back downriver to the Delaware-Chesapeake Canal, which connects the Delaware River and Chesapeake Bay, and during the forenoon of the next day she sailed through the canal to anchor in the bay. Later that afternoon she negotiated the lower reaches of the Potomac River, and soon after passing under the Potomac Bridge she anchored for the night off Quantico. Finally, during the morning watch on 18 October, *Devonshire* weighed anchor to make the final leg of

HMS *Devonshire* fires a Sea Slug missile. (*Crown Copyright/MoD*)

her passage and secure alongside a pier at Washington's Navy Yard. Once again during the five days that the ship spent in the city the hospitality was overwhelming, and on the two afternoons when her gangways were opened to the public some 12,000 people took the opportunity to look round. Leaving Washington during the forenoon of 23 October *Devonshire* retraced her course back downriver into Chesapeake Bay and after another night at anchor, during the following afternoon she entered the US Naval Base at Norfolk, Virginia. This time her stay lasted for less than 24 hours and during the forenoon of 25 October she left US waters to steam south for the Caribbean where for several days she carried out machinery trials. Six days after leaving Norfolk and having taken a detour to avoid the edge of a hurricane, *Devonshire* arrived at the Dutch island of Curacao where she put into Willemstad's New Harbour which, after the hectic days spent in US cities, proved to be more relaxing.

From Curacao *Devonshire* was scheduled to continue her machinery trials, combining them with a cruise to various Caribbean ports. However, two days out of Willemstad, during the evening of 6 November, she suffered a total power failure which took the engineers over two hours to rectify. At the time the ship was en route to San Juan, Puerto Rico, to undergo a 17-day maintenance period, which gave the opportunity for a full inspection. *Devonshire* left San Juan on 23 November to continue her trials, which were combined with weapons training and banyan beach outings at Bequia and Dominica. The ship's final port of call was Bridgetown, Barbados, where she arrived on the last day of November for a weekend visit. Finally on Monday 2 December, in company with *Wave Ruler*, *Devonshire* set course for home. Originally it had been intended that she would call at Palmas de Gran Canaria, but this was cancelled and at 0730 on

HMS Devonshire

Friday 13 December, a week earlier than scheduled, she anchored at Spithead. Three hours later she secured alongside Portsmouth's Fountain Lake Jetty.

During her four weeks alongside at Portsmouth *Devonshire* underwent some much-needed dockyard-assisted maintenance and the ship's company enjoyed some welcome leave, but by mid-January 1964 the ship was ready for sea again. After two days exercising off Portland she joined other ships of the Home Fleet, including her sister *Hampshire, Hermes, Leander* and *Llandaff*, for anti-submarine exercises in the South West Approaches. On the last day of January she returned to Portsmouth for further maintenance and it was early March before she put to sea again. On Friday 6 March, at Portland, she hoisted the flag of the C-in-C Home Fleet, Admiral Sir Charles Madden, who joined the ship for a NATO exercise code-named 'Magic Lantern' which, once again, saw *Devonshire* in the South West Approaches and the Western Atlantic. On conclusion of the first phase of the exercises *Devonshire* led the NATO fleet up the River Tagus to Lisbon for a long weekend visit. During her stay in the Portuguese capital another trials team was embarked, this time to carry out sea-worthiness trials which one member of the ship's company remembers thus: 'They had been carefully planned to destroy any feeling of well being. For almost two weeks we steamed into Atlantic waters just south of the Azores where, assisted by heavy seas, the ship was put through a programme of continuous heavy rolling.' However, by the end of March, with the weather having moderated it became more difficult to achieve the severe rolling, and *Devonshire* returned to Portsmouth Harbour.

On 26 April 1964, when *Devonshire* sailed on the final leg of the commission, she set course once again for the Caribbean. This time the transatlantic passage was broken by a short stop at Madeira where she disembarked another trials team, before continuing her passage to Bridgetown, Barbados and then on to the US Navy's missile firing ranges at Roosevelt Roads, Puerto Rico, where she took part in joint manoeuvres with US ships. At 1000 on Saturday 16 May there was a change of command when Captain David Williams RN arrived on board, just in time to witness a series of Sea Slug missile firings, and three days later, at 0900 on 20 May when the ship was at anchor off St Thomas, he took

Entering Portsmouth Harbour in March 1964 after exercises in the Atlantic Ocean.
(Maritime Photo Library)

Manoeuvring at speed. *(Crown Copyright/MoD)*

over from Howes who left by helicopter. After leaving St Thomas *Devonshire* carried out a cruise in the Caribbean area calling at St Vincent and Trinidad, but a proposed visit to British Guiana was cancelled. On 7 June she set course for Gibraltar, but en route was ordered to return direct to Portsmouth and nine days later she arrived alongside Fountain Lake Jetty to undergo a short maintenance period before participating with other Home Fleet ships in the 'Sea Days 64' displays in the Channel. These consisted of various demonstrations for senior officers from all three Services as well as MPs, but they were marred slightly by a collision between the destroyer *Diamond* and the frigate *Salisbury*. Later in July, after a period of maintenance, *Devonshire* made an official visit to Oslo before returning to Portsmouth in early August. The ship's final duty of the commission was to undergo shock trials at Spithead, which took place between 10 and 17 August. These entailed being secured to buoys before underwater mines were detonated at varying distances from the hull. By the evening of 17 August, however, with the trials completed, *Devonshire* returned to Portsmouth Harbour and within days she had paid off. It was the end of her first commission.

Although an eight-month refit lay ahead, *Devonshire*'s second commission officially began

HMS Devonshire

in September 1964 with an advance party living on board in very uncomfortable conditions. This was the first long refit carried out on a County-class guided missile destroyer and for both the dockyard personnel and the ship's own engineers it was fraught with difficulty as they coped with new and unforeseen technical problems. One of the most demanding of these involved the removal and replacement of the gas turbine engines, which meant cutting holes in a number of deck heads in order to lift them out. As one member of the ship's company remembers: 'The refit was officially classified as a "clean refit", but what that meant remained a mystery. Admittedly it did start with all tiled decks being covered by hardboard, and bulkheads being "wall papered" with polythene, but large pieces of machinery still managed to end up emptying quantities of thick oil in the canteen flat, which then seemed to seep everywhere. The portable air compressor on the flight deck was in the habit of "walking about" and at frequent intervals disgorging dirty oil and water. However, we managed and domestic services continued to be provided on a limited scale. We all got to know our jobs on board and, most importantly, the rum queue sorted itself out into its correct order of precedence.'

By the end of February 1965 *Devonshire*'s refit had been completed and on 1 March, after a final inspection, she left Portsmouth to carry out post-refit trials in the Channel, during which, as one member of the ship's company remembers: 'Damage control exercises reared their ugly head, full-power trials were successfully accomplished, we had a fire in the boiler room, the butcher locked himself in the fridge, the after heads were blocked and we had our first water shortage.' She then steamed north to Rosyth and on 8 April, after her final post-refit inspection by the C-in-C Portsmouth, the ship was once again declared 'operational', which meant she could proceed to Portland and introduce herself to the Flag Officer Sea Training for a brief insight into the rigours of the work-up, before returning to Portsmouth for seasonal leave.

Following this *Devonshire* steamed round to Cardigan Bay and the Aberporth missile range where she successfully fired both Sea Slug and Sea Cat missiles. A call at Devonport was needed for the repair of missile loading equipment, and at this point she hoisted the flag of the C-in-C Plymouth before steaming north to the River Mersey to lead the 20th Anniversary celebrations of the ending of the Battle of the Atlantic. During her stay in Liverpool the ship's ceremonial guard was put through its paces and a platoon of the seamen marched through the city to an enthusiastic reception by the local people which, that same weekend, was matched only by the welcome accorded to Liverpool City Football Club when they brought the FA Cup to the city.

After leaving Liverpool a brief stop was made at Devonport to replenish the missile stock before *Devonshire* presented herself at Portland to the 'tender mercies' of FOST's staff. The ship's arduous work-up in the Channel and Lyme Bay was broken by a weekend at Torquay and on completion a Families Day was held, followed on Friday 16 July by the Commissioning Ceremony at Portsmouth. The first 12 months of *Devonshire*'s second commission were to be spent on the Far East Station, based at Singapore, where the fleet had been built up to an unprecedented strength in response to the Indonesian Government's implacable opposition to the British-sponsored Federation of Malaysia, which had united the former Colonies and Protectorates in the area. The new Federation consisted of Malaya, Singapore, North Borneo (Sabah) and Sarawak and it was the inclusion of the latter two which had infuriated the Indonesian Government. The Confrontation with Indonesia had begun with a rebellion in December 1962 in the small, oil-rich State of Brunei, which had not actually been included in the Malaysian Federation, but no sooner had that initial rebellion been dealt with than Confrontation with Indonesia began.

As far as the Navy was concerned the two commando carriers *Albion* and *Bulwark*, together with their helicopter squadrons and Royal Marines, would form the spearhead for operations against

both Indonesian guerrillas and regular soldiers who infiltrated Sabah and Sarawak, but the Indonesian Navy had some powerful ships, particularly the ex-Soviet cruiser *Ordzhonikidze*[1], which had been renamed *Irian*, as well as five former Soviet Skoryy Class destroyers and an assorted collection of older frigates. To counter the threat posed by this force and to patrol the long Malaysian coastline, it was necessary to build up the Navy's Far East Fleet and *Devonshire* was to form part of what would be the largest British fleet ever to be stationed at Singapore since the opening of the Naval Base in 1938.

At 1845 on 15 July 1965 the ship's Flight arrived from Portland and seven days later, after a 48-hour delay due to a defective condenser, *Devonshire* slipped her moorings at South Railway Jetty and steamed out of Portsmouth Harbour to farewells from relatives and friends gathered on the Round Tower and along the seafront at Old Portsmouth. After a calm and sunny passage to Gibraltar the destroyer steamed into the Mediterranean where a proposed visit to Athens was cancelled due to civil unrest and Naples was substituted. After her south-bound transit of the Suez Canal she steamed to Aden where, on 7 August, she relieved her sister *London* to become the Navy's guided missile destroyer on the Far East Station. During the short stay at Aden a laundry crew was transferred from *London* and six students who were homeward bound to their homes on the island of Socotra were embarked as passengers.

After leaving Aden *Devonshire*'s passage east was made via Gan and Socotra, with a full Crossing the Line ceremony taking place in the Indian Ocean, and she arrived in the Singapore Naval Base in late August. Soon after her arrival on station she took part in the fleet exercise 'Guard Rail' in the South China Sea, before steaming on to Hong Kong to prepare for an official visit to Japan. During her stay in Hong Kong the colony was battered by the particularly fierce Typhoon Rose, during which *Devonshire* was ordered to sea to spend a rough 24 hours circumnavigating the fringes of the storm. During her visit to Japan the destroyer flew the flag of Vice-Admiral H. M. Norton, Flag Officer, Second-in-Command, Far East Station (FO2), and it was timed to coincide with a two-week British Exhibition of Trade and Culture, which was billed as the biggest of its kind in Asia. Among the attractions were the Regimental Band of the Argyll and Sutherland Highlanders, and a red double-decker London bus. The destroyer reached Tokyo on 17 September, but no sooner had she arrived alongside, just a few hours before the opening of the Trade Fair, than she had to sail again to ride out Typhoon Trix in Tokyo Bay, along with approximately 300 other vessels. *Devonshire* was able to anchor in the relatively shallow waters of Tokyo Bay, one member of the ship's company remembering, '...an exciting night with wind speeds exceeding 80 knots at times and during which 270 orders were rung down on the engine room telegraph.' Fortunately, after 24 hours the storm had subsided and *Devonshire* was able to return to her berth in the city. Our ship's company member takes up the story once again: 'Those in the know went to Yokohama for their runs ashore and the Peanut Bar appeared to hold a *Devonshire* reunion on most evenings. As the days passed the runs ashore moved from the Ginza area to the outlying districts of Shibuya-ku and Shinjuko-ku and never were so many health spa baths taken by so many men in such a short time. Sightseeing tours of Tokyo were popular too, as was a special trip on board a replica Japanese pirate ship which ferried men across Tokyo Bay to the Funabashi Centre, a big amusement park where they mingled with over 50,000 Japanese holiday-makers and enjoyed free refreshments and entertainment, which included go-kart races against Japanese teams.' During the stay *Devonshire* was visited by her royal sponsor who was in Japan for the exhibition.

On leaving Tokyo *Devonshire* steamed into her third typhoon, but despite this she arrived back in Hong Kong on schedule on 1 October. Her return,

---

[1] *Ordzhonikidze* had hit the world headlines in May 1956 when, during a visit to Portsmouth, the ex-naval diver Cdr Lionel "Buster" Crabb RNR had gone missing while attempting to inspect the Soviet cruiser's underwater hull.

HMS Devonshire

HMS *Devonshire* refuels from RFA *Wave Ruler*. *(Ken Kelly Collection)*

HMS *Devonshire* and her sister ship *Kent* at sea together *(Ken Kelly Collection)*

County Class GMDs

November 1965 and *Devonshire* closes RFA *Regent* during Exercise Ocean Safari in the North Sea.
(George Mortimore, Action Photos)

however, was limited to just a few days, for during a routine inspection of the underwater hull the ship's divers discovered serious damage to one of the propeller shaft bearings; after temporary repairs *Devonshire* sailed for Singapore where she underwent a period of dry docking.

On Sunday 7 November, with her post-docking trials over, *Devonshire* once again hoisted the flag of FOF2, FES, this time, Vice-Admiral P. J. Hill-Norton, and set course south for Australian waters, where she would lead the Royal Navy's contribution to 'Exercise Warrior', which also involved Australian, New Zealand and US Navy ships. It had been known for some weeks that *Devonshire* would take part in the manoeuvres and the Royal Navy's task group was to have been led by *Ark Royal*, but in late October a boiler room fire on board the aircraft carrier meant that she had to be withdrawn and *Devonshire* took over as the flagship of a force which also included *Barossa*, *Euryalus*, *Whitby* and the RFAs *Fort Duquesne* and *Fort Langley*. The main exercise began in the Coral Sea and continued as the ships made their way towards the east coast of Australia. Once again our ship's company mem-

ber takes up the story: 'Having crossed the equator, stirred the Christmas pudding and sent off all our Christmas cards we settled down to "Exercise Warrior". This was being fought out between Capitalist Blue Force led by Mr Frenzies and the People's Democratic Republic Orange Force led by Dr Meccano. During the exercise, as we gradually made our way southwards, we in *Devonshire* featured for both sides.' On 26 November, almost three weeks after leaving Singapore, the participating ships formed up outside Sydney Harbour to be led by *Devonshire* through the Heads, under the Harbour Bridge and round Cockatoo Island to their berths in Woolloomooloo Bay. Most members of the destroyer's ship's company will remember the tremendous hospitality shown by the people of Sydney and visitors to the ship included the touring MCC cricket team. Departure from Sydney came on 8 December, when *Devonshire* set course for Melbourne where two days later she arrived alongside Station Pier to find her new commanding officer, Captain Geoffrey C. Leslie RN, waiting to take over command. Once again the ship's company enjoyed the lavish hospitality of the local people

HMS Devonshire

before sailing again on 15 December, this time into strong winds and heavy seas to join *Euryalus* for the six-day passage to Fremantle where they were scheduled to join *Ark Royal*. Christmas Day was celebrated in sweltering temperatures and on 28 December when *Devonshire* sailed for Singapore, hundreds of newly made friends arrived to see the ship off. Our ship's company member remembers: 'The jetty and the harbour mole were packed with crowds all waving, some tearful, with car horns hooting and headlights flashing.'

The passage to Singapore was made in company with *Ark Royal* and *Devonshire* was able to exercise with the carrier in her true role as DLG and to the relief of most, FO2 and his staff transferred to the carrier, which eased the crowded conditions on board. At the stroke of midnight, which heralded in the new year, the two ships were in the Indian Ocean, close to the Cocos Islands. On her return to the naval base at Singapore *Devonshire* began a 'Docking and Essential Defects' refit period, but with the Far East Fleet now consisting of over 100 ships, shore accommodation at HMS *Terror* was in short supply. Most of the ship's company went ashore to the Royal Marines Barracks at Simbang, some six miles away from the naval base, with many officers setting up residence in various hotels on both Singapore Island and Johore Bahru.

It was early March 1966 when *Devonshire* put to sea again and having completed a week of trials she hoisted the flag of FOF2, Rear-Admiral C. P. Mills, and set course for the North Borneo coast to carry out a combined goodwill and operational cruise. The first stop was the port of Kuching where

An excellent view of *Devonshire* leaving port, with her ship's company manning ship and her Wessex helicopter on the flight deck. *(Crown Copyright/MoD)*

County Class GMDs

The County-class were large ships - *Devonshire* towers above this two storey warehouse.
(Ken Kelly Collection)

Devonshire became the largest ship to steam up the Sarawak River as far as Sejinkat, where she anchored for Admiral Mills to be flown ashore on official calls. From the Sarawak River the destroyer made her way to Labuan where 200 Army personnel were given a break from routine and taken for a day at sea, but unfortunately the visit was marred by the accidental death of a Petty Officer. The third port of call was Jesselton (Kota Kinabalu) where a children's party was held on board for a planned 80 guests, but in the event almost 300 youngsters turned up. In the best naval tradition everyone turned to with a will and all the orphans were catered for. The final ports of call were Sudat and Tawau and after leaving the latter a naval gunfire support exercise was carried out, the accuracy of which greatly impressed the observers ashore. In the event this exercise had to be cut short so that *Devonshire* could race to answer a distress call from a Hong Kong-registered freighter, MV *Carina* which, with a cargo of oil, nuts, coffee and live cattle, had grounded on a reef in the Celebes Sea. Steaming at 30 knots *Devonshire* was the first relief vessel to arrive on the scene and a boarding party quickly established that the stricken vessel was stuck fast on the reef and so severely damaged that

she could not be salvaged. Even as *Devonshire*'s boarding party were carrying out their survey hordes of Filipino pirates were gathering round the wreck, waiting for the ship to be abandoned when they could literally strip it bare. While this was going on the Australian frigate *Derwent* arrived to take over the salvage work and *Devonshire*'s main task was to transfer the crew and their possessions to the frigate, before setting course for the American naval base at Subic Bay to join a six-nation SEATO exercise.

The exercise, hosted by Thailand, was the biggest and most wide-ranging in SEATO's 12-year existence and it ranged from Manila to Okinawa and Bangkok. It involved some 45 ships and 1,500 personnel from the navies of the USA, Britain, Thailand, the Philippines, Australia and New Zealand. The main manoeuvres involved trade protection and the escorting of convoys, but a typhoon sweeping across the area caused severe weather conditions which made replenishment-at-sea exercises extremely hazardous. During the course of the manoeuvres *Devonshire* steamed to Okinawa for a brief visit and to carry out Sea Slug firings, before moving on to the US naval base at Yokosuka. After leaving Japanese waters *Devonshire* steamed

HMS Devonshire

through a very misty Taiwan Strait to Hong Kong where Admiral Mills struck his flag and the ship returned to Singapore to prepare for sea and harbour inspections. The busy few weeks which followed clearly paid off, for when *Devonshire* left the Singapore area for Hong Kong, FO2 signalled: 'Harbour Inspection completed. I was very pleased to see such a clean and smart ship which reflects great credit on you all. Appearance at Divisions was good. Well done.'

HMS *Devonshire*'s last visit of the commission to Hong Kong lasted only four days, and after returning to Singapore on 11 June preparations for the passage home began. Six days later she slipped her moorings and left Singapore for Aden, Suez and Malta. The final stopover was at Gibraltar and after an uneventful last leg of the passage the ship anchored in Plymouth Sound to drop off the West Country 'natives' before continuing her passage along the south coast. On Friday 15 July 1966, *Devonshire* arrived in Portsmouth Harbour, where families and friends were waiting to greet the ship. During her 12 months east of Suez she had steamed some 60,000 miles, but the commission was not yet over.

At the end of August 1966, with seasonal leave having been taken, *Devonshire* left Portsmouth to take part in Plymouth Navy Days, before setting course up Channel for an important Baltic cruise. Flying the flag of the C-in-C Home Fleet, Admiral Sir John Frewen, the destroyer would make a number of high-profile visits to Baltic ports, On 30 August, as *Devonshire* was off the south coast and about to enter the Strait of Dover, the ship's Flight picked up the C-in-C, after which *Devonshire* steamed north to the mouth of the River Elbe for a northbound transit of the Kiel Canal. It was while she was in the Elbe Estuary that *Devonshire* was involved in a minor collision with the 21,138-ton, BP oil tanker SS *British Sovereign*. Fortunately, there were no casualties and damage was limited to dents and scratches in the paintwork and the destroyer was able to continue her passage. In Leningrad when she was opened to the public large crowds took the opportunity to go on board the ship, and the ship's company entertained local children to a party. The C-in-C had meetings with his Russian counterparts, and the visit was declared a resounding success. As one officer remembers: 'The salute to the C-in-C from the Russian Fleet based at Kronstadt was a memorable sight as we steamed up the Neva River in the gathering dusk. Nowhere in the world had we aroused so much interest ashore. It was a common sight to see two or

On 28 September 1976, after a boiler room explosion the day before, the destroyer put into Lisbon.
(Author's Collection)

The unconventional lines of the County-class are clearly seen in this image. Although the flight deck was large enough to accommodate a Wessex, moving the aircraft on deck was quite a challenge. (Crown Copyright/MoD)

three groups of the ship's company ashore surrounded by 40 or 50 curious citizens of Leningrad plying them with questions. Our hosts in the Russian Navy looked after us well. Sightseeing trips were the order of the day with visits to the Hermitage, the Winter and Summer Palaces, all of which were unforgettable experiences. As was the Vodka which was bought for us and by us.'

After leaving Leningrad *Devonshire* called at Helsinki and finally Gdynia where, in the words of the same officer, '...the welcoming ceremony by ships of the Polish Navy was an indication of how well organised the preparations for our visit had been. Gdynia will always be remembered by *Devonshire*'s ship's company for the excellent runs ashore and for the fascinating way the old parts of the town had been rebuilt after the Second World War.' After her visit to Poland *Devonshire* returned to Portsmouth and on completion of the commission on 19 October the ship was placed in dockyard hands for a refit.

Originally it had been intended that *Devonshire* and her sister ships, *Hampshire, Kent* and *London*, as in the second phase of the County-class building programme (*Fife, Glamorgan, Antrim* and *Norfolk*), would be equipped with a new Mark II Sea Slug missile system which would fire higher, further and horizontally, giving it a surface-to-surface capability. It would also be capable of destroying the latest Soviet designed missiles. In the event, however, neither *Devonshire* nor the other three ships of the first phase would receive the improved weapons system and although *Devonshire*'s refit lasted for some eight months there were no major structural alterations. On 20 June 1967, *Devonshire*'s new commanding officer, Captain R. K. N. Emden DSC RN, was appointed to the ship and three days later she was recommissioned at Portsmouth for what would eventually be another deployment to the Far East Station. Prior to sailing east, however,

HMS Devonshire

Devonshire underwent a gruelling work-up at Portland, which began in July and was broken only for a short visit to Devonport and the summer leave period. This was followed by Sea Slug firings off Aberporth and runs ashore at Fishguard where, after a day on the missile ranges, the destroyer anchored. There were also short refuelling breaks at Milford Haven and a passage north to Invergordon for fleet manoeuvres. Finally, on 1 December 1967, *Devonshire* sailed for the overseas leg of her General Service Commission and three days later she called at Gibraltar. With the Suez Canal having been closed for six months the Navy's warships had become used to plying the longer Cape route to the Far East and during the passage south down the west coast of Africa *Devonshire* refuelled at Freetown and shortly afterwards 'Crossed the Line' with all due ceremony.

Arriving in Simonstown in plenty of time for Christmas many members of the ship's company were able to spend a few days with local families, while others went further afield to Cape Town. The generous hospitality shown to the men was in part repaid with a party on board for 100 under-privileged children, while on the official side at a reception given for the Mayor and members of the Simonstown municipality, Captain Emden was presented with a framed photograph, taken in 1908 of the sixth *Devonshire*, the four-funnelled first class armoured cruiser, at anchor in Simons Bay. On 27 December *Devonshire* left Simonstown to steam north into the Arabian Sea and two days later she officially joined the Far East Fleet. Off South Yemen she joined a task group, which included the aircraft carrier *Eagle*, which was standing by in case it became necessary to evacuate British nationals from the oil refinery at Little Aden. New Year celebrations were held at sea, with the captain and senior officers being entertained in the junior ratings' dining hall, where the 500,000th meal of the commission was served.

On 15 January 1968, with tensions in newly independent Aden having eased, *Devonshire*, *Phoebe* and RFAs *Tarbatness* and *Tidepool* were detached from the task group for a welcome break in the form of a four-day visit to the Seychelles, after which *Devonshire* steamed to the island of Gan where she hoisted the flag of FO2, Rear-Admiral E. B. Ashmore, to begin a series of strenuous Indian Ocean exercises. Other ships involved in the manoeuvres included *Triumph, Dido, Euryalus, Zest* and RFA *Olna* and on conclusion the force set course for Australia. On 17 February, as *Devonshire* steamed through Sydney Heads she was greeted by large crowds gathered on the sheer cliff-top of North Head while a flotilla of small boats followed up-harbour to the Australian naval base at Garden Island. Having been at sea for the best part of a month the destroyer's ship's company took every opportunity for shore leave and recreation. When *Devonshire* and the other ships were opened to the public nearly 10,000 people visited them and once again parties were given for disabled children. With the arrival in Sydney of the heavy repair ship *Triumph*, in preparation for an exercise period off Australia's east coast, *Devonshire* was able to undergo an assisted maintenance period.

On 6 March *Devonshire*'s three-week visit to Sydney came to an end and for several days after leaving harbour she exercised with HMAS *Parramatta* and *Vendetta*, before transferring FO2 to *Euryalus* for his official visit to New Zealand and then, steaming by way of Australia's south coast, setting course for Singapore, where on 19 March she arrived at the naval base. *Devonshire*'s stopover at Singapore lasted for just ten days before she sailed for Hong Kong where she hoisted the flag of the C-in-C FES, Vice-Admiral W. D. O'Brien, and set course for Japan to visit Tokyo and Kobe.

Following her high-profile visit to Japan and a brief return to Hong Kong *Devonshire* had been due to take part in a multi-national SEATO exercise, but in the event this was cancelled and instead she carried out a busy weapons training period off the US naval base at Subic Bay. Also involved in these manoeuvres were *Barrosa, Caprice, Carysfort, Dido, Euryalus, Llandaff* and *Zest*, together with the Canadian ships *Qu'Apelle* and *Saskatchewan*, the submarines *Rorqual* and USS *Ronquil*, and two RFAs. As well as the naval ships the RAF's 205

Squadron based at Singapore's RAF Changi (now the island's main international airport) also took part in manoeuvres which were mainly directed towards anti-submarine and anti-aircraft warfare. For the ship's company there was a short break at Subic Bay, where for the younger members the nearby town of Olongapo proved an eye-opener. Once the exercises were completed the whole force steamed north to Hong Kong for the wash-up, after which *Devonshire* returned to Singapore to carry out a six-week dockyard-assisted maintenance period, which also afforded the opportunity of station leave.

In July 1968 *Devonshire*'s annual inspection was carried out by FO2 and his staff then five days later, on 29 July, the ship left Singapore to begin her passage home. En route calls were made at Gan and Diego Suarez, and *Devonshire* also took her turn on the Beira Patrol. There was a final call at Simonstown, and refuelling stops at Dakar and Gibraltar before, finally, on 12 September 1968, after an absence of nine months, she arrived back at Portsmouth. Soon after her arrival the ship's company was reduced to no more than a care-and-maintenance party and the ship herself was placed in dockyard hands to undergo a major refit.

One of the first jobs to be tackled by Portsmouth Dockyard was the cutting of two large 13ft by 9ft holes in the hull, to provide easy access to the lower decks for the removal and replacement of the gas turbine propulsion machinery. With the refit planned for completion in late 1970 a naval spokesman commented: 'All parts of the ship, the fixtures and fittings, will be brought up to an "as new" condition and improvements in design since the ship joined the fleet in 1962 will be incorporated.'

On 2 January 1971 *Devonshire*'s new commanding officer, Captain S. R. Sandford RN, joined the ship and at 0900 on Tuesday 26 January the ship was recommissioned for sea trials, which began in earnest on 8 February when the destroyer left Portsmouth and steamed into a foggy and murky Channel. The trials continued until the last week of March when, once again, the ship was taken over by Portsmouth Dockyard, this time for rectification of defects which had arisen. Finally, however, on Tuesday 25 May, *Devonshire* was recommissioned back into the fleet. The guest of honour at the ceremony was Admiral Sir John Frewen who, some five years previously, had flown his flag in the ship for the official visit to Leningrad. Two days after the ceremony and after embarking a contingent of sea cadets from Jersey, the destroyer left Portsmouth to carry out a full-power trial and gunnery exercises followed by an overnight passage to the island of Jersey for a four-day courtesy visit to St Helier, which was Captain Sandford's home town.

During July 1971 *Devonshire* underwent a series of trials from Portsmouth, and in late August while taking part in Navy Days at the base she attracted over 17,000 visitors. During the first week of September a Families Day was held on board, after which the trials resumed with the ship day running from Portsmouth. Later in the month she steamed south to Gibraltar for flying and propeller noise trials, during which she exercised with the frigate *Tenby*. On 11 October, with the trials completed, *Devonshire* returned to Portsmouth to prepare for a gruelling seven-week work-up at Portland, which ended on 16 December when the ship returned to Portsmouth, in plenty of time for the Christmas and New Year leave period.

On Friday 21 January 1972, with seasonal leave and maintenance completed, *Devonshire* left Portsmouth to make a fast, 24-knot passage to Copenhagen to represent the Royal Navy at the funeral of King Frederick IX of Denmark. After a choppy passage north, at 0830 on 23 January *Devonshire* arrived in thick fog and sub-zero temperatures alongside Copenhagen's Langelinie Quay. The funeral took place the next day with the ship's funeral contingent forming part of the escort for the bier between Christiansborg Palace and the city's main railway station. Next morning the destroyer left Copenhagen for Devonport where she embarked Sea Slug missiles in readiness for weapons systems trials off Aberporth.

HMS *Devonshire*'s missile firing trials took place during the first two weeks of February, with runs

HMS Devonshire

HMS *Devonshire* at Spithead for the 1977 Silver Jubilee Fleet Review.
(Maritime Photo Library)

ashore at Fishguard and refuelling stops at Milford Haven. In the middle of the month, with the missile firing completed, the ship returned to Portsmouth, but eight days later she was at sea again for a 24-hour passage to London. She arrived off the Nore during the morning of 25 February and embarked the Thames pilot before making the two-hour passage upriver and under Tower Bridge to the Pool of London where she secured alongside the museum ship *Belfast*. At that time she was the largest operational warship to sail so far up the River Thames. For Captain Sandford it must have been a nostalgic few days, for he had once served as *Belfast*'s Executive Officer. Perhaps the most unusual gathering during the ship's visit was for all the landlords and barmaids from London public houses named the 'Devonshire Arms'. Needless to say reciprocal visits were made to the various licensed premises by members of the ship's company.

On 29 February *Devonshire* left the capital to steam back downriver and set course for Scottish waters and a major naval exercise in the North Sea, which included a weekend visit to Rosyth. By the third week of March, however, she was back at Portsmouth for dry docking and maintenance prior to sailing for the Far East. In mid-May the ship sailed to carry out a short trials programme which ended at Portland and on 19 May, after an overnight passage, she embarked families at Spithead for the trip back into Portsmouth Harbour. Three days later, at 1440 on Monday 22 May, she slipped her moorings at Fountain Lake Jetty and set course for Simonstown. After steaming through gale force winds and heavy seas in the Bay of Biscay, off the coast of Portugal she encountered a Soviet task force headed by the helicopter carrier *Leningrad*, which provided a good photo opportunity for *Devonshire*'s own helicopter. During the morning of 26 May she rendezvoused with the frigate *Lincoln* and in the early forenoon both ships secured alongside at Las Palmas, Gran Canarias, for a short visit. From Las Palmas *Devonshire* steamed south with both *Lincoln* and RFA *Tideflow*, and during 29 May the three ships crossed the equator, the event being marked with due ceremony. On 3 June *Devonshire* made another short stop when she anchored for the day off Jamestown, St Helena, which allowed for a short period of leave for both watches. That afternoon saw the arrival of the passenger liner *Southampton Castle* with mail, and

when the destroyer was opened to the public both local people and cruise passengers looked round the ship. The visit came to an end at 0045 on 4 June when *Devonshire* weighed anchor to resume her course for Simonstown, where she and *Lincoln* arrived four days later.

With a seven-day break at the Cape there was time for the ship's company to relax and on 13 June, at Simonstown Dockyard Church, Captain Sandford who was a widower, found time to get married. The ship's commander acted as Best Man and Commander (S) gave the bride away, leading to comments being made that this was probably the only time the supply branch had been known to give anything away. The event was well supported by the ship's company, with the Reception being held in the wardroom and attended by the officers, members of Number 3 Mess, Presidents and Leading Hands of all messdecks and the Band. The remainder of the ship's company celebrated with the order 'Splice the main brace!'

After leaving Simonstown on 15 June *Devonshire* steamed north into a choppy Indian Ocean and after an anti-aircraft exercise with South African Buccaneer bombers, she set course for the coast of Mozambique and the Beira Patrol, which by that time was in its seventh year and with no quick end in sight. *Devonshire* arrived off Beira during the early hours of 19 June where she took over from *Cleopatra*, which quickly headed south on her way home to Devonport. In the words of one member of *Devonshire*'s ship's company: 'As she steamed past us on her way south and home …it was quite clear that they were delighted to be going, "31 days to Guzz" and other less printable slogans were on display. Even her Wasp helicopter entered into the spirit of things by giving a short flying display and behaving and sounding just like a bee in a fit.' Apart from a day at anchor to allow the engine room department to repair a main steam line defect, *Devonshire* spent her 25-day patrol, during which she challenged over 100 merchant ships, slowly steaming up and down the Mozambique coastline, some 30 miles off the port of Beira. To help while away the hours an intensive programme of sports,

raffles and fishing competitions was organised. As well as the sports there was the '*Devonshire* Fayre', with stalls and competitions, and a ship's concert. At 0815 on 14 July, however, the frigate *Rothesay* arrived to relieve her on the patrol and at noon *Devonshire* set course for Singapore. Eleven days later she was steaming past fleets of small local fishing boats as she entered the Johore Strait on Singapore's east coast. Soon special sea duty men were closed up, the Guard and Band paraded and the upper decks were manned as the ship berthed alongside what was now the ANZUK basin of the former Singapore Naval Base, most of it now being a commercial shipyard. For the ship's company it was the first run ashore for 40 days.

Although the old naval base had shrunk considerably, there was still a lot to offer with a NAAFI shop and the swimming pool still intact. For *Devonshire*'s ship's company there was an eight-day break in Singapore before she joined *Lowestoft* and RFA *Green Rover* for exercises with RAF helicopters and RAAF Hunter fighters, after which she headed north for Japan. Steaming at a steady 20 knots *Devonshire* passed close to the island of Hainan and during the forenoon of 9 August, having managed to avoid a particularly severe typhoon, she arrived at the Japanese port of Ito, on the eastern shore of the Izu Peninsula, south of Tokyo. The town has been described as similar to Torquay, a mixture of seaside resort and fishing port, and *Devonshire*'s visit coincided with the local Anjin Festival, to celebrate the arrival of the British sailor William Adams who came in a Dutch ship in the latter half of the sixteenth century. He is regarded as the founder of the modern shipping industry in Japan, with his memory being honoured annually at a 'commemoration stone'. The ceremony itself took place on 10 August, with *Devonshire* firing a 15-gun salute and landing a ceremonial guard for the occasion. With the formal ceremonies over there was a carnival procession in which the destroyer's Guard and Band took part, and amongst the drum majorettes and Japanese character floats Captain Sandford took the part of William Adams, riding on a miniature sailing ship. That evening there was a

HMS Devonshire

huge fireworks display which, in the words of one ship's company member, 'made 5 November and Guy Fawkes Night look rather like half-starved amateurs.' The memorable visit came to an end on 14 August when *Devonshire* sailed south to the Subic Bay exercise areas off the Philippines.

Once again *Devonshire*'s passage saw her dodging a typhoon and after experiencing some extremely rough weather, five days later she arrived at the US naval base at Subic Bay for a weekend break before putting to sea for three days of weapons training on the US Navy's range. By 27 August the ship had returned to Singapore where she underwent routine maintenance and played host to a number of VIP visitors, including the First Sea Lord and a Parliamentary delegation. The ship's assisted maintenance period was carried out by the Fleet Maintenance Group and included a complete inspection of the boilers, the renewal of a propeller shaft bearing and a complete overhaul of most main machinery valves and fittings. Weapons and electrical work included the overhaul of radar and radar aerials as well as the missile and gunnery systems. The whole of the hull and much of the superstructure was repainted and some improvements were made to messdeck accommodation. In the early 1970s, with continuous commissions having been introduced, the ship's company was relieved progressively rather than all at the same time and during this maintenance period 50 officers and men left the ship for the UK, their places having been taken by personnel flown out to Singapore. On 18 September 1972, with the maintenance programme completed and having embarked the Commodore, ANZUK Naval Force, Commodore S. N. Clayden DSC, *Devonshire* sailed for Bangkok.

During her passage north the ship's company was put through the rigours of a mini-work-up, with a wide range of evolutions, including Sea Cat and gun firing against pilotless drones launched from RFA *Green Rove*r, damage control and other exercises. On 21 September *Devonshire* arrived off the entrance to the Chao Phraya River and soon she had crossed the bar and was steaming upriver. After 25 miles of dodging barges, water taxis and fishing boats, the destroyer secured alongside dolphin moorings at Khlong Toei, about five miles from Bangkok city centre. During her four-day visit the ship was opened to visitors and the ship's company entertained a large group of underprivileged children to the traditional party on board. Coaches bussed the liberty men to and from the city centre, which made the journey into Bangkok somewhat easier. When *Devonshire* left the Thai capital she rendezvoused with HMAS *Onslow* for exercises in the South China Sea, before steaming north for Hong Kong and on to Manila to carry out joint manoeuvres with the US Navy, after which she returned to Hong Kong for Admiral's Inspection.

On 11 November *Devonshire* left Hong Kong to return briefly to the Singapore exercise areas in the South China Sea, before setting course for Fremantle, via Bali, and after ten days in Western Australia, during which time the ship's company were hospitably entertained, the ship left for home. After a brief call at Mauritius, Christmas was spent at Cape Town, after which she steamed north through the Atlantic Ocean in company with *Lincoln*. There was a 24-hour stopover at Gibraltar and during the afternoon of Wednesday 17 January 1973 she anchored at Spithead to await Customs clearance. Next forenoon *Devonshire* weighed anchor to steam up harbour to secure alongside Portsmouth's Fountain Lake Jetty where, complete with large 'Welcome Home' banners, families and friends were waiting to greet her.

Following her arrival at Portsmouth *Devonshire* underwent a nine and a half-week docking and maintenance period, and on 23 January there was a change of command when Captain Peter W. Buchanan RN took over the ship. On 26 March the destroyer sailed to undergo post-refit trials in the Channel and weapons training at Portland. In May 1973 *Devonshire* joined *Ark Royal* in Lyme Bay to act as the carrier's planeguard escort and on 5 May, in company with *Ark Royal, Rothesay, Diomede, Minerva* and the RFAs *Cherryleaf* and *Resource*, she set course for the transatlantic passage to the US Navy's exercise areas off Puerto Rico. The first stage of the crossing involved joint exercises with

the French Navy, which included the aircraft carrier *Foch*, which *Devonshire* had to locate and attack. On 14 May she arrived off the US base at Roosevelt Roads and later the same day the exercises on the US Atlantic Fleet's Weapons Range began. During the evening of 19 May, while acting as planeguard to *Ark Royal*, the destroyer's sea boat recovered a survivor from one of the carrier's Gannet aircraft which had ditched, the other being picked up by the SAR helicopter. The exercises ended in early June with a visit to Fort Lauderdale, followed by further manoeuvres and a nine-day visit to Philadelphia. On 30 June, after leaving the USA, *Devonshire* again rendezvoused with *Ark Royal* and her group for the return passage to home waters and the Benbecula area off the Outer Hebrides where she carried out an intensive programme of live gunnery and missile firing. During this period she also received two distress signals. The first, on 14 July, was from a Danish fishing vessel which was on fire, but before *Devonshire* reached her the fire was extinguished and the destroyer was stood down. The second came the next day when the survey ship *Bembridge* signalled for help, but once again the request was cancelled before she reached the scene. The exercise period ended on 16 July when *Devonshire* secured alongside her sister *Kent* in Rosyth Dockyard.

The seven-day break in the Fife naval base ended on 23 July, when *Devonshire* joined *Ark Royal, Bulwark, Bristol, Fife, Kent* and 20 other ships in a demonstration of sea power for the Secretary of State for Defence. During the manoeuvres *Devonshire* once again acted as planeguard to *Ark Royal* as she flew her Buccaneer and Phantom aircraft. She also gave an impressive gunnery display and *Bulwark* demonstrated the landing of Royal Marines by helicopter. This major exercise ended on 25 July when *Devonshire* began her passage south to Portsmouth, arriving at Spithead the following morning. Shortly afterwards families were embarked, before the ship sailed for a dramatic Families Day, which involved manoeuvres with *Bristol* and *Kent*. By 1615, however, she had secured alongside Fountain Lake Jetty and the first long-leave parties had left the ship.

During her period alongside that summer the ship took part in Navy Days at Portsmouth, and over the three days of the holiday weekend she attracted some 28,641 visitors. By 3 September, however, with her maintenance programme complete and all leave having been taken, *Devonshire* embarked a Parliamentary delegation and sailed from Portsmouth to join *Bulwark* and *Blake* at Portland for three days of weapons training. In mid-September, in company with the frigate Plymouth, she sailed for Gibraltar and the Mediterranean where, after refuelling at Malta, she joined the NATO exercise 'Deep Furrow', which at that time was the largest maritime exercise conducted in the eastern Mediterranean. Its main purpose was to land a large amphibious force in south-west Turkey, as a demonstration of the organisation's ability to reinforce and defend its southern flank against an external aggressor. Britain's contribution to the landings came in the form of 41 and 42 Commando in *Bulwark, Intrepid* and the RFA landing ships S*ir Galahad* and *Sir Lancelot*. *Devonshire*'s role was to support the aircraft carrier group and after rendezvousing with USS *Independence* early on 21 September she, together with a US Navy and a Turkish destroyer, provided an escort screen for the carrier, which included fending off 'attacks' by submarines, aircraft and fast missile boats which were hidden among the Greek islands. Nine days later, with the exercise concluded, *Devonshire* and *Intrepid* entered the Dardanelles to anchor off Istanbul.

During October *Devonshire* remained in the western Mediterranean, operating from Gibraltar as she carried out a week-long period of anti-submarine exercises with *Sealion, Porpoise* and *Onslaught*. In early November she took part in joint manoeuvres with French and Italian ships, which saw her under 'attack' by French Super Étendard aircraft, and making a five-day visit to Toulon. On 21 November, after leaving the French port, *Devonshire* sailed for Malta to undergo a short maintenance period and on 5 December after leaving Grand Harbour, she exercised with the subma-

HMS Devonshire

HMS *Devonshire* dressed overall for the Silver Jubilee Fleet Review at Spithead in the summer of 1977. *(Syd Goodman Collection)*

rine *Sealion* before sailing home to Portsmouth, where she arrived nine days later to secure alongside Norfolk at Fountain Lake Jetty.

On Monday 14 January 1974, *Devonshire* sailed from Portsmouth and after making a very brief stop at Devonport to replenish her Sea Slug missile stock, she joined *Blake* for a transatlantic crossing. The other ships in the deployment to the Caribbean were *Bulwark, Brighton, Ashanti, Bacchante, Kent, Nubian, Torquay, Whitby, Fearless*, the submarine *Narwhal* and two RFAs. They were leaving behind the harsh winter of 1974 for a welcome break in the sun. *Blake*, wearing the flag of Vice-Admiral I. G. Raikes, Flag Officer First Flotilla, and *Devonshire*, had an extremely rough Atlantic crossing, with one of the destroyer's motor cutters being damaged beyond repair by the mountainous seas. On 24 January, however, the weather was calm, warm and sunny for the arrival at Bermuda and after steaming south the fleet began a series of exercises in the Caribbean, with *Ashanti* and *Bacchante* standing by to steam to the island of Grenada where, prior to Independence, rioting had broken out. On completion of the exercises *Blake* and *Devonshire* visited the southern US city of New Orleans, after which the fleet reassembled off Virgin Gorda for evolutions and recreational activities, and to bid farewell to the First Sea Lord, Admiral Michael Pollock. The farewell ceremony took the form of a steam past, with the First Sea Lord embarked in *Bulwark* and with ships' companies manning and cheering ship as they passed the commando carrier from astern. With the ceremony over *Devonshire* visited the islands of St Lucia and San Juan, before rejoining the fleet, now without *Bulwark*, for 'Exercise Safe Passage', after which she made a four-day visit to the US naval base at Norfolk, Virginia. Finally, on 18 March, *Devonshire* left the USA and in company with *Blake, Bacchante, Kent* and the German frigate *Augsberg*, began the passage home to Portsmouth. HM Ships *Blake* and *Devonshire* arrived at Spithead at just after midnight on 29 March and later during the forenoon the destroyer steamed up harbour to secure alongside South Railway Jetty.

It was 6 May when *Devonshire* put to sea again and after 48 hours off Portland she set course for the North Sea where she joined *Llandaff* and *Yarmouth* for anti-submarine exercises, with *Grampus* providing the prey. On 12 May the three ships steamed into the historic wartime anchorage of Scapa Flow to join other NATO ships, including *Whitby* and two Dutch destroyers, for 'JMC' (Joint Maritime Course) exercises in the North Sea. These ended with a visit to Bordeaux and, in company with *Bristol*, a Sea Day during which personnel from the National Defence College witnessed various manoeuvres and evolutions off the Isle of Wight. Returning to Portsmouth in late May *Devonshire* spent three weeks undergoing maintenance before sailing south to Gibraltar where, with *Blake, Bristol, Lynx* and the submarine *Swiftsure*, she took part in the anti-submarine exercise 'Zoom Too'.

On 11 July, with the exercise concluded, *Devonshire* underwent her sea inspection by the Flag Officer Second Flotilla, her old CO, Rear-Admiral Sandford, after which she secured alongside Gibraltar's South Mole. Five days later, however, during the evening of Tuesday 16 July, Sandford returned to the ship for an urgent conference. Although the ship's company were not party to the proceedings it was clear when all liberty men were recalled and the ship was placed under 'Sailing Orders' that something was afoot and the rumours began circulating round the ship. At 2359 that night *Devonshire* sailed for Malta and the ship's ultimate destination became more widely known. The previous day on the island of Cyprus, backed by the Greek military junta, the Greek officered Cypriot National Guard had staged a military coup and overthrown President Makarios, who was replaced by a former EOKA who was a fanatical supporter of the 'Enosis' policy – the union of Cyprus with the Greek Republic. Initially it was thought that Makarios had been murdered, but as *Devonshire* steamed towards Malta he was located and flown to safety in an RAF transport aircraft. Intelligence reports received in London strongly indicated that Turkey, which would not tolerate any attempts by Greece to annex Cyprus, was about to invade and occupy the north-east tip of the island, which was populated by the minority Turkish Cypriot population. This speculation was reinforced by the fact that Turkey was massing troops, tanks and artillery on its southern coast. With riots in major Cypriot towns, including Famagusta, Larnaca, Limassol and Nicosia, the situation for thousands of British ex-pats and holidaymakers was becoming more and more dangerous and plans were being made for a naval task force to evacuate British nationals from the island. On 20 July the fears of a Turkish invasion became a reality and suddenly large numbers of Britons were caught up in the fierce fighting between the Turkish Army and Greek Cypriot irregulars.

Meanwhile, during the afternoon of 20 July, *Devonshire* rendezvoused in Larnaca Bay with *Hermes*, which had embarked 900 Royal Marines of 41 Commando, and with the frigates *Andromeda* and *Rhyl*. As the Royal Navy ships began patrolling off the coast they were watched closely by a Soviet Kotlin-class destroyer and next day as fighting on the island intensified, some of the thousands of ex-pat Britons and holidaymakers were evacuated to the British military bases at Dhekalia, but there were still over 1,500 people gathered on beaches and in nearby fields, waiting to be rescued. During the forenoon of 23 July the naval ships began embarking the refugees and *Devonshire* took on her first passengers from Morphu Bay, most of whom were later transferred to the base area at Dhekalia and to *Hermes*. During the days which followed there were some gruesome incidents, including the discovery by *Devonshire*'s sea boat of seven bodies floating in the sea, all of which were landed at Dhekalia. By 28 July a UN-brokered ceasefire had been accepted by both sides and *Devonshire*'s patrol of the coastline became more relaxed. In the event she had taken on board 197 refugees in what had been an international relief effort, with Royal Navy, Soviet and US naval ships helping to evacuate the refugees. *Devonshire* remained on patrol off Cyprus throughout most of the month of August, but on the 26th she was withdrawn and two days later she refuelled at Malta before beginning her passage home. On 2 September, with a long refit ahead of her, the destroyer put into Devonport to disembark her Sea Slug missiles and two days later she called at Portland to embark families and friends for the six-hour passage to Portsmouth. Finally, at 1700 on 4 September, she arrived alongside Portsmouth Dockyard's Fountain Lake Jetty where, as soon as the families were ashore, de-ammunitioning and de-storing began. Just over two weeks later *Devonshire* was paid off into dockyard hands. Ahead lay an eight-month refit.

On 10 March 1975, as *Devonshire*'s refit neared completion, her new commanding officer, Captain Stephen A. Stuart RN, was appointed and soon afterwards her ship's company was brought up to strength. On Thursday 29 May, at a ceremony alongside the ship at Fountain Lake Jetty, *Devonshire* was rededicated with her sponsor Princess Alexandra as guest of honour. Following the rededication ceremony *Devonshire* remained alongside at Portsmouth until 18 June, when she put to sea to begin her post-refit trials in the Channel, with a weekend visit to Guernsey at the end of the month. The trials continued until 17 July when the ship returned to Portsmouth to give leave and to take part in Navy Days.

On 26 August *Devonshire* left Portsmouth to continue her trials and in the third week of September she secured alongside at Portland to begin her work-up. As always the six weeks of relentless exercises and evolutions were gruelling, but on 16 October she completed her sea inspection and put in to Devonport for a weekend break. The third week of October saw the destroyer steaming south in company with *Hampshire* for Gibraltar, with both ships carrying out Sea Slug firings en route. For *Devonshire* the first week of November was spent day running from Gibraltar, then on 7 November she headed back to home waters and the North Sea for 'Exercise Ocean Safari' which was NATO's largest exercise of the year. Watched over by a Soviet cruiser the large NATO task force, which also included *Blake* and USS *Independence*, as well as air and surface forces of eight nations, staged a large-scale anti-submarine exercise. On completion of these manoeuvres *Devonshire* spent five days at Rosyth and six days at Newcastle upon Tyne, before returning to Portsmouth in early December.

In mid-January 1976, *Devonshire* once again sailed into the North Sea, this time in company with *Blake*, to take part in the 'JMC 761' exercise, which ended with visits to Rosyth and Hamburg. By mid-February she was back at Portsmouth where, on 20 February, there was a change of command with Captain Antony L. L. Skinner taking over from Stuart. She remained at Portsmouth until 2 April, when she sailed for the Mediterranean where she joined the NATO on-call force in the area. Leaving Gibraltar on 9 April she steamed east to Istanbul and from there to Cagliari, Toulon and Naples, before taking part in a NATO exercise which ended at Malta, where *Devonshire* underwent a 12-day maintenance period. On 23 May *Devonshire* left Grand Harbour for the most important visit of the deployment, which had been arranged at a high political level some months earlier. Flying the flag of Vice-Admiral A. S. Morton, Flag Officer First Flotilla, the destroyer was to make a five-day official visit to Odessa, the first for ten years by a

On 12 January 1978 *Devonshire* steamed up the River Thames for a farewell visit to London. Here she is seen off Gravesend. *(World Ship Society)*

British warship to a Soviet port. It was part of an exchange which saw the Soviet destroyer *Obrazsovyy* visiting Portsmouth. Of *Devonshire*'s visit one member of her ship's company remembers it thus: 'The kindness of the local people left an overriding memory and the four-day programme was packed with official functions, visits, tours, sports fixtures, opera and even ballet performances. One of the pleasures almost forgotten in England was the sight of shapely girls in miniskirts. Some of the lads got to know the lasses and there were a few tears shed on the quay when the ship sailed.' *Devonshire* left her quay, close to the Potemkin Steps, on 1 June and next day she called at the Romanian port of Constanta for a three-day visit. In the Middle East, however, by 10 June fighting in refugee camps between Lebanese Army forces and Palestinian militias was raising fears for the safety of foreign nationals in Lebanon and for over a week *Devonshire* cruised off the Cypriot coast in case she were needed to evacuate Britons from the war-torn region. On 18 June, having been stood down, she returned to Malta to undergo a four-week maintenance period, during which she was visited by the C-in-C Fleet, Admiral Sir John Treacher.

On 16 July *Devonshire* left Malta to steam west for Gibraltar where she spent two days weapons training before returning to home waters and undergoing Customs clearance in Plymouth Sound before arriving alongside Portsmouth's Fountain Lake Jetty during the forenoon of 4 August. During her period alongside *Devonshire* took part in Navy Days where she attracted almost 20,000 visitors. She left for sea again on 8 September 1976, to carry out a programme of weapons training ahead of a three-month deployment with *Antrim, Bacchante, Charybdis, Naiad, Yarmouth* and three RFAs. The group would be commanded by the Flag Officer First Flotilla and during the deployment it would take part in the NATO exercise 'Display

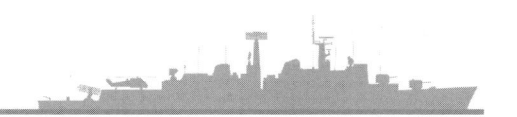

Determination' in the eastern Atlantic and the Mediterranean. Later the ships would be involved in a CENTO exercise along with the submarine *Osiris*, and in the Indian Ocean they would be joined by Iranian, Pakistani, Turkish and US naval ships. Among the countries on the itinerary were Portugal, Kenya, the Seychelles, Pakistan, Bahrain, Dubai, Egypt and Italy, and home again for Christmas.

At 1000 on Saturday 25 September, flying the flag of Vice-Admiral Morton, *Devonshire* left Portsmouth to rendezvous with *Ark Royal*, *Andromeda* and other ships of the group to begin 'Exercise Team Work'. Two days later, however, at 2037 on 27 September, when the ship was some 60 miles off Portugal's Cape Mondego, there was an explosion in the boiler room and all power was lost. The ship's company immediately went to Emergency Stations and as all way was lost, the destroyer was lying helpless in the water. Fortunately, there were no injuries, but it was 2230 before she was under way again and escorted by *Bacchante* she limped to the mouth of the River Tagus and upriver to Lisbon where, at 0950 on 28 September, she secured alongside *Antrim*. It was clear that *Devonshire*'s part in the deployment was over, and during the 48 hours she spent in the Portuguese capital FOF1 and his staff transferred to *Antrim*, while down below the engineers surveyed the damaged boiler room. Finally, during the forenoon of 1 October, escorted by the frigate *Lincoln*, *Devonshire* sailed for Devonport where she was de-ammunitioned. She returned to Portsmouth during the afternoon of 6 October.

HMS *Devonshire* remained undergoing repairs at Portsmouth for just over three weeks, but on 29 October she was once again ready for sea, and by the first week of November she was taking part in exercise 'JMC 764' in the North Sea, in company with *Glamorgan* and the cruiser *Tiger*. The exercises took them into Norwegian waters and to the old wartime anchorage at Scapa Flow, ending on 19 November at Rosyth. From here *Devonshire* made an 11-day 'Meet the Navy' visit to Middlesbrough, where she secured alongside the city's docks for a very hectic stay; the local press reported that they

A nice shot of *Devonshire* leaving Portsmouth on 17 July 1978. *(Leo Van Ginderen)*

August 1980 and *Devonshire* is laid up at Portsmouth. A proposed sale to Egypt had fallen through and the ship was providing a ready source of spares for her operational sisters. *(James W. Goss)*

had never seen such a busy warship. Each afternoon she was opened to the public and some 600 children from 15 schools in the area toured the ship and attended naval careers forums on board. When she left the city *Devonshire* rendezvoused with *Glamorgan*, which had made a similar visit to Newcastle, for weapons training in the Channel and Western Approaches. On 13 December, while in the Western Approaches, the ship's Wessex helicopter was lost over the side, with the tragic loss of its flight commander. Three days later *Devonshire* returned to Portsmouth.

For *Devonshire* 1977 was to be the ship's last full year of operational service and this got under way with 'Exercise Springtrain' off Gibraltar where, with her sisters *Antrim, Glamorgan* and *Norfolk*, she fired Sea Slug missiles off the North African coast. Back in Portsmouth, on 18 April, there was a final change of command when Captain C. A. F. Buchanan RN took over. After a period of dry docking and a mini work-up at Portland, June 1977 saw

the ship at Spithead for the Silver Jubilee Fleet Review, where she took her place in line with other ships of the First Flotilla, between *Antrim* and *Blake*. During July 1977 *Devonshire* took part in exercises in the Channel off Portland, calling at Torquay, before heading north for more exercises in the Norwegian Sea and visiting Rosyth and Stavanger. The autumn saw her in the Western Approaches taking part in 'Exercise Ocean Safari' and paying a brief visit to Esbjerg. During this period *Devonshire* joined *Ark Royal* to assist with her work-up and in November the destroyer paid a visit to Cardiff. By the end of the year, however, it was apparent that *Devonshire*'s operational career was drawing to a close, for it had been made clear that the first four County-class destroyers would not be modernised and *Hampshire* had already been withdrawn. As for *Devonshire*, rumours were circulating that Egypt was interested in acquiring her, but for the immediate future January 1978 saw the destroyer involved in 'Exercise Spring Train' from

HMS Devonshire

HMS *Devonshire* remained laid up at Portsmouth until July 1984. (*K.J. Harrow*)

Gibraltar. Also taking part were *Hermes, Arrow, Yarmouth*, the submarines *Churchill, Oracle* and the Dutch submarine *Tijgerhaai*. Alongside *Devonshire* were her sisters *Antrim, London* and *Kent*, with the four supporting RFAs *Olmeda, Olna, Resource* and *Stromness*, all hampered in the manoeuvres by bad weather.

In April 1978 came *Devonshire*'s last major deployment when she joined *Ark Royal*, also nearing the end of her service, and the RFAs *Olmeda* and *Resource*, for a transatlantic passage to the Caribbean. During this period *Devonshire* and *Ark Royal* took part in exercises off Puerto Rico and visited Guadeloupe, Antigua and Barbuda. At Antigua the Hollywood film star James Coburn paid a visit to the ship. There were manoeuvres with *Ark Royal, Antelope* and the RFAs and during 'Exercise Solid Shield' off the east coast of the USA *Ark Royal* and *Devonshire* found themselves up against USS *John F. Kennedy*. The destroyer fired her last Sea Slug missile off Puerto Rico and visited Grand Cayman, West Palm Beach and Charleston, before returning home for a short visit to Torbay.

HMS *Devonshire*'s last day at sea under her own power came on Tuesday 18 July 1978 when, with her sponsor, families and friends on board, she put to sea for a Families Day. Altogether some 800 guests were embarked and most of them saw the ship's Wessex helicopter put on an air display which, unfortunately, went wrong when the aircraft got a little too close to the ship and a rotor blade touched one of the davits, shattering the blade and sending the helicopter plunging into the sea. Luckily no one was injured and the guests all saw the helicopter's crew safely rescued. Next day *Devonshire* was paid off at Portsmouth, the hauling down of the White Ensign being marked by a final parade when, after Captain Buchanan had been piped ashore, he took the salute at Divisions and a march past on the jetty. The ship's Volunteer Band played Sunset as the Ensign was lowered for the last time and at the end of proceedings Captain and Mrs Buchanan were cheered by the ship's company, who lined the route from the dockyard. There was even a final 'Up Sprits' to mark the farewell.

With *Devonshire* having been reduced to

Reserve, negotiations with Egypt over the sale, which also included *Lincoln* and *Salisbury*, dragged on. It was thought the sale, if it went through, would provide work for British shipyards, with a modernisation refit at Vosper Thornycroft's Southampton yard. The refit was to have included a new flight deck for two Lynx helicopters and new missile systems. By November 1979, however, it was clear that Egypt was having second thoughts about the deal and soon afterwards came the news that it was not going to be completed. In the wake of the US-brokered Camp David Agreement Egypt had revised its future defence requirements.

HMS *Devonshire* remained laid up at Portsmouth, providing a readily available source of spares for her operational sisters. The end came in July 1984, when she was towed out into the eastern Atlantic to perform her final duty as a target ship. First a Sea Harrier armed with a Sea Eagle missile launched from *Illustrious* made a low-altitude attack and scored a direct hit, causing extensive damage. Finally, however, the submarine *Splendid* finished her off with a Tigerfish torpedo which quickly sank the destroyer and sent her to the bottom of the Atlantic Ocean.

The end came for *Devonshire* on 17 July 1984, when she was towed out into the eastern Atlantic to perform her final duty as a target ship. This photograph shows the extensive damage caused by a Sea Eagle missiles fired by a Sea Harrier from HMS *Illustrious*. *(World Ship Society)*

HMS Devonshire

A Tigerfish torpedo, fired by the submarine HMS *Splendid*, hit *Devonshire's* starboard side, abaft the hangar, breaking the ship's back and sending her to the bottom. The lower photographs, taken through *Splendid's* periscope, show *Devonshire* down by the stern and listing heavily. Shortly after these were taken her bows rose out of the water and she disappeared beneath the waves, stern-first. *(Crown Copyright/MoD 1984)*

Commanding Officers:

Captain Peter Howes DSC RN	8 January 1962
Captain David Williams RN	16 May 1964
Captain Geoffrey C. Leslie RN	8 December 1965
Captain Richard K. N. Emden DSC RN	20 June 1967
Captain Sefton R. Sandford RN	2 January 1971
Captain Peter W. Buchanan RN	23 January 1973
Captain Stephen A. Stuart RN	10 March 1975
Captain Antony L. L. Skinner RN	20 February 1976
Captain Colin A. F. Buchanan RN	18 April 1977

Battle Honours:

Ushant	1747	Martinique	1762
Finisterre	1747	Havana	1762
Louisburg	1758	Norway	1940
Quebec	1759	Arctic	1941

Chapter Two

HMS Hampshire
1963 - 1976

On 16 March 1961, at John Brown and Company's shipyard on the River Clyde, *Hampshire* took to the water for the first time. This photograph shows her as she is about to be towed to the fitting-out basin
(T. Ferrers-Walker)

Thursday 26 March 1959 was a blustery, showery spring day on the River Clyde, but during one of the rare sunny intervals a small ceremony took place, at which the first keel plates for John Brown & Company's Yard Number 711 were laid on the slipway. The ship was to be the second of the County-class destroyers and her keel was laid only 17 days after that of the first one. However, building work on this second ship proceeded at a slower pace and it was March 1961 before the ship was ready to be launched. As an indication of the importance of the County-class destroyers it had been agreed that the first four vessels would be launched by members of the royal family and an invitation was sent to the Queen Mother at Clarence House, but as she was attending a meeting of Commonwealth Prime Ministers at the time Princess Margaret was asked if she would perform the ceremony and she accepted the invitation. The launch took place at noon on Thursday 16 March 1961, when the fifth HMS *Hampshire* was sent down the slipway into the River Clyde.

The first three *Hampshire*s were all Fourth Raters, the first built in 1653, the second in 1698 and the third in 1741. The fourth *Hampshire* was a twin-screw cruiser of some 10,850 tons, launched in 1903. In June 1916, while sailing alone and in very heavy seas on passage from Scapa Flow to Russia, she was lost to a mine off Orkney. She was at the time conveying Lord Kitchener from Scapa Flow to Northern Russia and even today, almost 100 years on, controversy surrounds the loss of the ship, with conspiracy theorists still alleging dark deeds and official cover-ups.

It was some 15 months after the launching ceremony, on 1 June 1962, that *Hampshire*'s first commanding officer, Captain R. White CBE RN, was appointed and five months later the ship underwent her initial builder's trials, which involved the first transit of the River Clyde. With the trials over the ship returned to John Brown's shipyard at Clydebank, where fitting out was completed. It was, however, another nine months before *Hampshire* was ready for service and at 1509 on Wednesday 13 March 1963, at John Brown's shipyard, she was commissioned for service '...on the Home Station and east of Suez.' Next morning the main draft of the ship's company arrived and joined the ship and at Reveille on 15 March the ship was placed under 'Special Commissioning Routine' for the day. At 1130 the ship's company fell in on the jetty for the Commissioning Service and soon afterwards the ship's sponsor Princess Margaret and her husband Lord Snowdon arrived. Captain White read the Commissioning Warrant, the Pendant was hoisted and in his speech to those assembled he declared: 'Clydebank should take particular pride in HMS *Hampshire* because the workmanship and finish are of a magnificent standard. The sea trials have proved her to be an outstanding ship. All concerned with her should have a feeling of satisfaction and pride of achievement.' Next day, at 1300 on Saturday 16 March, *Hampshire* slipped her moorings and steamed slowly downriver to begin her final acceptance trials in the Firth of Clyde. The second day of the trials saw *Hampshire* in the Atlantic Ocean where she was able to take a minor role in an anti-submarine exercise involving the

Taken on 27 August 1962, this photograph shows *Hampshire* alongside her fitting-out berth at John Brown's yard. It would be another seven months before she was completed and commissioned. (*World Ship Society*)

Hampshire leaves the River Clyde for the first time on 29 November 1962 to undergo her initial builder's trials. Her Sea Cat missile launchers have not been fitted yet and, flying the Red Ensign, she is under the command of John Brown's trials master. *(World Ship Society)*

frigates *Falmouth* and *Hardy* and the submarine *Onslaught*. Later that day, having been formally accepted into naval service, *Hampshire* anchored off Greenock where John Brown's trials party disembarked before the destroyer set course south. Two days later, having carried out consumption trials, *Hampshire* anchored briefly in Cawsand Bay, before making her way via Torbay and Portland, to Portsmouth.

During April, as *Hampshire* lay alongside Middle Slip Jetty, stores and ammunition were embarked and on 3 May the ship was opened to families of ship's company members. Finally, on 13 May, she sailed for trials in the Channel which continued to mid-June, when she returned to Portsmouth. On Tuesday 18 June, *Hampshire* had the sombre duty of committing the body of the late Admiral of the Fleet Viscount Cunningham to the deep. Cunningham had collapsed and died on his way from London to his home in Bishops Waltham some six days earlier and *Hampshire* was chosen for the funeral service. At 1430 the procession lined up in the Royal Naval Barracks, the pall bearers being Admiral of the Fleet Sir Caspar John (First Sea Lord), Admiral Sir Wilfred Woods (C-in-C Portsmouth), Admiral Sir Royston Wright (Second Sea Lord), Vice-Admiral Sir Michael Villiers (Fourth Sea Lord), Vice-Admiral Frank H. E. Hopkins (Fifth Sea Lord), Admiral of the Fleet Sir George Creasy, Vice-Admiral Sir Geoffrey Barnard and the Commandant-General of the Royal Marines, Lieutenant-General M. C. Cartwright-Taylor. The cortège arrived on board *Hampshire* at 1530 and 20 minutes later the ship sailed to a point

County Class GMDs

A close-up view of *Hampshire's* twin Sea Slug missiles launcher.....
(Courtesy of John Lambert)

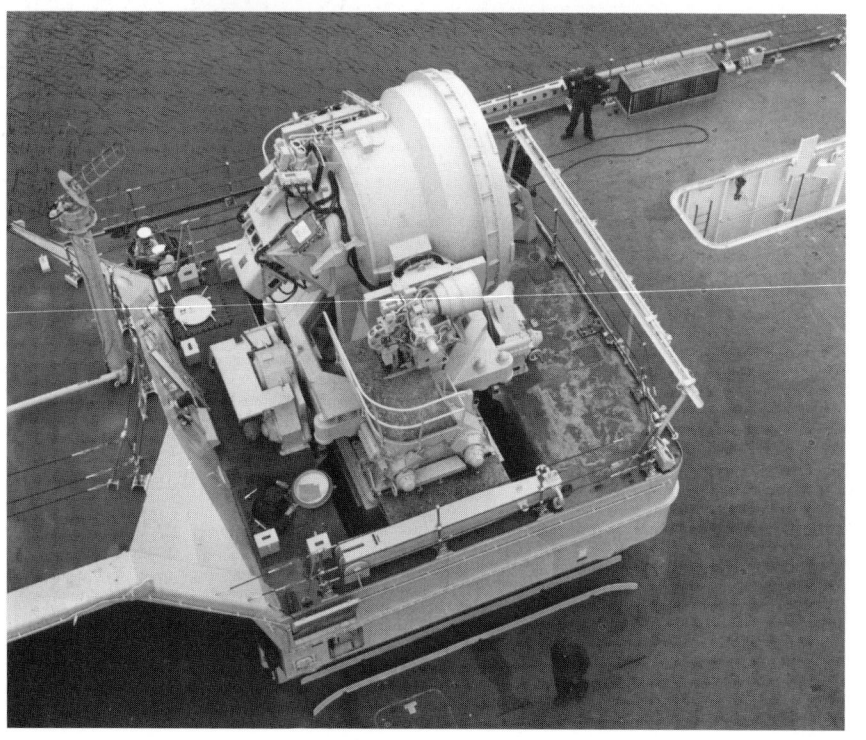

....and her Type 901 guidance radar aerial.
(Courtesy of John Lambert)

HMS Hampshire

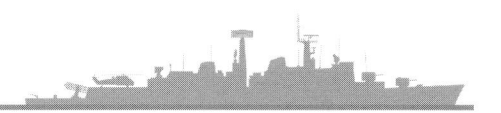

(Right) A close-up view of *Hampshire's* Type 965 'bedstead' radar aerial (AKE-1) on top of her mainmast. At the time this was the standard RN long range air-search radar.
(Courtesy of John Lambert)

(Below) A Wessex HAS1 helicopter on *Hampshire's* flight deck with her main rotor blades folded.
(Courtesy of John Lambert)

March 1963, and *Hampshire* undergoes her final acceptance trials in the Clyde area. *(Courtesy of John Lambert)*

some three and a half miles south of the Nab Tower where, at 1700, the funeral service took place. An hour later *Hampshire* had anchored at Spithead and next day she returned to Portsmouth Harbour.

HMS *Hampshire* continued her trials in the first week of July and during the evening of 10 July she hoisted the flag of Flag Officer Flotillas, Vice-Admiral F. R. Twiss. Leaving Spithead at 1030 on 11 July, she spent the best part of the day carrying out manoeuvres south of the Isle of Wight with King Paul of the Hellenes embarked as part of his three-day State Visit. During these exercises the destroyer was joined by ships of the 2nd Frigate Squadron and the fast attack craft *Brave Borderer* and *Brave Swordsman*, with Sea Vixens from RNAS Yeovilton making low-level fly-pasts, on one occasion at just 40 feet over *Hampshire*'s masthead. The day ended with King Paul taking the salute at a ceremonial steam-past and he left the ship at 1511. Eight months after the visit King Paul died and three years later when his son was deposed Greece became a Republic. *Hampshire* ran another day of trials followed by a three-day visit to Le Havre before she returned to Portsmouth. During the holiday weekend of early August the ship took part in Navy Days; as one of the main attractions over 31,000 people visited her.

By the last week of August 1963 *Hampshire* was ready for sea again and after leaving Portsmouth she set course for the missile ranges at Aberporth where she remained until the end of the month. Then she and other ships of the Home Fleet, including *Hermes, Tiger, Leander, Llandaff* and the newly commissioned nuclear-powered submarine *Dreadnought*, took part in a series of exercises in the Channel. On 1 September she hoisted the flag of Rear-Admiral D. E. F. Gibson, Flag Officer Aircraft Carriers, for 12 days of exercises code-named

'Unison'. These took place in Lyme Bay and the Channel and gained a great deal of publicity when, after reassuring local fishermen that 'normal fishing' could be continued during the naval manoeuvres, six live depth charges were 'lost' some eight miles south of Berry Head and all shipping had to be cleared from the area. During the exercises intensive anti-submarine operations were carried out, with *Dreadnought* and *Porpoise* acting as the targets for the surface ships and aircraft. The manoeuvres ended with a display for senior officers of Commonwealth Services, after which *Hampshire* returned to Portsmouth to undergo a three-week assisted-maintenance period. During the last three weeks of October and into November *Hampshire* operated in the Aberporth area, and underwent her work-up at Portland, which ended on 15 November with a successful inspection.

In late October 1963 it had been announced that *Hampshire* and her sister *Kent*, which had been commissioned at Belfast on 15 August, would be sent to reinforce the fleet at Singapore in response to the Indonesian Government's policy of Confrontation to the newly formed Federation of Malaysia. Before that, however, the destroyer was scheduled to take part in two major exercises in home waters and the first of these began on the last day of November when the ship sailed for Lough Foyle on Ireland's north coast. The main exercise, code-named 'Limejug', began in earnest two days later when *Hampshire* rendezvoused with *Hermes*, *Devonshire*, *Leander*, *Berwick* and *Porpoise*, for anti-submarine manoeuvres in the Atlantic Ocean off Ireland's north-west coast. Six days into the exercises *Hampshire* responded to a distress call from the trawler *Margaret Wicks* which had gone aground off Islay and she stood by as coastguards rescued the crew. On 11 December, however,

On 17 March 1963 *Hampshire* was accepted into service with the Royal Navy and soon after that the White Ensign was hoisted for the first time. Here she is seen off Greenock. *(Courtesy of John Lambert)*

A good stern view of Hampshire *at anchor in Tor Bay during exercise 'Unison' off the south coast.*
(World Ship Society)

Hampshire was detached from the exercise suffering from a defective turbo-generator; she returned to Portsmouth, where she gave leave and underwent a four-week maintenance period. The second major exercise began on 17 January 1964 when, flying the flag of Flag Officer Flotillas (Home), *Hampshire* left Portsmouth for the Portland exercise areas. Next day, with *Hermes, Devonshire, Leander* and *Llandaff*, she headed out for 'Exercise Phoenix' in the Western Approaches, which lasted for 12 days before the destroyer returned to Portsmouth. On 4 February 1964, at a small ceremony on board, the Lord Lieutenant of the County of Hampshire presented to the ship a silver replica of Winchester's statue of King Alfred. Next day the ship sailed for a five-day visit to the northern Spanish port of Ferrol before returning to Portsmouth to prepare for her service east of Suez.

On Friday 6 March, *Hampshire* left Portsmouth to spend a week off Aberporth, before putting in to Devonport to replenish her missile outfit. On 15 March she left Plymouth Sound to set course for Gibraltar, Malta and the Suez Canal. Arriving in Aden on 2 April she refuelled and set course for Gan, where she refuelled again from the hulk RFA *Wave Victor* before finally arriving at the Singapore Naval Base on 13 April, and officially joining the Far East Station. On her arrival *Hampshire* underwent a short period of self-maintenance before joining *Hermes* for exercises in the South China Sea and the passage to Hong Kong where the destroyer hoisted the flag of Vice-Admiral Sir Desmond Dreyer, the C-in-C Far East Station. After only a short weekend break in Hong Kong *Hampshire*, accompanied by the Australian frigates *Parramatta* and *Yarra*, sailed for an official visit to Japanese ports. The first of these was Kure which, during the Korean War, had seen a variety of Royal Navy warships and from there *Hampshire* steamed through the Inland Sea to Tokyo, where she secured alongside the city's prestigious Harumi Wharf. The visit to Tokyo was a more formal affair than the call at Kure and at one official function on board there were Ambassadors to six Commonwealth countries on board. From Tokyo *Hampshire* rejoined *Parramatta* and *Yarra* for exercises with the US Navy off Okinawa. During her return passage to Singapore, while steaming through a severe tropical storm, the ship's Medical Officer, assisted by the MO from RFA *Tideflow* which was also in company, performed an emergency appendectomy on an officer who had been taken ill. Three days later the ship arrived at Singapore Naval Base to undergo a three-week assisted-maintenance period.

On 23 June, with the maintenance work completed, *Hampshire* hoisted the flag of the C-in-C British Far East Command[1], Admiral Sir Varyl Begg, and next day she sailed for the exercise areas in the South China Sea. During the weeks which followed *Hampshire*, in company with other ships on station including *Centaur, Dido, Berwick, Cavendish*, HMNZS *Tarangi*, the submarine *Anchorite* and RFAs *Fort Duquesne* and *Fort Sandusky*, participated in a series of major exercises which began with 'Exercise Buttercup' off Penang. This was quickly followed in late July by the FOTEX exercises in the Strait of Malacca and South China Sea, then after a break of five days by 'Exercise Stopwatch'. This intensive activity was staged as a warning to the Indonesian Government which, with its policy of Confrontation, had raised the political and military tensions in the area and had actually carried out landings in south-west Malaya involving Indonesian irregulars. During late August *Hampshire* underwent routine maintenance but the increased tensions with Indonesia meant that a series of proposed visits to Australian ports, which she was to have made in company with *Berwick* and *Dido*, were cancelled and most of September was spent patrolling the Strait of Malacca, between Singapore and Penang. Early October, however, saw the ship in Hong Kong and later that month she returned to Singapore to undergo a second assisted-maintenance period.

It was during this period alongside at Singapore that preparations began for the ship's second commission, with some longer-serving members of the ship's company leaving for the UK by air and their places being taken by the advance party who had flown out to Singapore. There was also a change of command when, on 11 November, Captain F. W. Hayden DSC RN took over from Captain White who had left the ship the previous day. Six days later, with the maintenance period completed, *Hampshire* left Singapore for home. Steaming by way of Gan, Aden and Suez, she called at Gibraltar on 10 December and cleared Customs on 15 December in Plymouth Sound. Next day, at 0930, she secured alongside Portsmouth's Pitch House Jetty. Although the Far East deployment was over, the commission was not quite finished and in mid-January 1965 she spent two weeks off Aberporth, returning to Portsmouth in early February. The commission finally ended on 3 March when the old ship's company left the ship and next day a new draft joined from the RNB.

HMS *Hampshire* remained in dockyard hands for six months, with all her machinery and weapons systems undergoing a thorough overhaul. On 9 September she underwent her post-refit inspection and four days later she steamed out to Spithead for three days of underwater trials when she was subjected to mines being detonated about three quarters of a mile off both her port and starboard beams. Finally, at 1400 on Friday 1 October *Hampshire* was recommissioned in a ceremony which was held alongside the ship on Fountain Lake Jetty. She had been due to sail for post-refit trials the following day, but a defect in the forced lubrication system of her main gearing delayed her programme by five weeks and it was 5 November before she was able to put to sea. Initial trials took place in the Channel, but in early December she steamed south to continue them in the warmer waters off Gibraltar and the western Mediterranean. In the early hours of 13 December, while at anchor in Gibraltar Bay, the

---

[1] The British C-in-C Far East Command was an appointment which lasted from 1963 to 1971 and it involved the overall command of all British, Australian and New Zealand armed forces in the Far East.

destroyer was ordered to go to the assistance of the Spanish merchantman SS *Tarratolla*, which was on fire close to Alboran Island, but en route to the stricken ship the order was cancelled and three days later *Hampshire* sailed for Portsmouth to give leave and to carry out maintenance.

The new year of 1966 began for *Hampshire* on 18 January when she carried out a mini shake-down at Portland, before hoisting the flag of the C-in-C Home Fleet, Admiral Sir John Frewen, and conveying him to the French naval base at Brest where he was attending an important conference. After returning him to Portsmouth the next day, the ship then headed to Portland from where she operated for the whole of February and into March. During the latter half of March there were exercises with *Fearless* and missile firings at Aberporth, with two overnight visits to Belfast. On Thursday 21 April, *Hampshire* left Portsmouth bound for Gibraltar and the Far East Station. At that time President Sukarno of Indonesia, who had initiated the policy of Confrontation with Malaysia, had been relegated by the country's Army to a mere figurehead with General Suharto being effectively in control of government. He had immediately begun negotiations to end the conflict, so on 9 May, when *Hampshire* arrived in the Strait of Malacca, Confrontation was all but over, but for the time being the strength of the Far East Fleet would remain at a high level.

Within a week of her arrival in Singapore *Hampshire* took part in a major international naval exercise in the Subic Bay area with *Devonshire, Ajax, Dido, Salisbury, Chichester, Melbourne, Vampire, Otago*, USS *Yorktown, Walker* and *Bridget*. These manoeuvres were interrupted only by a brief visit to Manila and then continued until the end of May when the 'wash-up' took place off Bangkok. On 7 June, having hoisted the flag of the C-in-C Far East Station, *Hampshire* and *Chichester* set course for Hong Kong. On 20 June, with the destroyer alongside Hong Kong's North Arm, there was a change of command when Captain Ian D.

Flying the flag of the C-in-C Far East Station, Vice-Admiral Sir Desmond Dreyer, *Hampshire* is seen here in Japanese waters in 1964. *(Ken Kelly Collection)*

McLaughlan DSC RN took over the ship from Hayden. Seven days later, shortly after leaving Hong Kong, the destroyer suffered a main propulsion machinery breakdown which necessitated a return to the Colony for four days of repairs. Following her return to Singapore *Hampshire* hoisted the Flag of FO2, FES, Rear-Admiral C. P. Mills, before making two short visits to Malaysian ports, the first being Penang, where she anchored off Georgetown, and the second being Port Swettenham (now Port Kelang). She then returned to Singapore to undergo a six-week dockyard-assisted maintenance period, which included three weeks in dry dock, during which time the ship's company moved ashore into the spacious and airy accommodation at HMS *Terror*.

On 24 August *Hampshire* put to sea again to carry out trials, after which she returned to the dockyard for further work on her main propulsion machinery. It was the last day of September when, in company with *Bulwark, Victorious, Arethusa, Cleopatra, London, Kent,* HMAS *Sydney* and *Vampire*, she sailed for the Subic Bay exercise areas to carry out manoeuvres with US Navy ships. These were concluded in the second week of October with a convoy escort exercise south to Australian waters. Originally *Hampshire*, in company with *Arethusa, Cleopatra, Leander* and the submarine *Oberon*, had been scheduled to visit Sydney, but on 26 October, two days beforehand, *Kent* suffered machinery defects which required dry docking and *Hampshire* took over her sister's programme, securing alongside Melbourne's Inner Station Pier on 29 October at the start of a 13-day visit. At that time the programme of visits to Australian ports by the Royal Navy ships was the biggest since the end of the Second World War and the local people showed their appreciation when she was opened to the public for two days with some 4,500 visitors going on board to look over the ship. On 11 November *Hampshire* sailed to rendezvous with *Victorious* and other ships for two days of manoeuvres before the destroyer put into Adelaide's inner harbour for a seven-day visit to the port, after which she rendezvoused with the naval task force for more exercises, which included the landing of 42 Commando, Royal Marines, in the Shoalwater area. On conclusion of the manoeuvres she returned to Singapore.

On 17 December *Hampshire* left Singapore in company with *Arethusa, Llandaff* and *Londonderry* for exercises in local waters and next day her Medical Officer and sickbay staff were required to carry out an emergency appendectomy on a rating who was flown across from *Londonderry*. The operation was a complete success and three days later *Hampshire* and *Londonderry* put into Hong Kong, where they would spend the Christmas holiday. The new year, however, was spent at sea en route back to Singapore and on 30 January 1967, flying the flag of FO2, *Hampshire* left Singapore for a five-day official visit to Manila, after which she joined *Victorious* and *Leopard* for manoeuvres in the Subic Bay area. Four days after leaving Manila *Hampshire* returned to Hong Kong where the advance party for the ship's third commission joined the ship and the first phase of the second commission left by air for home. After leaving Hong Kong *Hampshire* returned to Singapore to undergo maintenance after which, on 11 March, she left the naval base to make a ten-day passage, via Gan, to Aden where she stayed just long enough to refuel, before setting course for the Red Sea and Suez.

Arriving in Suez Bay on 24 March, *Hampshire* made her northbound transit of the Suez Canal and pausing briefly in the Great Bitter Lake, she entered the Mediterranean at just before midnight the same day. Three days later she made a refuelling stop at Malta and another at Gibraltar, before arriving in Plymouth Sound for Customs clearance on 2 April. Next forenoon she secured alongside Portsmouth's South Railway Jetty where families were waiting to greet her. It was not, however, the end of the commission for the ship had been chosen to lead a series of official visits to the USA, but during the first dog watch on 9 May an explosion and fire in the Gas Turbine Control Room almost put paid to her scheduled departure. Fortunately the ship's own fire and emergency parties, assisted by the Dockyard and City Fire Brigades, were able to contain the outbreak and limit any damage. Although two ratings were treated for minor injuries, by 18 May all the damage had been repaired and that forenoon, flying the flag of FO2 Western Fleet, *Hampshire* left Portsmouth to rendezvous with *Euryalus*, *Torquay* and RFA *Tidepool* before setting course across the Atlantic bound for Canada. On 26 May *Hampshire* anchored at the mouth of the St Lawrence River and next morning she began her 34-hour passage of the river and seaway to secure alongside Montreal's City Harbour. From Montreal she returned to the St Lawrence Seaway and into Lake Ontario to Toronto and from there to Port Dalhousie on the Canadian/US border, where she negotiated the Welland Canal which joins Lakes Ontario and Erie, bypassing the Niagara River and Falls. Entering Lake Erie at Welland the destroyer steamed across to the mouth of the Detroit River for a three-hour transit to Detroit's smaller neighbour, Windsor, on the opposite side of the river, where she secured alongside at Dieppe Gardens. The visit lasted four days, after which *Hampshire* negotiated the series of rivers, lakes, canals and seaway on her passage to Halifax, Nova Scotia. This was the final port of call after which she recrossed the Atlantic, arriving alongside at Portsmouth on 4 July. Six days later she began three days of manoeuvres in the Lyme Bay area, but when she returned to Portsmouth on 13 July it was the end of the commission and she would spend five months alongside there and high and dry in C Lock.

On 6 November 1967, Captain Richard J. Trowbridge RN took command of the ship. In 1935 Trowbridge had joined the Navy as a Boy Seaman and was commissioned as a Sub-Lieutenant in December 1940. In the post-war years he commanded the destroyer *Carysfort* and the Fishery Protection Squadron. Six weeks after he joined *Hampshire*, the ship was recommissioned at 1130 on Saturday 16 December, with the official guests including the Flag Officer, Flotillas, Western Fleet. Two days after the ceremony *Hampshire* put to sea to begin her post-refit trials, followed by her work-up at Portland and missile firings off the Welsh coast. During this hectic period there were only short weekend breaks and over the first weekend of June she took part in Rosyth Navy Days. Following this she joined *Danae, Decoy, Jaguar, Juno, Naiad* and *Zulu* for various exercises and manoeuvres off Orkney. These ended when the whole force anchored in the old wartime base at Scapa Flow where, by 1968, there were very few reminders that this had once been a vitally important strategic base for the Royal Navy. After leaving Scapa Flow *Hampshire* returned south to Portsmouth and for the rest of June she stayed close to home, undergoing day-running exercises in the Channel.

HMS *Hampshire*'s first foreign run ashore of the commission came in early July when, flying the flag of Flag Officer Flotillas, she made a five-day visit to the Swedish port of Malmo, after which she steamed to Rosyth to join 50 other ships of the Western Fleet as they gathered for 'Exercise Seaforth'. It had been well over ten years since such a display of naval strength had been seen in Scottish waters and among other ships present were *Kent* (flag C-in-C Western Fleet, Admiral Sir John Bush), *Bulwark* (Flag Officer Aircraft Carriers), *Undaunted* (Flag Officer Sea Training), *Aisne, Arethusa, Cleopatra, Danae, Eskimo, Galatea, Juno, Keppel, Relentless, Rhyl* and the submarines *Otter* and *Walrus*. As well as undergoing a series of exercises and manoeuvres at sea, there was also a full programme of sporting activities from which *Hampshire* emerged as 'Cock of the Fleet'. It was said that the competitive spirit was so infectious that seven admirals and ten captains entered the veterans' races. The finale of 'Exercise Seaforth' began on 1 August when, watched by hundreds of early risers at vantage points along the Forth Road Bridge, the ships of the fleet left their berths at Rosyth to steam into the North Sea. Once east of the Bass Rock *Kent* slowed to eight knots to allow each ship in turn to steam past on either side of the flagship in salute to the retiring First Sea Lord, Admiral Sir Varyl Begg. Sweeping by that day the array of warships included the elderly Battle-class destroyer *Aisne*, on her last commission, as well as the handsome Leander-class frigates *Danae* and *Juno*, both on their first commissions. Overhead a Shackleton

HMS Hampshire

A fine aerial view of *Hampshire* at sea showing the layout of the two twin 4.5-inch turrets.
(Crown Copyright/MoD)

County Class GMDs

On 26 April 1966, en route to the Far East, *Hampshire* called briefly at Grand Harbour, Malta. *(Michael Cassar)*

After having navigated Canada's St Lawrence River in May 1967, *Hampshire* visited Montreal's City Harbour. *(Syd Goodman Collection)*

and six Buccaneers of 800 Squadron roared over the fleet at just above masthead height. At midday, with the ceremony over, *Hampshire* set course for Portsmouth and arrived alongside 24 hours later.

On 9 September, with summer leave and maintenance completed, *Hampshire* sailed to join *Eagle*, *Arethusa*, *Argonaut* and other ships, including the Canadian aircraft carrier *Bonaventure*, for a nine-nation NATO exercise code-named 'Silver Tower'. These manoeuvres, lasting 17 days, took the ships deep into Arctic waters where, as always in those days, the Soviet Navy took a close interest in proceedings with long-range 'Bears' and 'Badgers' flying overhead[2], and two Kotlin-class destroyers, accompanied by ocean-going trawlers, continually trailing the NATO fleet. By Saturday 28 September *Hampshire* had returned to Portsmouth to undergo a period of maintenance before her next major exercise. It was 21 October when she next put to sea, this time to rendezvous with *Arethusa, Valiant* and two RFAs, for the passage to Gibraltar where they joined other ships before setting course for Malta. They were heading for the largest NATO exercise in the Mediterranean for many years, involving more than 50 warships from France, Greece, Italy, Britain and the USA in wide-ranging manoeuvres designed to improve co-ordination and readiness in the area. The Royal Navy sent 17 warships in addition to *Hampshire* (flag Vice-Admiral A. M. Lewis, FO Flotillas). These were: *Barrosa, Cavalier, Juno, Mohawk, Jaguar, Leopard, Sirius, Troubridge, Valiant, Oracle, Grampus, Alliance* and five RFAs. Under the overall command of the Italian Admiral Luciano Sotgui, 'Exercise Eden Apple' lasted for two weeks and once again the large NATO presence attracted a great deal of interest from the Soviet Navy, including their latest helicopter carrier *Moskva*. Aircraft from all participating nations took part, including RAF formations and 800, 849 and 899 Squadrons from *Eagle*, which was refitting at Devonport. *Hampshire*'s ship's company enjoyed runs ashore at Malta and Naples before their return home to Portsmouth. The destroyer's homecoming during the morning of 5 December presented an impressive sight rarely seen these days as she led *Kent, Cambrian, Arethusa, Leopard, Sirius, Jaguar* and RFA *Olmeda* into harbour.

On 16 January 1969 there was another change of command when Captain Richard P. Clayton RN, who had left *Kent* as she began a long refit, took over from Trowbridge and five days later, flying the flag of FO Flotillas, Vice-Admiral Lewis, *Hampshire* sailed for Portland to join *Arethusa, Juno* and other ships of the Western Fleet to take part in an Anglo-French exercise in the Channel and Western Approaches. Five days later, however, *Hampshire* in company with *Arethusa, Juno*, the submarines *Narwhal* and *Otus* and RFAs *Lyness* and *Olwen*, set course for the Caribbean. The squadron was on a goodwill tour of five South American countries which would take them through the Panama Canal, down the west coast of South America and up the east coast. The first port of call was Bridgetown and from there they steamed west to Panama. On 16 February *Hampshire* completed her transit of the canal and entered the Pacific Ocean then two days later, as she steamed towards Callao, the equator was crossed with due ceremony. On 21 February she arrived at the port, which serves the Peruvian capital Lima. At Callao Admiral Lewis and Captain Clayton laid a wreath to the Peruvian national hero, Almirante Grau, and afterwards a ceremonial guard made up of men from *Hampshire, Arethusa* and *Juno* marched through the city. When opened to the public all three ships proved to be popular attractions. From Callao the squadron steamed south towards Valparaiso, carrying out an anti-submarine exercise 'Albion', with *Narwhal* and *Otus* en route, after which they anchored in Bahia Tongoi for two hours during the evening of 4 March while officials from the Chilean city of Coquimbo were welcomed aboard. They arrived in Valparaiso two days later and during the four-day visit *Hampshire*'s emergency party put on an impressive display when they tackled a large fire in the docks and had it well under control by the

---

[2] The 'Bear' was the NATO reporting name for the Tupolev 95 and the 'Badger' was the Tupolev 16. They were two very successful post-war Soviet bombers.

time the fire brigade arrived.

After leaving Valparaiso the squadron split up for visits to Buenos Aires, Mar del Plata, the Falkland Islands and Montevideo. However, before going their separate ways, just 12 hours after leaving Valparaiso they passed Coronel where speed was reduced and wreaths were laid in memory of the 1,800 men who lost their lives when the cruisers *Good Hope* and *Monmouth* were sunk in November 1914, the Navy's first major setback of the Great War. Five days later *Hampshire* rounded Cape Horn and on 16 March she passed the Falkland Islands. Next came a joint exercise with the Argentinean Navy, after which she steamed up the River Plate to secure alongside in Buenos Aires for a ten-day self-maintenance period. At this time the Argentine invasion of the Falkland Islands was still 13 years into the future and in 1969 relations between Britain and the South American country were good so many ex-*Hampshire*'s have happy and pleasant memories of the visit. After leaving Buenos Aires on the last day of March *Hampshire*'s final South American port of call was Rio de Janeiro, after which she rejoined *Arethusa* and *Juno* for some final manoeuvres before the latter set course for the Indian Ocean, while *Hampshire* and *Arethusa* began their passage home via Gibraltar. Finally, on 25 April, *Hampshire* secured alongside Portsmouth's Fountain Lake Jetty to undergo a five-week maintenance period.

On 2 June 1969, *Hampshire* left Portsmouth to join *Andromeda*, *Defender* and the submarine *Osiris* to carry out exercises in the North Sea and the Baltic, with visits to Gothenburg and Copenhagen. In July she spent ten days off the missile ranges at Aberporth and three days at Devonport, before steaming to Portland to join other ships of the Western Fleet for a rehearsal of the Fleet Review which was due to be held in Tor Bay later that month. The Review itself was spread over four days, beginning on 26 July when *Hampshire* and 39 other ships anchored in the bay during the afternoon. The largest warship present was the aircraft carrier *Eagle* (flag C-in-C Western Fleet) along with *Blake*, *Glamorgan*, *Diana*, 11 frigates, eight submarines, a variety of smaller ships and four RFAs. On 27 July 20 of the ships, including *Hampshire*, were opened to the public and on the third and fourth days the Queen visited a number of them, including *Hampshire*, and the Review ended with the fleet saluting the royal yacht with a steam past. With the ceremonies over *Hampshire* anchored off Brighton Pier for a three-day visit to the seaside resort and shortly before sailing on 1 August families were embarked for a day at sea, which included helicopter flying and gunnery displays. Finally, *Hampshire* secured alongside Portsmouth's Fountain Lake Jetty later in the afternoon to give leave and for maintenance. During Navy Days that summer she attracted well over 23,000 visitors.

The final leg of *Hampshire*'s commission began on 15 September 1969, when she left Portsmouth for weapons training in the Portland area and seven days later, after a weekend spent at Devonport, she sailed for Gibraltar and the Mediterranean. It had been announced that *Hampshire*, together with the aircraft carrier *Eagle* and the frigate *Aurora*, was taking part in a routine NATO exercise 'Deep Furrow' in the eastern Mediterranean and Aegean Sea. This was in response to the closure by Spain of the border and telephone links with Gibraltar and with large crowds demonstrating on the Spanish side of the border, it had been decided to increase the Navy's presence at Gibraltar and both *Eagle* and *Hampshire* spent a week in the area, where they also monitored Soviet naval activity. On 1 October, in response to calls for assistance after severe flooding in Tunisia following four days of non-stop torrential rain which had taken the lives of 500 people and left 100,000 homeless, *Hampshire* put into the port of La Goullette, close to Tunis city, where working parties assisted with flood relief duties.

On 4 October *Hampshire* left Tunisia and steamed to Malta to carry out an eight-day self-maintenance period, before joining *Eagle*, *Aurora* and four RFAs for 'Exercise Deep Furrow' which began off south-west Crete and then moved into the Aegean Sea. The exercise ended during the afternoon of 29 October, after which *Hampshire* made

HMS Hampshire

HMS *Hampshire* and other ships of the Western Fleet steam past the Royal Yacht during the July 1969 Fleet Review in Tor Bay. *(World Ship Society)*

her way back to Gibraltar. At this time she exercised with *Charybdis, Decoy* and *Scarborough* in local waters before making a five-day visit to Toulon and returning east to Malta. On 6 December, however, she left Grand Harbour to make a six-day passage back to Portsmouth where she paid off in early January 1970. Soon her ship's company had been reduced to just a small care and maintenance party whose job it was to prepare the ship for a period in reserve, followed by a long refit.

For over three years *Hampshire* lay in Portsmouth Dockyard's No 3 basin or in C Lock and at one stage, with shortages of manpower in the Navy and the fact that rapid advances in technology were fast making her and her sisters outdated, it was rumoured that she might not sail again. It was during this period laid up at Portsmouth that *Hampshire*'s care and maintenance party heard that 80-year-old Walter Farden, who had served in the old cruiser *Hampshire* when she had been sunk by a mine and lost off Orkney in 1916 and who was believed to be the last survivor of that tragedy, was in Chichester Hospital. The party visited the elderly survivor, a gesture which was much appreciated as it gave him an opportunity to talk over old times. The final six months of *Hampshire*'s lay-up period were spent in dockyard hands as the destroyer underwent a refit which would prepare her for further operational service.

By March 1973 *Hampshire* was back alongside the sea wall at Fountain Lake Jetty and on 21 May her new commanding officer, Captain Peter I. F. Beeson MVO RN, was appointed. That same month the ship's main engines were warmed through and turned for the first time since 1970 and on 4 June *Hampshire*'s complement was brought up to trials strength. Seven days later the ship left Portsmouth to begin 17 days of main machinery trials, but on 28 June, with a major defect having developed, she returned to Portsmouth and the dry dock, where she

County Class GMDs

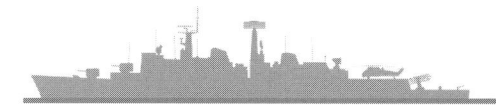

Floodlit in Malta's Grand Harbour during her Mediterranean deployment of October 1974, *Hampshire* presents an impressive sight. *(Crown Copyright/MoD 1974)*

remained until the second week of August. She was then moved back to Fountain Lake Jetty, where she took part in Navy Days and attracted some 9,900 visitors. On 31 August *Hampshire* was recommissioned and three days later she began her acceptance trials, which were successfully completed on 12 September. Next day she took a number of VIPs to sea for a day of displays, after which she returned to Portsmouth Dockyard.

HMS *Hampshire*'s first official duty of the new commission came on 20 September when she steamed north, via the Kiel Canal, to Stockholm, where she represented the Royal Navy at the funeral of King Gustav. During the return passage through the North Sea she was diverted to a point some 60 miles off the Norfolk coast to investigate a Soviet trawler which had been sailing too close to the new oil rigs which were springing up around the North Sea. On her arrival the trawler had disappeared and *Hampshire* resumed her passage to Portsmouth.

During October *Hampshire* continued her trials from Portsmouth, but in early November she steamed south to Gibraltar where she monitored Soviet naval movements through the Strait and exercised with her sister *Norfolk*, and *Argonaut*. By the end of the month she had returned to Portsmouth to give leave and to prepare for her work-up which was scheduled to begin at Portland on 10 January 1974. The destroyer's first sea work-up got under way on 21 January in a Channel which was being lashed by severe gale force winds and heavy seas. On one occasion, after her 'board and tow' exercise with RFA *Olwen* had been cancelled by Force 10 winds in the Portland area, a signal was intercepted from the Cypriot-registered coaster *Zodiac Steve* to the effect that she had suffered an engine room fire and was drifting out of control some 17 miles off Portland. *Hampshire* was immediately sent to the scene and on arrival found that the fire had been contained by the closing of all engine room hatches. The destroyer's helicopter quickly evacuated the coaster's Chief Engineer who was flown to Portland and the cancelled 'board and

HMS Hampshire

tow' operation was now carried out for real. It was not long before *Hampshire* had towed the coaster to the safety of Portland Harbour, where Admiralty tugs took over and the vessel was safely anchored. *Hampshire*'s work-up was completed successfully on 20 February, after which she steamed to Devonport to embark her outfit of Sea Slug missiles. She then proceeded to the Aberporth area to carry out test firings, which continued through to mid-March when she returned to Portsmouth to give leave.

On 1 April 1974 *Hampshire* left Portsmouth and steamed north to the Clyde area for anti-submarine exercises with *Andrew*, the last British submarine to carry a 4-inch deck gun, before heading south for Gibraltar and the Mediterranean. Leaving Gibraltar on 9 April *Hampshire* rendezvoused with *Llandaff* for the passage east and a five-day visit to Split in what was then Yugoslavia (now Croatia). At the end of April *Hampshire*, *Hermes*, *Fearless*, *Achilles*, *Lowestoft*, the submarine *Opportune* and three RFAs joined the NATO exercise 'Dawn Patrol', which altogether involved some 60 ships from six nations. Beginning off Crete the exercise involved a major amphibious landing, but during the morning watch on 4 May there was real-life drama when a Turkish Starfighter which was 'attacking' the splash target being towed by *Hampshire* crashed into the sea just astern of the destroyer. During its attack the aircraft could be seen diving at what appeared to be too steep an angle and it only pulled out of the dive when close to the ship's stern. Lookouts then reported seeing a parachute some miles away and the exercise quickly took the form of a search-and-rescue operation. In the event just seven minutes after leaving the destroyer's deck *Hampshire*'s Wessex helicopter, affectionately known to all as 'Humphrey', had winched the pilot from his dinghy and flown him to *Hermes*. For *Hampshire* and *Lowestoft* the exercise ended at Naples and from there the two ships steamed to Malta, where *Hampshire* undertook a ten-day self-maintenance period, before returning via Gibraltar to Portsmouth.

During June *Hampshire*, in company with *Yarmouth*, steamed north to Kiel for 'Kieler Woche', followed by a visit to the Swedish port of Helsingborg before returning south to Portland and Portsmouth. In early July she steamed up Southampton Water to the city's docks for a 'Meet the Navy' programme, which involved local schools and Sea Cadets. This was concluded with a day at sea for Sea Cadets and local VIPs. Later that month, flying the flag of the C-in-C Fleet, Admiral Sir Terence Lewin, she paid a five-day visit to Brest, before returning to Portsmouth to undergo six weeks of maintenance. Since recommissioning in August 1973 she had travelled some 30,000 miles.

On 2 September 1974 *Hampshire* left Portsmouth to steam south for Gibraltar and then to Malta. From there she made her way to the troubled island of Cyprus where the Turkish Army had invaded the northern section of the island. By that time British nationals had been evacuated, but until the end of the month *Hampshire* remained in the vicinity of Akrotiri Bay. After a short visit to Capri and Naples, where the C-in-C Fleet once again hoisted his flag, she returned to Malta. In mid-October *Hampshire* joined *Ark Royal* for exercises in the central Mediterranean, which included two days at anchor in the Bay of Porto Di Stefano, Sardinia. Following a weekend visit to Ajaccio in early November *Hampshire* steamed west to Gibraltar, from where she took part in exercises with the cruiser *Tiger* and the submarine *Sovereign*, as well as a multi-national exercise with French and Dutch ships. On 28 November she returned once again to Portsmouth.

On 3 January 1975 there was a final change of command when Captain Michael C. Henry RN took over the ship and four days later, during the forenoon of 7 January, *Hampshire* left Portsmouth to rendezvous with *Ark Royal, Fearless, Tartar* and the RFAs *Olwen* and *Resource*, for a transatlantic crossing to the US Navy's base at Roosevelt Roads, Puerto Rico. During the 11-day crossing helicopter crews from *Ark Royal*, *Hampshire* and *Resource* took part in a search-and-rescue competition, which involved precision winching a simulated 'man overboard' and a high-line transfer. In the event *Ark*

On 14 May 1975 *Hampshire* left Rio de Janeiro to join the carrier *Ark Royal* for exercise 'Brasex' before setting course for home. *(Crown Copyright/MoD 1975)*

Royal's helicopter crew won, but only by the narrowest of margins over *Hampshire*'s crew. During the exercises with *Ark Royal* and *Fearless* on the 'Atlantic Fleet Weapons Range' *Hampshire* carried out Sea Slug firings and for recreation there were visits to Virgin Gorda Island and Vieques Island. On 6 February *Hampshire* left the exercise area for the city of Charleston, South Carolina. During the ship's nine-day visit one guest on board was the renowned Second World War US General Mark Clark, who also invited a number of officers to his home.

From Charleston *Hampshire* returned to Puerto Rico to join *Ark Royal* for 'Exercise Landtreadex' an arduous three weeks of manoeuvres, which ended with a six-day break in Nassau. On 4 April, two days after leaving the Bahamas, *Hampshire* arrived at the US naval base in Norfolk, Virginia, for a 20-day period of self-maintenance. During the final week of this period, back in London the Government's Defence Review was announced and among the cuts which were to be made came the news that within 12 months *Hampshire* was to be withdrawn from operational service. The reason given was the fact that she had not been modernised, but the high manpower requirements in respect of the County-class destroyers were well known and there is no doubt that this also was a major factor in the decision making process.

After leaving Norfolk *Hampshire* joined *Ark Royal* to steam south for Brazilian waters where they rendezvoused with a squadron which included *Blake, Leander, Achilles, Diomede, Falmouth, Lowestoft*, the submarine *Warspite* and four RFAs, which were returning from a Far Eastern deployment, before the whole force carried out weapons training exercises with Brazilian Navy ships, which included *Maria E. Barnos, Esperito Santo* and *Naranhao*. This part of the deployment also included a seven-day visit to Rio de Janeiro where

HMS Hampshire

Hampshire was opened to the public and in the course of one afternoon some 5,000 people visited the ship. On 14 May, when *Hampshire* left Rio she took part in 'Exercise Brasex' with Brazilian ships after which, in company with *Blake* and *Leander*, she set course for Gibraltar and home. During the transatlantic crossing *Hampshire* was subjected to Admiral's inspection and on 1 June she arrived in Gibraltar where she remained for eight days before returning to the UK and, during the evening of 11 June, anchoring at Spithead. Next forenoon, having embarked families, *Hampshire* steamed up harbour to secure alongside Fountain Lake Jetty.

Staying just long enough for essential maintenance, on 25 June *Hampshire* left Portsmouth to steam north to the Clyde area where she undertook anti-submarine exercises. These were followed in July by a six-day visit to Birkenhead, before she returned to Portsmouth in time for Navy Days, when over 18,000 people visited the ship. In mid-September she carried out weapons training and acted as planeguard for *Ark Royal*. Later in the month she joined *Blake, Ariadne, Norfolk* (Flag FOF1) and *Scylla* for exercises in the Atlantic off the western islands of Scotland, after which she once again returned to Portsmouth where she hoisted the flag of the C-in-C Fleet, Admiral Sir John Treacher. On 10 October *Hampshire* paid a five-day visit to Swansea and later in the month she exercised with Dutch ships in the Atlantic as far south as Gibraltar. After spending most of November undergoing maintenance at Portsmouth, during the first week of December she assisted the destroyer *Bristol* with her work-up, before steaming up the River Scheldt for a weekend visit to Antwerp, before assisting the new frigate *Amazon* with her work-up and then returning to Portsmouth in time for Christmas.

The final phase of *Hampshire*'s career began on Tuesday 6 January 1976, when she left Portsmouth to join exercises with French ships in the Bay of Biscay, before steaming south to Gibraltar from

In late 1976, shortly before she paid off for the last time, *Hampshire* made a farewell visit to London. Here she is seen secured alongside the preserved cruiser *Belfast* in the Pool of London. *(Maritime Photo Library)*

County Class GMDs

In early June 1976 *Hampshire* left Portsmouth for Chatham, where all reusable equipment was stripped.
(James W. Goss)

Hampshire's final resting place, the shipbreaker's yard at Briton Ferry, South Wales. This photograph, taken soon after her arrival in the summer of 1979, shows her high and dry and awaiting the cutting torches.
(T. Ferrers-Walker Collection)

HMS Hampshire

where she operated for the rest of the month. In mid-February, with *Kent*, the cruiser *Blake, Ark Royal* and a Dutch naval force, she took part in 'Exercise Springtrain' in the Atlantic Ocean. The end of that exercise saw most of the ships making a transatlantic crossing for the exercise areas at Puerto Rico, but *Hampshire* remained in the Gibraltar area where she exercised with the submarine *Cachalot*. The first few days of March saw *Hampshire* exercising from Gibraltar before, on 5 March, she joined *Keppel* for the passage east for what was to be a four-day farewell visit to Malta. After leaving Grand Harbour *Hampshire* returned to Gibraltar, but only stayed long enough to refuel before steaming north, first to Devonport and then to Portsmouth where, during the forenoon of 19 March she secured alongside Norfolk at Fountain Lake Jetty. *Hampshire*'s last ten days of active service began on 22 March when she sailed from Portsmouth to carry out a farewell visit to London. Next forenoon, after a three-hour passage up the River Thames and under Tower Bridge, she secured alongside the museum ship *Belfast* in the Pool of London. That same evening her sponsor Princess Margaret attended a reception aboard and for four consecutive days the ship was opened to the public. At 1300 on 28 March *Hampshire* slipped her moorings and retraced her route downriver to make a coastal passage back to the Solent for a farewell visit to her adopted county city of Southampton where, at 0930 on 29 March, she secured alongside the port's prestigious Queen Elizabeth II Terminal in the Eastern Docks. Next day, at 1730, there was a farewell ceremony on the quay alongside the ship which was attended by civic dignitaries from the county of *Hampshire* and senior officers of the Royal Hampshire Regiment. Finally, at 1000 on the last day of March, *Hampshire* slipped her moorings and set course for Portsmouth. As she steamed down Southampton Water the ship's Wessex helicopter, 'Humphrey', flew off the ship for the last time and at just before midday families were embarked at Spithead for the last leg of the passage home. An hour later *Hampshire* had secured alongside Middle Slip Jetty and 'Finished With Engines' was rung down to the Machinery Control Room.

Within hours of her arrival in Portsmouth *Hampshire*'s executive officer, Commander Hugh Hart-Dyke, who later commanded *Coventry* during the Falklands War, had relieved Captain Henry, and the ship's complement was drastically reduced. There were rumours that the ship might be sold to a foreign navy, but these came to nothing and in early June 1976 she slipped quietly out of Portsmouth Harbour bound for Chatham to be de-equipped and de-stored before disposal. The end for *Hampshire* came in April 1979 when she was sold to the shipbreaking company of Thomas W. Ward and towed to the Welsh port of Briton Ferry at the mouth of the River Neath. By the summer of 1980 she had ceased to exist.

Commanding Officers:

Captain Robert White CBE RN	1 June 1962
Captain Frederick W. Hayden DSC RN	11 November 1964
Captain Ian D. McLaughlan DSC RN	11 June 1966
Captain Richard J. Trowbridge RN	6 November 1967
Captain Richard P. Clayton RN	16 January 1969
Captain Peter I. F. Beeson MVO RN	21 May 1973
Captain Michael C. Henry RN	3 January 1975

Battle Honours:

Gabbard	1653	Schooneveld	1673
Santa Cruz	1657	Texel	1673
Lowestoft	1665	Orfordness	1666
Jutland	1916		

Chapter Three

HMS KENT
1963 - 1997

On 27 September 1961, *Kent* was launched from Harland and Wolff's shipyard at Belfast. Here she is seen taking to the waters of the Lagan for the first time. (*World Ship Society*)

The third ship of the County-class to be commissioned, beating her sister *London* by just three months, was HMS *Kent*. Her keel had been laid on 1 March 1960 at the Abercorn Yard of Harland & Wolff Ltd in Belfast, close to the slipway where the P&O passenger liner *Canberra* was waiting to be launched. With a great deal of the metal prefabrication work having already been carried out and the steel plate having been stockpiled alongside the slipway, building work on the new destroyer proceeded quickly and by September 1961 she was ready to take to the water. The ceremony took place at 1300 on Wednesday 27 September, when Princess Marina, Duchess of Kent, named the ship and sent the hull down into the waters of the River Lagan. Some idea of government thinking at the time came when the First Lord of the Admiralty, in a speech following the launch, told his audience that the new destroyer would be one of six ships which, with aircraft carriers, would form the backbone of the Navy's defence against air and submarine attacks. Clearly, at that stage there had been no firm decision to build the last two County-class ships. It was also apparent that the Admiralty was still very much wedded to the idea of the fleet aircraft carrier, but it would be two years before serious planning work on the ill-fated CVA-01 began, and by the time it did get under way it soon fell victim to defence cuts, having been vetoed by the RAF's 'bomber lobby'.

The fitting-out work on *Kent* took longer than the first stage of construction on the slipway, but on 12 March 1963 the destroyer's first commanding officer Captain John G. Wells DSC RN was appointed.

County Class GMDs

HMS *Kent* at sea in August 1963 following her final acceptance trials. She arrived at Portsmouth for the first time on 26 August. *(Crown Copyright/MoD 1963)*

It was not the first time he had commissioned an HMS *Kent*, for as a sub-lieutenant in June 1928 he had commissioned the 10,000-ton County-class cruiser of that name. By mid-August 1963 over half of *Kent*'s complement of 488 officers and ratings had joined the ship and on 14 August *Kent* herself was moved to the Stormont Wharf in the Victoria Channel. At 1430 the next day all hands not on watch mustered on the jetty for the commissioning ceremony, which was attended by the C-in-C Home Fleet, Admiral Sir Charles Madden who, as a young sub-lieutenant, had served in the cruiser *Kent*. As well as a number of VIP guests an Army contingent from the Queen's Own Buffs, the Royal Kent Regiment, also attended the ceremony.

Two days later, at 0900 on Saturday 17 August, *Kent* left her berth to undergo her final acceptance trials in the Irish Sea and the Firth of Clyde. These were completed successfully and at 1800 the same day she was formally accepted from Harland & Wolff. Later that evening the ship anchored in Carrickfergus Bay for the night and next day *Kent*'s machinery trials began in earnest, with short overnight breaks off Peel, Isle of Man, at Loch Ewe, Plymouth Sound, Weymouth Bay and St Helen's Bay on the Isle of Wight. Finally, during the forenoon of 26 August she secured alongside Portsmouth's North Corner Jetty. Although she did not open for Navy Days that month, during the last weekend of August the ship was opened to private guests.

On 6 October *Kent* steamed out to a Spithead anchorage where a Wessex helicopter practised deck landings and four days later she returned to Portsmouth Dockyard. Six days after this she made the short passage to Chatham Dockyard, where she secured in No 3 basin. On 18 October she was visited by her sponsor and next day, as well as being opened to the public, there was a ceremony on board when the ship's bell from the pre-war cruiser HMS *Kent* was presented; this had been in the safe-keeping of the Royal Marines Barracks at Deal since 1948. During the afternoon a contingent from the 'HMS *Kent* Association', some of whose members had served in the cruiser of that name between 1903 and 1920, visited the ship. With the ceremonial duties over, *Kent* remained at Chatham for the weekend before embarking a party of Harland & Wolff engineers for the ship's main machinery trials which took place in the Channel during 23 and 24 October. Unfortunately, during the trials it became apparent that there were defects in the starboard main feed governor, for which Harland & Wolff accepted responsibility, but it meant that the ship had to return to Portsmouth for repairs which lasted for two weeks.

HMS *Kent*'s main trials began on 11 November and continued into the first week of December when the ship returned to Portsmouth to give leave. During the seasonal break a reunion lunch was held on board for officers who had commissioned the cruiser *Kent* in 1928 and among those present were three Admirals, including Admiral of the Fleet Sir Philip Vian. Other visitors included more men from the 'HMS *Kent* Association', including a retired Captain who, as a Petty Officer, had fought at the Battle of the Falkland Islands, and 86-year-old Lieutenant Herbert Kentsbeer who, as a Boy Seaman, had commissioned the seventh *Kent* in 1901. In mid-January *Kent* joined *Hampshire* (Flag Officer Flotillas, Home) and *London* to steam north for Rosyth, where the three ships carried out flying trials with a Whirlwind helicopter. In early February *Kent* steamed further north into the Arctic Circle for cold weather trials, which ended with a three-day visit to Tromso before the ship returned via Rosyth to Portsmouth. The second week of March saw *Kent* at Portland and beginning a gruelling ten-week work-up period, during which she was assisted by *Ajax* and *Corunna*. *Kent*'s final sea inspection took place during 13 and 14 May and by the forenoon of the second day she had disembarked Flag Officer Sea Training and his staff and had set course for Devonport, where she secured alongside the cruiser *Tiger* and loaded a full outfit of Sea Slug missiles. Five days later she steamed round to the Welsh coast to carry out a ten-day programme of missile firing on the Aberporth ranges, broken only by a 37-hour visit to Belfast.

By now reports were circulating to the effect that

Kent would be among a number of naval ships which were being sent east to augment Britain's naval strength in the Far East Fleet, based at Singapore. Indonesia had reacted violently to the British-sponsored Federation of Malaysia, which was bringing together Britain's former colonial possessions in South-East Asia, namely Malaya, Singapore and the territories of Sarawak and North Borneo (Sabah). This had resulted in an armed Confrontation which manifested itself initially during the closing weeks of 1962 with an armed revolt in Brunei. Thanks to the timely intervention of the commando carrier *Albion* the rebellion was quickly quashed, but no sooner had it been dealt with than the Indonesian Army began incursions into British North Borneo and Sarawak, and in April 1963 the colonial 'brush fire war' became known euphemistically as Confrontation. The Indonesian Navy had acquired a Sverdlov-class cruiser, INS *Irian*, formerly *Ordzhonikidze*, which together with a strong destroyer and frigate force far outweighed the small coastal force operated by Malaya and Singapore, so as far as the Royal Navy was concerned it also required a significant presence in the Far East. HMS *Kent* was in fact bound for Singapore and on 30 May 1964 she secured alongside Chatham Dockyard's No 3 basin to begin a six-week period of dockyard-assisted maintenance, while the ship's company took foreign service leave. That same day there was also a change of command when Captain Andrew M. Lewis RN took over from Wells. Sadly the ship's first long period of dockyard maintenance was marred by the death of a dockyard worker, who was killed when heavy equipment fell on to him from a crane.

The maintenance period ended on 14 July and next day *Kent* sailed for Devonport to embark Sea Slug missiles, then three days later she left for Gibraltar and the Mediterranean. Pausing briefly at Gibraltar to refuel and carry out exercises with *Brighton* off Malta, *Kent* arrived in Port Said during the afternoon of 30 July and at just before midnight she began her transit of the Suez Canal. By the next afternoon she was steaming south through the Red Sea, bound for Aden where, to everyone's relief, only three days were spent at the port. By 12 August she was at Gan and refuelling from the hulk *Wave Victor* in Gan Lagoon. Five days later she secured alongside Singapore Naval Base and officially joined the Far East Fleet.

HMS *Kent*'s arrival in the Far East coincided with a period of heightened tension in the Confrontation with Indonesia and, after a failed summit meeting between President Sukarno and the Malaysian Prime Minister Tungku Abdul Rahman, Indonesia actually landed an infiltration party of its regular soldiers on the south-west coast of Malaya. For *Kent* and other ships at the naval base this increased tension meant increased vigilance around all the ship, with ships' divers, augmented by divers from HMS *Terror*, making regular checks on all ships' underwater hulls.

On 1 September *Kent* left Singapore Naval Base to rendezvous with the aircraft carrier *Centaur* and RFA *Resurgent* for local exercises before setting course for Hong Kong. However, next day when the ships were just south of Pulau Tioman, the passage to Hong Kong was cancelled and *Kent* was ordered to patrol the Strait of Malacca. It transpired that a force of some 96 Indonesian paratroopers had landed in the area around Labis, on the main trunk road through Malaya's Johore State and roughly halfway between Yong Peng and Segamat. In the event the Indonesians were quickly dealt with by the Malaysian Army, but this was a serious escalation from the cross-border incursions on the island of Borneo. For most of September *Kent*, together with *Centaur*, *Ajax*, *Berwick*, *Vampire* and *Vendetta*, patrolled the strait between Malaysia and Sumatra, but with the close proximity of the two coastlines and with literally hundreds of fishing boats and merchant ships of all sizes in the area it was virtually impossible to monitor all the shipping. In the second week of September a force of 50 Indonesian troops landed on the Kesang River, just north of Muar in northern Johore, but once again they were quickly dealt with by the Malaysian Army. Finally, on 10 October, after exercising with the submarines *Anchorite* and *Amphion* and the frigate *Loch Fada*, the frigate *Falmouth* joined *Kent* for the postponed visit to Hong Kong, where they arrived four days later.

HMS *Kent*'s first visit to Hong Kong lasted for just eight days before she returned to the naval base at Singapore where, on 30 October, she hoisted the flag of FO2, Rear-Admiral P. J Hill-Norton. Two weeks later she left Singapore for a week's tour of ports in Sarawak and North Borneo, including Kuching, Labuan, Jesselton (Kota Kinabalu) and Tawau. Although shore leave was granted at each stop the towns were small with limited facilities and leave usually ended before midnight. After leaving Tawau on 25 November *Kent* steamed across the Sulu Sea to the US Naval Base at Subic Bay, a run ashore which, once experienced, was never forgotten. This four-day visit was followed by joint exercises with US Navy ships in the Subic Bay exercise areas, after which *Kent* returned to Singapore for ten days of maintenance, then with the minesweepers bearing the brunt of the coastal patrols in the Strait of Malacca and around Malaysian North Borneo, *Kent* was able to return to Hong Kong for a popular Christmas and New Year break.

For *Kent* the new year of 1965 began on 8 January when she left Hong Kong to rendezvous with other ships of the Far East Fleet, including *Victorious*, *Caesar*, HMNZS *Otago* and the submarine *Amphion*, for joint manoeuvres in the South China Sea and the Pacific, which took them as far afield as Okinawa; for *Kent* these ended on the last day of January at Hong Kong. In mid-February she was once again in the South China Sea, this time assisting *Victorious* with FO2's sea inspection. The exercise ended on 24 February when *Kent* returned to Singapore to undergo a three-week dockyard-assisted maintenance period. Although the Confrontation

On 17 October 1963 *Kent* arrived alongside Chatham Dockyard's No3 Basin for her first visit to the Kent naval base. *(Syd Goodman Collection)*

A fine aerial view of Kent manoeuvring at speed. *(Author's Collection)*

with Indonesia would continue until September 1966, Kent's role in the conflict was virtually at an end and on 16 March 1965 she left Singapore to take part in the annual FOTEX manoeuvres, which took the form of anti-aircraft, anti-submarine and convoy escort exercises. Altogether some 40 ships of the Royal Navy, the RAN and RNZN and the fledgling Malaysian Navy took part, including *Eagle*, *Victorious*, *Bulwark* and HMAS *Melbourne*. During the manoeuvres Kent flew the flag of the C-in-C Far East Station, Vice-Admiral Sir Frank Twiss, but on 23 March he and his staff transferred to *Eagle* and Kent anchored off Singapore before, on the last day of the month, setting course for home via the Pacific Ocean.

HMS *Kent*'s 11-week passage home to Portsmouth was intended as a flag-showing tour of US, Canadian and Caribbean ports and her first three visits evoked memories of the Second World War in the Pacific. Seven days after leaving Singapore she put into the island of Guam for 24 hours and six days later she arrived at Midway Island, literally just a sandy island atoll consisting of a US naval base. This time she remained only long enough to refuel before setting course for the highlight of the Pacific leg, the US Naval Base at Pearl Harbor, where she spent six days. Back at sea for seven days she carried out tracking exercises with US Navy aircraft, before arriving at the Canadian Naval Base at Esquimalt, from where she made the short passage to Vancouver for a five-day visit. Steaming south from Canadian waters, at 0815 on 12 May *Kent* passed under San Francisco's Golden Gate Bridge to secure alongside the harbour's No 17 berth, which gave liberty men easy access to the city itself. As always during visits of HM ships to the USA the hospitality shown towards the ship's company was generous. On 17 May *Kent* once again passed under the Golden Gate Bridge, this time bound for the naval base at San Diego, where she arrived alongside three days later. She stayed for just three days, after which she exercised with US Navy ships in the Pacific Ocean and then set course for the Panama Canal. As she arrived alongside Balboa's refuelling pier at 0830 on 31 May, waiting to join the ship was her new commanding officer, Captain R. A. Begg RN, who had flown out from London to relieve Lewis. No sooner had he arrived on board than he had the task of taking the destroyer through the Panama Canal and by 1930 that same day the ship was in the Caribbean and heading for Barbados. *Kent*'s call at Bridgetown was scheduled to last 48 hours, but machinery defects kept her there for five days, before she sailed for Portsmouth. Finally, at 0300 on 17 June, St Catherine's Light on the Isle of Wight was sighted and two hours later she anchored at Spithead. Later that day, having embarked the men's families, *Kent* moved up harbour to secure alongside Portsmouth Dockyard's Middle Slip Jetty. In July she steamed round to the Welsh coast for both Sea Slug and Sea Cat firings and gunnery practice, and these were followed by Home Fleet exercises with *Tiger* and *Dido* and a seven-day visit to Belfast, where some 18,000 people visited the ship. On 5 August, as she left Belfast, *Kent* embarked a group of civic dignitaries from the city and from Harland & Wolff's shipyard, to watch her, in company with *Tiger*, being put through her paces. Next day she steamed into the Firth of Clyde to anchor at the Tail of the Bank, where she joined 70 other ships of the Home Fleet, including the 10th Minesweeping Squadron, manned by men of the Royal Naval Reserve.

The last major event of *Kent*'s first commission was the Royal Review of the Home Fleet in the Firth of Clyde. The previous Clyde review had been in 1947, when three battleships had dominated proceedings, but 18 years later the light fleet carrier *Centaur* was the biggest ship present. The review proceedings were to last several days and during the forenoon of 10 August *Kent* received a brief visit from the Queen. The review itself took place on the next day, when the royal yacht *Britannia* steamed down the rows of warships which, as well as *Centaur* and *Kent*, included the cruiser *Lion*, the depot ship *Maidstone* and the nuclear-powered submarine *Dreadnought*. During the evening of 12 August *Kent* left the Firth of Clyde to join *Tiger, Centaur, Dido, Berwick, Wolverton, Iveston, Brave Borderer, Brave Swordsman*, the submarine *Oracle* and RFA *Olynthus*, to make a joint visit to Merseyside on one of the biggest flag-showing operations to the river. *Kent* was flying the flag of FO2 Home Fleet, Rear-Admiral J. O. C. Hayes, and she led the way upriver to a berth in Liverpool's Brocklebank Dock, off Bootle's Regent Road. Once alongside, FO2's flag was struck and the ship's company enjoyed some warm hospitality during the five-day stopover, which was primarily a recruiting drive. During the early evening of 12 August, when *Kent* left the River Mersey, she made a 30-hour passage to Devonport where, over a period of five days, she was de-ammunitioned before steaming round to Chatham in time to take part in Navy Days, before paying off.

HMS *Kent* remained there in dockyard hands for five months and on 31 January 1966 the Admiral Superintendent at Chatham made his completion date inspection. At noon on Friday 4 March *Kent* was recommissioned and three days later she began her post-refit trials in the Channel while day running from Portsmouth. In April, however, she ventured further north to the Moray Firth area and the east coast of Scotland, before beginning her work-up at Portland. For six gruelling weeks *Kent* exercised in the Channel and Lyme Bay, with assistance being provided by *Ashanti, Cleopatra, Eastbourne*,

Leopard and *Russell*. During the final phase in early June she was able to help the carrier *Victorious*, which was also carrying out her work-up from Portland. On 13 June the First Lord of the Admiralty, whilst visiting ships working up off Portland, transferred by jackstay from *Cleopatra* to *Kent*, from where he was flown ashore. Next day *Kent* successfully completed her work-up period and steamed round to the missile ranges on the Welsh coast where she carried out day-running exercises from Fishguard. On 2 July, as a fully operational ship, she returned to Chatham to give leave and prepare for foreign service.

On 8 August 1966 *Kent* left Chatham bound for the Far East and on 20 August, after a weekend in Gibraltar and 24 hours in Malta, she arrived in Port Said. As well as embarking the pilot and the searchlight, "Mr Mohammed Ali", the doyen of the port's gully-gully men, also went aboard to stage his incredible performance of magician's tricks. That night, at just before midnight, *Kent* led the southbound convoy into the Suez Canal and next morning she anchored in the Great Bitter Lake for eight hours. By 1835, however, she was steaming south to Aden where she made an eight-hour stop, which was quite long enough for most on board, before continuing the passage via RFA *Wave Victor* in Gan Lagoon. She arrived at Singapore Naval Base during the forenoon of 3 September, having completed the 9,000-mile passage in just 23 days.

With the Indonesian Confrontation over, the political situation in Singapore and Malaysia had relaxed somewhat, but within days of her arrival the C-in-C altered *Kent*'s itinerary in order to fly his flag in the destroyer for an official visit to Tokyo. This alteration in plan meant a great deal of hard work had to be carried out on essential maintenance, but on 12 September *Kent* sailed from Singapore to make a fast passage to Japanese waters. While off Luzon she delivered mail to HMS *Victorious*, which was exercising with USS *Oriskany*, and despite some rough weather from two typhoons, during the forenoon of 19 September *Kent* arrived alongside Tokyo's Harumi Pier. Whilst

HMS *Kent* at sea in the mid-1960s. (*World Ship Society*)

HMS Kent

The County-class were large ships with good seakeeping abilities and long range and were ideal blue-water ships. *Kent* is seen with crew manning the decks for a ceremonial sailpast. *(Crown Copyright/MoD)*

the senior officers were engaged in what appeared to be a never-ending round of official and ceremonial functions, the ship's company enjoyed coach tours, barbecue and swimming parties, and many sporting fixtures. This generous hospitality was reciprocated with a wardroom party and a party for 50 orphan children from one of the city's charitable orphanages. The ship was also opened to the public and over 9,000 people took advantage of the opportunity to look round. The liberty men who sampled Tokyo's nightlife found it to be on an incredibly lavish scale, but with high prices to match. The visit came to an end on Saturday 24 September when *Kent* sailed for Hong Kong. Within hours of her leaving Tokyo, however, it became apparent that two particularly violent typhoons lay between the ship and her destination, and having secured all her decks she had a particularly rough four-day passage, at one stage passing within 20 miles of the most severe weather.

After six days in Hong Kong *Kent* joined *Victorious, Bulwark, Hampshire, Arethusa, Cleopatra, Leander,* the submarine *Oberon* and four RFAs, to begin joint exercises with US and Australian ships in the Subic Bay area. These amphibious, anti-submarine and convoy escort manoeuvres took the force into Australian waters and ended with a series of visits, with *Kent* due to

A Sea Slug missile being transferred from a supply ship to Kent. *The four solid propellent motors, which jettison after burn-out, can be seen around the outside of the missile.* (Hawker Siddeley Ltd)

visit Melbourne and *Hampshire* scheduled to call at Sydney. However, four days before the end of the exercises *Kent* suffered mechanical faults which necessitated dry docking so she and *Hampshire* exchanged itineraries and on 28 October *Kent* arrived in Sydney and went straight into the Captain Cook Graving Dock where she remained for ten days. On 7 November she left Sydney to join *Victorious* and the other ships for another phase of exercises, this time off Australia's south coast, which for *Kent* ended on 18 November with an eight-day visit to Fremantle. By 3 December *Kent* was back at Singapore Naval Base, where preparations were made for a ten-week refit period.

During the refit her ship's company moved ashore for a five-week stay in HMS *Terror*, with its excellent swimming and sports facilities. On 11 January 1967, Captain Begg relinquished his command, and at 0800 the next day Captain B. D. O. McIntyre DSO RN assumed command of the ship which, at that time, was high and dry in the graving dock. On 11 February, when *Kent* emerged from her refit it was to carry out trials with the Australian destroyer *Duchess* before taking part in the annual FOTEX manoeuvres in the South China Sea and Strait of Malacca in early March. Also present were *Victorious, Arethusa, Blackpool, Fearless, Falmouth, Leander, Llandaff, Londonderry*, HMAS *Duchess* and *Vampire*. By the end of the month most of the force was operating in the Subic Bay exercise areas and on 1 April *Kent* arrived to spend a week in the US naval base there. Following this she paid a visit to Hong Kong before returning to Singapore for a further maintenance period.

On 24 May *Kent* left Singapore to begin her long passage home via the Indian Ocean and South American ports. In company with *Arethusa* her first port of call was Port Louis, Mauritius, where she arrived on 3 June. Although at this time political tensions in the Middle East were high the Suez Canal was still open. However, by the time she left Port Louis three days later Israel had launched sudden and unexpected attacks on all its Arab neighbours, resulting in an immediate closure of the Suez Canal. Unlike the Suez Crisis of 1956 when the canal had closed for just four months, this time it would remain shut off for eight years. For *Kent* this made no difference to her schedule for she was returning home via Cape Town and South America, and as a result she and *Arethusa* became the first Royal Navy ships to call at either Cape Town or Simonstown, both of which became strategically important ports during the period the Suez Canal was closed. The two warships steamed into Table Bay during the forenoon of 12 June and only the weather lacked any warmth. It was a wintry day after a weekend of violent storms and as they arrived in Cape Town offers of hospitality flooded into the ships. With *Kent*'s commission nearing its end during the visit, one-third of the destroyer's complement was changed, with some 150 officers and men flying out to join the ship and the same number returning home by air.

HMS *Kent*, Arethusa and RFA *Olynthus* left Cape Town during the afternoon of 17 June and steamed straight into severe gales and mountainous seas, which resulted in the cancellation of planned exercises which were to have been held in South African waters. Five days later the three ships paused briefly off the volcanic island of Tristan da Cunha, where helicopters from the two warships landed mail, stores and other items which were needed by the islanders. From the lonely Atlantic island *Kent* and *Arethusa* continued their transatlantic passage west and finally arrived at Montevideo on 28 June. The five days here were followed by seven days in Buenos Aires and another five days in Rio de Janeiro, in what were high-profile flag-showing visits. Between each port of call came joint exercises with Argentine and Brazilian naval ships, including the cruiser *Nueve de Julio* (ex-USS *Boise*), and during the exercises they were joined by HMS *Lynx*, the West Indies guardship. By 1 August, however, *Kent* was back in home waters and steaming up-Channel and by the afternoon of 3 August she had secured to a buoy off Sheerness. Next forenoon some 400 relatives and friends of the ship's company were embarked for the final passage up the River Medway and at just before noon *Kent* secured alongside Chatham Dockyard's No 3 basin. For most members of the ship's company there was leave to come, but for the ship herself there was one more duty before the end of the commission.

During the last week of August *Kent* took part in Chatham's Navy Days and on 6 September she sailed for Devonport to embark a full outfit of Sea Slug missiles, before spending almost two weeks off the Aberporth missile ranges. On 19 September, however, she returned to Devonport where all her remaining missiles were disembarked and next day after a fast passage up-Channel she once again secured alongside Chatham's No 3 basin. This time it was the end of the commission and by mid-October the remaining two-thirds of the old complement had left the ship. For *Kent* herself a five-month refit lay ahead during which, on 21 March, Captain I. G. Raikes CBE RN took over command of the ship. By 10 April 1968 her new ship's company had been brought up to full strength and everything was ready for the new commission.

Thursday 11 April 1968 dawned at Chatham with a sharp ground frost and thick mist, but this soon gave way to sunshine and at 1045 the ship's company fell in on the jetty alongside the ship. As well as families and friends of the ship's company there were VIP guests, including the Flag Officer Medway, Rear-Admiral W. J. Parker, and Major-General C. H. Tarver CB CBE DSO, the deputy colonel of the Queen's Regiment. The Commissioning Warrant was read by Captain Raikes and the specially baked cake was cut by Mrs Raikes. Six days later *Kent* left Chatham and steamed round to Spithead from where she began

HMS *Kent* looks very smart as she makes a ceremonial entry into Portland, possibly at the start of a work up period under the auspices of Flag Officer Sea Training. *(Crown Copyright/MoD)*

her post-refit trials, which continued into May, and in early June she began her work-up at Portland. As always the weeks spent at Portland were arduous and gruelling as the ship and her company were put through their paces with little time for rest and relaxation. Assisting *Kent* with the various exercises and evolutions was the frigate *Cleopatra* and on 23 July the destroyer successfully completed her final inspection by Flag Officer Sea Training. Next day she sailed for Rosyth where she joined 50 ships of the Western Fleet which, in June 1967 after the disbandment of the Mediterranean Fleet, had replaced the Home Fleet.

The reason for the gathering at Rosyth, the biggest since the Spithead Review of 1953, was to allow flag officers and commanding officers to discuss the latest naval matters and for the ships themselves to participate in a comprehensive programme of harbour training as well as a full range of sporting activities for Fleet championships. Ships taking part ranged from the command ship *Bulwark*, the guided missile destroyers *Hampshire* and *Kent*, the destroyers *Aisne* and *Cavalier*, to 25 frigates, six submarines, three survey ships, a minelayer, eight minesweepers and six RFAs. The C-in-C Western Fleet, Admiral Sir John Bush, arrived in Rosyth on 26 July and hoisted his flag in *Kent*. The grand finale of the assembly came on 1 August when, beginning at 0400 and at five-minute intervals, ships of the fleet left Rosyth for a display of close-formation manoeuvres. Embarked in *Kent* as guests of the C-in-C were the First Sea Lord and the

Secretary of State for the Navy.

As the ships steamed down the Forth towards the open sea the sun shone on the whole spectacle and created a magnificent sight, particularly appropriate with a lot of media attention at the time focusing on the country's diminishing Navy. Once into the North Sea *Kent* slowed to eight knots and each ship in turn steamed past in salute. There was all the appropriate ceremonial with ships' companies manning the decks, but it was said the most original touches were shown by *Keppel* and *Galatea*, both of which had a piper on the forecastle. The original itinerary had also included a fly-past, but because of fog this event was cancelled and on completion of the manoeuvres *Kent* set course for a four-day goodwill visit to the German port of Bremen. En route she received the following signal from the First Sea Lord: 'I have much enjoyed my visit and I have been greatly encouraged to find the Western Fleet in such good heart. I was delighted to have the chance of spending the final day at sea with you. I thought "Exercise Seaforth" went splendidly and the appearance and manoeuvring of the fleet were first class. I am sorry that fog stopped play. Many thanks for such a happy and memorable send-off.' Eleven days later Begg was succeeded by Admiral Sir Michael Le Fanu.

After spending an extended weekend at Bremen *Kent* returned to Chatham to give leave, undergo maintenance and also take part in the Medway town's Navy Days, during which she attracted over 23,000 visitors. At 1945 on 3 September 1968, the day after the Navy Days weekend, the alarms sounded as a serious fire broke out in the boiler

HM Ships *Kent* and *Fearless* alongside the South Mole, Gibraltar, in October 1968 for the talks between Prime Minister Harold Wilson and Ian Smith of Rhodesia on the future of that country. (*Author's Collection*)

room uptakes. The ship's own fire parties, together with the Dockyard Fire Brigade, took two and a half hours to extinguish the conflagration, but as damage was only superficial she was able to sail on 6 September for Portsmouth and Devonport to embark her full outfit of missiles and ammunition in readiness for the start of the NATO exercise 'Silver Tower' in mid-September. The manoeuvres involved ships and aircraft from nine NATO countries and consisted of anti-aircraft, anti-submarine and convoy escort exercises in an area ranging from the Bay of Biscay to deep within the Arctic Circle. *Kent* was due to leave Devonport during the afternoon of Sunday 15 September to join the aircraft carrier *Eagle* for the start of the exercises the next day. However, at 1205 that day, just hours before she was due to sail, a serious explosion occurred in the starboard boiler which, although there were no casualties, caused considerable damage. For three days Devonport Dockyard toiled to carry out the necessary repairs and during the afternoon of 18 September *Kent* finally left Devonport to join the exercise. However, dockyard employees were still on board and finishing off the boiler repairs, so the ship was limited to a maximum speed of 24 knots for short periods and a sustained speed of just 18 knots. At 0130 the next day, as she steamed to join the exercise, fire broke out in some boiler room lagging but fortunately this was soon extinguished and a few hours later she joined the anti-submarine exercises in the Bay of Biscay. On Saturday 21 September, closely watched by a Soviet ocean rescue tug, *Kent* joined Dutch ships close to Land's End to form a convoy escort force. However, within 48 hours of that phase of the exercise starting, her commanding officer Captain Raikes was taken ill with appendicitis, and during the forenoon of 24 September the destroyer put into Plymouth Sound where both he and the mail were landed. The ship's Executive Officer, Commander W. Morgan, assumed command of the ship for the conclusion of the exercise just over 24 hours later, then in compa-

HMS *Kent* in Malta's Grand Harbour. In the foreground is one of the ubiquitous Maltese water taxis which were popular with naval personnel. They were known colloquially as 'Daysos' - derived from the Maltese 'Dhajsa'.
(Michael Cassar)

ny with the frigates *Mohawk* and *Zulu*, *Kent* secured alongside at Rosyth Dockyard, where repair work to her boiler continued. Four days later Captain R. P. Clayton RN assumed temporary command of the ship and later that afternoon Flag Officer Flotillas, Western Fleet, Vice-Admiral A. M. Lewis, hoisted his flag and *Kent* sailed for two days of missile firing off the Welsh coast followed by a four-day passage to Gibraltar. Together with the assault ship *Fearless*, the destroyer was about to be thrust into the spotlight of the world's media.

Ever since the Crown Colony of Southern Rhodesia had, in November 1965, unilaterally declared its independence from Britain in the face of worldwide opposition, politicians in Britain, the USA and southern Africa had been looking for ways of legalising the situation. The illegal declaration of Independence had been made in order to keep in power a minority government which represented some 200,000 people of European origin who were only second generation colonial settlers, in the face of implacable opposition from the four million indigenous people. In December 1966 their leader Ian Smith met British Prime Minister Harold Wilson aboard the cruiser *Tiger* off Gibraltar, but Smith's intransigence in refusing to accept the inevitable meant that the talks had been bound to fail. Less than a year later, after unofficial and secret meetings between government representatives from Britain and Rhodesia, it was thought that there would be another opportunity to settle the issue of Rhodesia's independence, for as Harold Wilson told reporters at the time, he believed the meeting planned for October 1968 would be the last chance for agreement before Rhodesian nationalist parties began a long and bitter armed conflict, which would inevitably end in defeat for the white minority population of the country. The diplomatic meetings had been arranged to take place on board *Fearless* at Gibraltar, with Harold Wilson and his delegation living aboard the assault ship. The Rhodesian delegation, led by Ian Smith, would live on board *Kent* which was to be secured alongside *Fearless*.

HMS *Kent* left Fishguard at 1800 on 4 October and setting course south she rendezvoused with *Fearless* some 38 hours later off the Spanish coast. The two ships arrived in Gibraltar during the afternoon of 8 October where they secured alongside the dockyard's South Mole. The first delegation to arrive during the afternoon of 9 October was the British negotiating team led by Harold Wilson, while the Rhodesian team, accompanied by the British-appointed Governor, Sir Humphrey Gibbs, arrived later in the day, having been flown by the RAF from Salisbury (Harare). The talks began that evening, with Wilson and Smith spending half an hour alone before calling in their aides, and continued over four days. It soon became clear that the two sides were deadlocked from the start, mainly over the basic principle that there could be no legal independence before elections which would include the majority of the country's citizens. By the end of Saturday 12 October it was quite obvious that no agreement could be reached and the last day of the conference saw Wilson and Smith attend a church service on board *Fearless*, before beginning a final round of talks. At 2230, however, the conference ended just short of total collapse and Ian Smith, together with his delegates, left *Kent* to return to Rhodesia. The scene was set for a hardening of opinion on both sides and a bloody guerrilla war which inevitably ended with majority rule and a legacy of bitterness, the consequences of which remain today.

Meanwhile, at midday on Monday 14 October, Harold Wilson cleared lower deck of the ships' companies of both *Fearless* and *Kent* on the latter's flight deck to personally thank them for providing the conference facilities and he concluded his speech by ordering that the main brace be spliced. Later that afternoon, with all the VIPs having departed, *Fearless* left harbour and *Kent* began a 17-day assisted maintenance period at Gibraltar. One task which received urgent attention was the replacement of a turbo-generator which had been the cause of a number of sailing delays. *Kent* finally sailed during the afternoon of 31 October and set course for Malta, where she joined other ships of the Western Fleet to prepare for a series of NATO exercises designed to improve co-ordination and readiness. Altogether the manoeuvres would bring together more than 50 ships from five nations, which included France, Greece, Italy and the USA. (Although France was not a member of NATO's integrated command her ships took part in various exercises). The Royal Navy's contribution of 17 warships included *Kent* (Flag Officer Flotillas Western Fleet), *Hampshire, Barrosa, Arethusa, Juno, Mohawk, Zulu, Cavalier, Jaguar, Leopard, Sirius, Troubridge* and the submarines *Alliance, Oracle, Osiris* and *Valiant*. The manoeuvres which began on 5 November were under the overall command of Italy's Admiral Luciano Sotgui, whose headquarters were in Malta. Code-named 'Eden Apple' the exercise came at a time when Soviet naval forces in the Mediterranean had been steadily building up. It opened with an RAF and a naval air squadron engaged in an anti-submarine search operation, co-ordinated with the surface ships. Six days into the exercise the submarine *Alliance* suffered a fire while submerged and she had to be escorted to Toulon by a French destroyer. For *Kent* the exercise ended on 16 November at Naples and soon after berthing at the port the Italian destroyer *Intrepido* collided with her, but fortunately there were no injuries and damage to both ships was superficial. Six days later *Kent* had returned to Malta where FOF's flag was transferred to *Hampshire*. On 26 November *Kent* and *Cavalier* left Malta to steam west for Gibraltar where they joined *Arethusa, Sirius, Leopard, Jaguar* and *Barrosa* for the passage home, where *Kent* arrived in Portsmouth Harbour on 5 December. Three days later, having embarked relatives, the destroyer put to sea for a Families Day, after which she set course for Chatham, where she would spend Christmas and New Year.

On 21 January, Captain Raikes, now recovered from his emergency appendectomy, visited his command prior to taking over again. Two days later *Kent* made a 24-hour passage to Portsmouth and on 27 January Captain Raikes resumed his command of the destroyer. Next day *Kent* left for Portland to carry out a mini work-up, before setting course for the River Elbe and a five-day courtesy visit to Hamburg, which was always a popular run ashore. After leaving Germany *Kent* returned to a stormy North Sea to spend the rest of February off the Welsh coast. During March, in company with *Llandaff, Tartar* and the submarine *Sealion*, *Kent* took part in the anti-submarine exercise 'Razor Sharp' in the Western Atlantic, which ended with a visit to Lisbon, following which she returned to Chatham for leave and maintenance.

In late April, flying the flag of the C-in-C Western Fleet, Admiral Sir John Bush, *Kent* and the frigate *Duncan* paid a five-day visit to Belgium. While *Kent* steamed up the River Scheldt to Antwerp, *Duncan* meanwhile negotiated the huge Zenne Canal, via Mechelen to the inland city of Brussels. In his NATO role as Allied C-in-C Channel and Southern North Sea, Bush was received by the Belgian King at the Royal Palace in Brussels. At Antwerp on board *Kent* there was a reception in honour of the Prince of Liege and when the destroyer was opened to the public, in the space of just four hours 5,512 people and one dog visited the ship.

After leaving Antwerp and carrying out main machinery trials *Kent* spent ten days of May on a 'Meet the Navy' cruise, which took her to Belfast's Stormont Wharf, close to where she had been built. This four-day visit ended with a day at sea for 180 schoolboys and press representatives. After leaving Ireland *Kent* made the short passage to the River Clyde's Yorkhill Basin, close to Glasgow's city centre. Here, over the weekend of 16 May, nearly 22,000 people visited the ship and when she sailed on 19 May another 200 schoolboys were treated to a day at sea. Their adventure ended with disembarkation in the Firth of Clyde before, in company with *Defender*, the destroyer set course for the Baltic for visits to Oslo and Stockholm.

On 23 May, during her four-day visit to Oslo, King Olaf of Norway toured the ship and 3,000 local people also turned up when the gangways were opened to visitors. During the visit to Stockholm the C-in-C struck his flag and finally, on 5 June, *Kent* paid a three-day visit to Newcastle upon Tyne, before steaming south to Devonport for

HMS Kent

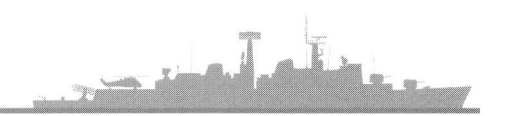

(Above and below) HMS *Kent* in the Firth of Clyde during May 1969. *(Maritime Photo Library)*

de-ammunitioning. On 11 June she arrived alongside Portsmouth's Fountain Lake Jetty and six days later Captain Raikes relinquished his command, being driven away from the ship in a horse-drawn carriage. On 20 June 1969 the ship's company members who were still with the ship moved to RNB and *Kent* paid off into dockyard hands to undergo a long refit, which it was estimated would last for three years.

During her long period in Portsmouth Dockyard *Kent* was manned only by a care and maintenance party and with all her machinery and equipment being overhauled and modernised the ship was a chaos of pipes and equipment. In the event it was just over three years before the ship took on a more organised feel and on 26 June 1972 the ship's company moved back on board from the barracks. On 1 July Captain A. R. Rawbone AFC RN joined the ship and took command, but *Kent* was not yet ready for sea and it was not until the last week of July that she was able to sail to carry out her post-refit trials; these lasted for a month before the ship returned to dry dock for further work and adjustments. In mid-October, after leaving dry dock, *Kent* returned to Fountain Lake Jetty for yet more dockyard work to be carried out and it was the second week of December before she was ready for recommissioning.

HMS *Kent* was recommissioned on Friday 8 December 1972 and for those members of the ship's company who had been on board through what was sometimes a very tedious period, often in uncomfortable conditions, it was a relief to see normality returning to the ship. Altogether there were some 1,200 guests for the ceremony, who were mainly families of ship's company members, while the VIPs included the Duchess of Kent, who had launched the ship, and the C-in-C Naval Home Command. After the ceremony the commissioning cake was cut by Mrs Rawbone, who was assisted by the youngest rating, 16-year-old JMEM Michael Erswell. By 1400 the proceedings were over and the VIP guests had departed, but the ship remained firmly alongside Fountain Lake Jetty.

On 15 January 1973 *Kent* put to sea to begin her post-refit trials which would continue through to mid-April. During the latter part of this period she steamed south to Gibraltar with a weekend break at Palma, Majorca included in early April. While operating from Gibraltar the ship carried out a number of exercises in preparation for her work-up at Portland, including a full-scale disaster exercise which also involved many of the Rock residents. On conclusion of the trials she returned to Portsmouth and on 7 May, after seasonal leave had

A very good stern view of *Kent* taken in August 1969 when she was in refit at Portsmouth. *(James W. Goss)*

HMS Kent

In this photograph, taken on 3 September 1973, *Kent* is shown leaving Portsmouth for Lisbon, Portugal.
(Derek Fox)

been taken, began her work-up at Portland. During the exercises she was assisted by *Tiger, Bacchante, Hermione* and the German destroyer *Bayern*, and throughout the hectic six-week period there was just a two-day break when the ship took part in Portland's Navy Days. Finally, on 21 June, she completed her last inspections and later that day she arrived at Devonport for a ten-day break, before undergoing Sea Slug firings off the Welsh coast. By the second week of July *Kent* was fully operational again and she steamed north to the old wartime anchorage at Scapa Flow to prepare for a major exercise code-named 'Sally Forth', which also included *Ark Royal, Bulwark, Devonshire, Fife, Bristol* and *Nubian*. It was an impressive display of sea power which was observed by the Secretary of State for Defence and senior NATO officers. The government minister used the occasion to make a statement regarding the future of the Harrier aircraft as it related to the Navy, two of which demonstrated their VTOL capabilities from the commando carrier *Bulwark*. The main purpose of the exercise was to show senior NATO officers the contribution the Royal Navy, Royal Marines and the RAF could make to the organisation. All three of the County-class destroyers present were deployed in an anti-submarine role, with their Wessex helicopters used as submarine hunters. On 26 July *Kent* returned to Spithead and after a Families Day at sea off the Isle of Wight she returned to Portsmouth to give leave and to take part in Navy Days.

On 3 September *Kent* put to sea again this time to exercise with the frigate *Berwick* which was about to pay off at Gibraltar before a long refit, when her ship's company would transfer to *Lowestoft*. For *Kent* there was a weekend visit to Lisbon before she took part in two major exercises, 'Quicksilver' and 'Swiftmove', both of which also included *Hermes, Andromeda* and the US Navy's *John F. Kennedy* and the heavy cruiser *Newport News* which was nearing the end of her career. Most of the manoeuvres took place in the Norwegian Sea, and both *Kent* and *Hermes* were closely shadowed by a Soviet Kanin-class destroyer 252; she suffered a fire on board while shadowing *Hermes* and in order to prevent an explosion fired off a torpedo from her starboard torpedo tubes. Needless to say the fire-fighting operations were closely watched by the

County Class GMDs

HMS *Kent* arriving at Vancouver during May 1974. *(Michael Cassar)*

NATO ships and all offers of assistance were turned down. For *Kent* the exercises ended with a weekend in Oslo, before she returned to Chatham, where she hoisted the flag of FOF1 for a six-day official visit to Antwerp for the 'Europalia 73' Belgian arts festival, for which *Kent* provided personnel for a military tattoo. By the end of October *Kent* had returned to Portsmouth to undergo a five-week maintenance period prior to a seven-month overseas deployment.

On 3 December 1973 *Kent* left Portsmouth and after 24 hours off Portland she set course for Gibraltar and the Mediterranean, arriving in Malta ten days later, where Captain John B. Robathan RN, took over command. After spending Christmas back at Gibraltar and paying a four-day visit to the Italian port of Livorno, on 2 February 1974 she joined *Blake*, *Nubian*, *Torquay* and *Whitby* to set course from Gibraltar to the Caribbean. Ten days later the group arrived at Virgin Gorda, where they rendezvoused with *Bulwark*, *Fearless* (FOF1), *Devonshire*, *Bacchante* (SNO WI), the submarine *Narwhal* and RFAs *Orangeleaf*, *Resource* and *Tidepool*. This gathering of 14 warships provided an excellent opportunity for competition and recreation after what had been a rough Atlantic crossing and it was also an opportunity for the outgoing First Sea Lord, Admiral Sir Michael Pollock, to review and bid farewell to the fleet before his retirement. Soon after her arrival *Kent* hoisted the flag of the C-in-C Fleet[1], Admiral Sir Terence Lewin, and on 15 February, after a busy programme of exercises, ship visits and inspections, the First Sea Lord embarked in *Bulwark* before, in two divisions and led by *Blake*, the ships steamed past the commando carrier with their upper decks manned before continuing their programme of exercises. *Bulwark* herself returned to Devonport to begin a refit, while *Kent* began a series of port visits in the Caribbean.

After calling at Barbados and San Juan, on 4 March *Kent*, *Blake*, *Bacchante* and *Devonshire* carried out a series of exercises before *Kent* and *Bacchante* set course for the Panama Canal and a scheduled visit to Valparaiso. However, even before they had reached the Panama Canal a foreign poli-

---

[1] In late 1971 the Western Fleet and Far East Fleet had been combined to form a single Fleet Command, which is more commonly known as Fleet.

cy change in London meant that the visit was cancelled at very short notice. Instead *Kent* visited Norfolk, Virginia, before arriving at Bermuda on 22 March. In early April, again in company with *Bacchante*, she finally made the Panama Canal transit to begin a series of visits to South and North American ports. Both ships visited the city of Callao where the programme included sea days for senior Peruvian naval officers, who were particularly interested in the operation of helicopters from warships. After leaving Callao and carrying out manoeuvres with the Peruvian Navy, *Bacchante* detached for a visit to Ecuador and *Kent* steamed north to the US naval base at San Diego. During her three-week visit to the base the ship underwent an assisted maintenance period, which gave the ship's company an excellent opportunity to travel in the area. Many were able to visit Mexico, which is only half an hour's drive away. Some of the more intrepid travellers got away on a five-day tour which took in the Grand Canyon and Phoenix, Arizona. On 20 May, after leaving San Diego, *Kent* passed under the Golden Gate Bridge at the start of a seven-day visit to San Francisco. Here the ship played host to members of the Variety Club of Great Britain, who were attending a convention in the city, and many functions were held which involved the entire ship's company.

Leaving San Francisco on the last day of May, *Kent* steamed north to Vancouver and during her stay in the Canadian city the ship's divers were called upon to recover the body of a deckhand from a tug which had capsized while assisting a freighter to dock. One of the divers was later commended for his courage by the city's coroner. After leaving Vancouver *Kent* steamed south to end her Pacific sojourn with a four-day visit to Acapulco. On 27 June, after an overnight stay at the Rodman Naval Base, Balboa, *Kent* made her return passage through the Panama Canal and three days later she called briefly at Puerto Rico to refuel and carry out Sea Slug firings at Roosevelt Roads, before setting out on her eastbound transatlantic crossing to home waters. Off Gibraltar she rendezvoused with *Devonshire*, *Norfolk* and *Brighton*, but the combined exercises were brief and on 12 July she sailed for home, arriving three days later in Devonport where she de-ammunitioned. On 18 July *Kent* arrived at Portsmouth to begin a 12-week maintenance period.

In the second week of October *Kent* left Portsmouth to carry out trials, during which she assisted with the search off the Isle of Wight for a seaman who had fallen overboard from the Finnish coaster *Presto*. In early November she was at Portland exercising with *Nubian*, but later that month she was ordered to Falmouth, where she stood by and escorted the cargo ship *Asiafreighter* out into the Western Approaches, to a position some 100 miles west of the Scilly Isles. The container ship had accumulated vast quantities of the highly toxic arsine gas and *Kent* kept all other vessels clear while the ship was ventilated and the cargo holds declared safe. On 25 November, with the operation successfully completed, *Kent* arrived alongside Devonport Dockyard. During the first and second weeks of December there was just time to fit in a five-day visit to Kiel, before returning to Portsmouth on 11 December.

For *Kent* the new year of 1975 began in the last week of January when she made her way north via the Clyde and Campbeltown, to Rosyth. No sooner had she left the latter port, however, than a fire in the HP Air Compressor caused the loss of power supplies to the evaporators and the port boiler. The subsequent reduction in speed meant a late arrival at Rosyth, where she joined *Antrim* and *Eastbourne* for JMC 751 exercises. These manoeuvres ended on the last day of February at Rosyth and five days later *Kent* returned to Portsmouth.

On Monday 10 March *Kent* left Portsmouth bound for Gibraltar and the Mediterranean, where she rendezvoused with *Ashanti* and the submarine *Rorqual*, before arriving in Grand Harbour on 19 March. After undergoing a short maintenance period, in early April, *Kent* left Malta to visit Trieste, before joining RFA *Black Rover* to make the passage of the Dardanelles and the Bosporus into the Black Sea, where she cruised for three days before returning to the Mediterranean. The short foray into

County Class GMDs

During manoeuvres at Spithead during May 1976, *Kent* is passed by a BH7 military hovercraft (above) and overflown by a Buccaneer (below). *(George Mortimore, Action Photos)*

The fast patrol boats *Cutlass* and *Scimitar* about to leave *Kent* behind during Spithead manoeuvres in May 1976. (*George Mortimore, Action Photos*)

the Black Sea was a political demonstration of NATO's right to gain entrance into those waters. After rendezvousing with *Juno*, the two ships shadowed a Soviet naval force, which included a Sverdlov-class cruiser and a submarine, the latter providing good practice for sonar tracking. After meeting and carrying out joint manoeuvres with *Bulwark* the three ships put into Gibraltar, where for three weeks *Kent* was guardship.

On 22 May, *Kent* and *Juno* left Gibraltar for a short visit to Toulon before carrying out rehearsal exercises for 'Exercise Dawn Patrol' during which she escorted *Bulwark* for landings in the Gulf of Taranto. This was followed by the exercise itself which for *Kent* ended with a visit to Naples. Leaving Italy on 3 July she returned via Trieste to Gibraltar, before steaming home to Portsmouth in the company of the new Type 42 destroyer *Sheffield*. During her four-month absence she had steamed some 17,000 miles and visited Gibraltar, Malta, Trieste, Toulon, Naples and Tangiers. On 21 July, seven days after her return to Portsmouth, *Kent* hoisted the flag of FOF1 and steamed to Devonport and then to the Welsh coast for missile firings, before returning to Portsmouth for Navy Days, where she attracted over 20,000 visitors. On 30 September Captain John B. Hervey RN relieved Robathan. During September and October she visited Falmouth and Glasgow, before taking part in exercises between Cape Wrath and the Moray Firth with *Ark Royal*. On 16 October she sailed up the River Thames to secure alongside HMS *Belfast* in the Pool of London. During her seven days in the capital she received visits from her sponsor and veterans from the previous *Kent* as well as a group of show business personalities, including the actor Dennis Waterman. On 23 October, after leaving the River Thames *Kent* set course for the Western Mediterranean to take part in the French naval exercise 'Île d'Or' which included visits to Toulon. By

Refuelling astern from RFA *Green Rover*. (*George Mortimore, Action Photos*)

the end of November she had returned to home waters and in mid-December, after a five-day visit to Southampton, she returned to Portsmouth.

On 2 February 1976 *Kent* left Portsmouth and steaming into Force 10 gales and very heavy seas, set course once again for Malta, from where she shadowed Soviet warships in the Eastern Mediterranean. Later in the month she joined *Ark Royal, Blake, Antrim* and *Hampshire* off Gibraltar for 'Exercise Springtrain', which was followed by three weeks acting as guardship at Gibraltar, with a short visit to Casablanca, but on 26 March she returned to Portsmouth to undergo a six-week maintenance period. When *Kent* sailed again on 7 May she was wearing the flag of the C-in-C Fleet, Admiral Sir John Treacher; she was bound for the German naval base at Kiel, where the host ship, the destroyer FGS *Rommel*, organised social and sporting events. The C-in-C visited the German Fleet Headquarters and watched various demonstrations by fast patrol boats. When *Kent* left Kiel she was accompanied by *Rommel* as they steamed out via the Skagerrak to Rosyth to take part in an international North Sea exercise which included Norwegian, Danish, German and British warships. At the end of May *Kent* took part in Chatham Navy Days before discharging her Sea Slug missiles at Devonport. During the second week of June, while day running from Portsmouth, she joined *Antrim* and *Blake* for Staff College Sea Days in the Channel, then her last operational day at sea before beginning a long refit was spent with families embarked off the Isle of Wight. Finally, at 1645 on 11 June, she secured alongside Fountain Lake Jetty at Portsmouth, where de-ammunitioning and de-storing began and the ship was placed at extended notice for steam. Later that month the remaining ship's company moved to shore accommodation in RNB and *Kent* herself was towed into No 3 Basin. During *Kent*'s refit there was a further change in command, with Captain J. B. Hervey OBE RN being appointed to the ship, then on 10 August

1976, as *Kent* lay in No 13 dry dock at Portsmouth, Captain J. C. K. Slater MVO RN was appointed. The refit dragged on, with the ship's much-reduced company making the daily journey from RNB to the dockyard. It was October before *Kent* was moved out of dry dock to the basin and early December before she was shifted back to the sea wall at Fountain Lake Jetty. During her time in dockyard hands all the ship's machinery had been thoroughly overhauled and her accommodation modernised. On 21 April 1977, her sponsor the Duchess of Kent attended at Portsmouth where the ship was recommissioned.

During the summer of 1977 *Kent* carried out her post-refit trials and her work-up at Portland, and on an unseasonably chilly, wet and blustery 28 June she took part in the Silver Jubilee Review of the Fleet at Spithead. Next day, as the fleet dispersed, there was a steam past off the Isle of Wight, before *Kent* resumed her work-up. Also that summer there was an action-packed Families Day in the Channel for almost 700 guests, which included flying displays by helicopters, a demonstration by a hovercraft and a jackstay transfer with *Glamorgan*, which was also holding a similar Family event on board, and at the end of August she took part in Portsmouth Navy Days.

In early September *Kent* steamed round to the Welsh coast, before joining a task group which included *Hermes, Antrim, Sheffield, Arrow, Diomede* and RFAs *Resurgent* and *Tidesurge*, for a 'Westlant' (Western Atlantic) deployment which, as well as including exercises with US Navy ships, involved a large NATO exercise and visits to Bermuda and Norfolk, Virginia. In October, at the end of the deployment there came 'Exercise Ocean Safari 77', which involved some 60 surface ships and submarines, as well as 250 aircraft. The key part of this exercise was a transatlantic passage of a convoy towards the Western Approaches and the Channel. One group, having crossed the Atlantic, was joined by another group of warships and, in the face of 'enemy' surface ships, submarines and aircraft, made for the Channel. The attacks included strikes from *Ark Royal*'s aircraft, as well as from shore-based aircraft. In addition to *Kent* and *Hermes*, other Royal Navy ships involved included *Fife, Sheffield, Arrow, Charybdis, Diomede, Hermione, Plymouth* and the submarines *Churchill, Valiant, Finwhale, Opportune, Oracle* and *Osiris*. The convoy consisted of the two RFAs. For *Kent* the year ended with a visit to London, before she returned to Portsmouth where, on 22 December, Captain R. J. F. Turner RN took over command.

On Monday 23 January 1978 *Kent* left Portsmouth bound for Gibraltar, where she was to take part in 'Exercise Springtrain', an annual weapons training period taking place in the Western Mediterranean, also involving *Blake* (flag FOF1), *Hermes, Antrim, London, Devonshire, Arrow, Yarmouth* and the submarines *Churchill* and *Oracle*, as well as the Dutch submarine *Tijgerhaai* and four RFAs. These manoeuvres continued through to mid-February, after which *Kent* returned to home waters and carried out missile firings off the Welsh coast. In early May, following a maintenance period at Portsmouth, *Kent* sailed north to shadow a Soviet naval force which included the aircraft carrier *Kiev* and a strong escort. This duty took *Kent* well north of the Arctic Circle, where heavy snowstorms hampered the shadowing operations. By mid-April *Kent* had put into Rosyth Dockyard for a ten-day maintenance period, before joining the fleet exercise 'JMC 782', which also included *Sheffield, Minerva, Arrow* and *Diomede*. During the ten days of manoeuvres *Kent* and the other surface ships acted as targets and screens during a 'Perisher' course for submarine commanding officers. On 9 May, with the exercises concluded, *Kent* paid a six-day 'Meet the Navy' recruiting visit to Hull, after which she joined *Sheffield, Diomede* and *Arethusa* for a 14-day period of Scandinavian visits. *Kent*'s schedule included five days in Copenhagen, after which she rejoined the other three ships for a five-day courtesy visit to Stockholm, hoisting the flag of FOF2 here. After leaving the Swedish capital *Kent* carried out exercises in the Baltic, before returning once again to Portsmouth.

After a two-week maintenance break *Kent* spent

On 18 April 1980 *Kent* paid off at Portsmouth to become a harbour training ship. Here, flying her paying-off pennant, she is arriving back at the port. *(James W. Goss)*

the latter half of June day running from Portsmouth on Staff College Sea Days, which concluded with a Families Day, before she steamed north to the Clyde area for anti-submarine training. In mid-July she began an intensive five-day period of weapons training exercises in the South-West Approaches, which also involved *Hermes, Sheffield* and *Antelope*. On 14 July she returned to Portsmouth and four days later she joined her sister *Devonshire* on her last operational day at sea with her sponsor and 800 relatives of the ship's company on board. After leaving harbour *Kent*'s ship's company manned and cheered ship as she steamed past *Devonshire*, before the two destroyers put on a 'farewell display'. Two hours later *Devonshire*'s Wessex helicopter ditched into the sea some three miles from *Kent* and she co-ordinated the rescue of the crew. Luckily they were unhurt, but despite the best efforts of *Kent*'s divers to salvage the wreck, it eventually sank. With the manoeuvres over *Kent* spent four days in the Portland area, before steaming north to Scotland's east coast to take part in 'Exercise Priory', an air defence exercise with the RAF. However, severe weather curtailed the manoeuvres and two days later *Kent* returned to Portsmouth where she secured alongside the recently decommissioned *Devonshire* at the North West Wall.

After giving seasonal leave and taking part in Navy Days at Portsmouth, on 1 September *Kent* began a 15-week refit at Portsmouth. By mid-October, however, as a result of heavy workloads and the loss of capacity following a year of industrial unrest in the Royal Dockyards, in order to maintain operational commitments some maintenance and refit work was put out to commercial shipyards. One of the first ships to be thus affected was *Kent* and on 16 October, having been made ready for sea, she left Portsmouth to steam north for the River Tyne and the Wallsend Slipway and Engineering Company's shipyard, where her refit was to be completed. Soon after leaving Portsmouth, at just before midnight, red distress flares were sighted and after searching the area she found a small cabin cruiser which had run out of fuel. After towing the vessel for some six hours, the tow was transferred to the minesweeper *Crofton* and *Kent* was able to resume her passage north, arriving at Wallsend early in the morning of 19 October. Two days later the ship's company moved into accommodation ashore and the ship herself was moved into dry dock. It was the second week of December before the refit was completed and *Kent* left the River Tyne to make her way back to Portsmouth, where she arrived alongside Fountain Lake Jetty on 18 December.

The year 1979 would prove to be *Kent*'s last full year of operational service and it began in mid-January when she sailed for a mini work-up at Portland. On 25 February, in company with *Hermione*, she steamed south to Gibraltar for the annual weapons training, 'Exercise Springtrain', which that year also included *Norfolk, Naiad, Antelope, Aurora, Ashanti, Arethusa, Eskimo* and *Berwick*, which, while en route to Gibraltar, had rescued the crew of a German coaster which had lost all power and was wallowing helplessly in heavy seas. On 9 March, while at Gibraltar, there was a final change of command when Captain J. P. Gunning RN took over the ship from Turner. During these exercises *Kent* flew the flag of FOF1 and as soon as they were completed *Kent*, together with *Newcastle, Naiad, Eskimo, Ashanti* and the submarine *Warspite*, left Gibraltar for a 10,000-mile deployment to West Africa and South America. For *Kent* the first port of call was Lagos, Nigeria, where she spent four days before setting course for a rendezvous with *Warspite* off Ascension Island. At Clarence Bay, Ascension Island, *Kent, Ashanti* and *Warspite* paused for fuel and stores, before beginning the transatlantic passage to Brazilian waters. On 4 April the equator was crossed with full ceremony and two days later the whole group came together at Rio de Janeiro. For the Royal Marines Detachments from all the ships the break included a working visit to the Brazilian Army's jungle training area outside Rio, while the ships' companies enjoyed a variety of organised activities, which included banyans, sailing and trips to the top of Sugar Loaf Mountain, as well as general sightseeing around the city. Leaving Rio on 16 April the group joined Brazilian Navy ships and the Belgian Navy frigate *Wandelaar* for exercises and manoeuvres off South America, which ranged as far south as Porto Alegra. On 23 April, after a further break in Rio, *Kent, Eskimo, Newcastle* and *Warspite* sailed for Recife where they stayed for four days, after which they made an 11-day passage back to Gibraltar. On 17 May *Kent* arrived back alongside Portsmouth's Fountain Lake Jetty.

On 25 June, after a period of maintenance, *Kent* left Portsmouth to rendezvous with *Hermes, Fife, Lowestoft, Newcastle, Ashanti, Ardent, Sirius, Scylla* and *Eskimo* for 'Exercise Highwood', which began in the South West Approaches and continued up into the waters west of Iceland. It was mid-July when the exercise ended and *Kent* steamed south to take part in Portland's Navy Days, before returning to Portsmouth. It was at this time that rumours began to circulate to the effect that *Kent* was to be withdrawn from operational service to become a static training ship in Portsmouth Harbour. Rumours which were not denied.

During the autumn of 1979 *Kent* took part in the major NATO exercise code-named 'Ocean Safari' which took her to the Norwegian Sea and north of the Arctic Circle. The exercise was also accompanied by strong gale force winds and heavy seas. After a short break at Portsmouth the destroyer sailed for the Mediterranean where she visited the Italian port of Genoa and in early December she left Gibraltar to return to Portsmouth for seasonal leave and maintenance. The new year of 1980 saw *Kent* begin her final weeks of operational service on 21 January with a three-day shake-down period at Portland. During the early hours of 24 January she passed through the Strait of Dover to arrive at Rosyth the next day, and during the three weeks which followed she took part in fleet manoeuvres in the North Sea, ending these with a short visit to Esbjerg. After leaving Danish waters during the forenoon of 17 February, *Kent* steamed south to the River Thames and during the afternoon of the next day she secured alongside HMS *Belfast*. During her six days in the capital the ship was opened to the public with access by a special boat service from St Katherine's Dock. After leaving the Thames she steamed north to pay a four-day visit to Hull, before taking part in a North Sea exercise code-named 'Eastaxe'. This was followed by a five-day farewell visit to the County of Kent at Chatham and by a weekend break at Portsmouth before she hoisted the flag of FOF2 and set course for Gibraltar and the annual 'Springtrain' exercises. The final day of these exercises saw the ships carrying out high seas gunnery shoots and at 1617 on Thursday 27 March *Kent* fired her last Sea Slug missile. Four days later, with her operational career effectively over, she returned to Gibraltar. *Kent* left Gibraltar for the last time on 8 April to steam north, via Lisbon, for Devonport where, over a period of 48 hours, she was de-ammunitioned.

For eight years *Kent* was the Fleet Training Ship based at Portsmouth and while retaining her seagoing capabilities she made occasional short training voyages. She soon became a landmark feature in Portsmouth Harbour, secured alongside *Rame Head* in Fountain Lake, close to HMS *Excellent*. In January 1988, however, she was towed from Portsmouth to Devonport for conversion to a static harbour training ship and thereafter she became a permanent fixture in Portsmouth Harbour's Fountain Lake, where she secured alongside *Rame Head*. For five years *Kent* retained this role, but in

HMS *Kent* as a static harbour training ship alongside Whale Island, Portsmouth. (*T. Ferrers-Walker*)

1993 it was taken over by the defunct *Bristol* and *Kent* was reduced to reserve. The end came on Friday 14 November 1997 when the Russian ocean-going tug *Agat* towed her from Portsmouth Harbour on the first stage of a long voyage to India. She had been sold to a Hong Kong businessman for some £600,000 and despite initial difficulties with the tow she ended her days on a beach close to the city of Mumbai.

Commanding Officers:

Captain John G. Wells DSC RN	12 March 1963
Captain Andrew M. Lewis RN	30 May 1964
Captain Robin A. Begg RN	31 May 1965
Captain Bernard D. O. McIntyre DSO RN	11 January 1967
Captain Iwan G. Raikes CBE RN	21 March 1968
Captain Richard P. Clayton RN (Temporary)	28 September 1968
Captain Iwan G. Raikes RN	27 January 1969
Captain Alfred R. Rawbone AFC RN	1 July 1972
Captain John B. Robathan RN	17 December 1973
Captain John B. Hervey OBE RN	30 September 1975
Captain Jock C. K. Slater MVO RN	10 August 1976
Captain Richard J. F. Turner RN	22 December 1977
Captain John P. Gunning RN	9 March 1979
Captain Kenneth H. Forbes-Robertson RN	2 June 1980

Battle Honours:

Porto Farino	1655	Finisterre	1747
Lowestoft	1665	Egypt	1801
Orfordness	1666	Falklands	1914
Barfleur	1692	Atlantic	1940
Vigo	1702	Mediterranean	1940
Velez Malaga	1704	Arctic	1942-43
Cape Passero	1718	Normandy	1944

Chapter Four

HMS LONDON
1963 - 1982

In the summer of 1962 London lay alongside her fitting-out berth at Wallsend on the River Tyne.
(*Maritime Photo Library*)

On Friday 26 February 1960, a bitterly cold winter's day on the River Tyne, the first keel plates were laid for what would be the fourth of the County-class destroyers, in a small ceremony at the shipyard of Swan, Hunter & Wigham Richardson Ltd. Once work was under way good progress was made and by the winter of 1961 the hull was ready to be launched. It had already been announced that members of the royal family would launch the first four ships of the class, and so at 1430 on Thursday 7 December 1961, the Duchess of Gloucester named and launched HMS *London*, sending her down the slipway into the River Tyne. Three days before her launch the first naval personnel had travelled to Wallsend and by early 1963 their numbers had increased considerably.

By mid-April 1963, just 16 months after her launch, *London* was ready to undergo her builder's trials and these began on 18 April when, at 0750, she left her fitting-out berth at Wallsend to anchor in the North Sea, just off Tynemouth's northern breakwater. At this stage the ship was still under the control of Swan Hunter and manned largely by their personnel. Still flying the Red Ensign her first series of trials lasted for four days, during which time the machinery was put through its paces over the measured mile. On the afternoon of 22 April, *London* returned to her fitting-out berth at Wallsend and it was 2 May when she began the second phase

County Class GMDs

(Above and Below) HMS *London* leaving the River Tyne in May 1963 for the second phase of her builder's trials. *(Maritime Photo Library)*

of her trials; this time they lasted for three weeks, as she steamed up and down the coast, between Tyneside and Leith, often anchoring for the night off Berwick and returning to Wallsend at weekends. The last day of trials was on 22 May when, at 0145, *London* began a final six-hour full-power trial, and having completed this successfully, by 1000 she was back alongside the Wallsend shipyard for completion of her fitting out.

On 14 September that year *London*'s first commanding officer, Captain Josef C. Bartosik DSC RN, was appointed to the ship. It was an unusual appointment since Bartosik was Polish and one of only three Polish naval officers who had transferred to the Royal Navy at the end of the Second World War. He was born in Krakow, a city which was then part of the Austro-Hungarian Empire and which, in 1919 as a result of the Treaty of Versailles, became part of the newly independent Second Polish Republic. In 1935 he joined the Polish Naval Officer Cadet School in Warsaw, from which he graduated with distinction three years later. On 1 September 1939, when Germany invaded Poland, Bartosik was serving in the sail training schooner *Iskra*, which was off the coast of West Africa at the time. Eventually the schooner was left in the charge of a small care and maintenance party and the remainder of her company escaped to Britain, where they were drafted to Polish destroyers. Bartosik went to the powerful and modern destroyer *Blyskawica*, which took part in the evacuation from Norway and Atlantic convoy duties. His second ship was the destroyer *Garland*, which had been transferred to the Polish Navy and subsequently took part in both Arctic and Mediterranean convoy duties. It was during this period that Bartosik's gallantry and devotion to duty was recognised, with the award of the DSC. After a spell as staff officer to the Senior Polish Naval Officer, he returned to sea as the gunnery officer to *Blyskawica*, which took part in the Normandy landings. In early 1945 he was the gunnery officer of the Polish cruiser *Conrad* (formerly HMS *Danae*), which, after the German surrender, was sent to the naval base at Wilhelmshaven, which had been captured by the Polish 1st Armoured Division, and for the rest of that year she assisted with the transport of Red Cross supplies between Norway and Denmark. At the end of the war, being unwilling to return to a Soviet-dominated Poland, Bartosik applied for a commission in the Royal Navy and he was one of only three applicants to be accepted. His first appointment as gunnery lieutenant was to the battleship *Anson* and by 1952 he had been promoted to commander. He later commanded the destroyer *Comus* in the Far East, the frigate *Scarborough* and the 5th Frigate Squadron, as well as Naval Air Station Culdrose. Over the years Bartosik earned a reputation as a martinet, with an unorthodox and uncompromising style of leadership. His appointment to *London* in the autumn of 1963 would be his last seagoing command before promotion to flag rank.

Captain Josef C. Bartosik. *(Courtesy of John Simm)*

On 1 October 1963, some four months after her initial trials, *London* left Wallsend to carry out further engine trials, but faults were found in her gas turbines and it was another two days before she returned to Wallsend for the last time under the Red Ensign. During the forenoon of 11 November *London*'s final inspection got under way and that afternoon Captain Bartosik signed for and commissioned the ship. Next day the first Wessex helicop-

A good close-up view of *London's* twin Sea Slug missile launcher. (T. Ferrers-Walker)

ter landed on the flight deck and the main body of the ship's company, who had travelled from Portsmouth in special trains, arrived on board in three separate drafts. Finally, with all preparations complete, at 1100 on Thursday 14 November, a formal commissioning ceremony was held on the jetty alongside the ship with two Vice-Admirals among the guests of honour, one of whom, Sir Peter Cazalet, had commanded the cruiser *London* during the late 1940s. Representing the City of London was an Alderman and a former Lord Mayor and that evening there was a wardroom reception for Swan Hunter's managers and foremen.

At 0800 on 16 November, two days after the commissioning ceremony, *London* slipped her mooring ropes and put to sea for the first time under the White Ensign. After pausing for photographs off Tynemouth, she began five hours of acceptance trials which were completed at 1545, when Bartosik formally accepted the ship from the builders. An hour later, having disembarked Swan Hunter's trials party, *London* set course for the Firth of Forth. However, when she was off Longstone Light she suffered a total loss of power and was left drifting helplessly for almost an hour. Fortunately by 2100 she was under way again and by 0213 the next morning she had anchored off Inchkeith Island in the Firth of Forth where, with Force 8 gales sweeping the area, she remained for over 24 hours. Finally, however, with the winds and heavy seas having moderated, *London* weighed anchor and continued her passage north via the Pentland Firth before steaming south via Loch Ewe and Plymouth Sound to Portsmouth where, at 1130 on 25 November, she secured alongside South Railway Jetty.

HMS London

Two images showing the launch of a Sea Slug missile from *London*. *(Courtesy of John Simm)*

HMS *London* remained at Portsmouth until mid-January 1964, when she sailed to continue her trials. Two days into these she joined *Hampshire* and *Kent* in the Channel for a widely publicised aerial photo shoot with all three ships steaming and manoeuvring together. The sea trials from Portsmouth continued through February and March, described as a 'tuning and testing' period, which finally ended in mid-April, when she moved round to the Welsh coast to put her Sea Cat and Sea Slug missile systems through their paces. May and June were busy months for *London* as the ship carried out a strenuous work-up at Portland, during which her sponsor, the Duchess of Gloucester, paid a flying visit to the ship while it was anchored at Spithead. The work-up ended during the second week of June, with an overnight visit by the Duke of Edinburgh, who witnessed Sea Cat firings in

A distant view of *London* firing a Sea Slug missile. *(Crown Copyright/MoD)*

HMS *London* passing through the Miraflores Locks, Panama Canal (in the canal's centenary year) with HMS *Tiger* and the submarine HMS *Odin* in 1964. *(Courtesy of John Simm)*

Lyme Bay, and by the end of June *London* had returned to Portsmouth.

On 3 July 1964, *London* left Portsmouth for the River Thames on her first visit to the capital and in the early hours of the next day she began steaming upriver. By 0530 she had reached Tilbury and just over an hour later she secured to buoys in midriver at Greenwich. During the visit some 25 officers and 300 ratings, led by the Royal Marines Band, paraded through the streets of the City of London, where the Lord Mayor took the salute outside Mansion House, before they marched to the Guildhall for lunch. On the two days that the ship was opened to the public huge queues built up, with hundreds of people waiting patiently for a place in the one small tender which ferried them to and from the ship.

After leaving Greenwich during the afternoon of 10 July, *London* made a fast three-day passage to Gibraltar, before returning to Portsmouth for Navy Days during the first week of August, when some 20,000 people visited the ship. As soon as the holiday weekend was over *London* was shifted into dry dock, to emerge once again in mid-August, in time to take part in the Home Fleet Assembly at Portsmouth. It was the first time for many years that such an assembly had taken place and for ten days there were conferences, social gatherings and sporting events. Some 21 ships, led by the cruiser *Lion*, were present and as well as *London* they included *Agincourt, Aurora, Carysfort, Diamond, Dundas, Eskimo, Galatea, Leander, Puma, Relentless, Rhyl, Salisbury* and RFA *Olna*. The assembly ended on

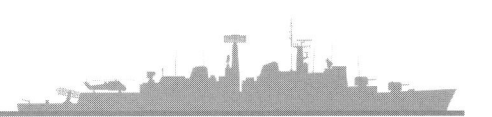

Testing the pre-wetting during the Panama Canal transit. *(Courtesy of John Simm)*

the last day of August when the ships of the fleet, minus *London* which was undergoing maintenance, made a ceremonial departure from Portsmouth Harbour.

In early September *London* carried out engine trials in the Channel before sailing to Devonport, from where she joined *Tiger* (flag C-in-C South Atlantic & South America Station), *Penelope* and RFA *Wave Chief* to form a special squadron on a 'showing the flag' cruise to South American ports. Although such cruises had been frequent prior to September 1939, in the post-war years they were few and far between, with the last such one having been made in 1961/62, when the cruiser *Lion* led a similar squadron. Apart from *London*, which would steam direct from South America to the Far East, the squadron would return home in time for Christmas.

After a six-day transatlantic passage the first port of call was the naval base at Ireland Island, Bermuda, where the frigate *Lynx* and the submarine *Odin* joined the squadron. From Bermuda *London* was temporarily detached to make a four-day visit to Houston, Texas, for a British Trade Fair in the city, but by 1 October she was at sea again and steaming to rejoin the squadron, which had just left its second South American port, Cartagena.

On 6 October the ships passed through the Panama Canal and next day they crossed the equator with full ceremony. At just after midday on 10 October they arrived at Peru's largest port, Callao, after which they steamed on to Valparaiso. During the first five days in the Chilean port the Royal Marines Detachments from all the ships put on a 'Beat Retreat' ceremony and a drill demonstration

HMS *London* receives a warm welcome in the Texas port of Houston.
(Courtesy of John Simm)

in the city's main square, where crowds packed the area to watch. When they were opened to the public over 12,000 people visited the four ships, with the queues for *London* and *Odin* being the longest. From Valparaiso the squadron exercised with the Chilean Navy, before steaming south to Punta Arenas, pausing on the way to lay a wreath close to the site of the disastrous Battle of Coronel where, just over 50 years previously, Admiral Craddock's squadron had been sunk by Graf Spee's powerful cruisers. On Thursday 29 October they arrived at Punta Arenas for an eight-day visit and once again the Royal Marines entertained the people of the city.

The final and possibly the most popular port of call on the South American continent was Rio de Janeiro, where the squadron arrived during the forenoon of 20 November for a seven-day visit, after which the C-in-C transferred his flag from *Tiger* to *London*. After leaving Rio *Tiger* led the squadron home via Dakar, while *London* set course for South Africa. On 1 December, as *London* passed Tristan da Cunha, the C-in-C was flown ashore by helicopter, but by mid-forenoon he was back on board and three days later the ship arrived in Simonstown to begin a three-week, dockyard-assisted maintenance period. Although she remained in South Africa during the Christmas period, on 30 December she left Simonstown bound for Singapore, via Mauritius and Gan.

During the ship's three-day visit to Port Louis, Mauritius, she received some 4,928 visitors over the space of one afternoon when she was opened to the public and the ship's Wessex helicopter answered a call for help from the Mauritius Broadcasting Corporation to lift into place six prefabricated sections of a 150-foot television mast onto a barely accessible 800-foot peak. Each section of the mast weighed three-quarters of a ton and at the time, as a cyclone passed to the north of the island, there was some very turbulent weather, with high winds and heavy rain lashing the island. As

HMS London

well as the inclement weather a major problem which had to be overcome was the earthing of some 18,000 volts of static electricity which had built up in the sections as they were flown to the site. The tricky task of guiding the helicopter into the correct position fell to Lieutenant John Walsh, who was in radio contact with the aircraft, but the most difficult job was carried out by Petty Officer Norman Anning, who, along with construction workers, climbed the mast and stayed for hours in an exposed position directing operations. The whole task was a race against the clock before the full force of the cyclone hit the island. In the event, on 8 January, before the heavy lift was completed, *London* had to put to sea in order to ride out the storm, but the naval personnel and radio engineers stuck to their job, successfully completing the task despite the weather. They then flew back to the ship, which by then had set course for Gan Lagoon, where she refuelled from the hulk RFA *Wave Victor*.

After only a three-hour pause at Gan, *London* made a non-stop passage across the Indian Ocean to the naval base at Singapore, where she secured alongside the Stores Basin to begin a four-week self-maintenance period. On 10 February 1965, *London* left Singapore to begin a busy six week schedule, which began with a two-day visit to Port

HMS *London (top right) in Simonstown Dockyard for Christmas 1964. Astern can be seen the South African Navy destroyer* SAS *Simon Van Der Stel (*ex HMS *Whelp) and the Type 12 frigate* SAS *President Pretorious. In the foreground are another pair of Type 12s,* SAS *President Kruger (inboard) and* SAS *President Steyn. To the right is the Loch-class frigate* SAS *Good Hope.*
(Courtesy of John Simm)

On 10 August 1965, as *London* steamed home at the end of her first commission, she went to the aid of an Italian-registered oil tanker, *Adriana Augusta*, which had suffered a major mechanical breakdown. Here *London* closes the tanker's stern in order to connect a hose and pump fresh water to the ship. *(Author's Collection)*

Swettenham (now Port Klang,) and from there she steamed into the South China Sea to join fleet exercises which also included the aircraft carrier *Victorious*, HMAS *Derwent* and *Ajax*, after which she steamed on to Hong Kong where she stayed until 2 March. After leaving Hong Kong *London* steamed to the mouth of the Chao Phraya River, where she made the three-hour passage upriver to the port area of Khlong Toei, which in those days was just outside the limits of Bangkok city. During the ship's three-day visit Thailand's controversial King Bhumibal made a visit for a couple of hours, after which his teenage son, the equally controversial Crown Prince Vajiralongkorn, remained on board for two days and disembarked during the afternoon of 13 March, as *London* reached the mouth of the Chao Phraya River on her way to the Gulf of Thailand. Here she joined *Eagle*, *Ajax*, *Derwent*, *Parramatta* and other ships of the fleet for the annual Fotex exercises in the South China Sea. These manoeuvres lasted over two weeks and took the fleet into the Strait of Malacca, north to Langkowi and ended with 'Operation Showpiece' off Singapore's south coast. This was a gunnery and air display staged as a signal to Indonesia that Britain intended to defend the recently created Federation of Malaysia.

In early April *London* was once again engaged in exercises and manoeuvres in the South China Sea, with recreational time at Pulau Tioman, the densely forested island situated some 20 miles off Endau on Malaya's east coast. When these exercises were over *London* returned to the naval base at Singapore and at the end of April, accompanied by *Caesar* and *Zest*, she sailed for Hong Kong where, during the first week of May, she underwent FO2's inspection. On leaving Hong Kong *London* joined *Victorious*, *Ajax*, *Cambrian*, *Euryalus* and the submarine *Amphion* for more exercises and manoeuvres in the South China Sea and around the Subic Bay area, which included a visit to the nearby US naval base. During these exercises *London* was called to assist *Amphion* whose Engineer Officer was injured, and who was quickly transferred to the destroyer by whaler. Next day *London* was put through her paces for FO2's sea inspection, before returning to Hong Kong at the end of June.

During the second week of July *London* and other ships of the fleet exercised with the fleet carrier *Ark Royal*, which had recently arrived in the Far East. Also involved in the exercises were *Ajax*, *Cambrian*, *Chichester* and *Euryalus*, but on 11 July *Ark Royal* suffered serious machinery problems and she was withdrawn from the manoeuvres. For over 24 hours, as the carrier's engineers struggled to carry out repairs, *London* stood by and preparations were made to take the carrier in tow, but in the event this was not required and on 16 August the destroyer returned to Singapore.

By mid-July *London*'s first commission was drawing to a close and on 20 July an advance recommissioning party who had flown out from the UK joined the ship, with a similar number of the original ship's company flying home. Seven days later *London* left Singapore to sail via Gan to Aden, where she arrived on 7 August. Forty-eight hours later, at 0630 on 9 August, she left harbour and set course to the westward to carry out exercises and trials whilst on passage. That forenoon, however, a signal was received from Flag Officer, Middle East, ordering *London* to close the 20,300-ton Italian oil tanker *Adriana Augusta*, which was en route from Cagliari to Kuwait and anchored in a position Lat 16°50'N/Lat 40°13'E, in order to supply her with drinking water, which appeared to be a simple task.

During the early hours of 10 August, as *London* steamed towards the tanker, the situation appeared to be much more serious when a signal was received from *Adriana Augusta* to the effect that the ship had no water at all and that all her main and auxiliary machinery had suffered a major breakdown. On board *London* as the gas turbines were started and speed was increased it was estimated that she would reach the tanker's position during the forenoon of that day. In the meantime, however, as *London* steamed at 28 knots towards *Adriana Augusta* the ship's helicopter, carrying three senior officers and 15 gallons of drinking water, flew to the stricken tanker. According to one of the officers present: 'The water was very quickly consumed by a parched and very thirsty Italian crew.' As *London* made her way to the tanker's position three more helicopter lifts transported the necessary engine room, electrical and communications ratings, as well as more drinking water to the ship.

By 1245 *London* was some four and a half miles from the tanker and because of the lack of soundings charted in the area, as well as numerous pinnacles and coral patches detected by sonar, she approached the vessel with some caution. By 1330, however, the destroyer was lying close to the tanker's stern and a hose supported on a 2½-inch jackstay was being passed across. Pumping of fresh water to the Italian ship began at 1400 and despite a 30-knot wind and a choppy sea, it continued all afternoon. During this operation the domestic water supplies on board *London* herself were rationed and by 1900 some 65 tons had been transferred to the oil tanker. *London* was then able to slip the hose and steam to seawards to patrol within radio contact of *Adriana Augusta*. In the meantime the team of engineers and electricians who had been flown over to the tanker had managed to repair the tanker's port boiler, a turbo-generator and her fresh water pumps with virtually no help from a heat-exhausted crew and working in swelteringly hot conditions throughout the night. By 0400 the stricken ship should have been capable of raising steam, but unfortunately, further technical problems prevented this and at 0600, having been relieved by the destroyer *Cambrian*, all *London*'s equipment and personnel were airlifted back to the ship and by 0745 she was continuing her passage home.

On 14 August she passed through the Suez Canal and took part in an exercise off Malta, before continuing to Gibraltar, where she paused for three days, before arriving at Spithead during the evening of 25 August. Next day, having cleared Customs, *London* steamed up harbour and at 1300 she secured alongside Portsmouth Dockyard's South Railway Jetty. She had arrived home in time to take part in Navy Days, where she attracted some 18,000 visitors, and during the last two weeks of September she exercised off Portland and the Welsh coast. The first two weeks of November saw *London* taking part in anti-submarine exercises and noise ranging trials in the Firth of Clyde, but by the middle of that month she had returned to Portsmouth and had paid off. During her commission *London* had steamed some 60,000 miles and ahead of her now lay a 30-week refit which would keep her out of commission until the spring of 1966.

On 17 February 1966 there was a change of command when Captain David N. Forbes took over from Bartosik, but it was mid-April before *London* was ready for sea and moved from the basin to the sea wall at Fountain Lake Jetty. Five weeks later, at 1115 on 20 May, the ship was recommissioned and three days after that, for the first time since mid-October 1965, she put to sea to begin post-refit trials in the Channel. These continued through to mid-June, then during the latter half of the month she operated in the North Sea, off the Scottish coast, calling at Invergordon before returning to the Channel and Portland to begin her work-up. Throughout this busy period she was assisted by *Caprice*, *Diana* and *Llandaff*, and on 9 August, just as soon as her final inspections were over, she steamed north once again, this time to join *Ark Royal* in the Moray Firth. At the end of August she returned to Portsmouth for Navy Days and on 12 September, flying the flag of FO2 Home Fleet, she sailed for the Baltic. *London*, her sister *Devonshire* and RFA *Oleander* were scheduled to make a number of goodwill visits to Baltic ports, with *Devonshire* (flag C-in-C Home Fleet) visiting Leningrad (St Petersburg), Helsinki and Gdynia, after which the C-in-C would transfer his flag to *London* for a five-day visit to Stockholm. Following this *London* returned via the Baltic Sound to the Welsh coast, before returning to Portsmouth in mid-October.

On 24 October 1966, *London* left Portsmouth to carry out a four-week deployment to the Mediterranean, which saw her visiting Civitavecchia, Piraeus and Malta, before returning home via Gibraltar and Portland. On 12 December, FO2 Home Fleet hoisted his flag and on 9 January 1967, with seasonal leave over, *London* sailed for

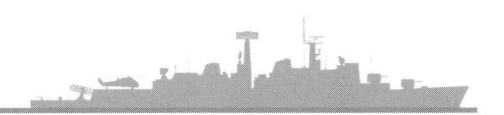

HMS *London* replenishes at sea from RFA *Fort Duquesne*, while the Leander-class frigate *Ajax*, awaits her turn. (*Syd Goodman Collection*)

the Caribbean. At sea she was joined by *Berwick*, *Phoebe*, *Zest* and RFA *Tidespring*, before the squadron set course for San Juan, where they joined a squadron from the Netherlands Navy which included the cruiser *De Zeven Provincien* and the destroyers *De Bitter*, *Noord Brabant* and *Zeeland*. Together the two groups carried out anti-submarine exercises, with USS *Thornback* acting as their prey. During this period *London* also visited Antigua, St Vincent and Barbados, before steaming north to Hamilton, Bermuda. Seven days later she sailed for home and after pausing briefly at Devonport, where FO2 struck his flag, on 9 February she secured alongside Portsmouth's Fountain Lake Jetty to begin a 17-week refit and maintenance period.

Five days into the refit, at 0400 on Sunday 12 March, fire broke out in the ship's main galley and it quickly became apparent that it was a serious situation. Within 15 minutes the Dockyard Fire Brigade was fighting the blaze and soon after that Portsmouth City Fire Brigade also arrived. In the event the fire was brought under control at 0620 and by 0700 it had been extinguished. The damage was confined chiefly to the galley itself, with surrounding areas affected mainly by smoke. Fortunately nobody had been injured, but in the galley itself most of the equipment and electrical wiring needed replacing. On 6 July, with the refit almost over, FO2 of the newly formed Western Fleet hoisted his flag in *London* and nine days later the ship left Portsmouth to begin a series of trials in the Channel. These ended on the last day of July when *London* sailed for the Baltic and the Swedish port of Sundsvall in the Gulf of Bothnia, where she spent six days before returning to Portsmouth by way of the Kiel Canal. Later in August she held a Families Day in the Channel before steaming round to the Welsh coast where, for the remainder of that month and the first week of September, broken by a weekend visit to Liverpool, she operated off the Aberporth missile range. By mid-September, however, she had returned to Portsmouth.

On Monday 2 October 1967, *London* left Portsmouth on the first stage of her passage to the

A nice aerial view of *London* at sea. *(Crown Copyright/MoD)*

Far East, but before leaving home waters she rendezvoused with *Aisne, Arethusa, Falmouth* and *Grenville* for exercises and manoeuvres between Plymouth and Gibraltar from where, after a 36-hour break, she steamed south on the long passage to Simonstown. The journey south was broken only by a six-hour refuelling stop at Freetown and, next day, by a light-hearted Crossing the Line ceremony. She arrived at the Cape on 20 October and remained at Simonstown for seven days, where essential maintenance was carried out, but on 27 October she steamed north into the Indian Ocean, bound for Aden.

HMS *London*'s presence off Aden was to reinforce the naval task force which had been deployed for the granting of Independence to the South Arabian Federation (Aden State and the surrounding Protectorates), which was set for midnight on Wednesday 29 November, by which time all British service personnel and their equipment would have to be withdrawn to ships of the task force, including *Eagle, Albion* and *Intrepid*. After refuelling from RFA *Tidereach* en route *London* arrived off Aden on 8 November and next day she joined other ships of the task force at anchor in the outer harbour. The ships were to provide for the British departure from Aden as well as the Army and Marines ashore and to remove huge quantities of stores and equipment to Bahrain. Preparations had also been made to evacuate European civilians should the security situation deteriorate around the date of Independence. Most of the Army personnel actually left Aden by RAF Air Support Command, with only the last units of the Royal Marines, who had been manning the final British perimeter around Khormaksar airfield, being evacuated by sea.

During the whole of November *London* and the other ships of the task force patrolled the waters around Aden and at sea there was little to indicate the drama which was unfolding ashore. On 12 November *London* assisted with an unsuccessful search for an officer lost overboard from RFA *Appleleaf* and six days later she provided medical assistance to the merchantman *Empire Architect*. In the event, at the end of November, the handover of power and the leave-taking passed without a hitch, but without the usual ceremonial which accompanied Britain's withdrawal from Empire. In this case it was confined to a review by the former Governor of detachments from all three services and the band played 'Fings Ain't Wot They Used to Be', but this was largely drowned out by the roar of an RAF Britannia aircraft which was waiting nearby to evacuate the Governor. At sea most of the task force remained on patrol for ten days after the handover of power, but once it became clear that the lives of European civilians still in Aden were not in any danger, the ships dispersed. On 9 December, after a day spent exercising with *Eagle* and replenishing from RFA *Tarbatness*, *London* set course for Mombasa where, four days later, she arrived alongside the depot ship *Forth*.

HMS *London* spent Christmas and New Year at Mombasa and on 29 December there was a change of command, when Captain Denis Jermain DSC RN took over from Forbes, who left the ship next day. Eight days later, during the forenoon of Saturday 6 January 1968, *London* left Kilindini Harbour and set course for Simonstown from where, after a weekend break, she set course across the Atlantic for the Caribbean island of Trinidad.

On 31 January, when she was some 16 hours'

During her 1967/68 deployment east of Suez, London follows Eagle during exercises in the Indian Ocean. The Commando Carrier Albion can also be seen in the background. (Author's Collection)

steaming from the island, FO2 Western Fleet, who had left the ship in Gibraltar while en route to Aden, rehoisted his flag and next forenoon *London* anchored at Port of Spain for a weekend visit. On leaving Trinidad she rendezvoused with other Royal Navy ships including *Aisne, Decoy, Falmouth, Juno* and the submarine *Walrus*, all of which had been operating in the area for some weeks, for exercises and manoeuvres before leading *Falmouth* and *Walrus* into the Venezuelan port of La Guira. After leaving Venezuela the squadron re-formed to carry out their own three-day exercise code-named 'Caribex', before *London* and *Falmouth* paid a short visit to Willemstad, Curacao, and then moved on for exercises with US Navy ships. *London*'s deployment ended with an eight-day visit to Bermuda after which she sailed for home on 4 March. After a seven-day Atlantic crossing she arrived off Portland, where her Wessex helicopter was disembarked, and that same evening she anchored at Spithead, before steaming up harbour the next day to secure alongside Fountain Lake Jetty. In just over five months she had steamed some 33,000 miles and during the period spent with the task force off Aden she was 48 days at sea without a break.

After undergoing two weeks' essential maintenance at Portsmouth, *London* hoisted the flag of the C-in-C Western Fleet, Admiral Sir John Bush, and left harbour to make the first of two 'diplomatic' visits, which took her to the French naval base at Brest, where the C-in-C was involved in a busy day of official meetings with his French counterparts. Then, after returning briefly to Portsmouth, *London* steamed up the Thames Estuary to secure to buoys in midriver off Greenwich. It was the ship's second visit to the capital and on this occasion 179 ratings were entertained at the city's Mansion House. By 6 April *London* was back at Portsmouth's Fountain Lake Jetty, where she paid off and began a 27-week refit which would see her in dockyard hands for six months.

HMS *London*'s first major refit came to an end during the second week of October and she was recommissioned on Friday 11 of that month, when strong winds and torrential rain were lashing the south coast, forcing everyone to take shelter in the ship's hangar for the ceremony. Just over two weeks later the ship left Portsmouth Harbour to begin a series of post-refit trials which lasted well into December. At 0812 on Friday 29 November, *London* left her Spithead anchorage, but before beginning her trials that day she rendezvoused in the Channel with the elderly Cunard passenger liner *Queen Elizabeth* which had been sold to an American company to be used as a tourist attraction at Port Everglades; at 1042 that forenoon, with her upper decks manned, *London* sailed by the veteran Cunarder in a ceremonial steam past. After escorting the former liner for a few miles *London* detached to continue her trials which saw her operating in the area between Land's End and the Channel Islands for the next few days. In early December she began day running from Spithead, before carrying out helicopter flying trials off Portland, but on 13 December she returned to Portsmouth for maintenance and to give seasonal leave.

The new year of 1969 saw *London* at Portland when, assisted by *Minerva* and *Yarmouth*, she underwent her work-up which took her through to the end of February; she then returned to Portsmouth for further maintenance and to give foreign service leave. On 9 April 1969, *London* hosted a Families Day, after which she returned to Portsmouth and three days later, having embarked the new Governor of Gibraltar, Admiral of the Fleet Sir Varyl Begg, she sailed for the Colony on the first stage of her passage east, which she made in company with *Defender*. The long passage south was broken at Freetown for a short refuelling stop and next day there was light-hearted fun with the Crossing the Line ceremony. On 1 May she reached Simonstown where there was a four-day break before she steamed north into the Indian Ocean and the Mozambique Channel where, during the afternoon of 9 May, she relieved *Diamond* on the Beira Patrol. *London*'s stint on the monotonous patrol did not last long and three days later she sailed for Malé and Astove Island, where she delivered some sup-

HMS London

A dramatic shot of *London* at sea. *(Crown Copyright/MoD)*

plies to the sole occupants, the British 'adventurer and businessman' Mark Veevers-Carter and his wife and three children. At Malé *London* hoisted the flag of FO2, Far East Station, before continuing her passage to Singapore, where she arrived on 24 May.

On arrival at Singapore *London* carried out maintenance, while at the same time in the South China Sea a large multinational SEATO exercise, codenamed 'Sea Spirit', was taking place some 650 miles west of Manila. Among the warships taking part were the frigates HMS *Cleopatra*, HMNZS *Blackpool*, the Australian aircraft carrier *Melbourne*, the US Navy's aircraft carrier *Kearsarge* and the destroyer, *Frank E. Evans*. At just before dawn on 2 June, tragedy struck when *Melbourne* collided with *Frank E. Evans*, slicing the destroyer in two. The forward section quickly sank, taking with it 74 members of her ship's company, but the after section remained afloat and was eventually secured alongside *Melbourne*. The manoeuvres were quickly abandoned as all the ships joined the rescue operation and in Singapore *London* was ordered to sail for the area to assist. It was 1000 before *London* was ready for sea and with *Ajax* she left for the rescue area, where she arrived at 1345 the next day. By that time, however, almost 36 hours had passed since the collision and there was little hope of finding any more survivors, although for two days both *London* and *Ajax* searched the area for bodies and wreckage, before continuing to the Subic Bay area where they joined the exercise. On 16 June, after two days at Olongapo, *London* and *Ajax* sailed for Japan.

Flying the flag of FO2, Vice-Admiral A. T. F. G. Griffin, the two ships were making high-profile goodwill visits to Japanese ports, with *London*

HMS *Rothsay* conducting a jackstay transfer with *London*. *(Courtesy of John Simm)*

spending four days in Yokohama and Hakodate. It was on 28 June, while she was at the latter port, that there was a change of command and Captain Peter G. Loasby DSC RN took over command from Jermain. Two days later both ships returned via Hong Kong to Singapore to join a large maritime and air exercise, code-named 'Julex 69'. The manoeuvres took place in the South China Sea and altogether some 31 vessels were involved. The Royal Navy's contingent was led by *London* (flag FO2) and also included *Ajax, Argonaut, Berry Head, Cleopatra, Danae, Fearless, Forth, Lincoln, Naiad*, the submarines *Cachalot, Onslaught* and *Rorqual*, as well as RFAs *Gold Ranger, Resurgent* and *Tidereach*. In addition there were ships from the Australian, New Zealand and Malaysian Navies and in the air were aircraft from the RAF, the RAAF, the RNZAF and the US Navy. During the 18-day exercise the ships were subjected to air, submarine and fast patrol boat attacks. The air defence exercises in particular allowed *London* ample opportunity to use her missile and tracking systems and with only two short breaks at Pulau Tioman the exercises continued until 24 July, when *London* led the Far East Fleet back into the naval base at Singapore.

Following her return to the naval base *London* underwent a three-week maintenance period, before making a short visit to Hong Kong and returning to Singapore. On Saturday 13 September, the new FO2 FES Rear-Admiral Terence T. H. Lewin transferred his flag from *Berry Head* to *London* and ten days later, in company with HMNZS *Otago*, the destroyer sailed for New Zealand. *London* had been chosen to represent the Royal Navy at celebrations marking the 200th anniversary of Captain James Cook's first landing at Poverty Bay. For Admiral Lewin the visit to New Zealand was of special interest, for he was a notable authority on the life of Captain Cook. Off New Zealand *London* and *Otago*

HMS London

A magnificent aerial view of *London* at sea, showing her upper deck layout in good detail.
(Crown Copyright/MoD)

joined *Argonaut*, HMNZS *Blackpool*, HMAS *Anzac*, the Canadian ships *Qu'Appelle* and *Saskatchewan* and USS *Hoel*, for joint manoeuvres in the area. After a 24-hour pause at Auckland, *London* visited Gisborne where, on the day of the Cook celebrations, two platoons of seamen marched in a parade through the town. After Gisborne *London* called at Wellington and Lyttleton, before steaming into Australian waters where she called at Hobart and Melbourne and took part in a multi-national exercise in the Jervis Bay area led by the aircraft carrier HMAS *Melbourne*. On 1 December *London* left Sydney Harbour and in company with *Galatea* and *Yarmouth* made the passage back to Singapore where she spent Christmas, then on 29 December she sailed for Gan.

After spending four days with the frigate *Leopard* on the Beira Patrol, *London* called at Simonstown and five days later, on 21 January 1970, she left South African waters to make the 13-day transatlantic passage to the Caribbean and Kingstown, St Vincent. From there she continued her passage north-west to the US naval base at San Juan where, in company with the submarine USS *Tullibee* and the aircraft carrier *America* she took part in a series of anti-aircraft and anti-submarine exercises. On 16 February, she left the exercise area to make a 15-day passage to Plymouth Sound, where the ship's Flight and the Fleet Air Arm personnel left the ship. Next day, at 1015 on Thursday 26 February, *London* secured alongside Portsmouth's Fountain Lake Jetty where she paid off.

For 27 weeks *London* remained in dockyard hands, but on Friday 26 June 1970 she was recommissioned, with the ceremony taking place beside the ship at Fountain Lake Jetty. The commissioning cake, which had been skilfully crafted by the galley staff, was a five-foot long model of the ship. Three days after the ceremony *London* began her post-refit trials in the Channel, which took her to St Peter Port and Torquay and during the afternoon of 7 August she steamed up the River Thames to secure at buoys off Greenwich. During her weekend visit to the capital 200 members of the ship's company were invited to a reception at the Guildhall and over two afternoons when the ship was opened to the public, some 2,000 people visited her. After leaving the Thames *London* returned to Portsmouth and during the Navy Days holiday weekend she attracted some 36,000 visitors. On Tuesday 1 September, there was a change of command when Captain Ronald S. Forrest RN took over from Loasby who was retiring after 37 years in the service. Next day *London* left Portsmouth for Portland to begin a hectic six weeks' work-up. During this period she operated with *Argonaut* and the submarine *Walrus* in the Western Approaches, and the work-up was successfully concluded on 14 October, with final inspections taking place that evening. Next morning the ship secured alongside at Devonport to embark a full outfit of missiles before returning to Portsmouth for a short maintenance period.

On Monday 26 October, when *London* left Portsmouth for the Mediterranean, she was flying the flag of Flag Officer Flotillas, Western Fleet, Rear-Admiral J. E. Pope. At sea she was joined by *Argonaut*, *Galatea*, *Juno*, *Rothesay*, *Scylla* and *Yarmouth* as they set course for the Mediterranean and a rendezvous with *Ark Royal* and *Exmouth* for 'Exercise Limejug', a joint Navy-RAF exercise in the first two weeks of November. The manoeuvres became world news when, at 1840 on 9 November, some 100 miles south of Cape Matapan, *Ark Royal* collided with the Soviet destroyer *Bravyy*. *Ark Royal* was about to begin a night-flying programme when *Bravyy* approached her starboard side and crossed her bows. The carrier's stem hit the destroyer's port quarter, but neither ship was seriously damaged. However, two seamen from *Bravyy* were thrown overboard and despite a thorough search by *London*, *Exmouth* and *Yarmouth* no trace of them was found. The ill-fated exercise ended at Malta's Grand Harbour during the afternoon of 13 November and Captain Forrest was appointed as the President of the Board of Inquiry set up to investigate the circumstances of the collision from the British viewpoint, with Commander A. E. Thompson taking temporary command of *London*. On 18 November *London* left Malta to make a fast passage home to the Welsh coast, where she spent

HMS *London* arrives at Malta's Grand Harbour in 1970. *(Syd Goodman Collection)*

four days off the Aberporth ranges before steaming north to the River Clyde for a five-day visit to Glasgow, where she secured alongside the city's Yorkhill Basin. After leaving the River Clyde *London* returned to the Aberporth ranges, but on 12 December she secured alongside at Portsmouth to give seasonal leave.

On Monday 18 January 1971, still wearing the flag of FOFWF, *London* left Portsmouth and was joined by *Norfolk*, *Hermione* and *Bacchante*, for two days of exercises off Portland before setting course for the Mediterranean where they joined the aircraft carrier *Eagle* for further exercises off Gibraltar. On 22 February, the group steamed westward to the Tyrrhenian Sea for joint manoeuvres with an Italian naval force, before visiting the port of Livorno. On 12 March they reached Malta, where they prepared to take part in the five-nation air and maritime exercise 'Dawn Patrol'. During her stay in Malta *London* played host to a television team who were filming a dance sequence with the popular group Pans People, who, danced their way around the quarterdeck, flight deck, Sea Cat launchers and gun turrets.

During March and April *London* and other ships of the Western Fleet put to sea on a number of occasions in order to rehearse manoeuvres, which for *London* included visits to Trieste and Civitavecchia. On 27 April the main exercise got under way, but three days later, during the afternoon of 30 April, the destroyer was detached to go to the aid of a Norwegian oil tanker, MV *Ronaville*, which had suffered an engine room explosion and fire resulting in a badly burned crew member in urgent need of medical attention. The ship was off the Libyan coast and some 200 miles away from *London*, but within an hour of setting course towards the tanker the Wessex helicopter carrying the ship's surgeon was launched and by 1640 it had returned with the casualty. *London* then increased speed and set course for Malta where the injured man could be transferred to hospital, but despite the best efforts of the medical staff, in the early hours of the following day he died from his injuries. Eight hours later *London* arrived in Malta and secured alongside Canteen Wharf where the man's body was landed. Later that afternoon *London* sailed to rejoin the exercise in the central Mediterranean, where she acted as escort to the Italian helicopter cruiser *Vittorio Veneto*. The exercises ended on 13 May, when *London* arrived in Naples for a five-day visit, after which she steamed west to Gibraltar to undergo a three-week self-maintenance period.

On 17 June, *London*, in company with the frigate *Chichester*, returned to Malta, from where they operated until the end of July. During this period *London* paid visits to Toulon and Marseilles and was the first Royal Navy ship to carry out Sea Slug firings at the French missile range off the Île du Levant, after which she returned, via Tunis, to Malta. At the end of July she took part in joint air and maritime exercises with RAF aircraft from Cyprus, which included a weekend at Famagusta. On 2 August, after leaving the Cypriot port, she steamed north to join an exercise with the Turkish Air Force, before negotiating the Dardanelles and the Bosporus to become the first Royal Navy ship to enter the Black Sea since the mid-1960s. During the time she spent in the landlocked sea she was constantly shadowed by a Soviet Kotlin-class destroyer, which stayed with her until she entered the Turkish port of Samsun and was waiting for her two days later when she sailed to return via Istanbul to Crete's Souda Bay. Although her stay was limited to less than 48 hours, for Captain Forrest it brought back memories of his wartime service in HMS *York*, which in 1941 had been sunk by enemy action while at anchor in the bay. On 17 August *London* left Crete to steam west to Gibraltar where, on 22 August, Admiral Pope struck his flag and was relieved as FOFWF by Vice-Admiral A. M. Power who hoisted his flag that same evening. Next day *London* led *Charybdis* and *Norfolk* to sea for the passage home, with *London* arriving alongside at Portsmouth in time for Navy Days, when she attracted over 30,000 visitors.

It was the last week of October 1971 before the dockyard completed their programme of rectifying defects in *London*'s main propulsion machinery and she was able to put to sea to carry out steam and gas turbine trials. At the end of that month FOFWF transferred his flag to *Antrim* for the duration of a North Sea exercise. On 10 November, *London* went to the aid of a French trawler, one of whose crewmen had been lost overboard between the Isle of Wight and Cherbourg. In the event the destroyer searched the area for six hours, but on a dark night with a choppy sea there was little hope of finding the man alive, and in the early hours of the following morning the search was called off. *London* continued her trials and weapons training in the Channel, and this included assisting *Dido* with her work-up, and also joining *Walrus* for anti-submarine exercises. On 22 November, with *Dundas*, she steamed north to Rosyth to take part in 'Exercise Highwood' which took them to the old wartime naval base and natural anchorage at Scapa Flow, where they refuelled at Lyness Pier before returning south to Portsmouth for the seasonal break.

On 6 January 1972, Vice-Admiral Power, who was now Flag Officer 1st Flotilla of the newly created Fleet Command (an amalgamation of the soon to be disbanded Far East Fleet and the Western Fleet) rehoisted his flag and 12 days later *London*, with *Ark Royal, Dido* and *Naiad* in company, set course for Bermuda and the US Navy's exercise areas off Puerto Rico. Six days into the passage, however, *Ark Royal* was ordered to make for the Crown Colony of British Honduras (now Belize), Britain's only colony in Central America, where a long-running border dispute with Guatemala had flared up and Guatemalan troops were reported to be massing on the border. *London* was ordered to accompany and provide support for the aircraft carrier, whose air group it was hoped would dissuade Guatemala from invading the small British colony.

A close-up view of *London's* starboard side. Note the Land Rover on deck. *(Maritime Photo Library)*

In the event, as they steamed towards British Honduras, the crisis was resolved by the politicians and *London* arrived at Bermuda on 29 January. Two days later she sailed to rendezvous with *Dido, Jupiter, Dreadnought* and the US submarine *Bluefish*, for an anti-submarine exercise, which for *London* was followed by a nine-day visit to Charleston, South Carolina. The main exercise of the deployment, code-named 'Lantreadex', began on 21 February when *London* joined *Ark Royal, Glamorgan, Dido, Jupiter*, three RFAs and ships of the US Navy. For *London* these manoeuvres were followed by an extended weekend visit to Port of Spain, Trinidad, before she rejoined the other ships for the transatlantic passage to Gibraltar. Here *London* carried out 14 days of maintenance before steaming on to Malta, where she was involved in an air defence exercise with aircraft from USS *Franklin D. Roosevelt*. Her stay in Malta, however, lasted for only nine days before she sailed for home,

arriving alongside in Portsmouth on 22 April.

HMS *London*'s commission still had some three months to run before she began a long refit, which had been delayed for some two years, and these last weeks of the commission would be more relaxed with the ship remaining in European waters. On 16 May, with *Bacchante* in company, she left Portsmouth for a 'Meet the Navy' visit to Newcastle upon Tyne, before steaming across the North Sea to transit the Kiel Canal. An international force of naval ships was gathering at Kiel for the annual 'Kieler Woche', during which *London*'s cutter crews acquitted themselves particularly well, coming in first and second in a competition with German, French, Dutch and Norwegian naval crews. After leaving Kiel the ship made a 48-hour stop at Invergordon, before steaming south to the Thames Estuary from where she made her way upriver. This time, however, instead of berthing at Greenwich she continued on towards the city and passed under Tower Bridge to secure alongside HMS *Belfast* in the Pool of London. During the five-day visit to the capital the ship received a steady stream of visitors, from the Lord Mayor of the City to the Pearly King and his daughter, the Pearly Princess. As a finale to the ship's visit 250 officers and men, led by the Royal Marines Band, marched through the city to the Guildhall, where the Lord Mayor gave a lunch in honour of the ship. Also present were all of *London*'s former commanding officers. On Wednesday 21 June, *London* made her way back down the River Thames and set course for Devonport where, over four days, she was de-ammunitioned. On 6 July she arrived in Portsmouth and ten days later she performed her final operational duty of the commission, shock trials in the mining grounds at Spithead. By 20 July these had been completed and *London* was placed at 'Extended Notice' for steam and paid off.

HMS *London* remained out of commission in Portsmouth Dockyard for over three years, but during this time no major modernisation work was carried out and it was on 5 May 1975 that her new commanding officer, Captain Peter D. Nichol RN, was appointed to the ship, which was still in dockyard hands, and remained so until mid-November, when she carried out three days of post-refit trials. It was during this period, after putting to sea for 55 hours of machinery trials, that *London* was ordered to a position in the Channel, Lat 52°28'N/Long 01°46'W, where the 4,400-ton MV *Gorizont*, ostensibly a Soviet fishing-factory ship, but in reality suspected to be a Soviet spy ship, had collided with a Moroccan freighter, MV *Ifni*. After the collision at 1915 on 25 November a distress call in Russian had been received by the coastguard. However, further messages from the Russian ship made it clear that no assistance was required and it was not long before at least seven Russian trawlers were on the scene and standing by the stricken vessel, which refused all other offers of assistance. Initially, during the night *Gorizont*'s crew, which included two injured men, were evacuated to the trawlers, but later seven men returned to the 'factory ship'. By the early hours of 26 November, however, *Gorizont* had partially sunk and there was only some 50 feet of her bow above water at which point her crew were once again evacuated. In the meantime the Moroccan ship *Ifni*, which had also been holed by the collision, was able to proceed slowly to Le Havre. When *London* arrived on the scene during the morning watch she found the bows of *Gorizont* still protruding from the water and the wreck surrounded by eight Soviet trawlers, which warned the destroyer to 'stay clear'. After searching the area for possible survivors *London* returned to the scene of the wreck which she illuminated with her searchlight while standing by. That forenoon *London* was relieved by *Penelope* and later in the day she returned to the dockyard. As for *Gorizont*, she eventually sank in some 38 fathoms of water.

During the forenoon of Friday 12 December 1975 *London* was recommissioned, but she did not put to sea until 12 January 1976, when she began a series of sea trials from Portsmouth and then from Gibraltar. It was mid-March before she began her work-up at Portland, which continued through to mid-May. On 15 June, flying the flag of the First Sea Lord, Admiral Sir Edward Ashmore and accompanied by the frigates *Bacchante* and *Lowestoft*, she left home waters and set course across the Atlantic for the USA. The three ships had been chosen to take part in America's bicentennial celebrations which included a naval review off New York. Before the review *London* visited Providence, Rhode Island, while *Bacchante* and *Lowestoft* called respectively at Wilmington and Bridgeport. On Friday 2 July, some 180 miles off New York, the three British warships rendezvoused with over 50 warships from 21 nations to form a 20-mile column, led by the cruiser USS *Wainwright*, the flagship of the US Navy's 2nd Fleet, and the aircraft carrier *Forrestal*. Next forenoon, to the sound of ships' horns, bells and sirens, the column entered New York Harbour, to be greeted by huge crowds in the city's Battery Park, the birthplace of the city in the days of the Dutch colony of Nieuw Amsterdam. Next day President Gerald Ford reviewed the international array of warships ahead of two days of festivals, parades and nautical flamboyance.

On 7 July *London* left New York and steamed directly to the Aberporth missile range, before returning via Plymouth Sound to Portsmouth. On 19 August the ship played host to the actress Susan Hampshire, who was on board to be presented with an inscribed deck plate from her sister ship *Hampshire*, which had been decommissioned and was awaiting the scrapyard. With *Hampshire* having been withdrawn, the long-term future for *London* did not look good.

In autumn 1976, *London*, flying the flag of FOF1, together with *Ark Royal* and *Fearless*, was assigned to the Commander Striking Fleet Atlantic, for a large NATO exercise code-named 'Team Work 76', which was designed to test the defences of Western Europe. As well as the three major Royal Navy warships, another 47 British vessels took part, including the frigates *Amazon*, *Berwick*, *Galatea*, *Gurkha*, *Llandaff* and *Salisbury*. In addition there was a large amphibious task force which included the RFAs *Sir Geraint*, *Sir Bedivere*, *Sir Percivale* and *Sir Tristram*, as well as *Resurgent* and *Grey Rover*. *London*'s role was to escort *Ark Royal*, which in turn provided air cover and protection for the large amphibious assault force, with rocket and bombing strikes by her Buccaneers and at higher altitudes her Phantom interceptors, directed by Gannets. Submarines, meanwhile, were kept at bay by Sea King helicopters.

As well as attracting the attention of the enemy (Orange) forces, which included RAF Vulcans, Buccaneers and Canberras, US F-104 Starfighters and Norwegian F-5 Freedom Fighters, *Ark Royal* also encountered 'Red Forces' of the Soviet Union, which overhead came in the form of Tu-95 Bear and Tu-16 Badger aircraft and at sea in the form of Polish and Russian intelligence-gathering ships and two Kresta-class cruisers, one of which, *Marshal Timoshenko*, kept a close watch on proceedings. These ended with a major amphibious landing near the Norwegian port town of Namsos, after which *London*, seven frigates and two RFAs visited Amsterdam. It was at this time that *London* joined NATO's Standing Naval Force Atlantic (inevitably

HMS *London* at Spithead in July 1977 for the Silver Jubilee Fleet Review. *(Maritime Photo Library)*

Dressed overall and with her ship's company manning ship, *London* presents an impressive sight at the Silver Jubilee Fleet Review. *(Ken Kelly Collection)*

given a typical naval acronym STANAVFOR-LANT) and in mid-November the commander of the force, Commodore John M. H. Cox, hoisted his broad pennant in *London*, which would be his flagship for the duration of the ship's secondment to the international force.

In January 1977, in her role as STANAVFORLANT's flagship, *London* was joined by five other ships of the squadron, including the destroyer HMCS *Annapolis*, for exercises in the Strait of Gibraltar and the Western Atlantic, which ended with a four-day break at Funchal, Madeira. They then returned to the area off Gibraltar where they were joined by *Antrim, Devonshire, Glamorgan, Norfolk* and the frigate *Cleopatra*, as well as other NATO ships, to begin 'Exercise Springtrain'. Early on in the manoeuvres *London* was called upon to help *Annapolis* which had suffered a mechanical fault in her aviation fuel supply,

leaving her with contaminated fuel. Her Sea King helicopter was too big to land on *London*'s flight deck and so that the Canadian ship did not lose valuable training time by returning to Gibraltar *London* helped out by rigging up an improvised 240-foot ship-to-ship jackstay and carrying out a 40-minute transfer of aviation fuel, which kept the Canadian Sea King airborne during the exercise. At this time, as well as putting into Madeira, *London* also visited Oporto, Lisbon and Cherbourg, after which Commodore Cox handed over the command of NATO's Standing Force Atlantic to the Dutch Navy at Den Helder. *London* then steamed up the River Thames to pay another official visit to the capital; her passage under Tower Bridge was delayed by over an hour when the bridge mechanism jammed, but eventually she was able to secure alongside HMS *Belfast*.

Once again *London*'s close links to the capital

city were confirmed, with visits being organised to the Tower of London, Parliament, the Stock Exchange and to two London football clubs. There was a luncheon at the Guildhall for 260 of the ship's officers and ratings and a party of 50, which included the ship's volunteer band, visited Great Ormond Street Hospital to entertain the children and present a £900 cheque for a medical research appeal. After leaving the River Thames *London* remained in home waters and during a short break at Scapa Flow the ship's divers located in 120 feet of clear water off the island of Cava, the wreck of the old German dreadnought battleship *Kronprinz Wilhelm*, which had been scuttled on 21 June 1919, but had never been raised. During the summer of 1977, flying the flag of FOF1, *London* took part in the Silver Jubilee Naval Review at Spithead, before returning to Portsmouth to give leave and undergo maintenance. On 9 August, at Portsmouth, there was a change of command when Captain David N. O'Sullivan took over from Nichol.

On 23 January 1978, after completing a mini work-up at Portland, *London* left Portsmouth to join *Blake* (Flag FOF1), *Hermes, Antrim, Devonshire, Kent, Arrow, Yarmouth*, the submarines *Churchill* and *Oracle* and the Dutch submarine *Tijgerhaai*, for 'Exercise Springtrain', which began in the Portland and Plymouth exercise areas and continued during the passage south to Gibraltar, where the main exercises took place in the Western Atlantic and Mediterranean. On completion there was a five-day break at Gibraltar, before *London* steamed north to Rosyth, carrying out a search-and-rescue exercise with Guernsey's lifeboat while en route. For 12 days in northern waters, and often through storm force winds and mountainous seas, *London*, *Blake*, *Devonshire* and three frigates took part in the training exercise JMC 781, with the only break being an overnight stay in Scapa Flow. In early April *London* left Portsmouth, once again bound for Gibraltar. This time, however, she stayed in the vicinity of the Rock for almost three weeks, carrying out day-running exercises in the Western Mediterranean, followed by a four-day visit to Madeira. On 29 April she secured alongside at Devonport for a short refu-

elling stop before sailing the same evening to join *Hermes*, which was bound for the USA via Gibraltar. At Gibraltar the two ships parted company and *London* set course for Malta and the NATO exercise 'Dawn Patrol', during which she acted as escort to USS *Forrestal*. On completion she paid a five-day visit to Naples before steaming west for Gibraltar where she was joined by *Norfolk, Apollo, Aurora, Maxton* and two RFAs for anti-submarine exercises with *Finwhale, Opportune, Osiris, Porpoise, Sealion*, the Canadian submarine *Ojibwa* and the USS *Sturgeon*. These manoeuvres took place in the approaches to the Mediterranean and a range of tactics was practised, both in support of and against, surface warships and submarines. The exercises ended with a steam-past salute by the submarines, after which *London* returned directly to Portsmouth, where she arrived alongside in mid-June.

HMS *London*'s stay in Portsmouth lasted for six weeks, which was long enough to give seasonal leave and carry out essential maintenance before, on 27 July, she sailed with *Fife, Active, Ajax, Andromeda, Charybdis, Plymouth*, the submarine *Swiftsure* and three RFAs for Bermuda and the US Navy's Western Atlantic exercise areas for joint manoeuvres with US ships. First, however, *London* visited the naval base at Bermuda's Ireland Island and Philadelphia, but on 21 August the force came together again and joined *Ark Royal* to take part in 'Exercise Common Effort', which began off the coast of the USA and continued across to the Azores and into home waters, where they were joined by *Hermes, Ardent* and *Sirius*, as well as Dutch warships and aircraft. The exercises continued under the code-name 'Northern Wedding', which unfortunately received a great deal of publicity after the loss of a Dutch reconnaissance aircraft and six of its 14 crew members. *London* and other ships were involved in the search for survivors, but on 20 September with the search having been called off, *London* put into Rosyth for a short break. On 25 September she sailed once again, this time to make two goodwill visits to Baltic ports. The first of these was a four-day call at the Polish port of Gdynia and the second, en route to Portsmouth, was to the Danish town of Aarhus. By 9 October she had returned to her base port and on 7 November, having carried out essential maintenance, she left Portsmouth to make a 24-hour coastal passage to the Thames Estuary and upriver to secure alongside HMS *Belfast* once more. During her six-day stay in the Pool of London the civic authorities laid on a lavish programme of entertainments, and on leaving the capital she returned via Portland to Portsmouth. On 20 November she sailed once again, this time for a six-day 'Meet the Navy' visit to Glasgow, where she secured alongside Yorkhill basin. On the last day of November she returned once again to Portsmouth.

On Thursday 28 December 1978, there was another change of command with Captain Thomas G. Ram RN taking over from O'Sullivan. *London* sailed again on 3 January 1979 and after carrying out weapons training in the Western Approaches in late January she was forced to return to Portsmouth for repairs to her main engine gearbox. By the second week of February she was at sea once again where she joined *Fife, Kent, Norfolk, Ariadne, Jupiter* and other ships, to steam south for Gibraltar for the annual 'Springtrain' series of exercises. These continued through to the end of February and concluded at Gibraltar, where for *London* there was a five-day break before she left harbour to steam east for a special duty at Malta.

The Royal Navy's naval base at Malta dated back to 1800, and for over 165 years it was the home of the powerful Mediterranean Fleet. In 1964 Malta gained its independence from Britain and soon afterwards a Defence Agreement was negotiated which allowed for the retention of the naval base. However, three years later, with Britain's role as a major world power behind her, her commitments east of Suez had decreased considerably and in June 1967 the Mediterranean Fleet was disbanded, with its assets being transferred to the newly created Western Fleet. Even so, a much reduced naval base at Grand Harbour was retained and in 1972 the Defence Agreement between the Maltese and British governments was renewed for a further seven years, with the annual cost being shared by Britain and the NATO countries. In 1974, however, Malta became a Republic and under its tough, skilful and confident Prime Minister, Dom Mintoff, it was moving away from its reliance on Britain and when the British government refused to increase the rental payments for military facilities on the island, Mintoff called for the withdrawal of all British forces stationed there. In reality, given Britain's much reduced world role, the withdrawal would almost certainly have come about anyway within ten years, but *London* was to be the last in a long line of British warships to use the base facilities at Grand Harbour. Thereafter, all Royal Navy visits to Malta would be as guests of the Maltese government.

HMS *London* arrived in Grand Harbour early in the forenoon of 9 March and, as countless British warships had done for many decades, she secured to head and stern buoys in Bighi Bay, where she hoisted the flag of Rear-Admiral O. N. A. Cecil CB, the last Flag Officer, Malta. During her three-week stay in Grand Harbour the ship welcomed on board a number of VIPs, including the President of Malta, Anton Buttigieg, the British Deputy Prime Minister, Michael Foot, and other civic dignitaries. At one stage the destroyer shifted her berth to go alongside Dockyard Creek to load stores and equipment, before returning to her buoys. During the evening of 31 March, just hours before the expiry of the Defence Agreement, *London* hosted a reception which was attended by the President of Malta, Michael Foot and Admiral Cecil. At midnight that night the Anglo/Maltese Military Agreement came to an end and next forenoon *London* prepared to make a ceremonial departure. This historic event is described by Michael Cassar and Joseph Bonnici, both of whom are expert historians in matters pertaining to the Royal Navy and its long relationship with Malta: 'There is something about the departure of ships which aircraft can never hope to rival. Aircraft leave in haste; ships choose speeds which give both the sailor and spectator time to savour the meaning of the moment. Thus it was at 1100 on Sunday 1 April 1979, when *London* literally loos-

HMS London

On 1 April 1979 *London* made a ceremonial departure from Malta. The event marked the withdrawal of the Royal Navy from its Mediterranean base. With a strong north-easterly gale blowing across the island of Malta, the proposed send-off by a flotilla of small boats had to be cancelled and in the event only the tug *St Rocco* was able to escort *London* to sea. In the upper image large crowds can be seen gathered on the High Bastion for the occasion. In the lower image, above the bridge, Admiral Cecil can be seen waving farewell. *(Michael Cassar)*

HMS *London* arriving at Antwerp in August 1981. *(Leo Van Ginderen)*

ened her ties and Britain's and slipped from No 8 buoy. It had been intended that a flotilla of small boats would escort her out of harbour and give her a memorable send-off, but a gregale blew up during the night and in the event only the tug *St Rocco*, a Maltese Armed Forces patrol boat and a solitary luzzo followed her past Imgerbeb Point. After passing the breakwater arms HMS *London* hove to outside the harbour and fired a 21-gun salute, while RAF Luqa's last solitary Nimrod flew low, dipping its wings in farewell.'

After leaving Malta *London* paused briefly at Augusta to disembark Admiral Cecil, who was also the NATO Commander South-East Mediterranean, before setting course for Gibraltar, where she paused for 36 hours before continuing her passage to Devonport where, over three days, she unloaded most of her ammunition. On 12 April she arrived at Portsmouth and by the end of the month she had paid off into dockyard hands to begin a 12-month refit. On 19 November 1979, Captain Ram relinquished his command and it was not until 10 April 1980, as the refit was nearing its end, that the ship's last CO, Captain John Garnier MVO RN, was appointed. By this time *London*'s ship's company had been brought up to full strength and during the forenoon of Friday 25 April 1980 the ship was recommissioned, with a rededication service being attended by the ship's sponsor, the Duchess of Gloucester.

On 12 May 1980, with the refit completed, *London* put to sea to begin her post-refit trials, first in the Channel and then, during June, she steamed south to Gibraltar where she remained until the first week of July. She then returned north to make a visit to Stavanger after which she held a Families Day off the Isle of Wight and continued her trials off Portland. In August she took part in Navy Days at Portsmouth, where she still attracted large crowds, and in mid-September, flying the flag of FOF2, she shadowed an East German survey ship, MV *Tropik*. After putting in to Devonport to embark a full outfit of Sea Slug missiles, she steamed round to Portland to begin her work-up.

HMS *London*'s work-up lasted until early November and during that time her training exercises took her into the North Sea to carry out aircraft ranging practice with RAF Canberras as far north as Newcastle, but mostly she operated in the Channel off Portland and she was assisted in this by *Minerva* and *Rhyl*. Her final sea inspection was on 6 November, after which she steamed round to Aberporth, where she remained for two weeks, before making a five-day visit to Liverpool. In early December *London* paid a short weekend visit to the French naval base at Brest, but by 11 December she had returned to Portsmouth to give leave.

The beginning of 1981 saw *London* lying alongside the destroyer *Bristol* at Portsmouth's Fountain Lake Jetty. Unknown to those on board, this was to be her final year of operational service with the Royal Navy, for a newly appointed Secretary of State for Defence was about to announce swingeing cuts to the Defence budget. Instituted in an atmosphere of single-minded political ideology in stripping public expenditure, which as far as Defence was concerned largely ignored the country's commitments, the Review ran from January to June 1981 and was extremely controversial. Following the three-month Falklands campaign in the spring of 1982, much of it was reversed, but for *London* there was to be no reprieve.

It was the second week of March 1981 before *London* was ready for sea again and her machinery trials off the Isle of Wight. On 16 March she left Portsmouth to carry out Sea Slug firing in the Channel and next day she received an emergency call from a Hunter aircraft which had crashed into the sea. The aircraft from the Fleet Requirements and Direction Unit at Yeovilton was carrying out a tracking exercise with *London* when it crashed some 12 miles off Start Point, Devon, Fortunately the pilot ejected safely and he was subsequently rescued by an RAF helicopter, which also collected *London*'s Medical Officer who gave first aid during the flight to RNH Stonehouse. After embarking a full outfit of Sea Slug missiles at Devonport, *London* steamed south to Gibraltar to take part in the annual 'Springtrain' exercises.

During the manoeuvres *London* flew the flag of the C-in-C Fleet, Admiral Sir James Eberle, as she led a force of destroyers and frigates, which included *Bristol, Ariadne, Argonaut, Euryalus, Minerva, Naiad, Rothesay, Bacchante, Lowestoft* and *Achilles* as well as the submarines *Sovereign* and *Otus*; they were also joined by the US Navy's frigate *Talbot*, RAF Hunter and Canberra aircraft and Royal Navy Buccaneers. On 3 April, when the force steamed into Gibraltar in line ahead, the sight must have brought back memories of the sea power of years gone by. During the exercises one of the Navy's firsts, the live firing of an Exocet missile, was carried by *Argonaut* – it was a weapons system which, just 12 months later, would become a familiar name to people the world over, but it would not be the Royal Navy firing them.

On 28 April, following her return from Gibraltar, *London* paid her final visit to the city of London, when once again she secured alongside *Belfast* in the Pool of London for an eight-day stay. During May she remained close to Portsmouth, but towards the end of the month she steamed round to Chatham for the last of the Navy Days at the Dockyard which was soon to close, after which she accompanied *Antrim* and *Cleopatra* to Bremen. Following a weekend at the German port the three ships joined a NATO exercise in the North Sea code-named 'Roebuck', which saw *London, Cleopatra* and *Plymouth* operating in the Shetland – Faroes gap and east of the Shetland Islands. This exercise ended at Rosyth, after which *London* returned to Portsmouth.

HMS *London*'s final weeks of operational service with the Royal Navy began on 18 August, when she steamed to Portland to carry out weapons training, before going north to the Faroes to join the NATO exercise 'Ocean Venture 81', which at the time were described as the biggest naval manoeuvres since the Second World War, and ranging from the Caribbean to the North Atlantic. For *London* the exercise ended with a five-day visit to the Belgian port of Antwerp. On Friday 18 September the ship began her last major deployment when she sailed for the Caribbean. During this period she visited Belize, Curacao and Martinique before arriving at St John's Harbour, Antigua, on 28 October. While *London* was present the island was granted independence from Britain and the ship's company took part in the ceremonial parades which were held to mark the occasion. On 13 November, after a brief visit to Barbados, *London* weighed anchor to head for the US Navy's exercise areas off Puerto Rico, where she joined USS *John F. Kennedy* and *Mount Whitney*, before visiting St Kitts and Dominica. The deployment ended on 30 November when *London* weighed anchor and left Dominica bound for home. By Wednesday 9 December the ship was once again in home waters where she joined *Brilliant, Glasgow* and *Cardiff* in the Western Approaches and between 0850 and 1302 that day she fired off her remaining 17 Sea Slug missiles to provide targets for the missile systems in the other three ships, after which she carried out a 4.5-inch throw-off shoot to provide targets for *Brilliant*'s Sea Wolf system. Next day she embarked press representatives to witness the last firing of a broadside by a Royal Navy warship. By this time she was in the Channel south of Tor Bay when, at 1043, she fired the first of six 4.5-inch broadsides. This was followed by five more broadsides. Later that evening *London* anchored at Spithead and next forenoon she steamed up harbour to secure alongside Portsmouth's South Railway Jetty. Three days later, at 1100 on 14 December, a short decommissioning service was held and the next forenoon the ship was towed out to Fareham Creek and secured alongside *Devonshire* where de-ammunitioning took place. Two days later she was returned to Fountain Lake Jetty to await her fate.

HMS *London* was just one of a number of ships which fell victim to the 1981 Defence Review, others being *Berwick, Brighton, Falmouth* and the ice patrol ship *Endurance*. Known at the time as the 'Big Pay-Off' after the Falklands War, many of the cuts would be reversed but for *London* it was the end of the line, for while she had been in the Caribbean, negotiations between the British and Pakistani Governments had been under way and the ship had in fact been sold to the Pakistani Navy. On 18 December Captain Garnier relinquished command and on the last day of 1981 the first Pakistani naval liaison team arrived on board to familiarise themselves with the ship.

After being refitted in Portsmouth, on 24 March 1982 the sale was completed and in May that year, after being renamed *Babur* and undergoing a series of trials, she left Portsmouth for her new base port at Karachi.

During her 12 years in service with the Pakistani Navy *Babur* had her Sea Slug missile system removed and her flight deck was extended and strengthened in order to operate Sea King helicopters. Her anti-aircraft protection was modernised by the addition of a Mk 15 Phalanx CIW System and three 35mm guns, but by 1993 she was well and truly outdated and after the acquisition by Pakistan of the two Type 21 frigates *Amazon* and *Ambuscade*, which were renamed *Babur* and *Tariq* respectively, the older *Babur* – ex-*London* was withdrawn from service and laid up. Finally, in 1995 she was sold for scrap.

HMS London

Two views of PNS *Babur* at Spithead while undergoing trials following her handover to the Pakistani Navy.
(Michael Lennon)

Commanding Officers:

Captain Jozef C. Bartok DSC RN	14 September 1963
Captain David N. Forbes RN	18 February 1966
Captain Denis Germaine DSC RN	29 December 1967
Captain Peter G. Loasby DSC RN	28 June 1969
Captain Ronald W. Forrest RN	1 September 1970
Captain Peter D. Nichol RN	5 May 1975
Captain David N. O'Sullivan RN	9 August 1977
Captain Thomas G. A. Ram RN	28 December 1978
Captain John Garnier MVO RN	10 April 1980

Battle Honours:

Kentish Knock	1652	Chesapeake	1781
Gabbard	1653	Groix	1795
Scheveningen	1653	Copenhagen	1801
Lowestoft	1665	Marengo	1806
Solebay	1672	Crimea	1854
Schooneveld	1673	Dardanelles	1915
Texel	1673	Atlantic	1941
Barfleur	1692	Arctic	1941-43

Chapter Five

HMS FIFE
1966 - 1987

On 31 August 1963, some 15 months after her keel was laid, *Fife's* hull begins to take shape on the stocks.
(World Ship Society)

On 31 May 1962, at the Govan shipyard of the Fairfield Shipbuilding and Engineering Company Ltd on the River Clyde, there were laid the first keel plates for the fifth of the County-class destroyers. HMS *Fife*, as she was to become, was the first ship to bear the name of the Scottish county which was the home to the dockyard at Rosyth on the Firth of Forth. She was also the first ship of the Royal Navy to bear the name and the first of what would to be the second batch of County-class destroyers. These would be fitted with the Mk II Sea Slug missile system which, unlike its predecessor, had a greater range and speed and also a limited anti-ship capability. In February 1964, led by Commander (E) E. R. May RN, the first naval personnel arrived in Govan to stand by the ship and four months later she was ready to be launched. The ceremony took place on Thursday 9 July 1964, when the Duchess of Fife sent the hull down the slipway into the River Clyde. In late September 1965, some 14 months after her launch, *Fife* began her contractor's sea trials, but she was still almost a year away from completion and it was mid-December that year before her first commanding officer, Captain Robert H. Graham MVO DSC RN, was appointed to the ship. Some six months later, on Tuesday 21 June 1966, an overcast day on the Clyde with frequent heavy showers,

County Class GMDs

Seen here in the Firth of Clyde, Fife is undergoing builder's trials. Flying the Red Ensign she is under the control of the Fairfield Shipbuilding and Engineering Company. *(Maritime Photo Library)*

the ship was commissioned. Fortunately, the rain held off long enough for the commissioning ceremony to be held on the jetty alongside and at 1355 the next day *Fife* slipped her moorings to steam down the Clyde for machinery trials in the Firth of Clyde and the Western Atlantic.

HMS *Fife*'s acceptance trials lasted for just under 36 hours and in the early hours of 23 June she returned to Greenock to disembark Fairfield's staff before setting course for Portsmouth. The passage south was made over four days, during which time further machinery trials were carried out. On reaching the south coast she paused briefly at Portland before steaming back down Channel as far as Les Casquets before returning to Weymouth Bay where she anchored during the evening of 25 June. Next afternoon she carried out further trials in the Channel before spending the night in St Helen's Roads and entering Portsmouth Harbour for the first time during the forenoon of Monday 27 June, securing alongside Fountain Lake Jetty.

Throughout July, August and September 1966, as *Fife* remained alongside at Portsmouth preparing for operational service, there was a constant stream of publicity about the new ship and the Mk II Sea Slug missiles with which she was armed. Also emphasised was the ship's 'action data automation', an early form of computer which had been developed from that fitted in the aircraft carrier *Eagle*. The equipment provided a defence system based on electronic computers which gave the height, bearing and range of potential targets, as well as automatic threat evaluations that recommended the best form of retaliatory action. It was said that the tasks performed automatically would otherwise have required 60 men. One announcement which received less coverage in the media, was the news that *Fife* was to temporarily have two women on board, although at that time not as members of the ship's company, but government scientific officers and experienced computer programmers who would initially operate the electronic equipment.

On Monday 3 October 1966 *Fife* finally put to sea to begin a long period of trials, during which time she operated from both Portsmouth and Portland. In mid-November, in company with the frigate

HMS Fife

Minerva, she operated in the Atlantic off the Azores and on 27 November left Ponta Delgada bound for Funchal, Madeira. Next day, however, the visit was cancelled and *Fife* was ordered to join HMS *Tiger* north of the Canary Islands and accompany the cruiser to Gibraltar. The two ships had been chosen as the venues for a vital diplomatic mission.

On 11 November 1965 the Crown Colony of Southern Rhodesia (now Zimbabwe), in an effort to avoid indigenous African majority rule, had issued a Unilateral Declaration of Independence from Britain. However, the breakaway State found it impossible to obtain any meaningful diplomatic recognition abroad and in November 1966 direct negotiations between the British Prime Minster, Harold Wilson, and the Prime Minister of Rhodesia, Ian Smith, were arranged to take place at sea on board *Tiger*. It was hoped that the talks would lead to a settlement which would not only be acceptable to the British government, but also to the US government and to the United Nations, all of which were insisting on the principle of 'unimpeded progress to majority rule'.

During the evening of 30 November *Fife* rendezvoused with *Tiger* and just over 24 hours later the two ships anchored in Gibraltar Bay. The first of the politicians to arrive in Gibraltar was Harold Wilson, who had flown out from Heathrow in an RAF Comet aircraft and he boarded *Tiger* soon after the ship anchored. In the early hours of 2 December, having flown from Salisbury (Harare) in an RAF aircraft, Ian Smith boarded *Tiger* and an hour later the cruiser weighed anchor and steamed into the Mediterranean where, at 0900, the diplomatic negotiations began. *Fife* weighed anchor at 0745 to join *Tiger* in a position Lat 35°43'N/Long 04°54'W, in the Alboran Sea, east of Ceuta, where she took station a mile off *Tiger*'s starboard beam. The meeting between the two leaders had been arranged to take place at sea in order to avoid the pressure of media publicity, but it was not long before the negotiations were making front page headlines the world over. While the talks between Wilson and Smith took place *Fife* remained on station off *Tiger*'s beam, but during the evening of Saturday 3 December the ships returned to Gibraltar, with *Tiger* anchoring in the bay and *Fife* securing alongside the south mole. Both leaders left

HMS *Fife* passes the Argentine Navy Sail Training Ship *Libertad* in the English Channel in June 1966.
(Crown Copyright/MoD 1966)

Tiger during the morning of 4 December, with a promise from Smith that his government would decide by 1000 the next day whether they would accept the proposals. There was, however, little optimism that there would be a settlement, which indeed proved to be the case. On Sunday 4 December the two leaders left Gibraltar by air and next day *Fife* sailed for Devonport, where she secured alongside to embark Sea Slug missiles before returning to Spithead for another week of exercises, she then proceeded to Portsmouth to give seasonal leave.

After a period of maintenance at Portsmouth, it was mid-February 1967 before *Fife* sailed to continue her trials and these took her through to the summer of that year. In May 1967 a diplomatic delegation of Soviet warships to Portsmouth, a reciprocal exchange for *Devonshire*'s visit to Leningrad (St Petersburg) in September 1966, was arranged for 6 June. The warship chosen to lead the mission was the brand new Kashin-class guided missile destroyer *Obraztsovyy*, the flagship of the Baltic Fleet. She was scheduled to arrive off Selsey Bill during the early morning of 6 June, where *Fife* had been ordered to meet and escort her through Spithead to South Railway Jetty in Portsmouth Harbour. HMS *Fife* duly set sail the day before and the two ships were within an hour of their rendezvous, when the visit was cancelled. Cold War politics had intervened following the outbreak of the Third Arab-Israeli War which had begun the previous day when Israel launched surprise attacks on Egypt, Syria and Jordan. The fighting had increased tensions between the Soviet Union and the Western powers, hence the cancellation of *Obraztsovyy*'s visit to Portsmouth. By midday on 6

HMS *Fife* with her original configuration of four 4.5-inch guns in twin turrets forward of the bridge. Her Type 965 'double bedstead' radar aerial easily distinguishes her from the earlier ships. *(Crown Copyright/MoD)*

June the Russian ship was steaming back to the Baltic and *Fife* had returned to Portsmouth Harbour. During the remainder of 1967 *Fife* continued her trials, usually on day-running exercises from Portsmouth, but during the last week of July there was a break in this routine when the ship steamed into the Baltic to make goodwill visits to Gothenburg and Copenhagen before returning to Portsmouth to resume her trials. On Friday 27 October, HMS *Fife* paid her first visit to the county of *Fife*, when she secured alongside the south arm of Rosyth Dockyard. During her four-day stay links which had been formed between the ship and the county were strengthened by reciprocal visits and social and recreational activities. A large framed painting of the ship passing under the Forth Rail Bridge, by the renowned naval artist Commodore Eric Tufnell RN, was presented by the county. During the latter half of that year she operated with *Chichester, Cleopatra, Diana* and *Wakeful*, and in November and December she spent several weeks off the Aberporth missile ranges, before returning to Portsmouth for docking and maintenance.

On 13 December 1967 there was a change of command when Captain Peter G. Lachlan MBE RN joined the ship, which at the time was high and dry in D lock. On 19 January 1968 *Fife* put to sea again to resume her trials, assisted by *Hampshire*, and these were concluded on 30 January. In early February she assisted *Glamorgan* with her trials before proceeding to Portland to begin her scheduled eight-week work-up. For two weeks all went well and during the morning of Thursday 22 February, *Fife* sailed to begin two days of intensive weapons training off Portland. During the afternoon of the second day, however, while the ship was carrying out 4.5-inch firings, fire broke out in the elevation motor of 'A' turret. Live ammunition was stacked in the hoists, racks and trays inside the turret, and Leading Seaman James Cragg, the captain of the turret, immediately ordered the crew of six out of the turret, knocked out the electricity supply and notified the bridge of the fire. The ship's company were ordered to Emergency Stations while a fire party tackled the blaze and, despite the danger, Cragg started to clear the ammunition from the turret, thus averting what could have been a catastrophic explosion. In the event, at 1640 with the blaze extinguished, *Fife* steamed safely to a buoy in Portland Harbour. Although the fire did not cause any serious disruption to the ship's programme, on 8 March a major fault developed in one of the turbo-generators and that afternoon *Fife* returned to Portsmouth for dry docking, when the generator was replaced lock, stock and barrel through a hole cut in the ship's side. Although the work-up had been cut short, with dockyard assistance the opportunity was taken to carry out other essential maintenance tasks, before the ship began the next leg of her General Service Commission, to the Far East. She and her sister *Glamorgan* were to sail by way of the USA and the Pacific Ocean, making a high-profile visit to Washington DC en route.

During the forenoon of Monday 6 April, *Fife* left Portsmouth to join *Glamorgan* which had left Devonport the same day. They reached the US East Coast during the afternoon of 14 April and for two days they anchored off the US Marine Corps base in Quantico Bay, in the Potomac River, before weighing anchor and steaming upriver to secure alongside Washington Navy Yard, situated on the Anacostia River about a mile south of Capitol Hill. During that afternoon when *Fife* was opened to the public some 8,500 people visited the ship and during the forenoon of Sunday 21 April the US Vice-President, Hubert Humphrey, paid a two-hour visit. After leaving Washington the two destroyers rendezvoused with the frigate *Leopard*, before all three ships secured alongside the Navy yard at Norfolk, Virginia, for a three-day visit. After leaving Norfolk *Leopard* was detached and she returned to Bermuda, while *Fife* and *Glamorgan* set course for Panama and the Pacific. During the forenoon of 4 May, after completing her transit of the Panama Canal, *Fife* set course for San Diego where, seven days later, she secured alongside the city's Broadway Pier. *Glamorgan*, meanwhile, continued north to San Francisco, before the two ships were reunited for visits to Esquimalt and Vancouver. At the end of May *Fife* visited Portland, Oregon, for that city's Rose Festival, after which the two ships rendezvoused for the passage across the Pacific Ocean. During the morning of 12 June the two ships arrived off the coast of Hawaii and at 0742 the C-in-C, FES, Vice-Admiral William O'Brien, landed on *Fife*'s flight deck and hoisted his flag, after which she led *Glamorgan* into the US naval base of Pearl Harbor for a five-day visit.

On 17 June *Fife* and *Glamorgan* left Pearl Harbor to make the long two-week passage to Singapore, but because of the crossing of the International Date Line the second anniversary of the commissioning was missed. During the long days at sea the C-in-C carried out an inspection of *Fife* and the two ships carried out joint gunnery, air defence, anti-submarine and replenishment at sea exercises. On 2 July, however, they arrived at Singapore Naval Base where *Fife* underwent a three-week dockyard-assisted maintenance period.

On 23 July *Fife* sailed to join *Albion*, *Devonshire*, *Glamorgan*, HMNZS *Otago* and the submarine *Rorqual* for anti-submarine and air defence exercises in the South China Sea, with weekends spent at anchor off Pulau Tioman. For the ship's company it was a very busy period, for as well as undergoing the intensive exercises they were also preparing the ship for FO2's Inspection. There was a setback during the evening of 5 August, however, when at 2135 fire broke out in the turbine compressor room and although it was extinguished in ten minutes, at 2220 it reignited. This time the blaze took longer to extinguish and at 2235, after suffering a complete loss of power, *Fife* was brought to a standstill in the water. In the event it was midnight before power was restored and the ship was able to get under way again. However, despite this setback, just ten hours later Vice-Admiral Edward Ashmore (FO2, FES) began his sea inspection as scheduled. Four days later *Fife* ended her 18 days at sea when she secured alongside the North Arm of Hong Kong's naval dockyard. *Fife*'s first visit to Hong Kong lasted for just four days, before she returned to Singapore to take part in more fleet exercises during which she embarked the C-in-C and the First Sea Lord, Admiral Sir Michael Le Fanu for a day, to observe a dress rehearsal for a major exercise scheduled to take place in the Coral Sea during September and October.

On 3 September *Fife* left Singapore Naval Base to join other ships of the Far East Fleet, including *Hermes* and *Caprice*, before setting course for Australian waters. Before the start of 'Exercise Coral Sands', which was due to begin later in the month, *Fife* was able to pay a ten-day visit to Sydney, before sailing on 23 September to join the manoeuvres. At the time 'Coral Sands' was the biggest amphibious exercise by the Far East Fleet since the end of the Second World War and involved over 50 British, Australian and New Zealand warships. After rendezvousing with *Caprice*, *Sydney*, *Anzac*, *Yarra*, *Duchess*, *Queenborough* and *Waikato*, the exercises began in earnest on the last day of September; also present were *Hermes,* which was still operating as an aircraft carrier, and the commando carrier *Albion*. For *Fife* the manoeuvres involved a fast, opposed passage of the Solomon Sea, followed by night encounter and RAS exercises. They ended on 13 October, when she and the heavy repair ship *Triumph* left the waters off Sydney and set course for New Zealand and the Pacific Ocean. Three days later they arrived in Auckland for a seven-day visit, before leaving for Lautoka on the Fijian island of Suva.

At 0215 on Saturday 26 October, when *Fife* was south of Matuku, a distress call was received from a small inter-island Fijian ferry. The stricken vessel was the 685-gross ton MV *Tui Lai*, a Norwegian-built ship dating from 1950. She had spent 17 years ferrying people and cargo round the Norwegian coast before being sold in September 1967 to the Maritime Co-operative Shipping Association of Suva. They refitted her as a three-class ship for the vital Fijian inter-island ferry routes and in April 1968, having been renamed *Tui Lai*, the vessel entered their service. On 25 October, while carrying some 42 passengers, including women and children, as well as 37 crew members and a cargo of copra, *Tui Lai* was on passage between Kabara and Suva and was passing the islands of Totoya and

Moala. At 2215, in a position Lat 18°55'S/Long 179°46'W, the ship struck the main reef off the north coast of Totoya Island. At first it was thought she might free herself by use of her main engines, but by 0215 on 26 October she was stuck fast with a 15° list to starboard and was taking in water. It was at this stage that she transmitted the distress call which was received by *Fife*.

By 0510 *Fife* had arrived off Totoya's north-eastern reef and had manoeuvred as close as she safely could to the stricken *Tui Lai*. Less than 15 minutes later her helicopter was airborne and flying the Executive Officer, the Shipwright Officer and a Radio Operator to the merchantman. They quickly ascertained that there was a very real danger of *Tui Lai* breaking up and so at 0600 with daybreak dawning, *Fife*'s helicopter began transferring all the passengers to the safety of the destroyer. At 0750 there was another attempt to free *Tui Lai* by use of her main engines, but just five minutes later, with the list and the flooding having increased, this too was abandoned. *Fife* then began passing a tow rope to the crippled ship, but all further attempts to refloat her failed and at 0944 the tow rope parted, taking with it two of *Fife*'s mooring bollards. At this point HMS *Puma*, which had been steaming independently from Newcastle, NSW to Suva, arrived on the scene to take over what had now become a salvage operation, but as the crippled ship had by that time moved beam on to the reef and the sea, it was decided to evacuate her 37-man crew, an operation which *Fife*'s helicopter accomplished in an hour and a half. At 1235 the wreck was abandoned and four hours later *Fife* arrived in Suva, where all her passengers were landed. The wreck of *Tui Lai* was eventually broken up in situ. *Fife* herself remained in Fijian waters for three days, during which time she paid a brief visit to Lautaka before joining *Caprice* for the passage to Pearl Harbor and the West Coast of North America.

HMS *Fife*'s visit to America's West Coast included calls at Long Beach and Acapulco before making her eastbound transit of the Panama Canal on 28 November. Prior to leaving Caribbean waters she exercised with the US Navy off Roosevelt Roads and made a two-day visit to Puerto Rico's capital San Juan, before sailing for home on 6 December. On 14 December the hills of Madeira were sighted as she passed within 15 miles of the island and four days later she arrived in Portsmouth Harbour, where she remained for 24 hours. She then departed for Chatham where she secured alongside the basin on 20 December. Ahead lay a seven-month refit.

On 30 May 1969 Captain W. David Scott RN took over command of *Fife* and just over six weeks later, with the refit completed, the ship was ready to recommission. The ceremony took place during the forenoon of Tuesday 15 July and three days later the ship left Chatham Dockyard to begin a series of post-refit trials, during which she operated from Portsmouth and Spithead. In mid-August she returned to Chatham to take part in Navy Days and at the end of September *Fife* was inspected by the C-in-C Western Fleet, after which she returned to the area around Spithead to continue her trials. In mid-October there was a short break in the routine when she paid a three-day visit to the German naval base at Wilhelmshaven, before returning to Portsmouth to continue her trials.

In mid-January 1970, after spending Christmas and the new year at Chatham, *Fife* sailed for Portland to begin a six-week work-up period which ended in late February when she returned to Chatham to undergo maintenance and give foreign service leave. On Wednesday 1 April *Fife* left home waters to make the passage to the Far East by way of Simonstown. During the passage south she called at the Moroccan port of Safi and at Lagos, Nigeria, with a traditional Crossing the Line ceremony being held on 17 April. Seven days later she arrived in Simonstown where there was a five-day break before *Fife* sailed into the Indian Ocean where, on the last day of April, she relieved the frigate *Nubian* and joined *Galatea* for a short stint on the Beira Patrol. On 5 May, however, after refuelling from RFA *Tideflow*, she left the patrol area to steam via Gan to Singapore. During her passage of the Strait of Malacca she rendezvoused with the submarine *Orpheus* to deliver mail and fresh provisions, before securing alongside *Triumph* at Singapore Naval Base the next day.

HMS *Fife* had arrived on the Far East Station just in time to participate in the annual Fotex exercises which as always took place in the South China Sea, with weekend recreational leave at Pulau Tioman. Also taking part were the frigates *Chichester*, *Euryalus* and *Plymouth*, with air defence exercises against RAF Lightning aircraft from RAF Tengah on Singapore Island. At the end of June *Fife* carried out firings of her Mk II Sea Slug missiles at a US Navy firing range off Manila. In October 1969 a Mk II missile fired by *Glamorgan* off the Welsh coast had crashed out of control and as a result all firings of the weapon were suspended. *Fife*'s firings were the first for eight months and no problems were encountered. On 1 July, with the exercises over, *Fife* left Singapore for Hong Kong to pay a fleeting visit before steaming on to the Japanese port of Kobe for the 'Expo 72' exhibition. From Japan she continued into the Pacific Ocean and during the evening of 26 July she stopped off Midway Island, where three hours' recreational leave was granted to all who could be spared. Later that evening *Fife* was once again under way and steaming towards Hawaii, where during the forenoon of 30 July she secured alongside the US Naval Base at Pearl Harbor. It was during the ship's stay here that *Fife*'s ship's company claimed the 'honour' of being the last Royal Navy personnel to have been issued with the daily tot of rum; given that the ship was some ten hours behind GMT and had only two days previously crossed the International Date Line, there was no doubt the 'honour' went to her.

After leaving Pearl Harbor on 3 August, *Fife* remained in Hawaiian waters and steamed to the US Navy's missile testing range some five miles west of Kekeha where she undertook a second series of Sea Slug Mk II firings. Three of the 20-foot missiles were fired, with their performance being monitored along the firing range. In the event Captain Scott was able to report to the Admiralty that 'everything functioned perfectly' and *Fife* set course for Long Beach and Acapulco. During the afternoon of 20 August she arrived at Balboa and next day she made her eastbound transit of the Panama Canal; after refuelling at San Juan she set course for Gibraltar.

The next leg of *Fife*'s General Service Commission took her into the Mediterranean where, based on Malta, she became part of the NATO Standing Force. On 3 September, after a short stop at Gibraltar, she assumed her new role and sailed for Malta from where she carried out day-running exercises in local waters for the next four weeks. On 19 October she made a four-day visit to the French naval base at Toulon and seven days later, when she returned to Malta, ships of the Western Fleet, including *Ark Royal*, *Albion*, *London*, a number of frigates and other NATO warships had gathered to prepare for 'Exercise Lime Jug 70'. The main exercises began on Thursday 5 November and four days later, some 100 miles south of Cape Matapan, *Ark Royal* collided with the Soviet destroyer *Bravyy*, which resulted in the deaths of two Soviet seamen. Five days later, during the afternoon of Saturday 14 November, when *Fife* was some 40 miles south of Crete, she suffered a major fire in her main gas turbine machinery room. The fire broke out at 1500 and burned for over three hours, during which time *Ark Royal* stood by while her helicopters transferred fire-fighting parties and their equipment to the destroyer. One member of the ship's company remembers the fire clearly: 'It was initially announced as being in the Gas Turbine Control Room, although it was in fact in the Gas Turbine Room itself. Damage Control Sections 2 & 3 were closed up and I belted off to HQ1, which was forward of the Greenies Mess and up by the Ops Room. As I had just completed a fire-fighting course at Whale Island, I remember being frustrated at not being involved, but as the fire took hold and the communications systems failed I was sent aft on message relaying errands. This was no easy task as the power systems had failed and we were down to the gloom of emergency lighting which, given the smoke, water and general mayhem, was barely sufficient. As I negotiated my way down the starboard passageway, just forward of the GTR I came upon a cook who was

HMS Fife

At the end of January 1971 *Fife* returned to Portsmouth from the Mediterranean, where she had suffered a major fire in her gas turbine machinery room.
(National Museum of the Royal Navy)

boundary cooling a 440-volt fuse panel which was still live, until it exploded off the bulkhead. I was on my way to the starboard Sea Slug magazine and on opening the watertight door I was confronted by the sight of a fire party boundary cooling the magazine, with the water actually boiling and giving off steam, which had almost filled the compartment.' Captain Scott's son Richard later recounted what his father had told him of the incident: 'He confirmed that the fire was almost catastrophic. Apparently a design fault left oil dripping down onto a very hot surface in the gas turbine room and this had ignited. Things were not helped by the fact that there were a lot of oxygen bottles stored nearby which started exploding and fed the fire. The seat of the fire was right underneath the Sea Slug magazine and it was touch and go. My father, who had been appointed to head the Inquiry into *Ark Royal*'s collision with a Soviet destroyer, during the exercise spent most of his time monitoring and watching the temperatures in the Sea Slug magazines. He really was on the verge of ordering that the whole lot be fired off in quick succession to save the ship from being blown apart.' The fire was eventually extinguished by rigging up piping and drenching the Gas Turbine Room with superheated steam from the boilers.

For most of this time *Fife* lay stopped in the water and it was not until 1912 that she was able to get under way again. Next day, during a lull in manoeuvres, *Fife* stopped for several hours to enable some temporary repairs to be carried out. Another ship's company member remembers: 'We sailed back to Malta under our own steam, albeit with a bit of a list to port, as a result of counter flooding as one of the oxygen cylinders had made a hole in the ship's side when it exploded.' During the forenoon of 17 October *Fife* arrived in Malta's Marsaxlokk Bay, where she secured alongside RFA *Regent* for further repairs. Three days later she secured alongside Parlatorio Wharf, Grand Harbour, for more permanent repairs, which were completed in mid-December. After undergoing machinery trials *Fife* returned to Malta for Christmas and the new year, then in mid-January 1971 she sailed for Portsmouth where she arrived alongside Pitch House Jetty on 30 January. Ahead lay a ten-month refit.

On 4 February 1971 there was another change of command when Captain George A. De. G. Kitchin RN took over the ship. Soon afterwards she was

HMS *Fife* departs Portsmouth in March 1972.
(National Museum of the Royal Navy)

shifted into dry dock and remained there until the summer. In the event it was mid-November before she was once again ready for sea, and for the rest of the year she was engaged on main machinery trials in home waters. On 11 January 1972 *Fife* left Portsmouth to head south for Gibraltar, from where she would continue the trials in the warmer weather of the Western Mediterranean. She remained in the Gibraltar area until the second week of February, and during this time she paid a four-day visit to Tangier, after which she set course for home waters and on 21 February she arrived off Portland. On 6 April, after completing her trials programme, *Fife* returned to Portland to begin her eight-week work-up period, during which she was assisted by *Achilles, Danae, Devonshire* and *Whitby* and in mid-May all five ships took part in an exercise in the Portland area. At the end of May, with her work-up completed, *Fife* returned to Portsmouth. During the summer months of 1972 *Fife* operated in Cardigan Bay and the Irish Sea, during which time she visited Douglas, Isle of Man, and went to the aid of an injured sailor in a small yacht off Onchan Head. In early July she exercised with *Ark Royal, Blake, Bulwark, Achilles, Andromeda, Brighton, Caprice, Engadine, Zulu* and *Lynx*, carrying out manoeuvres which took her from the Channel into the North Sea and up to Scapa Flow. The exercise, code-named 'West Hoe', ended at Devonport on 17 July when *Fife*, followed by *Bulwark, Blake, Achilles, Caprice* and *Lynx*, steamed into Plymouth Sound. Next day saw the arrival of *Ark Royal, Aurora*, and the Portuguese ship *Almirante da Silva*. In early August *Fife* visited Rosyth and during the second week of that month she returned to Portsmouth to give leave and play her part in Navy Days where, secured alongside *Blake* at Middle Slip Jetty, she attracted over 18,000 visitors.

On 10 September *Fife* left Portsmouth to join *Ark Royal, Albion, Blake* and other ships for the NATO exercise code-named 'Strong Express', which at the time was the largest amphibious exercise ever staged in northern waters. Initially *Fife* had the task of shadowing Soviet warships, after which she acted as escort to *Ark Royal*. The exercise was concluded with an amphibious landing of some 3,000 British, US and Dutch marines in Norway, after which there was a six-day wash-up at Rosyth. On 8 October, flying the flag of the C-in-C Fleet, Admiral Sir Edward Ashmore, *Fife* left Rosyth to pay a four-day visit to the German naval base at Wilhelmshaven, after which she returned to Portsmouth to prepare for a Mediterranean deployment.

Sailing from Portsmouth on 22 November, *Fife* set course for Gibraltar where, three days later, she became part of NATO's On Call Force, Mediterranean. During most of this period she flew the flag of FOF1, and after leaving Gibraltar on 27 November she took part in exercises with *Ark Royal*, *Arethusa* and USS *Forrestal* off Sardinia. There also was a four-day visit to Tunis, during which members of the ship's company took part in a wreath-laying ceremony at the Commonwealth War Graves Commission Cemetery at Medjez el Bat, where many members of the 8th Army are remembered. *Fife* finally arrived in Grand Harbour on 13 December, where she began a ten-day series of day-running exercises before returning to Malta to undergo an 11-day maintenance period. During this Christmas and new year break some 99 family members took the opportunity to fly out in a charter aircraft courtesy of the ship's Welfare Fund. Around 65 members of the ship's company who had been granted leave made up the passengers on its return flight to Luton. Despite fog causing some delays, by 3 January 1973 everyone was back on board as *Fife* left Malta to visit Villefranche and Civitavecchia. At the latter port some 80 officers and men travelled to Rome and were granted a 20-minute audience with Pope Paul VI. On 19 January *Fife* arrived in Gibraltar to begin a four-week docking and maintenance period.

On 16 February *Fife* was at sea again, where she joined *Ark Royal* to act as planeguard during manoeuvres in the Tyrrhenian Sea. At the end of the month she paid a seven-day visit to Naples, during which FOF1 struck his flag and left the ship to return home by air. It was on 3 March 1973, during *Fife*'s break in Naples, that Captain David J. Hallifax RN took command of the ship. For the remainder of March *Fife* exercised with *Ark Royal* and *Glamorgan*, with visits to Toulon and Gibraltar and on 23 March she returned to Grand Harbour to carry out a ten-day maintenance period, before exercising off Cyprus and visiting Famagusta, Crete and Piraeus. On 25 April *Fife*'s duties with the NATO On Call Force were drawing to a close and that afternoon she left Grand Harbour to sail via Gibraltar to Portsmouth where, during the forenoon of 4 May, she arrived alongside Fountain Lake Jetty.

On 4 June, flying the flag of the C-in-C Fleet, Admiral Sir Edward Ashmore, *Fife* left Portsmouth to be joined by *Arethusa*, *Gurkha* and *Plymouth* for visits to Baltic ports. *Fife* and *Arethusa* visited Copenhagen and Stockholm, where the Crown Prince of Sweden paid a short visit to the ship. The final port of call was Kiel, after which all four ships crossed the North Sea to Rosyth to prepare for a major fleet exercise. Leaving Rosyth during the forenoon of 4 July, *Fife* joined *Bulwark*, *Devonshire*, *Kent* and *Bristol*, as well as the frigates *Arethusa*, *Gurkha*, *Plymouth*, *Scylla*, *Whitby* and the submarines *Otter* and *Rorqual*, to carry out rehearsal exercises off north-east Scotland in preparation for the main event, 'Exercise Sally Forth 73', which involved the largest gathering of the fleet for some years. During the exercise *Fife* headed the screen which was protecting *Bulwark*, while the latter demonstrated the versatility of the Harrier 'Jump Jet', when two RAF aircraft showed their ability to lift off vertically from the commando carrier's flight deck. For *Fife* the manoeuvres ended on 13 July at Rosyth, and ten days later, in company with *Bristol* and *Devonshire*, she steamed south to Portsmouth to begin a ten-week refit. It was Wednesday 3 October 1973 when *Fife* put to sea again, and after carrying out day-running exercises from Spithead and Portland, on 22 October she left the Channel to steam north to Rosyth, before joining *Charybdis*, *Leopard*, *Andromeda* and *Lincoln*, for exercises in northern waters which ended on the last day of November at Portsmouth.

The new year of 1974 saw *Fife* wearing the flag of FO2, Rear-Admiral R. P. Clayton, and on 8 February she left Portsmouth to lead a deployment of eight ships, *Argonaut*, *Ariadne*, *Danae*, *Londonderry*, *Scylla* and the RFAs *Tarbatness*, *Tidereach* and *Tidespring* on a nine-month deployment to the Far East, Australia and New Zealand. From Gibraltar the group steamed non-stop round the Cape of Good Hope, with *Fife*'s first port of call being Port Elizabeth, where she spent seven days and within the space of two afternoons played host to almost 5,000 visitors. Leaving South African

HMS *Fife* returns to Portsmouth Harbour.
(World Ship Society)

waters *Fife* and her group steamed via the Seychelles and Gan to Singapore where, on 26 February, they secured alongside the Stores Basin in all that remained of what had been, until 1972, the British Naval Base, known then as the ANZUK Naval Base (Australia, New Zealand & United Kingdom Naval Base). From Singapore *Fife* steamed on to Hong Kong, where she underwent a 23-day maintenance period, before sailing back into the South China Sea and to the US Navy Subic Bay exercise area, where she was joined by *Chichester*, HMAS *Vendetta* and other ships of the group for joint manoeuvres with US warships.

From the waters around the Philippines *Fife* and her group steamed south to Australian and New Zealand ports, with *Fife* visiting Brisbane, Wellington and Auckland, before returning to Australia to spend seven days at Sydney. On 3 June, *Fife*, *Argonaut* and *Scylla* joined the Australian ships *Melbourne* and *Vampire* for 'Exercise Kangaroo 1' in the Coral Sea. At one stage this took *Fife* inside the Great Barrier Reef off Cape York Peninsula where, for a few hours, she anchored off Fife Island. During these exercises she carried out missile test firings and it was 27 June before she returned to the ANZUK base at Singapore. After her long period at sea *Fife* underwent a 14-day mainte-

nance period, during which time her fire-fighting parties assisted with a blaze aboard RFA *Derwentdale*. On 17 July *Fife* left Singapore on a 48-hour passage to the Indonesian capital of Jakarta, where she secured alongside in the city's docks at Tanjung Priok at the start of a five-day official visit. Although the Confrontation with Indonesia had been over for eight years, the visit of a British warship to an Indonesian port was still considered to be sensitive, but *Fife*'s stay was deemed a diplomatic success. Following her return to Singapore *Fife* joined local exercises with *Chichester* and HMAS *Stuart*, but on 1 August she set sail to lead the group on their homeward passage.

After making a 24-hour call at Georgetown, Penang, *Fife* joined the remainder of the group for the Indian Ocean crossing, via Diego Garcia and Mauritius, before carrying out exercises off southern Africa. On 28 August *Fife* led her group into Cape Town Harbour on what was a controversial seven-day visit to the South African port. With the South African regime enforcing its policy of Apartheid it had been British government policy to restrict visits by British warships to the country, but with the Suez Canal having been closed since 1967 it was impossible to boycott them altogether and the controversy over this particular visit was caused by a decision to carry out joint weapons training with the South African Navy. In the event, when the group left Cape Town on 4 September they spent 48 hours in the company of the South African frigate *President Kruger*, before setting course for Gibraltar. *Fife* finally arrived at Spithead in the early hours of 30 September and later that day she steamed up harbour to secure alongside Fountain Lake Jetty.

It was mid-November before *Fife* put to sea again and after making a five-day visit to Liverpool, she steamed north to Faslane before returning to Cardigan Bay for missile firings. On 12 December she returned to Portsmouth for Christmas and the New Year, and it was 20 January 1975 when she sailed north once again to visit Rosyth prior to an eight-day exercise. Following this she led a group of nine ships, including *Ashanti, Charybdis, Glamorgan, Hermione, Leopard, Norfolk* and *Nubian*, south to Gibraltar for 'Exercise Springtrain', which took her into the Mediterranean off Sardinia, with a six-day break at Genoa. By the end of March, however, she had returned to Portsmouth Dockyard.

On 11 April 1975 Captain David M. Eckersley-Maslin RN took over command of the ship from Hallifax, but during the rest of that month she remained at Portsmouth and it was 5 May before *Fife* put to sea again to visit Liverpool followed by

In 1975/76 *Fife* had 'B' turret removed and in its place was fitted a quadruple Exocet MM38 missile launcher. *(Crown Copyright/MoD)*

County Class GMDs

A dramatic view of *Fife* at sea. *(Crown Copyright/MoD)*

anti-submarine exercises with *Galatea, Tiger* and the submarine *Swiftsure*. After visiting her old base at Chatham *Fife* crossed the Channel to Bordeaux, before returning to Portsmouth and a Families Day at sea off the Isle of Wight. On 11 June she joined *Norfolk* and *Eskimo* off Portland, before steaming on into the North Sea to undertake an oil rig patrol, after which she continued on into the Baltic and the Gulf of Bothnia to visit the Swedish city of Sundsvall. On leaving the port she was shadowed by an East German Shershen-class patrol boat, but on 27 July she returned once again to Portsmouth Harbour. It would be almost 12 months before she put to sea again.

During *Fife*'s 11-month refit at Portsmouth, the major alteration to her appearance and to her weapons systems was the removal of 'B' gun turret, which was replaced with four MM38 Exocet missile launchers. The Exocet surface-launched missile system had been developed by the French Nord-Aviation aircraft manufacturer (later to become Aérospatiale) and was designed for attacking small to medium sized warships. Powered by a solid propellant engine, which allows a range of some 27 miles, after launching it is guided inertially until late in its flight when its own radar switches on and guides it onto the target. As a counter-measure against air defences around the target the missile maintains a very low altitude during its flight, skimming some three to six feet above the surface of the sea. In addition to the new weapons system, all *Fife*'s accommodation areas were refurbished and her machinery was overhauled. On 9 October Captain Eckersley-Maslin took command of the helicopter cruiser *Blake* and his place in *Fife* was taken by Commander J. F. T. G. (Sam) Salt RN. Finally, however, with the refit drawing to a close, in early March the ship's company moved back on board and five days later Captain Godfrey C. Lloyd RN took command of the ship.

On 12 April 1976 *Fife* was shifted back alongside the sea wall at Fountain Lake Jetty and on 26 May she underwent her final inspection by the Flag Officer, Portsmouth. Next day she put to sea to begin her post-refit trials, which continued until mid-June. During the forenoon of Friday 16 July a rededication service, attended by FOF2, Rear-Admiral J. D. E. Fieldhouse, was held and two days later *Fife* put to sea again to continue her trials and begin her work-up. Most of August was spent

HMS *Fife* at Spithead during the summer of 1977 for the Silver Jubilee Fleet Review. *(James W. Goss)*

HMS *Fife* at anchor in the Solent during the 1977 Silver Jubilee Fleet Review. *(Maritime Photo Library)*

alongside at Portsmouth, where she took part in Navy Days and attracted over 7,000 visitors. On 15 September she made a fast passage to Gibraltar and Malta where she rendezvoused with *Lincoln* and the submarine *Valiant* to carry our Exocet trials off Malta, and on 4 November she returned to Portsmouth.

In the period leading up to the end of the year *Fife* carried out further Exocet trials in home waters and in the new year of 1977 came a six-week work-up, in which she failed the final inspection. A senior officer who served in *Fife* at that time has stated: 'It was not a good year for the ship. In the new year, after a work-up at Portland she failed her final inspection, which did nothing for morale on board.' In June 1977 she took part in the Spithead Jubilee Review and shortly after this she escorted the royal yacht *Britannia* to Belfast Lough, from where her Wessex helicopter flew the Queen ashore to visit Hillsborough and the University of Ulster at Coleraine. On 19 September, at Portsmouth, there was a change of command when Captain Jeremy J. Black OBE RN took over. In his memoirs ('*There and Back*' 1984, Elliot Thompson) Captain Black speaks of his first priority as being to restore the overall morale of the ship's company and soon afterwards the ship returned to Portland for another round of exercises and a second inspection which this time was passed most satisfactorily. In the autumn of 1977 *Fife* took part in 'Exercise Ocean Safari', a large NATO exercise, the key element of which involved the passage towards the Channel of a convoy of supply ships. One group, having crossed the Atlantic, was joined in the Western Approaches by another small group, after which all the vessels made for the Channel in the face of 'enemy' surface ships, submarines and aircraft. The exercise, which took place in stormy weather, included attacks from *Ark Royal*'s aircraft on 'enemy' ships as well as on targets in Europe. During these manoeuvres *Fife* operated through Force 12 storms in the Denmark Strait while at the same time coming under constant 'attack' from aircraft and submarines. On occasions the weather conditions became so severe that the aircraft were grounded and in the words of Jeremy Black '...those at sea were more concerned with survival than make-believe wars'. In November *Fife* accompanied *Ark Royal* into the Mediterranean and although it was not sunbathing weather, the warmer climate enabled the ship's company to enjoy Civitavecchia. On leaving Italy *Fife* headed towards the Cote d' Azur to join French ships in an exercise codenamed 'Îles d'Or'. During the manoeuvres *Fife* and the French cruiser *Colbert*, which for the exercises had been designated as an 'enemy', joined forces to investigate a drifting life-raft which had been spotted by aircraft. Despite some adverse weather conditions *Fife*'s Wessex took off at night to check the raft, which in the event turned out to be empty. By early December *Fife* was back at Portsmouth and undergoing a dockyard-assisted maintenance period which would keep her out of service for the best part of four months.

On 3 April 1978 *Fife* left Portsmouth to carry out machinery trials in the Portland and Plymouth areas and, assisted by *Apollo, Ardent* and *Falmouth*, she carried out a successful work-up at Portland, before joining *Triumph, Eskimo, Sealion* and *Yarmouth* for Navy Days at Chatham followed by visits to Alborg and Amsterdam, where she hosted a meeting of the NATO Military Committee. On Thursday 27 July *Fife* left Portsmouth to join *London* for a transatlantic passage, via Ponta Delgada, to Bermuda, where she arrived on 5 August. There then followed an eight-day visit to Baltimore, after which she made the short passage to Norfolk, Virginia, where she joined *Ark Royal*, which had just completed a maintenance period, *Ajax, Active, Charybdis, London, Plymouth* and the submarine *Swiftsure*, plus three RFAs to join an extensive series of exercises. These were controlled by the US Navy's command ship *Mount Whitney*, and also included the cruiser *Virginia, Montgomery* and the destroyer *Luce*, as well as the German destroyer *Lütjens*. On 24 August they began 'Exercise Common Effort', a combined NATO exercise designed to reinforce US forces in Europe. It involved a fleet of American amphibious ships sailing east with a submarine screen and *Ark Royal*'s aircraft providing air defences. The exercise saw the ships steaming through stormy weather into the Arctic Circle where, at noon on 4 September, 'Exercise Northern Wedding' involving some 200 ships from NATO countries got under way in the Norwegian Sea as well as the North Sea in manoeuvres designed to test the various plans for the defence of northern Europe. With *Fife* and *Lütjens* acting as planeguard

On 14 September 1979 *Fife* returned home from the Caribbean at the end of a commission and it would be three years before she put to sea again. *(Ken Kelly Collection)*

County Class GMDs

HMS *Fife* at Plymouth Navy Days 1985 with the Leander-class frigate *Naiad* outboard. (*Author's Collection*)

for *Ark Royal*, two uninvited guests turned up who were nicknamed 'Flossie' and 'Ivan'. The former was a hurricane which swept in from the south-west and the latter, which came from the east, was a Russian shadowing Tu-95 Bear D aircraft. Also watching the exercise was the Russian Kresta-class cruiser *Admiral Makarov*. Among the 40 British ships taking part were *Hermes, Fearless*, three 'Sir-class' RFAs and *Bacchante* and *Berwick*. For *Fife* the exercise ended on 12 September, when she secured alongside at Rosyth for a four-day visit before steaming south to Portsmouth.

On 9 October, wearing the flag of FOF2, Rear-Admiral M. la T. Wemyss, *Fife* sailed north once again and was joined off the coast of Scotland by *Hermes, Antelope, Jupiter* and *Lowestoft* for anti-submarine exercises, before *Fife* steamed into the North Atlantic to carry out Exocet and Sea Slug firing trials. Following these she called at Plymouth Sound where FOF2 struck his flag and the ship continued her passage via the North Sea to Rosyth. During November she joined *Apollo* and *Euryalus* in a Joint Maritime Course in northern waters, and at this period she anchored briefly at the old wartime base of Scapa Flow. This was followed by some time in Cardigan Bay, after which she visited Hamburg where, according to one senior officer, everyone from Captain Black downwards visited the notorious Reeperbahn in the St Pauli district. On leaving the River Elbe and steaming through the

HMS Fife

Pentland Firth to the Clyde area, *Fife* exercised with the submarine *Valiant*, before steaming south via Devonport to Portsmouth for the seasonal break.

Four days before Christmas, on 21 December 1978, Captain Ronald G. Fry OBE RN relieved Black in command of the ship, but it was mid-February 1979 before *Fife* put to sea again and once more she was wearing the flag of FOF2, this time Rear-Admiral P. M. Stanford. After being joined by *London*, *Jupiter* and *Ashanti*, the group exercised with French ships before setting course for Gibraltar, where they would spend over three weeks taking part in the annual 'Springtrain' series of exercises, which included shadowing a powerful Soviet naval force, consisting of the aircraft carrier *Minsk*, two cruisers and a replenishment vessel, as they steamed north. *Fife* kept the force within her sights for 24 hours until she was off the mouth of the River Tagus, when she left the Soviet ships and made her way to Lisbon for five days. Following this she made her way back to Portsmouth, arriving alongside Pitch House Jetty during the forenoon of 23 March, but she remained only long enough to refuel before sailing north in company with *Blake*, *Intrepid*, *Brighton*, *Bacchante* and *Bristol* for 'Exercise Eastaxe' in the Norwegian Sea, during which *Fife* was diverted to Barra Head to shadow a Soviet cruiser round Rockall and into the

HMS *Fife* alongside at Chicago, USA, during the summer of 1987 while on a training cruise.
(Author's Collection)

County Class GMDs

HMS *Fife* sails under the Forth Rail Bridge to pay one of her periodic visits to Rosyth and the 'Kingdom of Fife'. *(Crown Copyright/MoD)*

Norwegian Sea, after which she steamed south to Rosyth and on to Portsmouth to begin a six-week maintenance period.

On Tuesday 15 May *Fife* sailed again to visit Hull, after which she returned briefly to Portsmouth to embark the Duke of Fife and sail north to the Clyde, from where she went on to make a four-day visit to Arhus, followed by a six-day visit to Cardiff. Following a training period in Cardigan Bay she joined *Hermes, Ardent, Jupiter* and other ships for 'Exercise Highwood', an amphibious exercise, which for *Fife* ended on 12 July when she was detached to return to Portsmouth from where, seven days later, she sailed for Bermuda. *Fife*'s arrival at the Ireland Island naval base marked the beginning of a Caribbean deployment which got under way with an eight-day visit to Port Canaveral, Florida, followed by Freeport, Bahamas and San Juan, with a Crossing the Line ceremony en route. The last two visits of the deployment were to Tortola and Antigua. On 27 August she left Antigua bound for Portsmouth, where she was to pay off at the end of her commission. However, a particularly heavy tropical cyclone had developed in the Atlantic off the Cape Verde Islands, the result being 'Hurricane David', with winds of up to 150 knots, which swept across the Caribbean devastating the island of Dominica. As she steamed out through heavy seas into the Atlantic, during the afternoon of 29 August *Fife* received a signal ordering her to turn round and head for the Dominican capital Roseau, to assist with relief operations. By that time *Fife* herself was steaming through mountainous seas and as she made the 48-hour passage her upper decks and weather decks were out of bounds to all but essential personnel. Finally, at 1245 on 31 August, she arrived at the Dominican capital.

The scene at Roseau which greeted *Fife*'s ship's company was one of almost complete devastation, which was described by one officer thus: 'It was as if a nuclear bomb had hit the island. Not a tree was left standing, half the buildings had been demolished and only a small number of those left had roofs. The people were immobilised by shock; severe injuries had been caused by corrugated iron scything from buildings; the hospital was devastated, there was no fresh water, no power, no communications. Dominica was dying.' As soon as the ship was safely moored Captain Fry met the Dominican Prime Minister, Oliver Seraphin, and it was agreed that the ship's company would assist in three major tasks; to restore the hospital, clear the tons of debris which were choking the reservoir and reopen the main road to the airport in the north of the island. Of the ship's complement of 480, at any one time some 400 were ashore working to restore essential services, while for those who remained on board, both food and water were rationed. The working parties ashore toiled for 18 hours a day, re-roofing vital buildings, burying bodies and toiling through the tropical rainforest with heavy packs and equipment to the earth-moving jobs at the reservoir. The key to the success of the whole operation was *Fife*'s Wessex 3 helicopter 'Humphrey', which flew continuously for ten hours a day on every day of the mission. Stripped of its sonar and radar to improve payload, the helicopter flew in hazardous conditions surveying the island, transporting supplies and working parties, evacuating casualties from field stations and ferrying the ship's surgeon as well as medical aid, to and from all parts of the island. In life-or-death casualty situations 'Humphrey' would often have to fly in steep-sided valleys and alight with only two wheels on the ground, while under constant threat of its engine being choked by the debris which littered the whole island. On 2 September *Fife* herself made a 36-hour passage to Bridgetown, Barbados, and back to pick up supplies for the beleaguered island. During the morning of 5 September, having unloaded the supplies, *Fife* put to sea to await 'Humphrey' and its crew and next day, with her mission completed, she sailed for Ponta Delgada and then Portsmouth where, ten days later than scheduled, she arrived alongside *Kent* at Pitch House Jetty, during the forenoon of Friday 14 September. It was the end of the commission and it would be over three years before she put to sea again.

Following her return to Portsmouth *Fife* was set for a complete change of role, to become the static Fleet Training Ship, with a permanent berth alongside HMS *Rame Head* at Whale Island, directly opposite Fountain Lake Jetty. On 12 October she received a visit from the grateful Dominican High Commissioner, who came to thank the ship's company for their assistance in the aftermath of the hurricane. Four days later Captain Fry relinquished his command and soon afterwards the ship's complement was reduced to 17 officers and 258 ratings. On 11 November *Fife* was shifted alongside *Rame Head* and eight days later the first 200 trainees boarded the ship. As a Fleet Training Ship *Fife*'s role was to consolidate different phases of the naval recruits' training courses, so that upon joining their first ship they could more quickly become effective members of a ship's company, with as little need as possible for further on-job training and supervision. Each trainee would spend between two and four weeks on board, and in addition up to 24 WEA Apprentices would be drafted to *Fife* as part of their year's sea training. Although she was secured firmly alongside *Rame Head*, she was in all respects a fully operational ship, working a normal ship's routine, with steam raised in order that trainees could carry out watchkeeping duties. Training on board was intense, with trainees being given a realistic idea of life on board an operational warship.

HMS *Fife*'s career as the Fleet Training Ship lasted for just over six months and on 29 May 1980 she was shifted back across Fountain Lake to secure alongside *Kent* once more, this time to transfer stores and equipment to her older sister as she prepared to take over the role of Fleet Training Ship from *Fife* on a more permanent basis. On 4 June *Fife* was towed round to No 3 basin to begin an extended refit. During this period her ship's company amounted to no more than a care and maintenance party and they were accommodated in the decommissioned Blackwood-class frigate *Hardy*, which was secured alongside *Fife*. During the course of this refit the destroyer was stripped down and virtually rebuilt with new equipment which would subsequently be tested in extensive trials. As well as giving her main and auxiliary machinery a complete overhaul, the ship's armament of Exocet, Sea Cat and Sea Slug missiles, as well as her twin 4.5-inch guns, were removed for overhaul and also supplemented by two triple torpedo tubes for launching Honeywell Mk 44 lightweight torpedoes. With a speed of 30 knots these had a range of some three nautical miles and with a 34kg warhead were intended primarily as an anti-submarine weapon. She was also fitted with a satellite communications system and updated radars. Finally all her accommodation spaces were completely refurbished and her hangar was adapted for use by a Westland Lynx HAS 2 helicopter (her old Wessex helicopter 'Humphrey' had played a prominent role in the Falklands campaign and was given a place of honour in the Fleet Air Arm Museum at Yeovilton). Originally the refit was scheduled to last until mid-1983, but because of the Falklands War the work was brought forward and was completed with the aim of getting the ship ready for sea by the end of 1982. On 7 September 1982, her new commanding officer, Captain Clifford J. Caughey RN, was appointed. By the end of November a full-strength ship's company had moved back on board and the ship was shifted back alongside the sea wall at Fountain Lake Jetty. Finally, at 1400 on Thursday 16 December 1982, *Fife* put to sea under her own steam to begin her post-refit trials.

With not long to go before Christmas, it was the new year of 1983 before the trials got under way in earnest, and these took her south to Gibraltar to the calmer waters of the western Mediterranean. By mid-March, however, she was back in Portsmouth and on the last day of the month she was recommissioned for the last time. The ceremony, which took place on the jetty alongside the ship, included a Scottish pipe and drum band, provided by *Fife*'s affiliated Army unit, the 4th Royal Tank Regiment, who also brought along a Scimitar armoured car. The commissioning cake was cut by Mrs Dorothy Caughey assisted by the youngest member of the ship's company, SEA Mark Waters.

Following the ceremony *Fife* resumed her trials and training exercises, which were finally completed on 10 June. Seven days later the ship was part of an international force which visited Kiel for the annual sailing regattas, after which she flew the flag of FOF1, Rear-Admiral R. W. F. Gerken, for Sea Slug firings off Aberporth. She then steamed north once again for training exercises in northern waters which ended at Rosyth, where *Fife* arrived in time for Navy Days. During the second half of July the ship took part in a major JMC exercise, which also involved *Abdiel*, *Lowestoft* and *Plumleaf*, after which she visited Copenhagen before returning to Portsmouth.

On 23 October, after a short training period at Portland, *Fife*, together with *Manchester*, *Apollo* and *Yarmouth*, sailed south for the Falkland Islands Protection Zone where, after a 26-day passage, they arrived in San Carlos Water. As *Fife* secured alongside MV *Alvega*, there to greet her was HMS *Bristol*'s volunteer band to give them a warm welcome. For *Bristol*, *Fife*'s arrival was all the more welcome because it meant that after five months away she could head for home, and soon afterwards *Fife*'s ship's company manned their upper decks to wish the Type 82 'bon voyage'. At the same time *Antrim*'s commanding officer Captain Caughey took over as the naval commander of the Task Unit Falkland Islands.

The South Atlantic deployment meant long periods at sea, often in severe weather conditions and, while on patrol, ship's companies remained at Defence Watches. Relaxation came with periods at anchor in Port William, or alongside the oiler *Alvega* in San Carlos Water. Christmas Day was spent at anchor off New Island and on 29 December *Fife* secured alongside *Alvega* once again. Three days later, on 1 January 1984, there was a change of command when Captain Jonathan J. R. Tod RN took over from Caughey. On 10 January, when *Fife* put to sea again from Port William Sound, her patrol took her to South Georgia where she anchored off Grytviken, Leith and in Stromness Bay, but by 20 January she was back in Port William. At 1110 on 28 January, while *Fife* was patrolling off the Falkland Islands, there was a trag-

HMS Fife

ic accident which marred what up to then had been a successful deployment. While working on the port Sea Cat launcher a young Weapons Engineering Apprentice, Jonathan Mills, suffered major burns when a missile accidentally ignited. Despite the fact that he was quickly flown the 150 miles ashore to hospital, four days later he died of his injuries.

HMS *Fife*'s stint in the South Atlantic ended during the forenoon of 11 February, when she was relieved by *Liverpool* and, once again in company with *Apollo, Manchester* and *Yarmouth* she set course for the Caribbean. The passage home was made by way of Barbados and Port Everglades, where she spent six days, then during the early evening of 17 March she anchored at Spithead. Next day she steamed up harbour to secure alongside Middle Slip Jetty at the start of what was to be an eight-week assisted maintenance period. By mid-May *Fife* was at sea again and after a training period at Portland, in early June she was involved in ceremonial duties which marked the 40th anniversary of the D-Day landings on the beaches of Normandy. On 5 June, having embarked a BBC TV crew and a number of D-Day veterans, *Fife* left Portsmouth and sailed for 'Utah Beach', from where, after disembarking her passengers, she headed east to collect first day covers from Arromanches before returning to 'Sword Beach' early on the morning of 6 June, where she joined *Britannia* and *Torquay*. HMS *Fife* was involved in a number of the ceremonies that day, with the ship's company providing street-liners at Bayeux and Arromanches, and also a ceremonial guard which, as part of a joint services contingent, marched through Caen. With the ceremonies over *Fife* returned to Portsmouth and five days later she and *Phoebe* steamed north to spend ten days at Kiel. During her passage home she visited Hull and, after Admiral's inspection in the North Sea, she proceeded to Rosyth where she celebrated her 20th birthday. This was followed by exercises from Portland and a Families Day off the Isle of Wight, before she returned to Portsmouth to undergo a refit which, apart from a week in early August when she acted as guardship at Cowes, kept her out of service until the end of the year.

Streaming her paying-off pennant and escorted by the RMAS tug *Bustler, Fife* enters Portsmouth Harbour to pay off on 28 June 1987.
(Walter Sartori)

In December 1984 and the first weeks of 1985 *Fife* underwent post-refit trials and training, and in the spring she joined her sister *Glamorgan* for a joint visit to Amsterdam and a joint Families Day off the Isle of Wight. For the remainder of 1985 *Fife* undertook duties as part of the Dartmouth Training Squadron, which took her to Dundee where, as well as renewing ties with the ancient 'Kingdom of Fife', she acted as guardship during the Royal Tay Yacht Club's Centenary Regatta. This was followed by a cruise to the Mediterranean with 86 officers under training. On 29 November 1985 there was a final change of command for *Fife* when Captain William J. Davis RN took over the ship. By the end of the year, however, she had returned to Portsmouth to begin a six-month refit which would re-equip her as the lead ship of the Dartmouth Training Squadron.

During the refit the ship's Sea Slug missile launcher and system were removed and replaced with a shed-like deckhouse, which served as a satellite navigation classroom with additional messdecks below it for officers and cadets under training. At least one of those messdecks was fitted with hammocks and the officers who were accommodated there were the last of the Navy's personnel to use such sleeping arrangements. By the time she had recommissioned in June 1986, with the imminent departure of *Glamorgan*, she was soon to become the last of the County-class destroyers to remain in active service with the Royal Navy. Her first visits after recommissioning were to Dundee and Rosyth and in September 1986 she took up her duties with the Dartmouth Training Squadron, starting with a cruise to the Mediterranean. This was followed by a Caribbean cruise, during which *Fife* visited Dominica, the island which, seven years earlier, she had helped to recover from the devastation caused by tropical storms. The ship was welcomed by the country's President and working parties of apprentices and officers under training were able to finish off the task of recovering an old museum cannon which had been washed down a mountainside during the storms of 1979.

In January 1987 she and *Intrepid*, which was also operating as a training ship, sailed first to the Canary Islands and then into the Mediterranean, where they went their separate ways before joining up again for a joint visit to Istanbul. In mid-March *Fife* paid a farewell visit to Scotland and the Kingdom of Fife, which had always had a soft spot for the ageing destroyer, where the local authority at Rosyth treated all the officers and men to valedictory honours for this final visit. At the same

The Chilean Naval Ship *Blanco Encalada* in August 1987, soon after her transfer to Chile.
(James W. Goss)

HMS Fife

Seen in August 1987 *Blanco Encalada* still carries *Fife's* name at her stern. Note the missing Sea Slug launcher and associated Type 901 director. *(Michael Lennon)*

time, however, a feeling of discomfort arose when it became known that like her sisters *Antrim*, *Glamorgan* and *Norfolk*, she was being sold to Chile, which at that time was ruled by the controversial Pinochet regime. After leaving Rosyth *Fife's* final cruise in Royal Navy service came in April 1987, when she led the frigate *Juno* on a deployment to North America and the Great Lakes, which included a visit to the city of Chicago. In June, on her return to home waters, she landed her officers under training at Dartmouth before steaming on to Portsmouth, where she was decommissioned.

On 12 August 1987 *Fife* was sold to the Chilean government and renamed *Blanco Encalada* and on her arrival at the Chilean port of Talcahuano, the site of that country's main naval base, she was refitted at the ASMAR shipyard. The previous removal of her Sea Slug missile system now allowed for the hangar to be enlarged and the flight deck to be extended to the stern of the ship, which in turn allowed her to carry and operate two French Cougar helicopters. In the mid 1990s *Blanco Encalada* was fitted with an Israeli Barak 1 surface-to-air missile system and in 2001, when the Type 42 destroyer *Edinburgh* was taking part in the international exercise 'Teamwork South', she joined three of the Royal Navy's old County-class destroyers, *Blanca Encalada* (*Fife*), *Prat* and *Cochrane* (*Norfolk* and *Antrim* respectively). During the course of the exercises several senior rates from *Edinburgh* managed to visit their old ship. Two years later, however, on 12 December 2003, *Blanco Encalada* was finally paid off, but it was some years later on 28 February 2007, having been sold to Turkish shipbreakers, that she arrived in the Adriatic port of Aliaga, the heartland of the Turkish shipbreaking industry, for demolition.

County Class GMDs

Two excellent shots of *Blanco Encalada* at sea, during exercise 'Teamwork South 99', showing how her flight-deck had been extended over the quarterdeck and with a traditional twin hangar with a door facing the flight-deck. The submarine is the Chilean Navy Oberon class CNS *O'Brien*. *(US Navy)*

HMS Fife

Blanco Encalada at the shipbreaker's yard at Aliaga, near Izmir, Turkey. In the lower image most of the forecastle structure up to the bridge has beeen removed.
(Selim San)

Commanding Officers:

Captain Robert H. Graham MVO DSC RN	14 December 1965
Captain Peter G. Lachlan MBE RN	13 December 1967
Captain W. David Scott RN	30 May 1969
Captain George A. de G. Kitchin RN	4 February 1971
Captain David J. Hallifax RN	3 March 1973
Captain David Eckersley-Maslin RN	11 April 1975
Captain Geoffrey C. Lloyd RN	15 March 1976
Captain Jeremy J. Black OBE RN	19 September 1977
Captain Ronald G. Fry OBE RN	21 December 1978
Captain Clifford J. Caughey RN	7 September 1982
Captain Jonathan J. R. Tod RN	1 January 1984
Captain William J. Davis RN	29 November 1985

Chapter Six

HMS Glamorgan
1966 - 1986

Glamorgan alongside her fitting-out berth on 25 August 1965. When this photograph was taken the advance party of naval personnel had arrived to stand by the ship as she neared completion. *(World Ship Society)*

For almost two years, between 13 September 1962 when the first keel plates were laid, and July 1964 when she was launched from Vickers Armstrong's shipyard at High Walker on the River Tyne, the sixth County-class destroyer was known anonymously as Yard Number 176. The launching ceremony took place on 9 July 1964 when Lady Brecon, the wife of the Minister of State for Welsh Affairs, named the ship *Glamorgan*, the first Royal Navy warship to bear the name, after one of the 13 historic counties of Wales.

During the wet summer of 1964 the ship lay in the fitting-out basin, with what was to become No 9 mess looking more like a swimming pool. The following winter the hull was covered in snow and during the first six months of 1965 there was a substantial increase in the numbers of naval personnel standing by the ship. One officer remembers those early days: 'In May 1965 the first seaman to arrive was Able Seaman Neal, who joined the ship with Leading Writer Jenkins. Between them they set up the Ship's Office and spent a great deal of their time chasing up lodging allowance and pay. There were days when our pay would arrive in the form of an unsigned cheque and the accompanying list would include people we didn't have, or several who were with us would be missed off. We were frequently indebted to the Vickers Cash Office who tided us

The ship's bell, HMS *Glamorgan*. (T. Ferrers-Walker)

over those embarrassing moments.'

On 16 August 1966 *Glamorgan's* first commanding officer, Captain Richard E Roe RN, joined the ship and eight weeks later, on 12 October, the advance party of the ship's company arrived on board. The commissioning ceremony took place on Friday 14 October 1966 and initially, as the day was dull and wet, arrangements were made to hold the ceremony in the hangar. That forenoon, following the first press conference held on board, an historic presentation took place, when a bronze plaque depicting images of *Turbinia* of 1894 and *Glamorgan*, the first and last ships to be powered by Parsons marine steam turbines was presented to Captain Roe. By 1966 the Parsons works at Wallsend had closed and the company was a member of the Richardson's Westgarth Group (ceased trading 1982). By 1400, however, the rain had cleared and an hour later the commissioning ceremony took place on the flight deck. After the speeches and the reading of the Commissioning Warrant, the alert was sounded and the White Ensign was hoisted for the first time. As soon as the flight deck ceremonial was over the guests went below to the Junior Rates dining hall where, assisted by the Master-at-Arms, the ship's sponsor, Lady Brecon, cut the commissioning cake. That evening a reception for civic dignitaries from the County of Glamorgan was held in the wardroom.

Glamorgan's acceptance trials began during the forenoon of Sunday 16 October when, at 1055, she slipped her moorings and left the River Tyne to undergo a day of non-stop trials and for Captain Roe '...an evening of non-stop discussion', which ended at 2015 when he accepted the ship from the builders although the port gas turbines had been troubled by excessive vibration. That evening, after disembarking most of the Vickers personnel, *Glamorgan* resumed her trials before sailing south to Spithead and Portland to continue testing her gas turbines. In the event it was the forenoon of 24 October before she arrived in Portsmouth Harbour for the first time.

On 29 November *Glamorgan* left Portsmouth for initial trials and her inaugural visit to Cardiff, but severe gales caused the cancellation of the visit and on 3 December she returned to Portsmouth where engineers from Vickers were waiting to examine the port gas turbine. While the ship underwent docking leave was given and it was the third week of January 1967 before *Glamorgan* put to sea to continue her machinery trials. During these, on the afternoon of 30 January, a power failure to the main engines forced lubrication pumps, left the ship drifting helplessly in the Channel between the Isle of Wight and Chichester for almost two hours, with the frigate *Eskimo* standing by in case a tow was required. The trials continued into February, but during the second week of that month she returned to Portsmouth for maintenance.

In mid-April *Glamorgan* was at sea once again and on 22 April she arrived at Cardiff for her delayed inaugural visit to the city. The highlights of the visit were a civic dinner at County Hall for 160 members of the ship's company and on the final day a gala ball at which Captain Roe chose 'Miss Glamorgan 1967'. In May 1967, wearing the flag of the C-in-C Home Fleet, Admiral Sir John Frewen, the ship left Portsmouth to be joined by *Delight* and *Zulu* for a passage into the North Sea and via the Kiel Canal to the Danish port of Arhus and then south again to Amsterdam, before returning to Portsmouth where the C-in-C struck his flag. For *Glamorgan* more trials lay ahead and at noon on 21 August, off the missile ranges at Aberporth, she fired her first Sea Slug Mk2 missile, and this was followed by air defence and anti-submarine exercises with the aircraft carrier *Eagle* and the submarine *Artful*. Towards the end of August, during exercises off Aberporth, she broke off to pay a weekend visit to Swansea. On 1 September, with her trials concluded, *Glamorgan* began a very hectic five-week work-up at Portland, where she was assisted by *Cleopatra*, *Penelope*, *Tartar* and *Ulster*. During the first week of October she successfully passed FOST's inspection and returned to Portsmouth. Five days later, at 0834 on 29 November, as she lay alongside Fountain Lake Jetty, the old destroyer *Corunna*, which had been paid off earlier in the year and was being towed to Fareham Creek, collided with *Glamorgan's* port side, causing some damage to the hull and various fittings. However, this did not prevent her from putting to sea on 6 January 1968 when, in place of her Wessex helicopter, she had a Dragonfly embarked for trials.

Most of January and February 1968 was spent in

HM Ships *Glamorgan* and *Triumph* exercising together in the South China Sea during Exercise Coral Sands in 1968. *(Author's Collection)*

HMS Glamorgan, flying the flag of the C-in-C Western Fleet, returns to Portsmouth Harbour following the NATO Fleet Review of May 1969. (James W. Goss)

the Irish Sea and off Aberporth, with weekends at anchor off Fishguard and refuelling breaks at Milford Haven. On 23 February, however, she returned to Portsmouth for docking and to give pre-deployment leave. With her sister *Fife* she was to undertake a high-profile visit to the USA, which included Washington DC. During the refit, however, unforeseen problems were encountered and at one stage it was thought the Washington visit might have to be cancelled, but in the event the ship was undocked on 30 March, after which the ship's company set to preparing her for sea. Six days later on 5 April, *Glamorgan* set sail at 1000, just an hour later than scheduled. After embarking Sea Slug missiles at Devonport she rendezvoused with *Fife* in the Channel and together with RFA *Olmeda* they set course for the USA.

The ultimate destination for the two destroyers was in fact the Far East, but with the Suez Canal closed to shipping they were sailing via the USA and Pacific Ocean. They arrived off the American coast during the forenoon of 14 April and after embarking the pilot they steamed into Chesapeake Bay to anchor in the Potomac River. Some 36 hours later, during which time the paintwork was touched up, they got under weigh and with *Fife* leading the way they steamed upriver to the Washington Navy Yard. During the six-day visit there were a number of high-profile VIP visitors to both ships, the most distinguished being the Vice-President, Hubert Humphrey, who during the forenoon on 21 April spent an hour and a half on board *Glamorgan*. During the afternoon on 22 April the two destroyers left Washington and on *Glamorgan's* itinerary were calls at Norfolk, Virginia and a brief overnight refuelling stop at Kingston, Jamaica. On 2 May the ships made their transit of the Panama Canal and two days later they left Rodman Naval Base. After entering the Pacific Ocean *Fife* visited San Diego while *Glamorgan* continued north to San Francisco, after which they rendezvoused for a joint visit to Vancouver and the Canadian naval base at Esquimalt. On Monday 19 May, two days after her arrival in Vancouver, there was a change of command when Captain Roe was relieved by Captain Ronald C. C. Greenlees RN. After leaving Esquimalt *Fife* visited Portland, Oregon, for the city's Rose Festival, while *Glamorgan* called at Seattle; when the ship was opened to the public there for just two afternoons, over 7,500 people visited her. During the forenoon of 4 June both ships left the US mainland to begin their passage across the Pacific Ocean, which was broken by a five-day visit to the US naval base at Pearl Harbor and a brief refuelling stop at Guam. Finally, during the early evening of 2 July they arrived at the Singapore Naval Base, where they joined the Far East Fleet.

On arrival at Singapore *Glamorgan* underwent a three-week maintenance period, assisted by Fleet Maintenance Staff from the heavy repair ship *Triumph*, but on 22 July she was once again ready for sea. She sailed that morning to join other ships, including *Defender*, *Diana*, *Euryalus*, *Grenville*, *Puma*, HMNZS *Otago* and HMAS *Vendetta*, as well as the submarines *Amphion* and *Rorqual*, for exercises and manoeuvres in the South China Sea, which included banyan breaks at Pulau Tioman. The programme of exercises extended into August, when they were joined by *Hermes*, and in mid-August they moved to the Strait of Malacca and the Andaman Sea, with a weekend break at Pulau Langkowi. At the end of August came a two-week break at Singapore, before *Glamorgan* once again joined the fleet to take part in what was at the time the largest maritime and amphibious exercise ever held in Australian waters. The manoeuvres took place over a wide area, ranging from the Solomon Islands in the Pacific Ocean, down to Sydney, NSW. More than 50 ships and 18,000 personnel from Britain, Australia, New Zealand and the USA, as well as 2,000 Royal Marines of No 3 Commando were involved. The exercise, code-named 'Coral Sands' and directed by Rear-Admiral D. C. Wells RAN, involved the 'destruction' of an enemy force who had invaded and occupied northern Queensland. Some 25 Royal Navy ships took part which in addition to *Glamorgan* included *Hermes*, *Albion*, *Intrepid*, *Triumph*, *Forth*, *Fife*, *Defender*, *Diana*, *Caprice*, *Euryalus* and *Puma* as well as the submarines *Andrew*, *Cachalot* and *Onslaught*. The various support craft included two SRN6 hovercraft, which were used to transport marines from various transports to the shore.

After leaving Singapore on 21 September *Glamorgan* joined *Euryalus*, HMNZS *Blackpool* and *Waikato*, and HMAS *Anzac* as escort to *Hermes*, which in the late 1960s was still operating as a fixed-wing aircraft carrier. After exercising in the South China Sea the carrier group replenished from RFA *Olna* before setting course for the Balabac Strait, steaming across the Sulu Sea, through the Sibutu Channel and into the Celebes Sea, where they rendezvoused with the amphibious force, which included *Albion*, *Intrepid*, *Triumph*, *Caprice* and RFA *Tidespring*. The whole task force then made its way to the Bismarck Sea where, at midnight on 30 September, off the Admiralty

HMS *Glamorgan* in Plymouth Sound during 1970. *(Crown Copyright/MoD 1970)*

On 28 November 1970 *Glamorgan* arrived at Malta. Here she is seen manoeuvring to No8 buoy in Grand Harbour. *(Michael Cassar)*

Islands, the amphibious phase of the exercise began. Following a helicopter assault by 800 Royal Marines on the coast in the area of Queensland's Shoalwater Bay, landing craft and hovercraft were used to put a further 1,200 Royal Marines ashore onto beaches of soft sand, with very rugged terrain further inland. As well as the troops, some 200 vehicles were also landed while escort ships, including *Glamorgan*, provided gunfire support. During the course of the exercise *Glamorgan* rendezvoused with a replenishment group, including RFAs *Fort Rosalie*, *Reliant*, *Tarbatness*, *Tidespring*, *Gold Ranger* and *Pearleaf*, and escorted them into the operating area to facilitate oiling, storing and ammunition transfers. Finally, with the exercise over, on 14 October *Hermes* led the main force of ships, including *Glamorgan*, into Sydney Harbour, where the latter secured alongside the cruiser wharf at Woolloomooloo.

Glamorgan's 17-day maintenance break in Sydney proved very popular with her ship's company, but on the last day of October she sailed to join *Hermes* and *Diana* for exercises in Jarvis Bay and then in the US Navy exercise areas at Subic Bay. In mid-November she arrived at Hong Kong to carry out a nine-day maintenance period, before undergoing Admiral's inspection and accompanying *Hermes* back to the naval base at Singapore. On 9 December 1968, during this period at Singapore, there was a change of command when Captain Stanley L. 'Mac' McArdle GM MVO RN took over from Greenlees. The son of a Royal Marines Colour Sergeant, McArdle was one of the few naval officers promoted from the lower deck who eventually achieved flag rank; he had actually joined the Navy as a Boy Seaman in 1938 and was commissioned in 1945. In January 1953, while serving as the First Lieutenant of the destroyer *Contest*, he was awarded the George Medal for the courageous rescue of survivors from the stricken ferry *Princess Victoria*, which sank during a fierce storm in the Irish Sea.

During the second week of January 1969 *Glamorgan* sailed for exercises in the South China Sea, during which she searched for, but failed to find any trace of, a merchantman reportedly on fire east of Singapore. On 10 January she left Singapore for Gan and then, via Mauritius, the coast of Mozambique where, on 22 January, she joined the frigate *Lincoln* on the Beira Patrol. *Glamorgan* spent three weeks on patrol off Mozambique, during which time after several rounds of inter-ship sports, she took the 'Beira Bucket' from *Lincoln*. Then during the afternoon of 11 February she was relieved by *Diana* and three days later she arrived at the South African naval base at Simonstown. Although *Glamorgan* had left the Far East Station she was not returning directly home and on 18 February, after exercising with the South African naval ships *Tafelberg*, *President Pretorious* and *President Steyn*, she set course into the Atlantic Ocean, bound for the Caribbean. After refuelling at Bridgetown, Barbados, *Glamorgan* steamed to Puerto Rico and the US Navy's missile firing ranges off the Roosevelt Roads Naval Base, where she spent two days carrying out Sea Slug firings. On 15 March she left for a ten-day passage home, arriving alongside at Devonport during the afternoon of 25 March and reaching Portsmouth two days later.

On her return to Portsmouth *Glamorgan* began a seven-week dockyard-assisted maintenance period, which ended in mid-May, when she hoisted the flag of the C-in-C Western Fleet, Admiral Sir John Bush, and steamed out to Spithead where a NATO fleet was assembling for a Royal Review on 16 May. In all a total of 63 warships from 12 countries took part in these celebrations for the 20th anniversary celebrations of NATO. The biggest ships present were the aircraft carriers USS *Wasp*, the newly converted helicopter cruiser HMS *Blake* and the Italian guided missile escort cruiser *Doria*. In addition to *Blake*, *Glamorgan* led a force of 12 Royal Navy ships made up of *Phoebe*, *Puma*, *Torquay*, *Tenby*, *Eastbourne*, *Wakeful*, the submarines *Alcide*, *Tiptoe* and *Olympus*, the minesweepers *Letterston* and *Shoulton* and RFA *Olmeda*. Following the review *Glamorgan* returned to Portsmouth where she remained until the last week of May, when she began a period of day running as she carried out various trials, before steaming to Devonport for ten days of maintenance. On 30 June *Glamorgan* left Devonport to make an overnight

HMS *Glamorgan* at sea with her Wessex helicopter ranged on the flight deck. *(Crown Copyright/MoD)*

County Class GMDs

HMS *Glamorgan* high and dry in Portsmouth Dockyard. *(T. Ferrers-Walker)*

passage to Holyhead, where later the next day she rendezvoused with the royal yacht *Britannia* for a week of ceremonial duties. In company with the frigate *Lincoln* she escorted the royal yacht to Llandudno, Swansea and Cardiff for the Prince of Wales' tour of Wales following his investiture on 1 July. The destroyer's entry into King's Dock, Swansea, on 3 July was particularly spectacular as it was timed to coincide with a Fleet Air Arm fly-past over the city. On 8 July, her royal escort duties over, *Glamorgan* returned to Portsmouth.

During the rest of July *Glamorgan* remained in home waters off the south coast and on 29 July, flying the flag of Vice-Admiral Sir Michael Pollock, Flag Officer Submarines, she took part in the Western Fleet Review off the coast of South Devon. Twenty-five ships, led by the aircraft carrier *Eagle* and including *Hampshire*, *Blake*, the nuclear-powered fleet submarines *Valiant* and *Warspite*, as well as six patrol submarines, minesweepers and RFAs, steamed past the royal yacht in winds which at one point reached gale force. With the review over *Glamorgan* returned to Portsmouth. During August the ship remained close to the south coast, taking part in Navy Days at Portland and Portsmouth then undergoing a six-week maintenance period at Devonport, after which most of October was spent off the missile firing ranges at Aberporth. During this time, in the Cardigan Bay area, one of the missiles went out of control and landed on farmland some nine miles inland from the coastal town of Borth, where it burst into flames. Although there had been no warhead on the missile it had landed close to a farmhouse and all further firings of the Mk2 Sea Slug were suspended pending a full investigation. The training exercises finally ended at Rosyth and during the first half of November *Glamorgan* spent five days in Newcastle upon Tyne, followed by visits to Copenhagen, Hamburg and Amsterdam, before she returned to the south coast where she exercised with *Llandaff*. Finally, on 11 December, she arrived in Liverpool's Huskisson Dock for a five-day visit to the city, after which she steamed north to the Clyde for exercises with the submarine *Onyx*, before returning to Devonport on 18 December, where she paid off.

On her arrival at Devonport *Glamorgan* was taken in hand by the dockyard for a long refit which would keep her out of commission for the best part of ten months. On 17 March 1970, just three months into the work, there was a change of command when Captain Raymond P. Dannreuther RN took over from McArdle. During the refit all the ship's main and auxiliary machinery and the accommodation areas were refurbished and by August 1970 she was in a fit state to be opened to the public for Navy Days. By Monday 5 October *Glamorgan* was once again ready for sea and that forenoon she sailed to begin her post-refit trials, followed by a three-week work-up at Portland. On 21 November she left Devonport bound for Gibraltar, where she rendezvoused with the frigate *Euryalus* and continued through the Mediterranean to Malta, from where the two ships operated until the second week of December when *Glamorgan* returned, via Gibraltar, to Devonport.

During the first months of 1971 *Glamorgan* remained in home waters, operating mainly from Portland, but also from Fishguard. During the third week of March she took part in anti-submarine exercises in the Atlantic Ocean with *Cachalot*, before returning to Cardigan Bay. In early April her missile-firing trials ended with a three-day visit to Cardiff.

On 1 June 1971 *Glamorgan* left Devonport to rendezvous with the aircraft carrier *Eagle* before setting course for Funchal, Madeira. The two ships were on the first leg of their passage by way of the Cape of Good Hope to join the Far East Fleet, which was about to be disbanded in favour of a new five-power agreement involving Britain, Singapore, Malaysia, Australia and New Zealand. This would replace the Anglo-Malaysian Defence Agreement and remove the main burden of responsibility for the defence of the area from Britain's shoulders. As for the mighty Singapore Naval Base, which had only been completed in 1938, just in time to be occupied by the Japanese, most of it was to be turned over to commercial interests, with just a small section of the old Stores Basin being utilized

County Class GMDs

With the Spanish town of Algeciras in the background and her Wessex helicopter on the flight deck, *Glamorgan* approaches Gibraltar. *(Crown Copyright/MoD)*

by what was known as the ANZUK Force (Australia, New Zealand, UK), with the Royal Navy's contribution being limited to just two frigates, the first being *Gurkha* and *Jaguar*. In addition to the small naval presence Britain was also retaining a battalion of troops and a limited number of RAF aircraft. However, even as arrangements for the main British withdrawal from Singapore were going ahead there was a great deal of speculation as to how long the new force would remain in being. (ANZUK was actually disbanded in 1974).

In early June 1971, *Eagle* and *Glamorgan* were on their long passage east and on 18 June the destroyer put into Port Elizabeth for a nine-day visit. On 3 July she refuelled from RFA *Wave Ruler* at Gan and five days later she secured alongside the repair ship *Triumph* in the Stores Basin at Singapore Naval Base. Pausing just long enough to carry out essential maintenance, on 21 July she sailed to join *Eagle* (flag FO2 FES), *Achilles*, *Danae*, *Jaguar* and the RFAs *Olna*, *Reliant* and *Resource*, for what was to be an eight-week visit to Australian and New Zealand ports.

After steaming via the Sunda Strait and the west coast of Australia, during their passage through the Great Australian Bight the squadron exercised with Australian warships before assembling off Sydney Heads during the early hours of 4 August. At 0800 that forenoon *Glamorgan* led *Achilles*, *Danae* and *Jaguar* through the Heads for the 14-mile trip up harbour, around Cockatoo Island, beneath the imposing sweep of the Sydney Harbour Bridge, to the dockyard at Garden Island, where *Glamorgan* secured alongside the cruiser wharf, being joined later in the day by *Eagle*. On leaving Australia *Glamorgan* acted as planeguard to *Eagle* during exercises in Jervis Bay, before making a rough passage of the Tasman Sea and the Cook Strait in

HMS Glamorgan

winds of up to 100mph, which forced her to shelter for three days in Tasman Bay. Finally, however, on 20 August she arrived at Lyttelton, which the ship's company voted the most hospitable port of the tour. On leaving here *Glamorgan* rejoined *Eagle* and the rest of the squadron for exercises in the Fremantle area, but on 8 September her time in Australia was cut short when she was forced to put into Geraldton for repairs to her rudder. She left five days later for a slow and sedate passage back to Singapore Naval Base for more permanent repairs.

Glamorgan remained in the dockyard until the second week of October, when she sailed for Hong Kong where, on 18 October, Captain Thomas H. E. Baird RN took command of the ship. Captain Dannreuther, who was retiring after more than 30 years' service, began his journey home courtesy of Jenny's Side Party who, having bedecked their sampan with bunting, carried him past the cheering ship's company and on to HMS *Tamar* where he transferred to more orthodox transport. Ten days later *Glamorgan* returned to Singapore to join the ceremonies marking the final withdrawal from the naval base, just 34 years after its completion.

The Army and RAF in Singapore had held their final parades on 29 October, but the naval ceremonies took place two days later and on 31 October, flying the flag of FO2 FES, Rear-Admiral David Williams, *Glamorgan* joined *Eagle*, *Albion*, *Triumph*, *Scylla*, *Arethusa*, *Achilles*, *Argonaut*, as well as Australian and New Zealand ships and five RFAs for a final steam-past. Altogether 16 ships took part, with *Glamorgan* leading the line as they steamed past RFA *Stromness*, from where the last C-in-C Far East Command, Air Chief Marshal Sir Brian Burnett, accompanied by the three High Commissioners from Britain, Australia and New Zealand, and the Deputy Prime Minister of Singapore (the Prime Minister Mr Lee Kuan Yew was in London), took the salute. Overhead flew Buccaneers, Sea Vixens and Gannets from *Eagle*, as well as Sea King, Wessex and Wasp helicopters

HMS *Glamorgan* enters Grand Harbour, Malta. *(Michael Cassar)*

County Class GMDs

At sea following the removal of B turret and its replacement by a quadruple Exocet missile launcher. In this image, the missile cannisters have yet to be embarked. (Crown Copyright/MoD)

from *Eagle*, *Albion*, *Triumph* and the escort vessels. Overall it was a low-key occasion and as soon as it was over the ships steamed into the Strait of Malacca to an area off Penang to begin 'Exercise Curtain Call', during which *Glamorgan* returned briefly to the Stores Basin of what was now the ANZUK base for minor repairs. By mid-November the fleet had left the area and soon afterwards *Glamorgan* made a dash across the Indian Ocean to the area around the Seychelles to assist the tanker RFA *Derwentdale*, whose engineers it transpired only wanted advice. On 22 November *Glamorgan* arrived in Kilindini Harbour, Mombasa, where she secured alongside the depot ship *Triumph* to begin a 14-day maintenance period.

Three days into her refit, with much of the main and auxiliary machinery opened for maintenance, *Glamorgan* received an unexpected order to proceed to sea as soon as possible, 'destination unknown.' For over 12 hours the ship's company worked non-stop to get the ship ready for sea and it was said that some of the engine room department were seen 'beachcombing the rubbish barge' for various pieces of machinery which had been discarded and were to have been replaced. Personnel who were just settling into the Silversands leave centre, some 70 miles up the coast, were hastily recalled to the ship and at 0930 on 26 November *Glamorgan* sailed south to Simonstown, where she paused to refuel. After leaving Simonstown the ship was ordered to make a transatlantic crossing, refuel at the Brazilian port of Recife and at Bridgetown, Barbados, before setting course for Hamilton, Bermuda, where she arrived during the afternoon of 15 December. During the passage the 'secret' of their hasty departure from Mombasa and their destination was disclosed. *Glamorgan* was to act as guardship at Bermuda during a summit meeting between the US President, Richard Nixon, and the British Prime Minister, Edward Heath, and although the political talks were held ashore at Government House, the summit dinner on 20 December, at the end of the 48-hour meeting of the two politicians and their staff, took place on board HMS *Glamorgan*. Heath and Nixon arrived on board at 2000 and left three hours later, but the ship herself remained at Bermuda for a further seven days before sailing for Chaguaramas, Trinidad, where, over a period of two weeks at the Swan Hunter dockyard, the maintenance period begun in Mombasa was completed.

Having seen the new year in at Trinidad, on 13 January 1972 *Glamorgan* left Chaguaramas to rendezvous with *Triumph*, *Minerva* and RFA *Olwen* and set course for the Argentine capital of Buenos Aires, making her seventh crossing of the equator en route. The 'mini-fleet', as it was known, was undertaking a defence equipment sales trip to both Argentina and Brazil and during the forenoon of 23 January the ships made their way up the River Plate to anchor two hours downriver from Buenos Aires. Next morning they completed their passage to secure alongside the city's docks. At that time a series of joint talks between Britain and Argentina over the future of the Falkland Islands had been going on since 1965, and in July 1971 they had succeeded in getting an air route opened between Port Stanley and Commodoro Rivadavia, which, interestingly, was operated by the Argentine Military Airline LADE.

After a seven-day visit to Buenos Aires, on the last day of January the ships made their way back down the River Plate to rendezvous with a Brazilian Navy squadron, led by the cruiser *Barroso* (ex-USS *Philadelphia*), which also included *Pernambuco*, *Aire*, *Paraiba*, *Araguary* and the submarine *Tamandare*, for three days of joint manoeuvres while en route to Rio de Janeiro. During the three-day passage Rear-Admiral Williams, FO2, flew his flag in *Glamorgan* which, as the temporary flagship of the mini-fleet, led the way into Rio's picturesque Guanabara Bay, from where, just visible through the heavy mist, was Sugarloaf Mountain. The visit to Rio lasted for five days, after which the mini-fleet steamed north via Bridgetown, Barbados, to Roosevelt Roads where, in the US Navy's Puerto Rico exercise areas, they joined *Ark Royal*, *Berwick*, *Jupiter* and US Navy ships for joint manoeuvres, which were concluded at the end of February with a two-day wash-up at Virgin Gorda. Following this *Glamorgan* made a ten-day visit to St John's, Antigua, then joined *Jupiter*, which had been serving with the Standing Naval Force, Atlantic, for the passage home.

When *Glamorgan* secured alongside No 5 Wharf in Devonport Dockyard during the afternoon of Thursday 16 March, she had been away for ten months, during which time she had steamed some 70,000 miles, visited 14 countries, taken part in the ceremonies marking the end of the independent British presence on Singapore Island and played host to a high-level summit meeting between the President of the USA and the British Prime Minister. On arrival in Plymouth Sound, for the final few miles of her homeward journey, she had embarked 450 friends and relatives of the ship's company and as she steamed up the Hamoaze to her berth in the dockyard they too lined the guardrails. Ahead lay an eight-week maintenance period.

It was mid-May before *Glamorgan* was ready for sea, and on 16 May she left Plymouth Sound for three days of trials before returning to the dockyard where she secured alongside the cruiser *Tiger*. During the summer of 1972 *Glamorgan* remained

The public swarm aboard the ship during Portland Navy Days. *(T.Ferrers-Walker)*

in home waters, but in mid-September she joined the assault ship *Intrepid* for passage to Gibraltar and the Mediterranean. On the last day of September *Glamorgan* began a five-day visit to Corfu, before steaming on to Malta's Grand Harbour from where, during the whole of October, she carried out a series of day-running exercises. In early November she visited the Italian naval base at Taranto and from there she joined the NATO exercise 'Endless Chain', which also involved US Navy and Italian ships. On completion of the exercise *Glamorgan* steamed home via Taranto, Palma and Casablanca, arriving alongside at Devonport on 1 December to begin an assisted maintenance period and to give leave.

The new year of 1973 began for *Glamorgan* with a four-day visit to Cardiff, during which FOF2 hoisted his flag for the passage south to Lisbon for the NATO exercise 'Sunny Seas' off the Portuguese coast, where she was joined by *Ark Royal*, *Tiger*, *Norfolk*, *Arethusa*, *Gurkha*, *Lowestoft*, *Diomede*, *Rorqual*, *Dreadnought* and *Conqueror*. The force also included ships from NATO's Standing Naval Force Atlantic, among them US, Dutch, Norwegian and Canadian vessels. In mid-February there was a break at Gibraltar, which saw one of the largest gatherings of British warships for many years and it coincided with the tightening of a four-year blockade of the Rock by the Spanish government, which sent its helicopter carrier *Dedalo* to shadow *Ark Royal* and *Glamorgan*. After leaving Gibraltar the fleet steamed into the Mediterranean to begin a series of training exercises during which *Glamorgan* acted as planeguard for *Ark Royal*. After a series of anti-submarine and amphibious exercises, on 24 February *Glamorgan* led *Cleopatra*, *Arethusa* and RFA *Olmeda* into La Spezia on a ten-day visit to the port. On leaving La Spezia the ships completed the final phase of the exercise and on 15 March *Glamorgan* returned to Devonport.

On 27 April 1973 *Glamorgan* put to sea again and she was ordered to proceed to the area around Eddystone Light to assist *Argonaut* in the search for 20 giant metal containers washed overboard from the German coaster MV *Belle Virtue*, which had sunk after being in collision with the Panamanian bulk carrier *Maritime Pioneer*. The containers, which were riding low in the water and were only just awash, posed a serious danger to shipping. At 1730 *Glamorgan* joined *Argonaut* at the scene of the collision and parties of seamen were sent in whalers to attempt to sink two of the containers that had been located, but at 2040, with darkness falling, these attempts were abandoned and *Glamorgan* set course for Lisbon, where she arrived on the last day of April.

Glamorgan's passage south marked the start of

HMS Glamorgan

The davits holding the Cheverton motor launch have been lowered into their launch position. The tubes in the foreground are the starboard Shipboard Torpedo Weapons System (STWS) mount.
(T. Ferrers-Walker)

her return to the Mediterranean and Malta, although after just four days in Grand Harbour she accompanied *Intrepid* to Istanbul, before sailing south to Cyprus where, on 28 May, she arrived off Dhekalia and joined *Intrepid*, *Bulwark*, *Berwick* and *Olmeda* for the NATO exercise 'Dawn Patrol' which included USS *Forrestal*, *Daniels* and *Marley*, and ended in Naples on 16 June. *Glamorgan* remained in the Mediterranean for a further 12 weeks, exercising mainly with US Navy ships, including the aircraft carrier *Independence*, acting as planeguard for her for two weeks. There were visits to Tunis and Corfu, and during the night of 7/8 August she shadowed a Soviet Kresta-class cruiser. By 17 August she was back at Gibraltar and four days later she left harbour to rendezvous with the nuclear-powered submarine *Valiant*. Just a few hours later, at 0155 on 22 August, *Valiant* signalled that she was in difficulty and so for the next seven hours *Glamorgan* escorted her slowly back to Gibraltar. At the end of August came a four-day visit to Tangier and during the first week of September she was limited to day running from Gibraltar. *Glamorgan's* commission was drawing to a close and during the forenoon of 10 September, after embarking the outgoing Governor of Gibraltar, Admiral-of-the-Fleet Sir Varyl Begg, *Glamorgan* sailed for Portsmouth where she secured alongside South Railway Jetty three days later. By the end of that month she had been paid off and was lying in No 3 basin where she began a six-month refit.

Glamorgan, like her sisters *Antrim* and *Norfolk*, was to be refitted to carry Exocet missiles and, like her two sisters, she had B turret removed and replaced with four rather featureless, but functional, MM38 canister-like missile launchers, with special deflectors to prevent damage to the bridge superstructure from the boosters. She also had her middle pair of boats removed and a triple STWS torpedo launcher fitted to the main deck on each side in their place. A large platform was added to the front of the main mast that spanned across the entire width of the ship to which was added a pair of SCOT radomes for long-range communications. On 11 February 1974, as the ship lay alongside in No 5 basin at Portsmouth Dockyard, her new commanding officer, Captain Kenneth Vause RN, was appointed to the ship. At this stage, however, the accommodation on board was uninhabitable and it was not until the end of March after the ship had been shifted to Fountain Lake Jetty, alongside *Hampshire*, that the ship's company was able to move back on board and the numbers of personnel were brought back to full strength. On 1 May the

HMS *Glamorgan* at Spithead for the 1977 Silver Jubilee Fleet Review. *(Maritime Photo Library)*

ship underwent basin trials and just over two weeks later she was inspected by the Flag Officer, Spithead, her old commanding officer from 1968/70, Rear-Admiral McArdle. Three days later she put to sea to begin her post-refit trials, which continued in the Channel right up to the end of the month. During the forenoon of 21 June 1974, with *Glamorgan* secured alongside South Railway Jetty, a rededication ceremony was held on the jetty alongside the ship, which was attended by the ship's sponsor, Lady Brecon, as well as Rear-Admiral McArdle and the Band of the Royal Welch Fusiliers. The recommissioning cake was cut and after the proceedings were concluded the ship was opened to families.

Three days after the rededication ceremony *Glamorgan* put to sea to continue her trials, which included a weekend visit to Cherbourg and Navy Days at Portsmouth. On Monday 2 September, having just returned to Portsmouth after a day at sea testing the Exocet equipment, she was ordered to sea at short notice into a very stormy Channel to assist in the search for the yacht *Morning Cloud*, which had gone missing on passage between Burnham-on-Crouch and Cowes. Although the yacht was owned by the former Prime Minister Edward Heath, he was not on board at the time, and in the event it transpired that the yacht had sunk in heavy seas off Shoreham with the loss of two crew members. That evening, having failed to find any trace of the yacht or its crew, *Glamorgan* anchored in St Helen's Roads off the Isle of Wight. Later that month she began her work-up at Portland, during which, on 18 October, she again went to the aid of another yacht which was in difficulty in Lyme Bay. This time, however, a boarding party was able to make repairs and the destroyer escorted the yacht safely into Portland Harbour before setting course for Portsmouth.

In early November *Glamorgan* paid a weekend visit to Swansea before spending a week in Cardigan Bay on the missile ranges. In the latter half of November, flying the flag of FOF2, she took part in a NATO exercise which began in the North Sea and took her around Iceland and into the Atlantic Ocean. Also taking part were *Hermes*, *Juno*, *Rhyl*, the RFAs *Retainer* and *Tidepool*, as well as Dutch and German warships. During these manoeuvres there was a short break in the old wartime base at Scapa Flow and five days later the exercises ended at Rosyth. During the first week of December *Glamorgan* made a five-day official visit to Cardiff, before returning to Portsmouth for the seasonal break.

On 28 January 1975 *Glamorgan* left Portsmouth to steam south to Gibraltar and on to the French naval base at Toulon, from where she carried out a week-long series of Exocet missile trials and firings on the nearby ranges. On 17 February she returned to Gibraltar where Rear-Admiral John Fieldhouse, FOF2, hoisted his flag for a series of exercises code-named 'Springex', which would evolve to become the annual 'Springtrain' exercises. Ships taking part on this occasion included *Berwick*, *Charybdis*, *Jupiter* and *Nubian*. With the exercises over *Glamorgan* paid a five-day visit to Naples, after which she was joined by *Nubian* for the passage home. During the last week of March she steamed north to Rosyth to take part in air-defence exercises in the North Sea and in mid-April she returned to Portsmouth to carry out a ten-week assisted maintenance period.

On 6 May Captain Robin E. de M. Leathes RN took over command of the ship from Baird and on 22 July *Glamorgan* left Portsmouth, again wearing the flag of FO2, bound for Gibraltar. This time she was leading five ships of the 8th Frigate Squadron: *Ajax*, *Berwick*, *Llandaff*, *Plymouth*, and *Rothesay*, as well as RFAs *Gold Rover*, *Tarbetness* and *Tidespring* on what was designated as the 'Group Three Deployment'. It would take the ships right round the world and the first port of call at Gibraltar saw *Glamorgan* delayed by an overheating gearbox. Upon their arrival at Malta the group exercised with the US Navy's aircraft carrier *John F. Kennedy*, and on 11 August they set course for Port Said where they arrived three days later and spent 36 hours before making their southbound transit of the Suez Canal. Once into the Indian Ocean the group split up to visit various ports, with *Glamorgan*, *Plymouth* and *Rothesay* calling at Bombay.

After exercising with Indian naval ships the group continued their passage east and on 10 September they secured alongside the old Stores Basin of the former ANZUK section of Sembawang Dockyard at Singapore to undergo a four-week maintenance period. On 6 October *Glamorgan* and *Plymouth* left Singapore to visit Port Klang on Malaya's west coast before proceeding to the Indonesian port of Surabaya. From there *Glamorgan* made a brief call at Bali, before the group came together again and headed south-east into the Timor Sea to join Australian Navy ships for 'Exercise Swift Swing', which for *Glamorgan* ended on 5 November at the port of Newcastle, New South Wales. Twelve days later she made the short passage south to Sydney, after which the group dispersed to various Australian ports, with *Glamorgan* visiting Hobart in time to see the end of the Sydney to Hobart yacht race.

Having spent both Christmas and New Year in the Tasmanian state capital *Glamorgan* led the group into New Zealand waters to begin a series of visits to ports there. *Glamorgan* visited Bluff, one of the most southerly towns in New Zealand, and Dunedin, also on the south island, then during the third week of January she led the group into the Pacific Ocean where, with *Llandaff* and *Jaguar*, she visited Tonga. After the group came together once again course was set for the US naval base at Hawaii's Pearl Harbor for a five-day visit. On 17 February they set course for the West Coast of the USA, but *Ajax*, which had suffered a major fire in her main switchboard while en route from Fiji, was left behind while the Pearl Harbor Navy shipyard carried out repairs.

On arrival off the US West Coast *Glamorgan* began her programme with a visit to San Diego where, after she had secured alongside the city's naval base, she received a visit from the C-in-C Fleet, Admiral Sir John Treacher. After leaving San Diego on 2 March the group once again reassembled to carry out a series of exercises with US and Canadian ships, including USS *Enterprise* and HMCS *Provider*, and these ended ten days later with a return to San Diego. For *Glamorgan* the high spot of the exercises was the firing of three Sea Slug missiles, two of them being fired at fast targets which they destroyed. The ten days of exercises

HMS *Glamorgan*, with her ship's company fell in at Procedure Alpha, arrives at Malta in April 1977.
(Crown Copyright/MoD 1977)

involved some 38 ships, including *Ajax* complete with a new switchboard which had been taken out of HMS *Dido* and flown to Pearl Harbor. On 15 March *Glamorgan* led the group out of San Diego to set course for the Panama Canal and the US Rodman Naval Base. Nine days later, after a 48-hour stopover at Rodman the group completed their transit of the Panama Canal and set course for La Guira. After leaving Venezuela all that remained was for the group to make its transatlantic crossing and during the morning of 14 April *Glamorgan* anchored at Spithead. Later, during the forenoon, she steamed up harbour to secure alongside South Railway Jetty to begin a 12-week maintenance period.

On 15 June 1976, as *Glamorgan* lay high and dry in C lock at Portsmouth Dockyard, there was a change of command when Captain Brian K. Shattock RN took over the ship from de Leathes and on 7 July she was ready for sea once again. Following trials she began her work-up at Portland, during which time she exercised with *Ambuscade*, *Antelope*, *Fife*, *Zulu* and the submarine *Orpheus*, and she also took part in Portland's Navy Days. At the end of July she arrived in Cardiff for a five-day official visit to the city and in early September, having taken part in Navy Days at Portsmouth, she navigated the River Scheldt to make a six-day visit to the port of Antwerp, after which she returned to Portland. During October *Glamorgan* continued to operate from Portland, but in early November she steamed north to Rosyth to join *Devonshire*, *Achilles*, *Antelope*, *Euryalus* and *Amazon* for a major NATO exercise in the North Sea, after which *Glamorgan* paid a ten-day visit to Newcastle upon Tyne. On 5 December she left the River Tyne to return to the Portland area where, for ten days, she joined *Devonshire*, *Newcastle*, *Galatea*, *Aurora* the submarine *Narwhal* and RFA *Resource*, for anti-submarine exercises. On 16 December she returned to Portsmouth where she secured alongside *Norfolk* at Fountain Lake Jetty. By the end of the year she had paid off to undergo a major refit.

Glamorgan's refit, which cost some £44 million, included a full hull survey, considerable improvements to the living accommodation, a complete re-tubing of all the ship's boilers and extensive work on the weapons and communications systems. On 7 October 1980, when she was high and dry in D lock, her new commanding officer, Captain Michael E. Barrow RN, joined the ship which 13 days later was towed from D lock to Fountain Lake Jetty. By mid-November the ship's company had been brought up to full strength and at 0945 on Friday 21 November, the ship's company fell in on the jetty alongside the ship for the start of the rededication ceremony. The guest of honour was the ship's sponsor, Lady Brecon, and other guests included the Lord Mayors of Cardiff and Swansea. The cake was cut by Mrs Judith Barrow, who was ably assisted by the youngest member of the ship's company, JWEM Philip Davey. The ceremony was completed by 1400 and 12 days later *Glamorgan* left harbour for the first time in almost four years to begin her post-refit trials.

After a break for the Christmas and New Year holidays *Glamorgan's* trials continued into January and February 1981 and on 20 February there was some relief in the form of a five-day visit to Cardiff. By early March she was back at Portsmouth. On 5 March, having spent the night at anchor off the Isle of Wight, *Glamorgan* spent most of the day exercising in the Channel then, at 1510, she received an emergency signal from the tug *Sea Rover*, which claimed to be off Beachy Head and sinking after being fired on. However, before the destroyer arrived on the scene it was learned that the tug was in fact the subject of a joint anti-drug smuggling operation by British and French Customs and that it was a French naval ship which had fired a warning shot when the vessel failed to stop. While *Sea Rover* was arrested and taken into Newhaven, *Glamorgan* returned to Spithead. During April and May *Glamorgan* remained in home waters and in June, with *Hermes*, *London*, *Glasgow*, *Coventry*, *Aurora* and *Plymouth*, she took part in two major NATO exercises in the Western Approaches, after which she and *Aurora* paid a nine-day visit to Kiel to represent the Royal Navy at the ever-popular 'Kieler Woche', when the regional capital of Schleswig-Holstein hosts its annual sailing regatta and festivities. After leaving Kiel *Glamorgan* returned via a fuelling stop at Dover to Portland and it is interesting to note that as she entered Portland Harbour she encountered the newly completed Argentine Navy Type 42 destroyer, *Santissimo Trinidad* which, some nine months later, would lead the Argentine invasion of the Falkland Islands.

It was in the summer of 1981 that the British Government's Defence White Paper, which proposed extensive cuts to the Royal Navy, including the sale of *Invincible*, was proving to be very controversial. Under Defence Secretary John Knott's plans two of the ships earmarked for decommissioning in 1983 were *Glamorgan* and *Norfolk*, with the ice patrol ship *Endurance*, which was the Navy's last representative in the South Atlantic. Perhaps more than any other it was the announcement of *Endurance's* withdrawal which was noted by the ruling military junta in Argentina, who saw that an opportunity might arise whereby they could wrest control of the Falkland Islands, South Georgia and other territories which made up Britain's Antarctic possessions. The idea was probably reinforced by the Foreign Secretary's willingness to discuss a possible transfer of power and a subsequent leaseback in respect of the Falkland Islands themselves.

For *Glamorgan's* ship's company this was all in the future and during two weeks in July the ship operated in the Cardigan Bay area in conjunction with RAF Canberra bombers carrying out trials, but by the middle of the month she had returned to Portsmouth to carry out maintenance and give leave. After taking part in Portsmouth's Navy Days and making a short visit to Amsterdam, *Glamorgan* returned to Portsmouth to prepare for her next major deployment, to the Persian Gulf and the Armilla Patrol, a response to the war between Iran and Iraq, designed to protect British, American and other shipping in the Persian Gulf area.

Glamorgan left Portsmouth on Monday 19 October 1981, and in company with *Ambuscade* and RFAs *Fort Austin* and *Pearleaf*, she set course for the Persian Gulf, via the Mediterranean. Whilst on passage the group conducted exercises with French and Portuguese warships and there was time for a short stopover in Naples, where FOF1, Rear-Admiral J. F. Woodward, and his staff joined the ship, having flown out from the UK. On 5 November, having exercised with Italian warships off Augusta, *Glamorgan* rendezvoused with *Ambuscade*, which had visited Corfu, the group arrived in Port Said, and by the evening of the next day they had cleared the Suez Canal. Before entering the Red Sea there was time for a short visit to the Jordanian port of Aqaba and off Djibouti they exercised with French warships. The next big event took place in the Indian Ocean, when the group met USS *Coral Sea*, *Ingersoll* and other US warships, as well as HM Ships *Diomede* and *Euryalus*, which were being relieved on patrol by *Glamorgan* and *Ambuscade*, for 'Exercise Gonzo'.

Admiral Woodward, in his book *One Hundred Days* describes how, during the exercises which followed, by a clever use of lights and signals *Glamorgan* managed to "sink" the aircraft carrier *Coral Sea*, but the destroyer's luck was to be short-lived. On 24 November, with the exercises over, *Glamorgan* set course for the Bahrain area and next day, whilst en route, she and *Ambuscade* anchored off the small Omani town of Bandar-Jissah for a post-exercise debrief. As the bay had not been surveyed since the mid-nineteenth century Lt-Cdr Ian Inskip, *Glamorgan's* navigating officer, took the precaution of having soundings taken all around the ship; these appeared to indicate that the destroyer was safely anchored over a flat, sandy sea bed. However, unknown to anyone the ship was almost directly over a large uncharted rock and at 1615 when she weighed anchor both propellers hit the rock which, according to the ship's log sent, 'large vibrations through ship' and caused serious damage to both propellers. The ship was quickly anchored again and divers were sent down to survey the damage. It was clear that *Glamorgan* would be unable to move under her own steam, but by 1745 *Ambuscade* had taken her in tow to the nearby port of Muscat where it was hoped temporary repairs could be carried out. In the event a team of clearance divers together with the ship's divers were able to ensure that *Glamorgan* could steam at reduced speed and on the last day of November she weighed anchor and set course for Suez and for home.

Glamorgan had originally been scheduled to remain on the Armilla Patrol until mid-February 1982, with Christmas being spent at Mombasa. Instead she was limping home at 13 knots sounding, as the late Lieutenant David Tinker described it '...very much like a washing machine.' As the destroyer made her way north the initial disappointment at not being able to take Christmas leave in Mombasa was replaced with the prospect of being at home with families over the festive season. On 9 December she passed through the Suez Canal and three days later she refuelled at Augusta. On 16 December she made an overnight stop at Gibraltar and during the forenoon of 21 December she secured alongside *Antrim* at Portsmouth's South Railway Jetty.

Glamorgan remained in dockyard hands for over seven weeks, of which half was spent in dry dock having new propellers fitted. Work was also carried out on the main gearboxes, plummer blocks and A brackets. On 10 February 1982 the ship was back alongside Fountain Lake Jetty and carrying out basin trials, and three days later she left Portsmouth for post-refit trials, during which her main propulsion machinery was put through its paces. Following this she steamed into the North Sea to take part in a major JMC exercise, in foul weather, which also involved *Invincible*, *Brilliant*, *Arethusa*, *Diomede*, *Broadsword*, RFA *Olmeda* and the Norwegian frigate *Trondheim*. The ocean phase took place in very heavy weather west of the Shetland Islands and ended on 26 February when

HMS Glamorgan

Glamorgan arrived back alongside at Leith, from where she steamed across the North Sea to the Belgian port of Antwerp. Following this she returned to Portsmouth to prepare for 'Exercise Springtrain', which was to take place from Gibraltar, with *Glamorgan* flying the flag of the C-in-C Fleet, Admiral Sir John Fieldhouse.

At 0852 on Wednesday 17 March *Glamorgan* left Portsmouth bound for Gibraltar. In all some 23 ships were taking part in the programme of exercises, the first phase of which took place en route. *Glamorgan* arrived in Gibraltar on 24 March and two days later the C-in-C Fleet hoisted his flag. However, while the ship's company were enjoying their runs ashore, events were unfolding in the South Atlantic which would have a major impact on world affairs. The sovereignty dispute between Britain and Argentina over control of the Falkland Islands was not new, but since the early 1970s the Argentines had been stepping up pressure for Britain to cede the islands to them. In 1974 the idea of a condominium, with joint sovereignty, was floated, but with the islanders refusing to take part in the diplomatic talks the idea was dropped. During the latter half of the 1970s there were a number of provocative acts by Argentina and the Argentine press campaigned vigorously for an invasion of the islands. In February 1976 an Argentine warship, the destroyer *Almirante Storni*, when some 80 miles south of the Falkland Islands, fired at the unarmed British Antarctic Research ship *Shackleton*. In response the British government stationed an ice-patrol ship HMS *Endurance* and a frigate in the area and at the same time the Defence Chiefs drew up a revised assessment of what would be required to dislodge and evict a determined Argentine invasion. However, at the same time reports in the press suggested that the British government was actively considering withdrawing *Endurance* from service. In early 1977 it became known that the Argentines had established a military presence in the South Sandwich Islands, but apart from a diplomatic protest Britain took no action. In late 1979 Britain was still searching for

18 March 1982 and *Glamorgan* leaves Portsmouth Harbour for Gibraltar and exercise 'Springtrain'. It would be July before she returned from the South Atlantic. *(James W. Goss)*

an agreement with Argentina and one of the options being discussed was a transfer of sovereignty, with a leaseback by the Falkland Islanders. When they were consulted, however, the islanders rejected the idea and by late 1981 the Argentine government was complaining about the lack of progress and their UN representative made a provocative speech referring to the 'illegal occupation' of the islands. He went on to express his government's hope that they would soon '...be able to report in due course to the General Assembly that this series of negotiations concerning the Malvinas, South Georgia and South Sandwich Islands, which will begin soon, was the last one.' There is no doubt that the British government's decision to withdraw the Royal Navy's last presence in the South Atlantic, HMS *Endurance*, was taken by the Argentine government as a sign of Britain's diminishing interest in its South Atlantic possessions.

Meanwhile, in Argentina, on 22 December 1981 in a military coup, General Leopold Galtieri had taken over from Roberto Viola as the President of Argentina, at the same time as retaining his position as C-in-C of the Army. Galtieri and his military junta were deeply unpopular in the country and beating nationalist drums and making threats to invade the Falkland Islands was a way of ensuring short-term popularity.

In late January 1982, about a month after Galtieri seized power, the Argentine government delivered a communication to the British Ambassador in Buenos Aires stating that the British recognition of Argentine sovereignty over the Falkland Islands remained an essential requirement for any 'solution' to the dispute. With the 150th anniversary of British rule over the Falkland Islands approaching, it was acknowledged that the Argentine government would want the occasion to be marked in some dramatic way, but at the UN in New York political negotiations dragged on. By March 1982, however, it was events on the island of South Georgia which began to overshadow the seemingly endless negotiations, when a hitherto unknown scrap metal dealer from Buenos Aires began to make the news in the British press. In 1978 Constantino Davidoff had been granted a contract to dismantle the disused whaling stations on South Georgia, an island which was virtually unknown to most Britons, and on 11 March 1982 he was transported to South Georgia in the Argentine Navy's transport *Bahia Buen Suceso*. Although Davidoff has vehemently denied it there was evidence that he was being used by the Argentine military to deliberately provoke an incident, for earlier that year the Argentine military had already begun planning for the invasion of the Falkland Islands and South Georgia. The plan provided for an invasion force of some 3,000 troops who would quickly overpower the token force of Royal Marines and then be back on the Argentine mainland within a few days, leaving behind an occupation force of some 500 troops. With the expulsion of the Marines and British government officials, it was also thought that within a week life on the islands would be back to normal. On a much more sinister note, there was also a draft plan to evict the whole population of the islands and replace them with Argentine settlers, and although it was shelved this part of the plan was never abandoned.

Meanwhile, on 16 March, the *Bahia Buen Suceso*, carrying Davidoff and his party, arrived off South Georgia and landed at Stromness Bay. Having failed to obtain landing permits in Buenos Aires, Davidoff and his party were instructed to obtain the necessary documents from the British Antarctic Survey team at Grytviken. However, they failed to do that and three days later the members of the BAS team noted that they had raised the Argentine flag and shots were fired. This was reported by radio to the Governor of the Falkland Islands who ordered that the flag be taken down and permits obtained. On 21 March, having unloaded stores, but having failed to obtain permits, the *Bahia Buen Suceso* sailed. By this time the incident had reached diplomatic level with the British government protesting to the Argentine government and insisting that the ship return to South Georgia and evacuate all of Davidoff's party. Next day, however, with the Argentinians still on South Georgia, HMS *Endurance* left Port Stanley to forcibly remove them and on 24 March a party of 22 Royal Marines was landed at Grytviken. It was at this point that what had been merely a diplomatic incident became a major crisis.

In response to the dispatch of *Endurance* the Argentine Navy sent their warship *Guerrico* to intercept and shadow her and at the same time a second Argentine supply ship, *Bahia Paraiso* arrived at Leith and landed a party of marines. For several days the two parties played a cat and mouse game, but by 28 March the main activity had moved back to the Falkland Islands, when an Argentine invasion fleet sailed from their bases on the mainland for the islands. Five days later the small force of Royal Marines at Port Stanley had been overwhelmed and the Argentine invasion of the islands was complete. From this point onwards the Argentine timetable did not go to plan and it must have quickly dawned on the ruling junta that they had completely misinterpreted the likely British reaction and in fact had made a huge error of judgment.

Meanwhile, at Gibraltar, as Lieutenant Commander Ian Inskip has said, '...we were well aware of the growing crisis', and at 0800 on 29 March, as the Argentine invasion fleet approached the Falkland Islands, the harbour training phase of 'Springtrain' ended and the ships sailed to carry out a variety of high-seas firing exercises in the Eastern Atlantic and Western Mediterranean. As well as *Glamorgan* (flag C-in-C), other ships taking part included *Antrim* (flag FOF1 Rear-Admiral Woodward), *Ariadne*, *Aurora*, *Battleaxe*, *Brilliant*, *Broadsword*, *Coventry*, *Dido*, *Euryalus*, *Galatea*, *Glasgow*, *Lowestoft*, *Plymouth*, *Rhyl*, *Sheffield* and *Yarmouth*, all of which were due to return to their UK base ports during the first and second weeks of April. That same evening, with the exercises barely under way, but with the crisis over the Falkland Islands deepening, Admiral Woodward flew over from *Antrim* and soon afterwards *Glamorgan* was detached to Gibraltar to land both men for urgent consultations with politicians and the Ministry of Defence in Whitehall, after which the destroyer rejoined the exercises.

During the afternoon of 31 March, both *Glamorgan* and *Antrim* carried out Sea Slug firings, but two days later, during the early hours of Friday 2 April, as Argentine warships were landing special forces and marines on the Falkland Islands, *Glamorgan*, *Antrim*, *Brilliant*, *Glasgow*, *Plymouth*, *Arrow*, *Coventry* and *Sheffield*, with RFAs

Not only did the ships of the Task Force have to contend with Argentine air attacks, but also the severe weather conditions in the South Atlantic.
(Cdr Ian Inskip)

County Class GMDs

Appleleaf and *Tidespring* in support, were ordered to sail south for Ascension Island as part of an advance group.

Although the Argentine junta had been sabre rattling for some months, the actual invasion of the Falkland Islands appears to have taken the British government and indeed the country by surprise. A photograph published in the world's media of Royal Marines being made to lie face down on the ground following their surrender caused a deep sense of national outrage and galvanised public opinion in a way which left British politicians with very little room for compromise. But it soon became clear that neither side was in any mood for compromise and instead of reducing troop numbers as had been planned, the junta was rapidly reinforcing its original invasion force, albeit with thousands of barely trained and often reluctant conscripts. Twenty-four hours after the occupation of the Falkland Islands an Argentine military force invaded South Georgia. The small force of defending Royal Marines not only shot down three helicopters, they also damaged the corvette *Guerrico*.

During the passage south, as diplomatic efforts to resolve the crisis continued apace, it never seriously looked as if either side would compromise. In all the newspapers the maps of these little-known islands became larger in scale and suddenly the town of Port Stanley, and even small settlements, became familiar names in almost every household throughout the country. At noon on 4 April Woodward shifted his flag from *Antrim* to

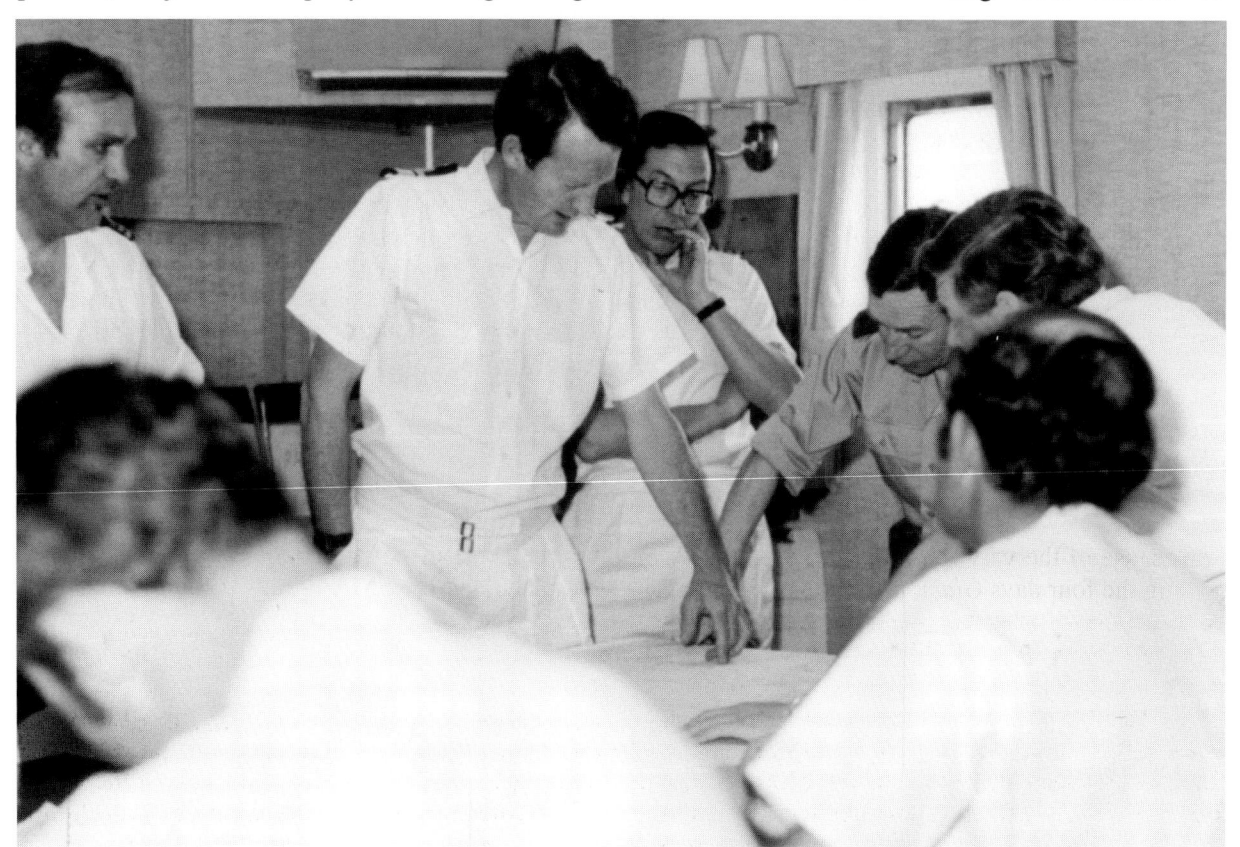

Rear-Admiral J. F. (Sandy) Woodward, the Task Force Commander, with his staff in the Captain's Day Cabin, which had been converted to a Staff Office, on board *Glamorgan*, before the flag transfer to *Antrim*.
(Cdr Ian Inskip)

HMS Glamorgan

Glamorgan, which gave him better communication facilities. As the vessels steamed south the seriousness of the situation became apparent when soft furnishings and much of the ships' plastic laminate Formica panelling was stripped out in order to minimise the danger from fire and deadly splinters.

On 3 April, the day after the invasion, the British government announced that a Task Force would be dispatched to retake the islands and two days later, amid great publicity, the first ships led by *Hermes* sailed from Portsmouth. By 6 April the mission to liberate the islands had been given the code name 'Operation Corporate' and it was on this day that the name and the ship's immediate destination, Ascension Island, first appears in *Glamorgan's* logs. Next day the British government declared a 200-mile exclusion zone around the Falkland Islands which, from 12 April, meant that any Argentine ships or aircraft within the zone could be sunk or shot down. On 12 April *Antrim*, *Plymouth* and *Tidespring* were detached to retake the island of South Georgia and despite the best efforts of the US Secretary of State, Alexander Haig, it was becoming increasingly clear that diplomatic efforts to find a solution were getting nowhere and military action was looking increasingly likely. *Glamorgan* arrived off Ascension Island on 11 April and although the island is over 3,000 miles from the Falkland Islands, it was to prove vital as a forward mounting base for the replenishment of ships and its airfield, Wideawake, would also prove invaluable for land-based aircraft operating in support of the fleet.

Because of the very real threat from submarines, during the four days *Glamorgan* was off Ascension, she remained under way, with stores and ammunition being transferred by helicopter. During the afternoon of 15 April *Glamorgan* rendezvoused with the newly arrived *Hermes*, the next day they were joined by *Invincible* and as they slowly made their way south they exercised together. During this period they were shadowed by an Argentine military Boeing 747, but with diplomatic efforts to settle the crisis still under way the rules of engagement did not allow it to be shot down and Harriers from *Hermes* had to escort the aircraft away. By 26 April South Georgia had been recaptured and by the end of the month, with the weather having deteriorated, the ships were at the edge of the Total Exclusion Zone (TEZ).

Glamorgan's long passage south with the rest of the Task Force had been no pleasure cruise, as the ship's company battled the elements and also got themselves and the weapons systems to combat readiness. At the outset, when they had been diverted from the 'Springtrain' exercises, few believed that they would actually go to war, but at the end of April, with diplomatic efforts to reach any agreement having failed and with the Argentine junta frantically attempting to reinforce and entrench their positions in the Falkland Islands, it became increasingly clear that the shooting war was about to begin in earnest, after which there would be no room for compromise. 1 May began with a lone bombing attack by an RAF Vulcan bomber, which delivered 21 1,000lb bombs onto Stanley airfield. Although it did not cause a great deal of damage, the raid sent a powerful message to the junta in Buenos Aires. *Glamorgan* also went into action that day when, after entering the TEZ in the forenoon and refuelling from RFA *Olmeda*, she was detached with *Alacrity* and *Arrow* to carry out a bombardment of Argentine military targets around Stanley.

As she steamed in towards the coast and left the carrier group to the eastward, smoke could be seen rising from the area around the airfield, which was the result of the Vulcan raid and a raid by Sea Harriers from *Hermes*. *Glamorgan* herself came within range of Argentine aircraft flying from the mainland and the FMA Pucara anti-insurgency aircraft, which were now based at airstrips on the Falkland Islands and which could pack a powerful punch in the form of two 500lb bombs, or one 1,000lb bomb. At just after 1500, when the Falkland Islands were sighted, *Glamorgan* went to Action Stations and at 1830 her log entry records: 'Proceeding towards gun line with *Arrow* and *Alacrity*.' By 1925 the three ships were within 18,000 yards of Stanley airfield and for the next 15 minutes they fired 50 salvoes each, after which they

Looking aft onto *Glamorgan's* flight deck during a severe Atlantic storm, showing damage to the ship's Wessex helicopter. *(Cdr Ian Inskip)*

headed seaward. During the bombardment there had been some counter-fire by Argentine artillery units and the patrol boat *Islas Malvinas* (later captured and renamed HMS *Tiger Bay*), but the latter was driven off by *Alacrity's* Lynx helicopter. As the ships headed back out to sea they came under attack by four Mirage Dagger jets, one of which loosed rockets and bombs at *Glamorgan*; all of them missed, but falling close to the stern the force of the explosions was felt throughout the ship. *Arrow*, however, had been hit by cannon fire which had left one man wounded. Lieutenant Commander Ian Inskip later met one of the Argentine pilots and he recalls the attack: 'Captain Dimeglio attempted to strafe us, but in order to release his bombs he had to stop firing and the shell splashes stopped short of our quarterdeck. We had been turning "very hard left" on the orders of the Principal Warfare Officer (PWO), but as that would take us into the minefield I countermanded the order to "Starboard 35". The sudden alteration of course probably upset the pilot's aim. However, two parachute retard, 1,000lb bombs, were released and they dropped into the sea on either side of the quarterdeck. The stern was lifted 17ft (the contents of the tiller flat watchkeeper's stomach only 15ft) and we were all well and truly shaken up'. Later, during the passage home, Ian took the opportunity to dive on both shafts and he found: '...the hull plating dished, the fairing plating to both A-brackets had been blown off, together with the port ropeguard assembly. There were also a few shrapnel holes in the rudders. Internally, the pillar in the tiller flat was bent and a shaft bearing housing was cracked'.

Just over five hours later, at 0100 on 2 May, *Glamorgan* and *Arrow* were back inshore and carrying out another bombardment, this time at Argentine troop concentrations. At 0137, as the destroyer opened to seaward, she was illuminated by starshell and onshore artillery opened ineffective fire, but by the forenoon she was back with the carrier group and replenishing from RFA *Resource*. Later that day the submarine *Conqueror* torpedoed and sank the elderly Argentine cruiser *General Belgrano* which, operating in conjunction with the aircraft carrier *Veinticinco de Mayo*, had approached to a position where it posed a very real and dangerous threat to the ships of the Task Force.

Much was later made of the fact that the cruiser was steaming away from the Task Force's position at the time of the sinking, but in fact it was irrelevant for a ship's course can be altered in an instant and, under cover of darkness, it would have been possible to escape detection as *Glamorgan* herself had done only a few months before when exercising with USS *Coral Sea*. That evening *Glamorgan's* third shore bombardment operation was cancelled.

With the sinking of *General Belgrano* and the subsequent heavy loss of life, the reality of war took on a new dimension, no longer could it be passed off as just a diplomatic crisis and the time for compromise was over. On 4 May came a shattering blow for the Royal Navy when, at 1420, the destroyer *Sheffield* was hit amidships by an air-

HMS *Glamorgan* bombards Argentine positions on Pebble Island during the morning of 15 May, during the SAS raid on the airfield. *(Cdr Ian Inskip)*

launched Exocet missile, killing 18 of her complement and causing severe damage which resulted in the ship being abandoned. When *Sheffield* was hit *Glamorgan* was some 12 miles away and during the afternoon smoke could be seen billowing from the stricken ship.

The first land action in the campaign to retake the Falklands came during the night of 14/15 May, with an SAS operation to raid the Argentine airfield on Pebble Island off the north shore of West Falkland. The operation was to have taken place the previous day, but it had been delayed and *Glamorgan* steamed though severe gales and heavy seas to a position some 10 to 15 miles away from Pebble Island, which she reached in the early hours of 15 May. Some hours beforehand helicopters from *Hermes* had landed an SAS detachment, whose aim was to destroy as many Pucara and T-34 Mentor aircraft which were based on the airstrip as possible. With the main British landings scheduled to take place on 21 May in the San Carlos area, the aircraft posed a threat to the success of the landings. In the event the SAS managed to lay explosive charges under each of the aircraft without being detected and once they had completed the task the raiding party opened fire on the aircraft with small arms and light anti-tank weapons, which was the cue for *Glamorgan* to provide naval gunfire support.

Glamorgan had been in her bombardment position since 0700 and soon afterwards she fired the first of 20 salvoes which, according to both British and Argentine accounts was accurate and devastating. One Argentine version indicates that their marines remained in their shelters during the bombardment, which ended at 0749 when *Glamorgan* left the area to steam through the heavy seas to rejoin the carrier battle group at just after midday. Altogether 11 aircraft were destroyed, with two of the SAS detachment being wounded, but all were safely evacuated back to *Hermes*.

During the early hours of 17 May *Glamorgan* carried out a bombardment of Argentine troop positions round Stanley, during which she fired 142 rounds, before rejoining the carrier group at 0910. These nightly bombardments of enemy troop positions became a regular feature of *Glamorgan's* routine, generating constant stress for the whole ship's company, but it has since been acknowledged that the ship played a vital role leading to the success of the campaign.

Friday 21 May was the date chosen for the main British landings at San Carlos Water on East Falkland. This was the most critical phase of the whole operation and any serious setbacks could have jeopardised the whole undertaking. During the evening of 20 May, moving at a speed of 11 knots and shrouded by thick fog, 11 ships of the amphibious force steamed slowly towards East Falkland. At around 1800 that evening the force reached the point at which there could be no turning back. Meanwhile, that same evening *Glamorgan*, still with the carrier battle group, replenished from RFAs *Tidepool* and *Regent* before detaching at just after 2000 to carry out a bombardment of the hills around Stanley in order to create a diversion and make it appear that the landings would be on the eastward and not the western shores of East Falkland. After approaching the coast and closing up to Action Stations at 0130, *Glamorgan* remained close to the shore for over two hours firing her main armament at Argentine positions and generally making a great deal of noise, keeping this up continuously until 0350, when she left to rejoin the carrier battle group and, as her log records: 'Proceed to Circle 4 *Hermes*.' Meanwhile, in San Carlos Water the main troop landings were under way. The first and most vital phase began with 40 Commando RM going ashore by landing craft, securing San Carlos Settlement and establishing defensive positions on the slopes of the coastal hills. Supporting bombardments were provided for the assaulting battalions by *Antrim*, *Ardent*, *Plymouth* and *Yarmouth*. Subsequent phases saw artillery being landed, together with more assault battalions. When daylight came *Glamorgan* was on picket duty with the carrier group and providing anti-aircraft and anti-submarine protection for *Hermes*, which was within range of Argentine Super Entendard aircraft and their Exocet missiles.

For a time during 22 May it seemed that

HMS Glamorgan

Glamorgan would relieve the damaged *Antrim* in San Carlos Water, but in the event the newly joined *Exeter* took on that duty. The landings at San Carlos saw the start of what was effectively an intensive three-day air battle, during which *Ardent*, *Antelope*, *Coventry* and *Atlantic Conveyor* were lost and a number of ships were damaged, including *Antrim*, but not one soldier was prevented from landing. To this day it remains a mystery as to how the great white liner *Canberra* came through unscathed.

During this period *Glamorgan* remained with the carrier group, but at 2050 on 25 May she was detached to carry out a bombardment of Stanley Airfield and some six hours later she arrived off the coast. At 0350 the destroyer fired the first ever Sea Slug missile at a shore target which Ian Inskip describes as exploding on the airfield in a huge fireball. The Sea Slug was quickly followed by 150, 4.5-inch shells at targets all round the airfield in order to disrupt any Argentine aircraft which might have landed there to refuel. Although there was some counter-battery fire from the Argentine artillery ashore, this caused no problems for *Glamorgan* and at 0415 the ship's log records: 'Clearing area to east. Fired on from astern.' Some 15 minutes later the ship was stood down from Action Stations and at 0940 she rejoined the carrier group.

Thursday 27 May was spent replenishing from RFAs *Olmeda* and *Regent* and in the early hours of Friday 28 May, *Glamorgan*, together with *Alacrity* and *Avenger*, closed the shore off Stanley in order to bombard troop concentrations in the area. The bombardment began at 0230 with the firing of a Sea Slug missile by *Glamorgan*, followed by salvoes from her 4.5-inch guns. At 0310 a second Sea Slug

HMS *Glamorgan* fires a Sea Slug missile. *(Cdr Ian Inskip)*

missile was fired in the direction of the Moody Brook area outside Stanley, which landed on target and damaged a number of Argentine aircraft. At 0350, with her own bombardment completed, *Glamorgan* supported the two frigates and when *Alacrity* came under fire from shore batteries the destroyer silenced them with her own gunfire. Two rounds of the enemy battery fire landed close to the destroyer, but by 0500 they were clearing the area. It is interesting to note that Ian Inskip points out in his book *Ordeal by Exocet*, that a highly skilled Argentine engineer officer, Captain Julio Perez, had by this time created a system for the launching of Exocet missiles from an improvised land-based launcher which had been set up in the Stanley area and in fact as *Glamorgan* set course to leave the area an unsuccessful attempt was made to fire one of the missiles.

Next day came the news that the settlements of Darwin and Goose Green had been captured and during the evening *Glamorgan*, in company with *Ambuscade*, once again closed the shore to bombard Stanley Airfield and any aircraft which were parked in the area. Once again the ships came under fire from artillery batteries ashore and as Ian Inskip recounts, it was heavy and accurate fire and at one stage the howitzer shells landed within 200 yards of the ship. Once again, however, the bombardment was successful and at 0730 the two ships withdrew to seaward and, in atrocious weather conditions, rejoined the carrier group. Soon after this *Glamorgan* was ordered eastward to a more secure area designated the 'Tug and Repair Area' (TARA) for some much needed maintenance, but just as she was leaving the main group an Argentine Super Entendard, escorted by Skyhawks, attacked the force with the last remaining air-launched Exocet missile. Although the attack failed, the smoke trail from the missile could be clearly seen and only prompt and efficient action by *Glamorgan* prevented it from locking onto the destroyer as its target.

During the 11 days spent in the relative safety of the repair area everyone was kept busy carrying out the essential repairs and maintenance, which included boiler cleaning, a difficult enough task when alongside in port, but in the stormy South Atlantic Ocean while still under way it was doubly challenging. However, despite the adverse conditions, the fact that the ship was away from the immediate danger zones allowed for a certain amount of relaxation from the continuous stresses of the previous four weeks. While *Glamorgan* was carrying out maintenance, the Army ashore was making steady progress towards Stanley, and although there were setbacks such as the disaster at Fitzroy when the landing ships *Sir Galahad* and *Sir Tristram* were bombed with heavy loss of life, there was no stopping the advance and by 10 June the main Argentine positions in and around Stanley were surrounded. The land to the west of them was occupied by two British brigades and the sea to the south, east and north was dominated by the Royal Navy. The scene was set for the final battles for Mount Longdon, Mount Harriet and Two Sisters, without which the Argentine position would be untenable. The plan was for a two-pronged attack on the mountains and *Glamorgan* was detailed to support 45 Commando RM, who were to take Two Sisters. The attack was scheduled to begin during the early hours of Saturday 12 June.

Thursday 10 June was *Glamorgan's* last full day in the maintenance area and at 1500 on the next day, after refuelling from *Tidepool*, she rejoined the carrier group and took station on *Hermes*. Two hours later, in company with *Yarmouth*, she detached from the main body to make a six-hour passage to the gun line south of Stanley and at just after 2300 the ship went to Action Stations. *Glamorgan's* log shows that she was on station and 20 minutes later *Yarmouth* arrived and was stationed a mile south of *Glamorgan*, with *Avenger* two miles east. The two frigates would be firing in support of troops assaulting Mount Longdon and Mount Harriet and the bombardment was opened at 0120. Some 27 minutes later *Glamorgan* began her bombardment and Captain Barrow recalled: 'We responded to calls throughout the night, detailed gunnery, relying very heavily on our navigation, firing rounds at ranges of six to seven miles, hoping not to hit our own troops. I'm glad to say we didn't, but I have to say we were firing as little as 200 metres from our own troops. There was a lot of kelp around, and a 155mm howitzer fired at us, rather ineffectively. As a result of the help we were able to give them, 45 Commando did take that mountain, but we had to stay rather longer than we should.'

Glamorgan's bombardment lasted throughout the night and at 0400 the ship's log records: 'Troops on the move. Fire unnecessary.' At 0515 it recorded: 'Troops in sight of final objective'; at 0600: 'Final target being engaged'; at 0617: 'Mission complete. Withdrawing to CVBG.' As Ian Inskip records, *Glamorgan* was supposed to be back with the carrier group by dawn and in the event daylight was fast approaching. Captain Barrow recalled: 'We knew that on the way back we had to skirt around a minefield and we also knew that there was probably a shore-based Exocet, removed from a destroyer in the Buenos Aires area, flown to the Falklands by Hercules and installed on some sort of wagon. We believed this to be in the vicinity of Pembroke Point, and so we had a large red circle drawn on our chart representing the extreme range of this missile.' As *Glamorgan* steamed away from the gun line her gas turbines were connected and she was quickly working up to 25 knots. Ian Inskip takes up the story: 'As we raced away from the gun line I kept my eyes glued to the bridge 999 display. I paid special attention to the direction of Cape Pembroke where intelligence had indicated an Exocet might be located. When nearly 18 miles from Cape Pembroke Point, although still in the charted danger zone, I made my planned alteration to port to start making ground towards the carriers whilst still retiring speedily towards the edge of the danger zone. I reasoned that, first, we were now hull down from the coastline south of Port Harriet. Our radar horizon was 11 miles and we were losing Cape Pembroke on radar, hence a radar on Cape Pembroke would be losing us. Secondly, if we were to be targeted from Cape Pembroke they would have already fired.'

However, with all the intelligence reports indicating that the Argentine missile was situated at Cape Pembroke, Ian Inskip could only base his calculations on that information. Captain Barrow again: 'It was, therefore, with some alarm that shortly after 0630, whilst proceeding at 24 knots towards the carrier, skirting around the edge of the red ring, my operations officer noted what looked like yet another round from a 155mm howitzer coming in my direction. We'd been seeing these on the radar, so it was no surprise, but at the same moment the officer of the watch, my navigating officer Commander Ian Inskip, noticed a flare coming from the same direction. A 155mm round doesn't have a flare, so it was quite obvious this was something else, and that in the next ten seconds, which was the time of this missile, we would have to do something about it. The navigating officer, of his own volition and quite correctly, turned the ship away from the oncoming Exocet missile, as there was no doubt that was what it was. This was the correct tactic for an approaching Exocet, which at that stage is searching with its radar head for a returning echo.'

At 0637 the entry in *Glamorgan's* log reads: 'Missile hit aft port side (Exocet). Large fire in hangar/galley.' Ian Inskip describes his experience as the missile hit the ship: 'On the bridge we heard a seemingly unremarkable thud, followed almost immediately by a "whooomph" as the fuelled helicopter in the hangar erupted into flame.' Ian goes on to say: 'To those closer to the explosion, it sounded equally as loud as a stun grenade and had a similar effect. People in the "Rhondda Valley" (the main passageway running the length of the ship) some 150ft away from the explosion were blown off their feet. I did not see the flash, having my head buried in the display hood. I looked up as the bridge echoed to alarm bells. Night turned into day as 100ft flames towered above masthead height.'

The missile had hit *Glamorgan* on the port side abaft the after funnel and detonated in the vicinity of the hangar, blasting a 10ft x 5ft hole in the hangar deck. The fully fuelled helicopter in the hangar exploded and a major fire developed there. The galley area on the deck below was devastated, with shattered Formica fragments flying through the air and causing horrific injuries. Thirteen members of *Glamorgan's* company were killed by the blast and

The damage to *Glamorgan's* hangar, caused by the Exocet missile which hit the ship in the closing stages of the Falklands War. It was only the fast reactions of the ship's Navigating Officer and the dedicated hard work of the ship's company that saved her. *(Author's Collection)*

one man later died of his injuries. Seventeen men suffered serious injuries, but the ship was still able to steam at reduced speed while all effort was put into fighting the fires and saving the ship. With the Sea Slug magazine flooded and with generators damaged, half the ship's power was lost and as the firefighters began boundary cooling of the hangar, increasing volumes of water from the hoses and from fractured firemain pipes began to affect the ship's stability as she took on a list of 12 degrees to port. By 0720 the hangar fire had been contained and free surface water in the main galley below had been restricted by the construction of a dwarf bulkhead and controlled by portable pumps. Counterflooding improved the ship's stability and by 0800 the list had been reduced to 4 degrees. It was 1025 before all the fires were extinguished and priority could be given to recovering bodies from the devastated area around the hangar and evacuating the wounded. All afternoon helicopters flew back and forth between *Glamorgan*, *Hermes* and *Invincible*, as wounded men were transferred to the two carriers and the ship herself, the first to survive an Exocet attack, was able to make her way back to the vicinity of the carrier group.

That evening, between 1915 and 1935, in a position 51°50.5'S 53°31.8'W, the funeral service was held for the 13 members of *Glamorgan's* company who had lost their lives. Ian Inskip describes the moving ceremony: 'As the sun set a short service was held on the flight deck. After the Last Post had been played on a bugle by a young Marine

Engineering Mechanic (E), who had only learned it that day, the bodies were slipped over the side from the quarterdeck. It was absolutely still apart from splash ...splash ...splash ...splash of our comrades. It seemed to go on and on and tears filled my eyes. Although my head was bowed I could see other men crying. It was a sad and most moving moment and it was not an easy task for Martin Culverwell (the Padre), but he performed the committal ceremony very well. It was a service which none of us would forget.'

Glamorgan had been escorted back to the carrier group by *Avenger* and *Yarmouth*, and at just before midnight the first repair parties were transferred by seaboat from the oilfield support ship *Stena Seaspread*, which had been taken up from trade and chartered by the MoD as a repair ship. The work of clearing the debris from the hangar and galley areas began almost immediately, with the repair ship providing the catering facilities. For four days, whenever weather conditions permitted, *Glamorgan* went alongside *Stena Seaspread* and gradually order was restored to the damaged areas. On 14 June, with all the high ground overlooking Stanley in British hands and the streets of the town crammed with demoralised Argentine troops, the end was in sight and later in the day came news of a ceasefire. In the early hours of the next morning the Argentine surrender was confirmed. Three days later, at 1530 on Friday 18 June, *Glamorgan* anchored in San Carlos Water where *Stena Seaspread* was able to secure alongside to resume the repairs in much calmer conditions. Next evening, having been ordered to return home,

A close-up of the Exocet damage, showing the hole made by the missile as it punched its way through the hangar deck. *(Author's Collection)*

County Class GMDs

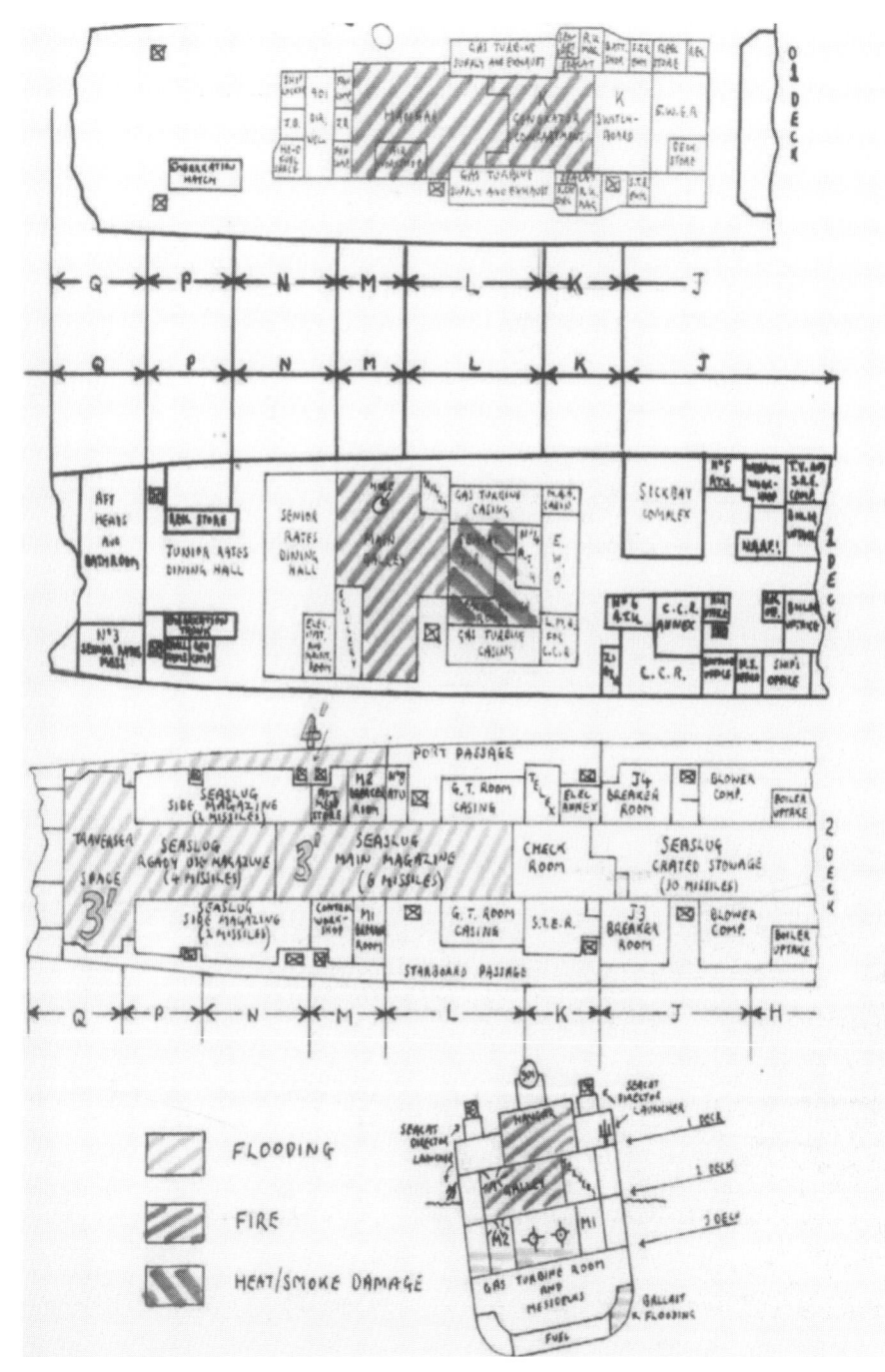

HMS *Glamorgan's* damage control state board at 0705 on 12 June, some 30 minutes after the Exocet hit, showing areas of fire, heat/smoke damage and flooding. It also shows the ship's list to port. *(Cdr Ian Inskip)*

An RAF Chinook helicopter removes Wessex helicopter, XT 486, from *Glamorgan's* flight deck at San Carlos Water after the Argentine surrender. The Wessex had been temporarily transferred to *Glamorgan* from RFA *Tidepool* as a replacement for its own Wessex, XM 837 (Willie) which had been destroyed in the Exocet attack.

(Cdr Ian Inskip)

County Class GMDs

Surrounded by a flotilla of small boats *Glamorgan* arrives home to Portsmouth after her war service in the South Atlantic. *(James W. Goss)*

Glamorgan weighed anchor to steam round to Berkeley Sound and Port William to prepare for her passage to Portsmouth. That afternoon, while at anchor, the Argentine hospital ship *Almirante Irizar* passed by on its way to Stanley in order to embark wounded soldiers for repatriation. As Ian Inskip records: 'She passed closed to our port side, cameras trained on our battle scarred hangar.' That same evening, at 2249, *Glamorgan* weighed anchor to return to the carrier group before beginning her passage home.

During the forenoon of 21 June, having transferred stores and embarked a handful of passengers, *Glamorgan* steamed past *Hermes* and fired a 13-gun salute to FOF1, then in company with HMS *Plymouth*, which had also suffered battle damage, she set course north. The passage home took them through the waters of the South Atlantic where, with winter setting in, ice and stormy weather was becoming a hazard, but by 29 June she had reached Ascension Island, where she went alongside MV *Alvega* to refuel. Later that afternoon the passage north was resumed and the next day she crossed the equator for the fifth time, with the crossing the line ceremony being held during the afternoon of 1 July. Nine days later, as she steamed up Channel, C-in-C Fleet joined the ship by helicopter and hoisted his flag on board. Finally, at 0800 on Saturday 10 July *Glamorgan* anchored at Spithead. Just over two hours later she weighed anchor and, escorted by a flotilla of small boats, made her way up harbour, past crowds of cheering people lining Southsea Seafront, the Round Tower and the harbour area. At 1058 *Glamorgan* was alongside the North West Wall where families were waiting to board the ship and at 1102 Ian Inskip rang off 'Finished with main engines'. *Glamorgan* was home, but the triumphal return was tempered by the fact that 14 members of her company had been lost.

Glamorgan's return to Portsmouth meant a long period in dockyard hands, during which time the ship would undergo major repairs to her battle dam-

HMS Glamorgan

HMS *Glamorgan* is seen here alongside Portsmouth dockyard's South West Wall soon after her return from the South Atlantic. This photograph, taken on 10 July, clearly shows the smoke-blackened and badly damaged hangar.
(James W. Goss)

age and at the end of July she was shifted to No 14 dry dock, where she remained for the rest of the year. On 2 November 1982 there was a change of command when Captain Christopher P. O. Burne CBE RN took over from Captain Barrow. During the Falklands campaign Burne had been appointed as the Senior Naval Officer of Naval Party 1710 on board the P&O liner *Canberra*, a largely unsung role of imposing naval discipline on the 400-strong civilian crew, a task which he carried out well, par-

This image shows the deck which was patched in the South Atlantic and the missing Sea Cat missile launcher and hangar door. Note the hangar roof has been forced upwards by the explosion caused at the time of the missile impact.
(T. Ferrers-Walker)

HMS *Glamorgan* in No14 dry dock at Portsmouth undergoing repairs to the battle damage sustained in the South Atlantic.
(Above: James W. Goss; Below: T. Ferrers-Walker)

ticularly when the liner was anchored in San Carlos Water and being subjected to air attacks, when his commentaries over the public address system did much to keep up morale. In 1978 he had been the first commanding officer of the ill-fated destroyer *Coventry*.

It was mid-January 1983 before *Glamorgan* was afloat again and during the forenoon of 23 January a rededication service was held. It was, however, 12 April before the rebuilt hangar and galley, and all other repairs had been completed. She had also been fitted with four twin 30mm and two single 20mm, close-range anti-aircraft guns. That same afternoon *Glamorgan* sailed to begin three months of trials and work-up exercises. Most of this period was spent in the Channel, from Portland and Portsmouth and it was a period of intense activity with little time for relaxation, although in late May there was a short two-day break at Le Havre. By mid-July, having completed her final Sea Week in company with *Antrim*, *Nottingham*, *Manchester* and *Warspite*, she steamed north to take part in a JMC exercise off the Orkneys and Shetlands, with a weekend break at Rosyth, before returning south to the Aberporth missile ranges, where she carried out 4.5-inch gunnery and Exocet firing. At the end of July, with the main exercise periods over, *Glamorgan* secured alongside the King's Dock, Swansea, for a six-day visit. During this break, in one four-hour spell when she was open to visitors, almost 5,000 people turned out to look over the ship. After leaving Swansea *Glamorgan* joined *Euryalus* for the passage to Portsmouth where, after a Families Day at sea, she secured alongside Fountain Lake Jetty to give leave and undergo maintenance.

On 19 September, when *Glamorgan* put to sea again, course was set south to Gibraltar where, until early October, she acted as guardship. During the passage home she exercised with French warships, shadowed a northbound group of Soviet warships and after rendezvousing with the P&O liner *Canberra*, which had been refitted and returned to cruising service for her owners, she carried out a high-speed steam past, much to the delight of *Canberra's* passengers. On 13 October she returned to Portsmouth to prepare for a deployment which would take her east of Suez.

Glamorgan left Portsmouth on Monday 14 November 1983, in company with the frigate *Brazen*, bound for the Persian Gulf where they were to be deployed on the Armilla Patrol. However, on 18 November while at Gibraltar, they were ordered to sail for the Eastern Mediterranean to an area some 30 miles off the city of Beirut. The two ships were to provide support for the British contingent of a multi-national peace-keeping force (USA, Britain and France) which was attempting to keep warring factions apart as civil war raged in Lebanon, with the added complication of preventing attacks on Lebanese forces by Israelis. During the five days the two ships spent patrolling off the coast working parties were employed ashore assisting the Army to make their barrack buildings secure from sniper fire and rockets. In addition the ships provided rest and recreation facilities to members of the Queen's Dragoon Guards. On 28 November, however, they were relieved by *Fearless* and, in company with RFA *Blue Rover*, they continued their passage to Suez and the Red Sea, arriving off Oman on 5 December.

After a week on patrol the three ships sailed south to the fresher waters of the Indian Ocean and the port of Mombasa, where they spent Christmas and New Year, before returning to the Persian Gulf. On 3 February, for just three days, *Glamorgan* hoisted the flag of the C-in-C Fleet, Admiral Sir William Staveley, for visits to Bahrain and Muscat, after which both *Glamorgan* and *Brazen* left for a break from the Persian Gulf to visit Colombo, Sri Lanka. *Glamorgan* also visited the Indian port of Cochin (Kochi) at the southern end of India's west coast, an unusual port of call for Royal Navy ships. In March, between exercises with a powerful group of US Navy warships led by USS *Ranger* and *Midway*, both *Glamorgan* and *Brazen* visited Karachi, but on 24 March the two ships left the Persian Gulf and steamed into the Gulf of Aden, where they exercised with *Rothesay* and *Aurora*, both of which were homeward-bound from a seven-month 'Orient

County Class GMDs

On 17 July 1986 *Glamorgan* paid a farewell visit to Swansea. Here she is being manoeuvred through the lock into the Prince of Wales dock. *(Syd Goodman Collection)*

Express' deployment. The whole group also exercised with the French Navy's Indian Ocean contingent off Djibouti, but on 1 April they anchored off Suez and next day made their northern transit of the Suez Canal. During her passage through the Mediterranean *Glamorgan* visited Rhodes and also made a brief call at Gibraltar. On 14 April 1984, having left Gibraltar the previous day, *Glamorgan's* final Sea Slug firings took place, when she launched her remaining 11 missiles as targets for *Exeter's* Sea Dart. In the event only seven of the missiles made successful flights, but to date there is no record as to whether any of them were engaged by *Exeter*. Next day her remaining 14 missiles were jettisoned into the sea, which marked the end of Sea Slug as a Royal Navy weapon. *Glamorgan* arrived at Spithead during the early evening of 17 April. Next forenoon she steamed up harbour to secure alongside Fountain Lake Jetty.

In mid-June 1984, flying the flag of FOF2, *Glamorgan* left Portsmouth, where she was joined by *Apollo* and *Brazen* to steam north for exercises in Arctic waters, which included a brief visit to Hanningsvag, the northernmost city on the Norwegian mainland which, in June, has virtually 24 hours of daylight. There were also visits to Tromso, where a team from the destroyer made a two-day climb of Mount Jekkevarre, the highest mountain in Arctic Norway, and the Danish port of Arhus. *Glamorgan* then returned to Portsmouth where, after a Families Day, she began a seven-week docking and maintenance period. It was during this break, on 21 August, that there was a change of command when Captain Rodney P. Warwick RN took over from Burne.

On 30 August, after taking part in Navy Days and carrying out post-refit trials, *Glamorgan* sailed from Portsmouth to call briefly at Dover, where she embarked Army personnel from the Welsh Guards, who were to form an honour guard for the ship's next visit to the Belgian port of Antwerp on the Scheldt River. The visit had been organised as part of the British contribution to the commemoration of the 40th anniversary of the liberation of Brussels in early September 1944. As the Welsh Guards were the first Allied troops to enter the city on 3 September that year, the regiment had been chosen to take part in a military parade in the city's Grand Place, which was attended by the Belgian Prime Minister and Britain's Minister of Defence. *Glamorgan's* visit to Antwerp lasted for seven days, after which she returned, via Dover where she disembarked the Welsh Guards, to Portsmouth.

During September and October *Glamorgan* remained close to the south coast, operating with a number of ships, including *Plymouth*, *Battleaxe* and the German frigates *Rheinland* and *Bremen*. During mid-October 1984 severe gales swept across Britain causing widespread damage and disruption, and at Portland, during the afternoon of 17 October

A late image of *Glamorgan*. Note the Land Rover and container on the flight deck and the 40mm Bofors abreast the after-funnel in place of the GWS 22 directors for the discarded Sea Cat missile system.
(Crown Copyright/MoD)

County Class GMDs

Glamorgan, Avenger and FGS *Bremen* returned to harbour early after exercising in the Channel. At 2330, as a Force 10 gale swept across Portland Harbour, *Bremen* began dragging her anchor. Ten minutes later the German ship started drifting onto *Glamorgan* and although she attempted to take avoiding action, *Bremen's* port screw fouled the destroyer's anchor cable and the two ships collided, with the frigate scraping along *Glamorgan's* port bow, causing damage to both the hull and guard rails. Both vessels then began to drift towards the north-east breakwater and it took almost an hour to cut *Glamorgan's* anchor cable and free her before she reached it. Fortunately, by that time tugs had arrived on the scene and they towed *Bremen* into the middle of the harbour, while *Glamorgan* and *Avenger* put to sea to ride out the storm. In the event the damage to *Glamorgan* was not serious and on 19 October she put into Portsmouth, where the dockyard soon had her ready for sea again. The end of October saw *Glamorgan* off Aberporth carrying out Exocet firings and from there she steamed north to Rosyth to join *Illustrious, Falmouth* and RFA *Fort Grange* for a JMC exercise in northern waters. By the last week of November *Glamorgan* had returned to Portsmouth to give leave and undergo maintenance.

After the Falklands War in 1982, both *Glamorgan* and *Fife*, instead of being placed on the disposals list, had been retained for what at the time was described as a 'prolonged period'. But not only did their age and outdated Sea Slug missile systems weigh heavily against them remaining with the fleet for any prolonged period, compared to the newer Type 42 destroyers they were manpower intensive and by the end of 1984 there were rumours of *Glamorgan's* impending demise. However, she was to have another full year of service and in early 1985 she joined *Invincible, Fearless, Fife, Newcastle, Jupiter* and *Yarmouth*, together with RFAs *Olwen, Fort Grange, Sir Bedivere* and *Sir Caradoc*, in northern waters for a NATO exercise which ranged from the Channel to the North Sea and the approaches to the Baltic Sea. Also involved were naval ships from the Netherlands and Norway and the exercises ended with the landing of 42 Commando RM on the Norwegian coast. After the manoeuvres *Fife* and *Glamorgan*, the last two County-class destroyers on active service, got together for a joint visit to Amsterdam. For *Glamorgan* this was followed by a visit to the Pool of London where she hosted a high-profile dinner to mark the retirement of the First Sea Lord, Admiral Sir John Fieldhouse. Before giving leave at Portsmouth she joined *Invincible* at sea for a joint Families Day off the Isle of Wight, the highlight of which was a flying display by Sea Harriers of 801 Squadron and Sea Kings of 820 Squadron.

Glamorgan's last major deployment came in early 1986, when she joined *Intrepid* with the Dartmouth Training Squadron at Rosyth to embark classes of apprentices and at Dartmouth where midshipmen joined the two ships, for a nine-week deployment to the Caribbean. Together with RFA *Plumleaf* they steamed via Ponta Delgada, first to Virgin Gorda then Bridgetown, Barbados, where they exercised with the Barbados Defence Forces, before proceeding to San Juan, Puerto Rico, and a very popular maintenance period at Mayport, Florida. The ships then recrossed the Atlantic for home. By mid-June *Glamorgan* was back at Portsmouth where, on the 21st of the month, there was a final change of command when Captain Hugh Peltor RN took over from Warwick. *Glamorgan* then went on to spend five days paying farewell visits to her 'parent' counties of Mid, West and South Glamorgan, when she visited Swansea. Among the formal farewells was a remembrance service in St Mary's Church, Swansea, which was attended by Captain Michael Barrow, where the 14 members of her ship's company who had been lost in the Falklands campaign were remembered. A memorial plaque which had been placed in *Glamorgan's* main passageway, the 'Rhondda Valley', was presented to the church, where it still occupies a place of honour. Captain Peltor also visited civic representatives in each of the three Glamorgan counties and presented framed photographs of the ship. There was a full programme of sporting activities and with her last goodbyes said

HMS Glamorgan

In service with the Chilean Navy as *Almirante Lattore*. Like *Prat*, she retained her Sea Slug system.
(Armada de Chile)

Glamorgan steamed north to Leith in time for the Commonwealth Games. In August she undertook her final duty as guardship for Cowes Week, before returning to Portsmouth where she was paid off.

In September 1986 *Glamorgan* was purchased by the Chilean government and on 3 October she was transferred to the Chilean Navy. On her arrival at the Talcahuano Naval Base she was renamed *Almirante Latorre*, but she was known as *Latorre*. Like *Prat* she retained her Sea Slug missile system and her original appearance remained basically unchanged. She operated both SA 319B Aerospatiale Alouette or Bell 206B helicopters and retained her flagship accommodation and facilities. *Latorre* served the Chilean Navy for 12 years, before finally being paid off and decommissioned on 31 December 1998. For seven years she lay in Reserve, but the end came on 11 April 2005 when, having been sold for scrap, she sank in the South Pacific Ocean, whilst under tow to the breaker's yard.

Commanding Officers:

Captain Richard E. Roe RN	16 August 1966
Captain Ronald C. C. Greenlees RN	19 May 1968
Captain Stanley L. McArdle GM MVO RN	9 December 1968
Captain Raymond P. Dannreuther RN	17 March 1970
Captain Thomas H. E. Baird RN	18 October 1971
Captain Kenneth Vause RN	11 February 1974
Captain Robin E. de M. Leathes RN	6 May 1975
Captain Brian K. Shattock RN	15 June 1976
Captain Michael E Barrow RN	7 October 1980
Captain Christopher P. O. Burne CBE RN	2 November 1982
Captain Rodney P. Warwick RN	21 August 1984
Captain Hugh Peltor RN	21 June 1986

Battle Honours:

Falkland Islands 1982

Roll of Honour

South Atlantic 1982:

Petty Officer Michael J. Adcock
Cook Brian Easton
Air Engineering Mechanic Mark Henderson
Air Engineering Mechanic Brian P. Hinge
Acting Chief Air Engineering Mechanic David Lee
Air Engineering Artificer Kelvin I. McCallum
Able Seaman David McCann
Cook Brian J. Malcolm
Marine Engineering Mechanic Terence W. Perkins
Leading Cook Mark A. Sambles
Leading Cook Anthony E. Sillence
Steward John D. Stroud
Lieutenant David H. R. Tinker
Petty Officer Colin P. Vickers

Chapter Seven

HMS NORFOLK
1970 - 1982

This photograph shows *Norfolk* immediately after her launch on 16 november 1967, as she is towed to her fitting-out berth. *(World Ship Society)*

HMS *Norfolk* was the penultimate ship of the County-class, but her career with the Royal Navy was short and after just 11 years' service she was sold to the Chilean Navy. Her story begins in August 1964, when the newly formed Ministry of Defence asked the Tyneside shipbuilders Swan, Hunter & Wigham Richardson to provide '...a tender for the construction and completion in all respects of one Guided Missile Destroyer'. In early November the resulting tender was duly submitted and on 6 January 1965, the estimate for some £7,500,000 was accepted by the MoD, with the first keel plates being laid on 15 March 1966. *Norfolk* was launched on 16 November 1967, with the naming ceremony being performed by the Duchess of Norfolk.

During 1968 and 1969 *Norfolk's* fitting out was delayed slightly by industrial problems which were dogging the shipbuilding industry generally at that time and her first period of sea trials was put back by some five weeks, eventually beginning on 5 April 1969. At that stage she was very much in the hands of the builders, but a small naval contingent, led by Commander (E) J. G. Richards, had been standing by the ship since October 1967 and they accompanied her during this first seagoing trials period in the North Sea. In July 1969 *Norfolk's* first commanding officer, Captain B. H. G. M. Baynham RN, was appointed and after that a steady stream of naval personnel travelled north to Wallsend, where they were accommodated in hotels, guest houses, 'digs' and even nearby Army married quarters in the Newcastle and Whitley Bay area. During this period the skeleton ship's company was kept busy. For

HMS *Norfolk* at anchor off Great Yarmouth during her initial trials programme.   *(Maritime Photo Library)*

the engineers there was the familiarisation with, and the inspection and testing of equipment; the seamen helped to store ship, while the 'buffer' supervised and checked various pieces of equipment and rigging; the Supply, Secretariat and Stores Department meanwhile was kept busy arranging the delivery of victualling supplies and working out menus. By early 1970, however, the ship was almost ready, but then her delivery voyage from the River Tyne to Portsmouth suffered a further three-day delay and she eventually left on Friday 6 March 1970 and arrived alongside Portsmouth's Fountain Lake Jetty early the next morning.

At 1115 on Saturday 7 March, in the Admiral's Day Cabin, Captain Baynham signed the acceptance documents and officially took the ship over from the builders. Then, some 15 minutes later, with the ship's company having fallen in on the quarterdeck, there was a short ceremony of acceptance, with the Red Ensign being lowered and the White Ensign hoisted. However, at this stage, although her ship's company had been brought up to full strength, there was still fitting-out work to complete and the ship herself was not yet ready for sea.

In the event it would be some three months before *Norfolk* began the next stage of her trials, but during the forenoon of Friday 29 May the commissioning ceremony was held on the jetty alongside the ship. The guest of honour was the ship's sponsor, the Duchess of Norfolk, with other VIPs including Rear-Admiral J. E. Pope, FOF Western Fleet, and Vice-Admiral Sir Ian McGeoch, as well as men who had served in the previous *Norfolk*, headed by Engineer Vice-Admiral Sir Lancelot Peile, who had won the DSO in the old cruiser during the *Bismarck* chase. There were also several COs from the old *Norfolk* and altogether almost a thousand guests attended the ceremony, most of whom were relatives and friends of the ship's company. The commissioning cake was cut by Mrs B. Baynham, wife of the commanding officer, and she was assisted by the ship's youngest rating, JEM Ralph Warner. Ten days after the ceremony, during the forenoon of Monday 8 June, *Norfolk* finally slipped her moorings at South Railway Jetty, to put to sea for the first time under the White Ensign at the start of a four-month programme of trials, most of which took place in the Channel and the North Sea. In August there was a break when she returned to Portsmouth to give leave and take part in Navy Days, when some 37,000 people visited the ship. Earlier in July, when she had been open to the public at Portland's Navy Days she had also attracted thousands of visitors. Mid-September 1970 saw *Norfolk* back in the North Sea and paying a five-day visit to the River Tyne, where she held an open day for Swan Hunter's staff, after which she crossed the North Sea to visit Bremen and the Danish port of Alborg, which was always a popular run ashore. During these first foreign visits *Norfolk* flew the flag of Flag Officer Flotillas, Western Fleet (FOFWF), but on 6 October she returned to Portsmouth where the flag was transferred to *London* and *Norfolk* began a long period of maintenance, which would take her through to the new year of 1971.

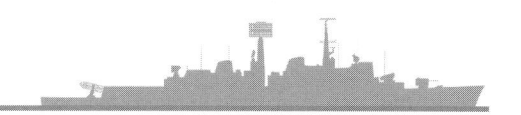

On Monday 11 January, *Norfolk* sailed for a Families Day at sea off the Isle of Wight, which included lunch and tea on board, with the highlight of the programme being the embarkation of the ship's Wessex helicopter. Then, after a series of local day-running exercises she sailed to join the submarine *Opossum* for exercises in the Channel. In mid-February, with the aircraft carrier *Eagle*, the frigate *Achilles* and *London*, she steamed south to Gibraltar for a month-long period of Mediterranean exercises, before she and *Achilles* returned to Portsmouth, where *Norfolk* spent a week in dry dock. Following her docking period she spent the next three months in home waters, during which time she operated off Portland with *Falmouth*, *Glamorgan* and *Minerva*, and off the missile range in Cardigan Bay before moving north to Rosyth. On

During her four-day visit to the county of Norfolk she anchored some 700 yards off Great Yarmouth's Britannia Pier. *(Maritime Photo Library)*

County Class GMDs

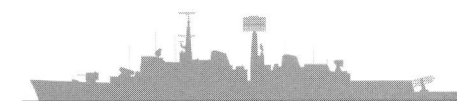

An impressive aerial view of *Norfolk* at sea during the early years of her career. She is still fitted with four 4.5-inch guns in twin turrets. *(Crown Copyright/MoD)*

17 August, having given seasonal leave, *Norfolk* hoisted the flag of FOFWF, Rear-Admiral Power, before sailing south to Gibraltar where the flag was transferred to *London*. *Norfolk* then joined *Leopard* for the passage east to Malta and the Eastern Mediterranean, where there were visits to Izmir and Souda Bay. During this Mediterranean deployment she also visited Toulon, Taranto and Genoa, which included a cruise which would have enhanced any travel brochure. She steamed between the islands of Elba and Corsica, through the Adriatic, about 30 miles off the Italian coast, past the volcanic island of Stromboli, through the Strait of Messina and north to Taranto. By the end of August 1971 the British government was negotiating with the Maltese government for continued use by Britain and other NATO countries of the island's military installations and while these negotiations were under way British warships avoided Malta for fear of disrupting the delicate talks. However, on 28 August *Norfolk* and *Leopard* paid a short 48-hour visit to Grand Harbour. The ship's ten-day period of self-maintenance, which would normally have been undertaken at Malta, was instead carried out at the Italian naval base of Taranto.

During the second week of October the first of a series of major NATO exercises, code-named 'Deep Furrow', began from Crete's Souda Bay, with a large multi-national force practising a major amphibious landing on the Greek island. During this exercise *Norfolk* acted as escort to the amphibious group, which included the commando carrier *Bulwark*. On 19 October, on conclusion of the exercises, *Norfolk*, accompanied by the destroyer HMS *Cavalier*, made a fast passage back to Gibraltar where *Norfolk* was dry docked for four days and underwent an assisted maintenance period. During the afternoon of 5 November, having completed a six-week course at RNC Dartmouth and having graduated as an Acting Sub-Lieutenant, the Prince of Wales joined the ship for eight months of sea training. Next day *Norfolk* sailed for her second exercise, which was with French warships and code-named 'Îl d'Or', during which *Norfolk* escorted the ageing helicopter carrier *Arromanches* (ex-HMS *Colossus*). With the exercise over there was a short break at Toulon before *Norfolk* and *Naiad* made a fast passage north to Plymouth Sound to refuel, embark stores and head north again, this time to the River Clyde area for 'Exercise Highwood', which took her north to Scapa Flow. Finally, after a very busy period she returned to Portsmouth for seasonal leave and maintenance.

It was mid-February 1972 when *Norfolk* sailed again and for six weeks she remained in home waters, with a three-day visit to Avonmouth. During most of this period the ship exercised from Portland into the Channel and the Western Approaches, operating with *Cavalier*, the frigate *Plymouth* and the Dutch destroyer *Utrecht*. In late March *Norfolk* and *Cavalier* acted as moving 'targets' for the fast patrol boats *Sabre* and *Scimitar*, and on 30 March *Norfolk* returned to Portsmouth. At this time there was a flurry of VIP visits, including the ship's sponsor, the Duchess of Norfolk, followed three days later by the Duke of Edinburgh. On 17 April, however, *Norfolk* sailed for an eight-week deployment to the Mediterranean, which began with joint exercises with the French Navy on their missile ranges off Toulon, during which she carried out Sea Slug firings. Following this she visited Ajaccio, before rendezvousing with the Italian helicopter cruiser *Andrea Doria* and the French destroyer *Cassard*, for the annual NATO exercise 'Dawn Patrol', the conclusion of which saw *Norfolk* off the east coast of Crete from where she made a fast passage back to the French naval base at Toulon, her fifth visit to the port in less than 12 months. This time, however, she remained at Toulon for 13 days carrying out routine maintenance, before steaming east to Malta, where she arrived on the last day of May for a five-day visit. On 5 June she sailed west once again and ten days later she secured alongside Portsmouth's Fountain Lake Jetty.

On Friday 30 June, for just over an hour, the Queen visited *Norfolk*, where her son the Prince of Wales gave her an informal tour round the bridge, the Operations Room, the Galley and a Seamen's mess deck, before being served tea in the wardroom and watching a missile handling display. On 14

HMS *Norfolk* at sea. Her Wessex HAS3 helicopter is ranged on the flight deck aft. *(Crown Copyright/MoD)*

July, the Prince of Wales left *Norfolk* for further courses and three days later there was a change of command when Captain John M. H. Cox RN took over the ship. His appointment came as *Norfolk* was seconded to the multinational NATO Standing Naval Force Atlantic (STANAVFORLANT), during which time she flew the broad pennant of the force's commanding officer, Commodore John D. E. Fieldhouse, and on 24 July she left Portsmouth for northern European waters and her first deployment in her new role.

These first duties with the NATO force consisted of a series of visits to Scandinavian ports and exercises with other NATO warships of the force, which included USS *Bigelow*, the German destroyer *Schleswig Holstein* and the Dutch destroyer *Amsterdam*. After being accompanied by her sister *Fife* to Trondheim, *Norfolk* went on to visit Harstadt, Narvik, Tromso and Stavanger, before crossing the North Sea to Newcastle upon Tyne where, in company with *Schleswig Holstein*, she spent four days. The two ships then recrossed the North Sea to the Dutch naval base at Den Helder, where they prepared for their first major exercise, 'Strong Express', in the North Sea. Also taking part in these manoeuvres were the powerful US Navy warships *John F. Kennedy* and *Little Rock*, as well as 26 other NATO warships, and after a short break at Bremen, the exercise finally ended on 10 October, which for *Norfolk* saw the start of a visit to Rosyth. Following this *Norfolk* was back in the North Sea, this time taking part in a JMC exercise, which took her to Scapa Flow and to the Belgian port of Antwerp. During November *Norfolk* remained in the North Sea, taking part in various multi-national exercises, including 'Exercise Yellow Bird' off Jutland, in the area of the famous battle which had taken place some 56 years earlier. Happily, by the latter years of the twentieth century the British and German warships were now firm allies. During this period *Norfolk* visited Frederikshavn, Copenhagen and Bergen, before the final multi-national anti-submarine exercise in late November with USS *Bigelow*, *Amsterdam*, the

HMS Norfolk

Norwegian frigate *Oslo* and the submarines HMS *Courageous* and the Swedish *Delfinen*. On 10 December, however, *Norfolk* returned to Portsmouth.

In January 1973 came the news that *Norfolk* would be taken in hand by Portsmouth Dockyard for a major refit, during which one of her 4.5-inch guns would be removed and the destroyer would become the first Royal Navy warship to be armed with the French Exocet ship-to-ship missile system. Before this, however, there were more multi-national exercises to lead and on 15 January 1973, having been joined by *Apollo*, *Glamorgan* and RFA *Tidespring*, she sailed south to Lisbon and 'Exercise Sunny Seas' in the Atlantic area between Gibraltar and Madeira as well as the Mediterranean. The exercise, which failed to live up to its name, involved a large force of naval ships, including *Ark Royal*, *Tiger*, *Fife* and *Glamorgan*, as well as ships from the US, France, Portugal, the Netherlands and Norway. *Norfolk's* part in the exercise ended in mid-February at Toulon, as did her tenure with the multi-national Standing Naval Force Atlantic, and after 48 hours on the Cardigan Bay missile range, and landing her Wessex helicopter at Portland, on 27 February she arrived alongside Portsmouth's Fountain Lake Jetty.

On 16 March 1973 Captain Cox relinquished his command and six days later the much reduced ship's company moved into shore accommodation at the Royal Naval Barracks. *Norfolk* herself was taken over by the dockyard and placed at six months' notice for steam. For seven months the ship remained in dockyard hands, during which time B 4.5-inch gun turret was removed in its entirety and replaced with a four-launcher Exocet MM38 missile system, the deadly effectiveness of which was belied by what appeared to be merely four over-large canisters. On 14 August the ship's new commanding officer, Captain Martin La T. Wemyss RN, was appointed and soon after that the ship's company moved back on board, having been brought back

After exercising in the Mediterranean with the fleet carrier *Eagle* and the destroyer *London*, on 27 February 1971 *Norfolk* entered Malta's Grand Harbour for the first time. She is shown here passing the breakwater.
(Michael Cassar)

up to full strength. By the end of September *Norfolk* was ready for sea and on Monday 1 October she left Portsmouth to begin her post-refit sea trials.

In the early hours of 5 October, just four days into her trials, *Norfolk* was in the Channel when she was called to the aid of the 1,525-gross ton Lebanese cargo reefer, MV *Barrad Crest*, which, fully loaded with bananas, was on passage between Surinam and the UK. During the evening of 4 October, when the vessel was some 20 miles east of Start Point, a fire started in her engine room and quickly took hold of the after end of the ship. The first vessel to reach the scene was a German merchantman, which took off most of the crew members and soon after this HMS *Leander* arrived and reported flames leaping from all parts of the superstructure. She sent a fire-fighting team over to the burning vessel, but it was obvious further assistance would be required and *Norfolk* arrived on the scene at 0130 on 5 October. Half an hour later, having dispatched two sea boats carrying firefighters and equipment to the crippled vessel, *Norfolk* manoeuvred to less than 20 yards from *Barrad Crest* to allow her hoses to be played onto the hull in an effort to cool it down. Meanwhile, during the night, as firefighters from *Norfolk* and *Leander* fought to control the blaze, *Achilles* arrived on the scene with large quantities of equipment and material which were transferred to the reefer. By daylight it appeared that the fires were just smouldering and well under control, and *Norfolk* prepared to take her in tow. Some 40 minutes later she began towing the stricken ship to the sheltered waters of Plymouth Sound, where the City's Fire Brigade could take over and finally dampen down the parts which were still smouldering. At 1646, having towed her to a position well inside Plymouth breakwater, *Norfolk* slipped the tow and handed *Barrad Crest* over to the MoD tugs *Advice* and *Superman*, after which she anchored in the Sound. Meanwhile, Plymouth City Fire Brigade took over responsibility for the fire on board the cargo ship which was now spontaneously erupting in several places, and therefore still a major threat. At 1830, however, with her task completed, *Norfolk* weighed anchor and put to sea. Her official log shows her passing the breakwater out of Plymouth Sound at 1840. Three minutes later there was a huge explosion as gases released by the burnt and overheated bananas in *Barrad Crest* blew out a large section of the side plating and forced off the cargo hatch cover. Debris was blown some 100 feet into the air and it is said that windows were rattled

Moored in Grand Harbour, the ship made an impressive sight at night once floodlit.
(Michael Cassar)

HMS Norfolk

for up to five miles inland. On board the reefer ten members of the City Fire Brigade and a dockyard employee were injured, but miraculously nobody was killed. Ambulances rushed to Millbay Docks to carry the injured to hospital and *Barrad Crest* was left to burn itself out. Eventually the gutted hulk was towed to Jennycliffe Bay where it was beached. As for *Norfolk* meanwhile, on leaving Plymouth Sound she returned to Spithead, from where she continued her trials through to mid-December, when she returned to Fountain Lake Jetty.

On 14 January 1974 *Norfolk* put to sea again to carry out Exocet familiarisation trials, although at this stage she did not actually fire any of the missiles, and following this she steamed on to Portland to undergo a three-week work-up period. When this was completed she paid courtesy visits to London, where she secured alongside HMS *Belfast*, then to Middlesbrough and Rosyth, from where she joined *Andromeda*, *Apollo*, *Plymouth*, RFA *Olwen*, as well as *Utrecht*, the frigate *Tjerk Hiddes* and the Portuguese frigate *Almirante Pereira De Silva*, for exercises in the North Sea. On 26 March, having carried out a two-week maintenance programme at Portsmouth, *Norfolk* steamed south to Gibraltar from where, after refuelling, she sailed for Toulon. During the whole of April and May she operated from Toulon on the French missile ranges, where she became the first Royal Navy warship to fire the Exocet missile. By the end of June her ship's company were as familiar with the city of Toulon as they were with Portsmouth, but this period in the ship's career was also punctuated by visits to Calvi, St Tropez and Genoa. On 3 July, with her Exocet trials over, *Norfolk* arrived in Malta for a five-day break before steaming west to Gibraltar, where she joined *Kent* for the passage home to Portsmouth.

On 1 September *Norfolk* again left Portsmouth to steam south to the Mediterranean and the French naval base at Toulon, where she spent another two months on the French Navy's missile ranges in the area. It was at Toulon, during the forenoon of 4 November, that the ship's next change of command took place, when Captain Ian R. Bowden MVO RN took over from Wemyss. Next day *Norfolk* left Toulon for Malta to carry out an 18-day maintenance period, before returning to Gibraltar to carry out Exocet firings in the Eastern Atlantic against targets towed by the tug *Robust*. By 17 December, however, she had returned to Portsmouth.

For *Norfolk* the new year of 1975 began at the end of January when, with *Antrim* and *Salisbury*, she carried out weapons training off Portland, before sailing south in February to join *Fife*, *Leopard*, *Hermione*, *Ashanti* and other ships for the annual 'Springtrain' series of exercises, which continued into March. On 6 March, in a position west of the Channel Islands, she provided medical assistance to the French trawler *La Fayette* and next day she arrived in Portsmouth to begin a nine-week dockyard-assisted maintenance and docking period.

It was 12 May before *Norfolk* put to sea again, and for the next four months she remained in home waters, exercising in the Channel and taking part in Portland Navy Days, before steaming north for Rosyth Navy Days and exercises in northern waters, which took her into the anchorage at Scapa Flow. These manoeuvres continued into July and for two days she was host to the US Ambassador, who was flown from London in the ship's Wessex helicopter, as an observer to the exercises. Following this she paid a six-day visit to Newcastle upon Tyne and during the passage south to Portsmouth she embarked a contingent of boys from the soon to be defunct training establishment HMS *Ganges*. At the end of August she took part in Portsmouth's Navy Days, before sailing north again, this time to the Skagerrak and the Swedish port city of Gothenburg. During this cruise she was accompanied by *Abdiel* and *Scylla*. The three ships were in Sweden for the ceremonial unveiling of a plaque by King Carl Gustav XVI, commemorating the British Admiral, Sir James Saumarez. During this period *Norfolk* flew the flag of FOF1 and for two hours on the day of the ceremony Carl Gustav, who was an honorary Admiral in the Royal Navy, flew his flag in *Norfolk*. After leaving Sweden and returning to Portsmouth there was only a brief pause before *Norfolk* was at sea again to join *Ark Royal*, *Blake* and *Hampshire* in the Channel, after

County Class GMDs

HMS *Norfolk* shows off her new surface-to-surface missile capability as four Exocet launchers have now replaced 'B' turret. *(Crown Copyright/MoD)*

which she took part in a multi-national North Sea exercise, during the course of which she again flew the flag of FOF1.

On 10 October *Norfolk* left Portsmouth to steam south to Gibraltar where, with the assistance of *Antrim*, she underwent FOF1's sea inspection, before continuing on to Malta. On arrival off Grand Harbour she paused briefly to hoist the flag of Rear-Admiral O. N. A. Cecil, the NATO Commander South East Mediterranean and Flag Officer Malta, before steaming on to the Egyptian port of Alexandria where, on 8 November, she was the first major British warship to visit for 13 years. The visit gave the ship's company the opportunity to visit Cairo and the Pyramids, and after leaving Alexandria *Norfolk* steamed south through the Suez Canal to set course for the French naval base at Djibouti in the Gulf of Aden. During the passage south through the Red Sea the ship's second helicopter pilot was taken ill with acute appendicitis and he had to be flown ashore to a hospital at Jeddah in Saudi Arabia. Meanwhile, after a three-day call at the barren, sun-bleached rocky French outpost of Djibouti, *Norfolk* retraced her course north and after transiting the Suez Canal she called at Piraeus, Malta, Civitavecchia and Gibraltar, from where, on 14 December, in company with *Ariadne*, she left for Portsmouth. During the passage through the Bay of Biscay the two ships encountered severe Atlantic storms, but despite the weather conditions *Norfolk's* helicopter could be launched in order to go to the aid of a Danish merchantman, MV *Susanne*, which had developed machinery problems. Two days later, on 18 December, *Norfolk* secured alongside at Portsmouth.

During the first six months of 1976 *Norfolk* did not stray far from home waters and on 9 March, while the ship was undergoing maintenance at Portsmouth, Captain William R. Canning RN took over the command. It was mid-April when she put to sea again to carry out weaponry drills and training in the Channel and in the Cardigan Bay area, but on 10 May *Norfolk* once again took over the command of NATO's Standing Naval Force Atlantic, before steaming into the North Sea to join her international force which included USS *Coontz*, HMNoS *Trondheim*, and HMNlS *Isaac Sweers*, FGS *Bayern*, HMCS *Assiniboine* and the Portuguese frigate *Magalhaes Correa*, to carry out anti-aircraft exercises. After these *Norfolk* put into Rosyth where she hoisted the broad pennant of the Commander STANAVFORLANT, Commodore John M. H. Cox who, back in 1972/73 had been *Norfolk's* commanding officer. One of the ship's officers remembers this time as being '...all at Portland work-up pace and for six months we worked flat out, both at sea and in harbour.'

Norfolk's first major exercise in her new role began six days after Cox took command and for a week the ships battled against each other and against some very heavy seas. During June the NATO force operated in the North Sea, carrying out anti-submarine and bombardment exercises, but there were also visits to Amsterdam, Den Helder, Wilhelmshaven and Kiel, which was always a very popular destination, to carry out an assisted maintenance period. After leaving Kiel during the third week of July *Norfolk* remained in German waters and with her NATO force carried out anti-submarine exercises in and around the Skagerrak. After a four-day visit to Oslo the force moved into the North Sea, where they were joined by *Danae* for exercises there and in the Norwegian Sea. Later in August, after visiting Narvik and Liverpool, *Norfolk* spent two weeks carrying out anti-submarine training exercises in the Clyde area, before joining the NATO force to lead a convoy escort exercise from the Western Approaches to Portland, where she arrived in time to assist *Diomede* with her final work-up inspections. This was quickly followed by exercises in the Western Approaches and a five-day visit to the inland city of Ghent in Belgium's East Flanders province. This involved navigating the River Scheldt and passing through the Westsluis Lock into the Terneuzen Canal, which provided a deep water link from the river to Ghent, where *Norfolk* secured alongside the city's Rigakaai. After leaving Ghent *Norfolk* returned to the Skagerrak, where she visited the Danish port of Alborg, before joining the NATO exercise 'Yellow

HMS *Norfolk* test fires an Exocet missile. A sea-skimming anti-ship missile it had a range of about 25nm. *(Ken Kelly Collection)*

Bird' in the western Baltic. Here she was closely shadowed by East German patrol boats, which almost followed her into Copenhagen and were waiting for her again when she left the Danish capital. Four days later, on 20 November, she secured alongside *London* at Cherbourg, where she relinquished her STANAVFORLANT duties and returned to Portsmouth.

It was the third week of January 1977 when *Norfolk* put to sea again and after exercising with *Diomede*, *Galatea* and *Rhyl* off Portland, on 24 January she sailed south for Gibraltar where she joined *London* and other ships for 'Exercise Locked Gate' in the eastern Atlantic, before steaming east into the Mediterranean to visit Genoa and to join French warships for exercises south of Toulon. By now, however, *Norfolk*'s commission was drawing to a close and after leaving Gibraltar on 3 March she steamed north for a four-day visit to Avonmouth, after which she returned to Portsmouth and paid off into dockyard hands. She would not put to sea again for over 12 months.

On Friday 15 July 1977, as *Norfolk* lay at extended notice for steam in No 3 basin of Portsmouth Dockyard, her new commanding officer, Captain Anthony J. Whetstone RN, was appointed to the ship, which at that point still had another eight full months in dockyard hands. During this refit updated computer displays were provided in the Operations Room, a new satellite communications system was installed and improvements were made to her main and auxiliary machinery. In the event it was the second week of March 1978 before basin trials were conducted on the main propulsion machinery and it was not until Monday 17 April that the ship was recommissioned. The rededication ceremony was held on the jetty alongside and the guest of honour was the ship's sponsor, the Duchess of Norfolk. The commissioning cake was cut by Mrs Whetstone, the wife of the commanding officer, assisted by the ship's youngest rating, JMEM R. McBride. Next day *Norfolk* left harbour to begin

HMS Norfolk

her post-refit trials, but these were dogged by gearbox problems and at one stage a minor fire in the gas turbine room. Having finally completed her trials *Norfolk* began her work-up in the Channel and Eastern Atlantic and in late May she paid a four-day visit to Bordeaux for British Week, during which she hosted a visit by a group of former Free French sailors who, during the Second World War, had served in the Royal Navy.

From Bordeaux *Norfolk* steamed south to Gibraltar, first to take part in a fleet exercise and secondly to carry out a series of Sea Cat firing trials. At 0750 on Monday 12 June she sailed to begin a day of missile firing, but at 1312 she was ordered to break off her exercises and alter course for a position some 14 miles south-east of Gibraltar, where two merchant ships had been involved in a collision at sea. The collision had taken place at 1107 that forenoon when, in thick fog, the 6,000-ton Algerian freighter MV *Ibn Batouta* had ploughed into the port side of the 11,000-ton American bulk carrier SS *Yellowstone*. The force of the collision had gouged a huge hole between the engine room and the main crew's mess deck of the US ship, almost splitting the bulk carrier in two. Five of *Yellowstone*'s crew were killed and two injured and at 1435, when *Norfolk* arrived at the scene, *Ibn Batouta*'s bow was still locked into *Yellowstone*'s port side. *Norfolk*'s helicopter was deployed to evacuate the injured seamen to hospital at Gibraltar and that afternoon the Shipwright Officer and a working party were put aboard *Ibn Batouta* in an attempt to separate the two ships. Meanwhile, a German salvage tug stood by in case her services were required. *Norfolk*'s boarding party worked through the night and at 0505, using her own engines and with the tug in place to assist, the slow process of separating the two ships began; finally, after six hours, at 1106 they were disengaged. With the salvage tug in attendance and *Ibn Batouta* able to leave under her own power, *Norfolk*'s working party was recovered, but the destroyer remained at the scene. Unfortunately, however, so great was the damage to *Yellowstone* that some three and a half hours after she had been pulled free the bulk carrier rolled over onto her port side and sank. In the event *Ibn Batouta* made it safely to Oran and *Norfolk* resumed her missile firing exercises. A subsequent US Board of Inquiry put the blame onto *Yellowstone*'s master for failing to properly use the ship's radar, which in turn had led her to cross the bow of *Ibn Batouta*. *Norfolk*'s final duty before leaving Gibraltar, for which she was joined by *Falmouth*, was to shadow a strong Soviet naval force in the Western Approaches, but on 26 June the two ships were back in Portsmouth Harbour.

During July and August *Norfolk* remained close to her home base, and on 1 September she steamed round to Portland to carry out a mini work-up. Two days into the exercises there was an opportunity to undertake a genuine emergency towing evolution after RFA *Olwen*, which was returning home from the Mediterranean, grounded on the Shambles sandbank outside Portland Harbour. For almost 12 hours efforts were made to free her by manoeuvring her main engines, but when it became clear that this would not work *Norfolk* passed a towing hawser and with the help of three tugs to steady her, she pulled the RFA back into deep water. Over the weeks which followed *Norfolk* conducted various exercises and evolutions with *Antelope*, *Berwick*, *Arrow*, *Euryalus*, *Falmouth* and the German frigate *Lübeck*. By the last week of October *Norfolk* had moved round to Cardigan Bay for Sea Cat missile firing, and it was at Fishguard on 28 October that Captain Anthony D. Hutton OBE RN relieved Whetstone in command of the ship.

On 30 October *Norfolk* left Cardigan Bay and after refuelling at Milford Haven she set course for Gibraltar and the Mediterranean for a long weekend visit to Genoa. On her return to Gibraltar, during the afternoon of 16 November she took over the tow of the old wartime destroyer turned frigate HMS *Undaunted*, from the tug *Cyclone* for an 18-hour tow to a position Lat 34°10' Long 11°08'W, in the eastern Atlantic, just under 200 miles west of the Strait of Gibraltar. The heading 'Daily Summary' in *Norfolk*'s official log for that day reads: 'Missile and Gunnex to sink *Undaunted*'. In fact *Undaunted*

On 9 February 1974 *Norfolk* steamed up the River Thames to secure alongside the preserved cruiser HMS *Belfast* in the Pool of London. Here she is making her way upriver and.... *(World Ship Society)*

had already been used as a target and had suffered extensive damage to her forecastle area on her starboard side, but it was left to *Norfolk* and the submarine *Swiftsure* to deliver the final blows. *Norfolk* fired the first shot when, at 1139, she launched an Exocet missile at *Undaunted* which hit the old frigate and tore a huge hole in her port superstructure amidships, but did not sink her. The destroyer followed this with both Sea Slug and Sea Cat missiles, but still *Undaunted* did not sink. At 1648 came *Swiftsure's* turn and she fired a salvo of torpedoes which missed. However, at 1728 she fired a second salvo which slammed into *Undaunted's* side and the force of the explosion broke the ship in two. Within four minutes the bow section had sunk, but it was 1751 before the stern disappeared beneath the waves. Next forenoon *Norfolk* secured alongside at Gibraltar and two days later she sailed for Portsmouth, arriving alongside during the forenoon of 24 November.

The new year of 1979 began with a short period of weapons training at Portland, a visit to Antwerp on 12 January, then anti-submarine exercises off Portland and a visit to Liverpool. On returning to Portsmouth she hoisted the flag of FOF2, Rear-Admiral P. Stanford, before joining *Alacrity* and *Falmouth* for an air defence exercise in the Western Approaches, which involved a variety of RAF aircraft, including Victors, Vulcans, Shackletons, Phantoms and Jaguars. On conclusion of the exercise *Norfolk* steamed up the River Thames to secure alongside *Belfast* in the Pool of London, before returning to Portsmouth to prepare for 'Exercise Springtrain' from Gibraltar. During these manoeuvres *Norfolk* again flew the flag of FOF2 and joining her were her sisters *Fife*, *London* and *Kent*, as well as the new Type 42 destroyer *Sheffield*, the frigates *Antelope*, *Arrow*, *Aurora*, *Arethusa*, *Ajax*, *Ashanti*, *Ariadne*, *Jupiter* and *Charybdis*, and the submarines *Churchill*, *Warspite* and *Odin*. The passage south through the Bay of Biscay was made in appalling weather, with *Arrow* and *Berwick* being called upon to rescue the crew of a sinking German coaster, MV *Paaschburg*. At the same time *Jupiter* rescued the crew of a Greek merchantman which had foundered off Cape St Vincent. At the end of the exercises *Norfolk* led *Arrow* and *Aurora* on a four-day visit to Rouen, before steaming to Devonport, from where she held a Families Day, before returning to Portsmouth.

On Tuesday 8 May 1979, after hoisting the flag of FOF2, *Norfolk* led *Arethusa*, *Arrow* and *Falmouth* out of Portsmouth Harbour at the start of a seven-month group deployment to the Mediterranean, the Indian Ocean, Australia, New Zealand and the Pacific. At sea they were joined by *Achilles*, *Dido* and the submarine *Courageous* for the first part of the deployment, then the RFAs *Black Rover*, *Fort Grange*, *Lyness* and *Olmeda*. After pausing briefly at Gibraltar the group steamed into the Mediterranean, where they took part in the NATO exercise 'Dawn Patrol', during which *Norfolk* escorted the French aircraft carrier *Clemenceau*. Later the group went their separate ways for a series of visits to Eastern Mediterranean ports, which took *Norfolk* and *Falmouth* to the Turkish city port of Izmir, where they anchored off Ataturk Square. On 1 June the group reassembled in the Eastern Mediterranean and six days later they made their southbound transit of the Suez Canal. During the passage down the Red Sea *Dido* and *Fort Grange* provided medical assistance to a Pakistani merchantman and on 15 June the group crossed the equator with due ceremony, before next day arriving at the Seychelles. After a brief pause the group steamed on, via Diego Garcia, to Fremantle, with the ten-day passage being livened up by an intership sports competition. On 4 July, after pausing in

.....passing under Tower Bridge. *(Crown Copyright/MoD 1974)*

Jurien Bay to spruce up the paintwork, the ships arrived in Fremantle, a visit which had been timed to coincide with the 150th anniversary celebrations of the founding of Western Australia.

Following the visit to Fremantle *Norfolk* led the group through an extremely rough Great Australian Bight to Hobart and Sydney where the group spent 17 days carrying out self-maintenance. On 7 August, after leading the group to sea from Sydney, *Norfolk*, *Arrow* and *Falmouth* joined HMAS *Melbourne*, *Hobart* and the submarine *Onslow*, for exercises in the Jarvis Bay area, before steaming on to Auckland where, during just one afternoon that *Norfolk* was opened to the public, some 6,000 people visited the ship. From Auckland the ships took part in 'Exercise Tasmanex', which also included US, Australian and New Zealand vessels. During the exercise Stanford took his group into the Pacific Ocean and in the closing stages of the exercise *Norfolk* was charged with 'defending' Norfolk Island, anchoring offshore during the afternoon of Friday 24 August for five hours. The island, which is one of Australia's dependent territories, was at that time populated by some 1,600 people, almost all of whom can trace their ancestry back to the HMS *Bounty* mutineers of 1789, before they were moved to Norfolk Island in 1874. During *Norfolk's* brief visit one of the guests of honour on board was Mr Fletcher Christian, a descendent of the mutineers' leader. Despite boisterous seas almost a quarter of the island's population came on board to visit the ship.

After leaving Norfolk Island the ship rejoined the group for manoeuvres with *Falmouth* and USS

On 3 September 1975 *Norfolk* conducted a six-day official visit to the Swedish port of Gothenburg, where King Carl Gustav visited the ship and unveiled a plaque to Admiral James Saumerez. *(Crown Copyright/MoD 1975)*

HMS Norfolk

HMS *Norfolk* leads *Arethusa*, *Arrow* and *Dido* out of Portsmouth Harbour for the Group Eight deployment. Later they would be joined by *Achilles* and *Falmouth*. *(Crown Copyright/MoD 1979)*

HMS *Norfolk* anchored off Ostend, Belgium, for the Belgian Royal Fleet Review of July 1980.
(Leo Van Ginderen)

Camden, before securing alongside at Suva on 27 August. From here *Norfolk* visited Tonga, before returning to Australian waters to exercise with RAN and RNZN ships and, with *Arrow* and *Falmouth*, to make a second visit to Sydney. The last Australian port of call for *Norfolk* was Brisbane, after which the group came together again for exercises during the passage to Singapore, which for *Norfolk* was made via Djakarta. It was 19 October when the group arrived alongside what had once been the Stores Basin of the Royal Navy's former naval base and which by then was the naval basin, part of the civilian-run Sembawang Dockyard. The ships were to undergo a 16-day maintenance period at Singapore and much of the work was carried out by men of the Fleet Maintenance Unit who had been flown out specially.

After leaving Singapore on 3 November the group split up again to visit a number of ports around the Indian Ocean area, with *Norfolk*, *Arrow* and *Dido* visiting the Indian port of Cochin which, even in the pre-Second World War days of the British Raj, rarely saw Royal Navy warships. After the four-day visit the group reassembled to make a fast passage home, although in the Mediterranean *Norfolk*, *Falmouth* and *Achilles* called at Piraeus, before transiting the Corinth Canal en route to Gibraltar, where there was a short refuelling stop before they continued the final leg of the deployment. *Norfolk* finally arrived at Spithead during the evening of 13 December and next forenoon she steamed up harbour to secure alongside Fountain Lake Jetty. During the seven months she had spent some 2,792 hours at sea and had steamed 38,500 miles.

On 15 January 1980, with the ship in refit, there was a change of command, with Captain Richard G. Sharpe OBE RN taking over from Hutton, but it was not until the end of March that the ship was ready for sea again. *Norfolk* finally left Portsmouth Dockyard on 31 March to undergo a two-month trials and work-up period at Portland, during which time she joined HNLMS *Utrecht* to shadow three Soviet ships in the North Sea and to carry out gunnery and missile firing exercises in the eastern Atlantic, which included firing Exocet missiles. This intensive exercise period concluded with a five-day visit to Amsterdam and a series of Staff College Sea Days from Portsmouth, during which she was accompanied by *Phoebe* and RFA *Olmeda*. In mid-June she steamed north to the German naval base at Kiel, before crossing the North Sea for Rosyth Navy Days. July began with a North Sea exercise which also involved *Bacchante*, *Minerva* and *Rhyl* as well as the RFAs *Fort Austin*, *Lyness* and *Pearleaf*. During these manoeuvres *Norfolk* shadowed a Soviet naval force round the Faroe Islands and later that month she was one of a number of warships which anchored off the port of Ostend to take part in a Belgian Navy Fleet Review. By the end of July she was back in Portsmouth for maintenance and Navy Days, during which she attracted some 23,500 visitors over the three open days. At the end of August, wearing the broad pennant of Commodore D. G. Armitage, *Norfolk* took over as the flagship of the NATO Standing Naval Force Atlantic.

Norfolk's first duties in the role that she had undertaken twice before took her into the North Sea to lead the NATO exercise 'Teamwork', which also involved USS *Iwo Jima*, HMCS *Valdez* and *Frazer*, the German frigate *Lübeck* and HNLMS *Van Galen*. These manoeuvres took the ships as far north as the Arctic Circle and back down to Devonport where, on 25 November, *Norfolk* began a three-week assisted maintenance period. On leaving Devonport she rejoined *Valdez* and *Van Galen*, and after undergoing FOF3's inspections she steamed back into the North Sea to lead another NATO exercise, which as well as the NATO force included the Type 42 destroyers *Cardiff* and *Newcastle*. On 9 November, as she lay at anchor in Scapa Flow, a remembrance service was held over the site of the wartime wreck of HMS *Royal Oak*. When this exercise was concluded there was time for visits to Wilhelmshaven and Rotterdam, before the whole NATO force put into Portsmouth for Christmas and New Year. Normally the NATO force would have dispersed to their respective base ports, but because of a political crisis in Poland, where a Gdansk shipyard worker Lech Walesa had formed a free Trade Union which was challenging the Soviet-backed Communist government, it was decided to keep the NATO ships together at Portsmouth for the seasonal holiday.

For *Norfolk* the new year of 1981, which was to be her last full year of service with the Royal Navy, began on 15 January when she led USS *Ricketts*, HMCS *Saguenay*, the German frigate *Braunschweig* and other ships of the NATO force to Gibraltar where they joined *Bulwark* and the submarines *Odin* and *Sceptre* for 'Exercise Test Gate', an anti-submarine exercise in the Eastern Atlantic, which enabled *Norfolk* and *Ricketts* to pay a five-day visit to Funchal, Madeira. At the end of the exercise *Norfolk* returned to Portsmouth, where she handed over her NATO role to *Antrim* and began an eight-week dockyard-assisted maintenance period.

When *Norfolk* left Portsmouth in late April 1981, she spent a short while on shakedown drills in the Portland area, before making a series of visits which began at Great Yarmouth and took her to Copenhagen, Stockholm, Luleå and Bremerhaven, before she returned to Portsmouth in mid-June for a Families Day. On 7 July there was a final change of command when Captain Brian W. Turner RN relieved Captain Sharpe and next day *Norfolk* sailed for the North Sea to carry out a patrol of the Forties oil fields, at the same time shadowing a powerful force of Soviet ships, which included the two cruisers *Sverdlov* and *Oktyabrskaya Revolutsiya*. The cat-and-mouse shadowing continued for a period of five days before the Soviet ships left the area and *Norfolk* put into Hull for a five-day visit; after putting to sea again on 20 July she rendezvoused with *Invincible* and *Apollo* for 'Exercise Eastaxe' in the North Sea. Three days later, however, after returning to Portsmouth, she secured alongside the redundant *Devonshire* moored at the dolphins, where equipment was transferred from *Norfolk* to the

At 1100 on Wednesday 17 February 1982, flying her paying-off pennant, *Norfolk* left Portsmouth for her delivery voyage to Chile. She was still under the White Ensign and during the 41-day passage to Talcahuano the reduced ship's company instructed Chilean navy personnel in all aspects of operations. She was actually handed over to Chile on 6 April 1982.
(*Michael Lennon*)

older ship. Next day she was shifted to South Railway Jetty where more stores and equipment were landed. On board the rumours regarding *Norfolk's* fate began to circulate. For more observant members of the ship's company a visit on 10 September by a delegation of senior Chilean naval officers provided a significant hint, particularly as they made a very detailed inspection of the ship. The answer came in early October 1981, when it was announced that both *Norfolk* and RFA *Tidepool* were being sold to the Chilean government. The controversial sale was a direct result of the even more controversial Defence Review which had ordered a drastic reduction of the Navy's surface fleet. However, *Norfolk's* service with the Royal Navy was not quite over and in mid-October she made a four-day visit to Amsterdam and took part in exercises in the Channel, but on 20 October she returned to Portsmouth Harbour where she was secured in No 3 basin.

On 9 November 1981 the first key Chilean naval personnel arrived on board and by the end of that month a full Chilean steaming crew had arrived to undergo familiarisation training by her now much reduced Royal Naval complement. On 7 December, with all but essential ammunition and stores having been landed, *Norfolk* sailed for three days of sea training in the Channel, which took place in atrocious weather conditions, and at one stage the ship was ordered to stand by in case she was required to assist a French oil tanker which was in difficulty. On her return to Portsmouth she was taken over by the dockyard for a month-long docking period.

On Friday 8 January 1982 Captain Turner hosted a dinner for all *Norfolk's* former commanding officers to commemorate the completion of the ship's service with the Royal Navy and later that month *Norfolk* sailed to begin a 12-day programme of sea

A good view of CNS *Capitán Prat* at sea. The Sea Slug launcher has been removed and the flight deck enlarged. A larger hangar has also been fitted with the hangar door facing the flight deck. *(Fernando Wilson Lazo)*

training for the Chilean ship's company. Finally, at 1100 on Wednesday 17 February, *Norfolk* left Portsmouth bound for her new career in Chile. During the long transatlantic passage, which was broken only for a short refuelling stop at Ponta Delgada in the Azores, the ship's Royal Navy personnel continued to train their Chilean counterparts. After 15 days the ship reached San Juan where there was a five-day break and after leaving Puerto Rico, *Norfolk* set course for the Panama Canal, which she transited on 11 March and spent four days at the US Rodman Naval Base. *Norfolk's* passage south from Panama was made via Arica and Valparaiso, but finally, during the forenoon of Tuesday 30 March she arrived at the main Chilean naval base at Talcahuano. Seven days later, at 1040 on Tuesday 6 April 1982, as Britain's Task Force sailed south from Portsmouth to retake the Falkland Islands, on *Norfolk's* quarterdeck at Talcahuano, the handover ceremony began and ended an hour later when the White Ensign was lowered and the Chilean Naval Ensign was raised.

For *Norfolk's* Royal Navy personnel all that remained was a flight home to London, but for the ship there was a refit in a local shipyard and she was renamed *Capitán Prat*. Initially she retained all her armament and in 1986 the Chilean government bought up all the Royal Navy's remaining stocks of Sea Slug missiles. In 1996 the Sea Cat missile system was replaced with the Israeli Barak SAM system and five years later the Sea Slug launcher was removed and the ship was rebuilt as a helicopter carrier, with the flight deck being extended right aft, to carry and operate Cougar attack helicopters. In the event *Capitán Prat's* career with the Chilean Navy lasted for 24 years before, in March 2006, she was laid up. Two years later, in September 2008, she was sold to Mexican shipbreakers.

Commanding Officers:

Captain Brian H. G. M. Baynham RN	1 July 1969
Captain James W. D. Cook RN	1 April 1971
Captain John M. H. Cox RN	17 July 1972
Captain Martin La T. Wemyss RN	14 August 1973
Captain Ian R. Bowden MVO RN	4 November 1974
Captain William R. Canning RN	9 March 1976
Captain Anthony J. Whetstone RN	15 July 1977
Captain Anthony D. Hutton OBE RN	28 October 1978
Captain Richard G. Sharpe OBE RN	15 January 1980
Captain Brian W. Turner RN	7 July 1981

Battle Honours:

Velez Malaga	1704	Arctic	1941-43
Atlantic	1941	North Africa	1942
Bismarck	1941	North Cape	1943
Norway	1945		

Chapter Eight

HMS Antrim
1970 - 1984

On 8 June 1968, some eight months after her launch, *Antrim* lies alongside her fitting-out berth at Fairfield's shipyard on the River Clyde. (*World Ship Society*)

On Thursday 19 October 1967, at the Govan shipyard of the Fairfield Shipbuilding Works, off the Govan Road, Glasgow, there was launched the last of the eight County-class destroyers, HMS *Antrim*. The naming ceremony was performed by Mrs Marjorie Mason, the wife of the then Minister of Defence, Roy Mason. The ship's keel had been laid some 21 months earlier, on 20 January 1966, and at the time of her launch it was expected that *Antrim* would be ready to undertake a General Service Commission east of Suez by April 1969. Unfortunately, industrial unrest in the shipbuilding industry resulted in delays and on the Clyde this was complicated by the fact that the smaller shipyards were organising themselves to merge into a single company, which was soon to become Upper Clyde Shipbuilders. Further setbacks were caused in the new year of 1969, when an explosion in one of the newly fitted main boilers caused a great deal of damage to the boiler casing and tubing.

In February 1970 the ship underwent builder's trials and in the first two weeks of October that year she carried out further sea trials. On board was *Antrim's* first commanding officer, Captain Hubert W. E. Hollins RN, who had been standing by the ship for six months and with him he had a full steaming crew of Royal Navy personnel. After

During February 1970 *Antrim* underwent her initial builder's trials in the Firth of Clyde. She is sailing under the Red Ensign and her Sea Cat missile launchers have not yet been fitted. *(Maritime Photo Library)*

anchoring at the Tail of the Bank the trials were delayed for 24 hours by gearbox problems, but next day after refuelling at Loch Striven she began her first machinery trials, which took her as far as Brodick Bay off the Isle of Arran. There then followed four days on the measured mile at Skelmorlie and a full day at sea after which she returned to Fairfield's basin at Govan on 10 October. At the end of the month *Antrim* spent another day at sea on trials, but it was the third week of November before she was ready to leave the builder's yard for her delivery voyage. That came at 2300 on Saturday 21 November when, having refuelled at Loch Striven Jetty, *Antrim* set course for Portsmouth, arriving alongside Fountain Lake Jetty at 0900 on Monday 23 November. Just over an hour later, at a ceremony attended by a piper from the Royal Irish Rangers, the regiment which was affiliated to the ship, *Antrim* was accepted into the Royal Navy.

Having been successfully delivered to Portsmouth *Antrim* remained firmly alongside until 3 February 1971, when she began her initial trials and shakedown period, which was punctuated by a weekend visit to the port of Rotterdam. During the forenoon of Tuesday 30 March *Antrim*'s commissioning ceremony was held and there were a number of special 'touches' which gave a very Irish flavour to the occasion, including pipers from the Royal Irish Rangers and sprigs of shamrocks flown specially from Ireland, which the ship's company wore on their cap ribbons. The guest of honour was Mrs Marjorie Mason, the ship's sponsor, and the commissioning cake was cut by Mrs Hollins and JMEM S. Wing. However, there still remained a great deal of work to be done storing and provisioning and preparing for a long period of testing and tuning of the ship's weapons systems, the electronic equipment and the main propulsion machinery. Meanwhile, ashore at RNAS Yeovilton, *Antrim*'s Flight and its Wessex helicopter were already undergoing their own work-up at both Yeovilton and Portland.

After spending the whole of April alongside at Portsmouth, on 3 May *Antrim* put to sea to embark her Wessex helicopter at Portland, before steaming into the Irish Sea to begin weapons training. At the end of May she returned to the River Clyde where she secured in Yorkhill Basin, just across the river from her birthplace at Fairfield's shipyard which was now part of Upper Clyde Shipbuilders. *Antrim's* weekend visit to Glasgow was an opportunity for the people of the city to see the ship they had built and on each day that she was opened to the public over 2,000 people visited her. From Glasgow *Antrim* made the short passage across to Portrush, County Antrim, for her first visit to the county after which she was named. Although the security situation severely restricted liberty men, she was able to take a contingent of Sea Cadets and Royal Irish Rangers to sea for a day. After leaving Portrush and refuelling at Faslane *Antrim* steamed round to the North Sea, to Invergordon, from where she continued her trials. However, on 12 June, following a main lubricating pump failure, the trials were curtailed and with her port propeller shaft locked she returned to Portsmouth at reduced speed. The repairs were completed on the last day of June and *Antrim* returned to the North Sea to continue her trials. During this period she visited the Norwegian naval base of Haakonsvern and the Belgian city of Antwerp. The visit to Antwerp came exactly 65 years after the previous HMS *Antrim*, a 10,850-ton cruiser which served between 1905 and 1922, visited the city in the first decade of the twentieth century. The city's press gave a great deal of publicity to the current visit while the 1906 newspaper headline, 'Never has the heart and soul of Antwerp been so aroused as by the coming of the *Antrim*' was much quoted. After leaving the River Scheldt *Antrim* returned briefly to Portland before returning to Portsmouth, where she held a Families Day off the Isle of Wight and secured alongside for seasonal leave. During Navy Days in August the ship attracted over 20,000 visitors.

On the last day of August *Antrim* left Portsmouth to continue her long programme of trials, training, testing and tuning the ship's machinery and weapons systems. For most of September and October she remained in and around the Portland area. On 6 September there was a change of command with Captain David A. Lorem RN taking over from Hollins, and she was on hand at Portland during the early hours of 29 September to provide medical assistance to the submarine *Alliance*, which had suffered a battery explosion which killed one man and injured 13 others. In mid-October *Antrim* completed her work-up and passed her final inspections, before spending 48 hours in the Cardigan Bay area and then steaming north via the Pentland Firth to Invergordon in order to take part in a North Sea exercise code-named 'Westaxe', which for *Antrim* meant hunting down the submarine *Opportune*. In mid-November *Antrim* spent ten days off the Aberporth missile ranges, before steaming north again to join an air defence exercise with *Jupiter* and *Londonderry*, but on 10 December she returned to Portsmouth.

On 17 January 1972 *Antrim* sailed south to Gibraltar, where she joined *Ashanti*, *Eastbourne*, *Scarborough* and *Tenby* from the Dartmouth Training Squadron for exercises in the Western Mediterranean and for a visit to Civitavecchia during which time she flew the flag of the C-in-C Fleet, Admiral Sir Edward Ashmore. Later she returned to Gibraltar where she again operated with the training squadron and the submarine *Grampus*. After remaining in the Gibraltar area until mid-March *Antrim* made her return to Portsmouth by way of Barcelona and Lisbon. At the former port she was the biggest Royal Navy ship to visit since 1963 and although the four-day stopover began in thick fog, the weather soon cleared to allow a full programme of social and sporting activities. Eight days after leaving Barcelona *Antrim* arrived off the mouth of the River Tagus, where thick fog once again hampered the ship's progress upriver. However, once alongside the magnificent hospitality offered by the city's British community was much appreciated. Despite the poor weather local interest in the *Antrim* was highlighted by the fact that in just three hours on the afternoon she was opened to the public, some 2,500 visitors toured the ship. On 23 March, having completed her first operational deployment, *Antrim* returned to Portsmouth to begin a nine-week dockyard-assisted maintenance period.

It was late May when *Antrim* left Portsmouth to carry out further trials and air defence exercises with Sea Vixens from RNAS Yeovilton, after which she sailed south to Gibraltar once again. This time, as well as revisiting Barcelona, she exercised with ships of the Italian Navy and the US Navy's 6th Fleet, which included tactical missile firings and mock attacks by aircraft from USS *John F. Kennedy*. She also visited St Raphael, Iraklion and Toulon, and on 27 June she assisted with the search for survivors of a US Navy helicopter crash. In the event the US Navy rescued the pilot, while *Antrim* recovered wreckage from around the crash site. On 18 August she visited Malta's Grand Harbour after which, in company with *Danae*, she passed through the Dardanelles to make a four-day weekend visit to Istanbul. *Antrim's* three-month Mediterranean deployment ended at Gibraltar with anti-submarine exercises with *Orpheus*, before she steamed home to Spithead where, during the forenoon of 14 September, she embarked families for the passage up harbour to South Railway Jetty.

During October and November *Antrim* remained in home waters, joining *Ark Royal*, *Apollo*, *Berwick*, *Caprice* and the submarine *Walrus* for 'Exercise Westaxe' in the Channel and Western Approaches. On 28 December, however, in company with *Mohawk*, she left Portsmouth for a nine-month deployment east of Suez. With the Suez Canal closed to shipping they steamed south by way of Funchal, Madeira, before making a long non-stop passage via the Cape of Good Hope to Durban, where there was just a 48-hour break before they continued north through the Indian Ocean to Kilindini Harbour, Mombasa. From Mombasa *Antrim* sailed north once again to the Gulf of Aden and into the Red Sea, to what was then the remote Ethiopian port of Massawa (now part of Eritrea). *Antrim* was at Massawa to take part in what was described in the press as one of the

A good aerial view of *Antrim* during her early career. *(Crown Copyright/MoD)*

HMS Antrim

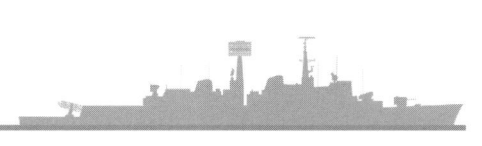

Another good image of *Antrim* with her original armament intact. Compare the flight deck markings with the previous image. *(Crown Copyright/MoD)*

strangest fleet occasions, Imperial Ethiopian Navy Days. The event was held over three days and on a commercial jetty in this Ethiopian outpost there were sporting, diplomatic and military events, all culminating in a passing-out parade for 11 midshipmen and a ceremonial steam-past. In addition to *Antrim* there were several foreign naval ships, including American, French and the Soviet destroyer *Skrytny*. For the visit *Antrim* flew the flag of Rear-Admiral R. J. Trowbridge and Emperor Haile Selassie's guest of honour was Princess Anne. During the evening of 10 February both VIPs dined on board *Antrim* and two days later came a 'Sea Day', when all the ships steamed past the Ethiopian royal yacht in which Haile Selassi and Princess Anne took the salute. *Antrim* also gave a demonstration of naval gunfire, when she bombarded a deserted island off the coast. At the time of the three-day event there was a great deal of criticism regarding the extravagance of the occasion in what was one of the world's poorest countries, but it would be the last such extravagance, for just 19 months later Haile Selassi was deposed.

Antrim had been due to leave Massawa during the forenoon of 13 February, but sailing was delayed by boiler failure. However, next day she secured alongside a berth at Port Sudan, where there were sporting fixtures, and for the less energetic a visit to the old port of Suakin. After leaving Port Sudan *Antrim* crossed the Red Sea to the Saudi Arabian port of Jeddah. During her three-day stopover at the pilgrim's seaport for Mecca, some 45 miles inland, one Muslim member of the ship's company was able to visit the holy city. Some sailors made a coach trip to Taif, which turned out to be a hair-raising two and a half-hour desert drive via a 5,000 foot escarpment, driven at high speed all the way. The passengers were, however, able to assist the coach driver when the vehicle burst a tyre en route. After leaving Jeddah *Antrim* spent six days at sea as she steamed down the Red Sea, across the Gulf of Aden and into the Indian Ocean to refuel alongside RFA

HMS *Antrim* enters Malta's Grand Harbour on 18 August 1972 during a Mediterranean deployment. *(Michael Cassar)*

Wave Ruler at Gan, after which there were six more days at sea before she arrived alongside the ANZUK naval base, now part of Sembawang Docks, in Singapore.

After a long-weekend break at Singapore, *Antrim* and *Mohawk* made a four-day visit to Bangkok before returning to Singapore to undergo a three-week maintenance period. When this was completed during the last week of April the two ships left for Hong Kong. During the stay there they were visited by the First Sea Lord, Admiral Sir Michael Pollock, after which *Antrim* began a series of visits to Far Eastern ports, including Kobe, Chinhae in South Korea and Sattahip, Thailand. It was at Sattahip on 23 May that a change of command took place, with Captain George A. F. Bower RN taking over from Loram, who left the ship next day. *Antrim* remained in the Sattahip area for several days undergoing exercises with the Thai Navy, but on 2 June she set course south to the US Navy's Subic Bay exercise areas off the Philippine Islands. The main purpose of the exercises was to give *Antrim* the opportunity to fire her Sea Slug missiles, but her arrival coincided with the monsoon season and a great deal of time was spent dodging heavy rain storms. Eventually, however, a successful firing was carried out against a pilotless target aircraft launched from a US fighter and, scoring a direct hit, she also took a shot at the drone's wreckage. Finally, after completing her missile-firing programme, *Antrim* put into the US Navy's base at Subic Bay, before returning to Hong Kong to carry out a three-week duty as the Colony's guardship. During this period she was called upon to sail at short notice to go to the aid of an oil drilling rig in the Taiwan Strait which had broken loose from its mooring, but in the event it was brought under control by tugs and *Antrim* returned to Hong Kong.

On 9 July *Antrim* left Hong Kong to return to Singapore on the first stage of her passage home, but soon after leaving the Colony her port steam turbine began overheating and to add to the problems one of her main boilers developed a defect so, with her steam turbines disconnected and using her

HMS Antrim

gas turbines, *Antrim* made her way slowly back to Hong Kong. Thirty-six hours later she was able to make the four-day passage to Singapore and when homeward-bound she called at Port Louis, Mauritius, after which she spent a week on the Beira Patrol, before calling at Durban and Simonstown. During her passage north through the Atlantic Ocean she refuelled at Freetown and spent 48 hours at Gibraltar, before arriving at Spithead during the evening of 26 September. Next forenoon she steamed up harbour to secure alongside Pitch House Jetty. *Antrim's* commission was drawing to a close, for she was about to be taken into dockyard hands to undergo a refit and an Exocet conversion. First, however, she had to disembark her Sea Slug missiles and this was done at Devonport during the second week of November. Finally, after a series of machinery trials in the Channel, on 16 November she returned to Portsmouth. Ten days later her ship's company moved to accommodation in the Royal Naval barracks and the ship was paid off.

During the months *Antrim* spent in dockyard hands her appearance was altered by a light tubular foremast carrying a Type 992Q radar scanner and B turret was removed, to be replaced by four Exocet MM38 canisters, with special deflectors to avoid damage to the bridge superstructure from the boosters. On 14 May 1974 the ship's new commanding officer, Captain Harry R. Keate RN, joined the ship. It was, however, the end of August before *Antrim* was ready for sea and on 6 September she began her post-refit trials which continued for the rest of the year, being broken at the end of October by a short visit to Brest. It was in January 1975 that Exocet trials began and later that month *Antrim* began her work-up at Portland, which continued throughout February. In March the ship joined *Kent* at Rosyth for a JMC exercise, before returning to Cardigan Bay for further Exocet and Sea Slug trials. During the last week of April there was a short exercise

When Antrim put to sea in the autumn of 1974 after a long refit, her twin 4.5-inch guns of 'B' turret had been replaced with a box-like structure of a quadruple Exocet missile launcher. *(Author's Collection)*

HMS *Antrim*, with her newly fitted Exocet missiles, leaves her berth alongside her sister ship *Kent* at Portsmouth's Fountain Lake Jetty on 28 October 1974 for a short visit to the French port of Brest, before beginning a programme of trials and work-up exercises. *(Derek Fox)*

period in the Clyde, before *Antrim* returned to Portsmouth.

On 19 May 1975, *Antrim* left Portsmouth to steam south to Gibraltar and on to Casablanca, before entering the Mediterranean and taking part in French naval exercises from Toulon, from where she steamed on to Civitavecchia, Malta and Trieste, before returning to Grand Harbour to undergo maintenance. The ship remained in the Mediterranean until mid-October and during this time she visited Cagliari, Naples, Cannes and Istanbul. In September she joined *Hermes*, *Norfolk*, *Ajax* and *Intrepid* for the NATO exercise 'Deep Express' in the eastern Mediterranean and on 20 October she left Gibraltar to steam home to Portsmouth.

On 12 November 1975, with the ship high and dry in dock, Captain R. Michael Burgoyne RN took over from Keate and it was mid-January before *Antrim* put to sea once again. For the next six months she remained very much in home waters, exercising with *Ark Royal*, *Yarmouth*, *Devonshire*, *Andromeda* and the submarine *Valiant*, as well as the German destroyer *Bayern*. On Monday 23 February 1976, *Antrim* sailed early from Portland to carry out machinery breakdown drills. Later in the day, when these had been successfully completed, in the boiler room, 17-year-old MEM2 William Wallace was on the lower plates hand pumping lubricating oil round the starboard fuel pump, which was being restarted, when there was an explosion just a few feet away from him, resulting in a large fire at that site and a number of secondary fires around both the starboard main feed pump and the standby fuel pump. Such was the intensity of the fires that there was a danger of a major conflagration which would have threatened the safety of the ship. Wallace shouted 'Fire' but quickly realised that he was the only person close to the blaze, so he attempted to reach the nearest fire extinguisher.

That, however, had been enveloped by the fire, so he plunged through the flames surrounding the starboard feed pump and in the process past the ladder which could have taken him to the immediate safety of the upper plates. Instead he went some 15 feet aft to find a gas-water extinguisher and, despite thick, choking black smoke in the whole area, he began extinguishing the fires. In doing so he prevented leaking diesel fuel from the standby fuel pump from reigniting, which is what had caused the initial explosion. By the time Wallace was relieved by a senior rating and a fire party he had already successfully extinguished the fires. There was no doubt in anyone's mind that his presence of mind and courage had prevented a potentially disastrous major fire and the ship was able to remain at sea, before returning to Portland three days later.

In June 1976, after a Families Day off the Isle of Wight, *Antrim* left Portsmouth for the Baltic to visit Stockholm and Luleå, returning to Rosyth via Århus. At Rosyth she took part in Navy Days, before sailing south to Portsmouth where she again took part in Navy Days. On 13 September, flying the flag of Vice-Admiral A. S. Morton, FOF1, she joined *Ark Royal*, *Andromeda* and *Bacchante* for exercises off Portland, before steaming south for 'Exercise Teamwork' in the eastern Atlantic. Two days after leaving Portland, during the afternoon of 27 September, *Antrim* was carrying out general drills some 60 miles off the Portuguese coast with *Bacchante* and *Devonshire*, when the latter suffered an explosion in her boiler room and lost all power. For some two hours, as *Devonshire* lay helpless in the water, both *Bacchante* and *Antrim* stood by the crippled ship, before escorting her to the mouth of the River Tagus and into Lisbon. Four days later *Antrim* left Lisbon to join *Ark Royal* for 'Exercise Display Determination' and the passage to Malta, which was the first stage of an eight-week deployment into the Indian Ocean.

HMS *Antrim* secured head and stern to No8 buoy in Grand Harbour, Malta, in June 1975. She has an awning rigged over her forecastle and floodlighting is in place. *(Michael Cassar)*

During the second week of February 1976 *Antrim* exercised in home waters with the aircraft carrier *Ark Royal*. In this photograph the two ships are in the Bristol Channel, about to carry out a jackstay transfer.
(*Crown Copyright/MoD 1976*)

On 7 October, having taken part in two major NATO exercises, and having left Malta's Marsaxlokk anchorage, *Antrim* was joined by *Bacchante*, *Charybdis*, *Naiad*, *Yarmouth* and the RFAs *Olna*, *Stromness* and *Black Rover*, before setting course for Port Said and a group deployment into the Indian Ocean. After leaving the Suez Canal during the evening of 12 October, the group steamed south to exercise with French naval ships off Djibouti before they entered the Indian Ocean. For *Antrim*, after leaving the Gulf of Aden there was a long passage south to the Seychelles, where she spent ten days, during which time the ship was visited by the President of the newly formed republic. After leaving the Seychelles *Antrim* steamed north once again as the ships regrouped for exercises with both the Pakistani and Iranian navies off Karachi, the latter's contribution being the frigate *Faramarz*, which had been built in Southampton by Vospers. The exercises, code-named 'Midlink', ended with visits to Karachi and to the southern Iranian port of Bandar Abbas in the Strait of Hormuz, which was the main base for the Iranian Navy. On leaving Iranian waters the group headed back to Suez, exercising en route with French ships. On 7 December they made their northbound transit of the Suez Canal, after which *Antrim* docked in Alexandria for three days before steaming home via Gibraltar. On 21 December she arrived back in Portsmouth.

On Monday 7 February 1977, *Antrim* put to sea again and after weapons training off Portland she steamed south for Gibraltar to join a NATO force with a strong Royal Navy contingent, including *Norfolk*, *London*, *Glamorgan*, *Devonshire* and *Cleopatra*, for exercises in the eastern Atlantic and eastern Mediterranean. This was followed by 'Exercise Springtrain' which also included *Achilles* and *Cleopatra*, before *Antrim* returned to Portsmouth. In mid-March she visited Copenhagen

HMS Antrim

before spending most of April in Cardigan Bay, carrying out missile firings, including Exocets.

During May, June and July 1977 *Antrim* remained close to home, with Navy Days at Chatham and a five-day visit to Hamburg. In early June she operated from Portsmouth with *Tiger*, *London* and *Glamorgan*, after which there was a Families Day with *London* off the Isle of Wight. On 28 June she formed part of the 1st Flotilla for the Silver Jubilee Fleet Review at Spithead, and at the start of July she steamed north for anti-submarine exercises in the Clyde area, but by the end of the first week she had returned to Portsmouth to give leave. On 19 August *Antrim* was sent north to carry out a fishery protection patrol and to shadow a Soviet naval force in the area of Bishops Rock. On the last day of August she left the patrol area to steam south, where she rendezvoused with *Hermes* (flag FOF1, Rear-Admiral R. R. Squires), *Kent*, *Sheffield*, *Arrow*, *Ambuscade*, *Diomede* and the RFAs *Stromness*, *Tidereach* and *Resurgent* for a 'Westlant' deployment to Bermuda, the USA and the Caribbean. During the passage, some 500 miles west of Ireland, *Stromness* rescued a lone British sailor who had been drifting for four days on an upturned dinghy. The man was transferred to *Ambuscade* for the passage home to Britain. Meanwhile, on 9 September the group arrived at Bermuda's Ireland Island naval base.

Three days after leaving Bermuda, on 15 September, *Hermes* led *Antrim*, *Tidereach* and *Resurgent* into Maryport, Florida and from there to exercises with the US Navy and assisting HMS *Penelope* with Seawolf missile firings. Following this she steamed on to the US Navy's base at Norfolk, Virginia, for a 16-day maintenance period, and, on 3 October 1977, a change of command, when Captain Gordon F. Walwyn CVO RN took over the ship. Nine days later the group departed,

HMS *Antrim* at speed. The colourful boats and black funnel tops and masts were soon to give way to all-over grey in the wake of the South Atlantic campaign in 1982. *(Crown Copyright/MoD)*

HMS *Antrim* floodlit at Stockholm in June 1976. Note the lighting on her Type 975 radar aerial.
(Syd Goodman Collection)

with *Antrim* visiting Nassau and Freeport, Bahamas. At Nassau she took over as escort to the royal yacht *Britannia*, which was carrying the Queen on a Jubilee tour of the Caribbean islands. These duties took *Antrim* from the Bahamas to the Virgin Islands, Antigua and Barbados. The passage home was made in company with the royal yacht. Just outside Ponta Delgada in the Azores she was detached from her escort duties and after refuelling at the Portuguese port she steamed direct to Rosyth, where she joined the NATO exercise 'Ocean Safari'. The exercise, designed to test NATO's ability to keep open Atlantic trade routes, involved 60 surface ships and submarines, together with 250 aircraft. As well as *Antrim* the Royal Navy's contribution included *Hermes*, *Blake*, *Fife*, *Kent*, *Sheffield*, *Arrow*, *Charybdis*, *Diomede*, *Hermione*, *Plymouth* and the submarines *Churchill*, *Valiant*, *Finwhale*, *Opportune*, *Oracle* and *Osiris*. There were also aircraft from *Ark Royal* and ships from the USA, Canada, the Netherlands, Norway, Portugal and Germany. *Antrim's* manoeuvres took her from the North Sea to the Western Approaches and it was mid-December when she finally arrived back in Portsmouth.

On 16 January 1978 *Antrim* left Portsmouth for Gibraltar and the annual series of 'Springtrain' exercises and as she approached the Rock she was ordered to shadow a Soviet research ship which had been 'loitering' off the Colony monitoring naval movements. At that time British and Spanish diplomatic relations over the issue of Gibraltar's sovereignty were not good and the Soviet government was pressing the Spanish to grant naval fuelling and base facilities at Algeciras overlooking Gibraltar Bay. In the event, when *Antrim* arrived on the scene the Soviet ship, *Odyssey*, was inside Gibraltar's territorial waters, but when it was ordered to leave it did so immediately.

'Exercise Springtrain' that year was led by HMS *Blake* (flag FOF1) and also present were *Hermes*, *Devonshire*, *London*, *Kent*, *Yarmouth* and the submarines *Churchill* and *Oracle*. Also taking part was the Dutch submarine *Tiggerhaai* and supporting them all were the RFAs *Olmeda*, *Olna*, *Resource* and *Stromness*. The three-week programme of exercises was beset by extremely rough weather conditions, with gale force winds and heavy seas, but on 13 February *Antrim* was detached to head north once again. Although she was due to begin a long refit there was just one more duty to perform and on 16 February she collected the Flag Officer Plymouth for a three-day weekend visit to Cherbourg, after which she returned to Portsmouth where she was paid off and taken over by the dockyard. She would not go to sea again for almost 18 months.

On 27 March 1979, with the ship in Portsmouth Dockyard's No 3 basin at extended notice for steam and her much reduced ship's company living ashore at RNB, there was a change of command, with Captain Michael F. Parry RN joining the ship. By this time the refit was coming to an end and by mid-May 1979 her ship's company was once again up to strength and the ship herself was back alongside the sea wall at Fountain Lake Jetty. Finally, during the forenoon of 24 July, *Antrim* left Portsmouth Harbour to begin her post refit trials in the exercise areas south of the Isle of Wight. After a break for seasonal leave *Antrim's* completion date inspection was held on 28 August and three days later a Families Day was held off the Isle of Wight after which the trials began in earnest and continued through to Christmas. In October, however, *Antrim* steamed south to Gibraltar where she flew the flag of FOF1 for three days and at the end of that month she sailed directly to Hamburg for a five-day visit to Hamburg, after which she resumed her trials from

HMS *Antrim* at Spithead in the summer of 1977 for the Silver Jubilee Fleet Review. *(Maritime Photo Library)*

During October 1977, while in the Mediterranean en route to the Indian Ocean, *Antrim* took part in exercise 'Display Determination'. She is seen here leading the frigates *Andromeda, Naiad, Bacchante, Charybdis* and *Yarmouth*. *(Crown Copyright/MoD 1977)*

Portsmouth.

In February and March 1980 *Antrim* carried out her work-up from Portland, where she joined *Ambuscade, Bacchante, Brighton, Glasgow* and the German destroyer *Emden*. Later in March the whole force moved into the North Sea, where they joined *Minerva, Scylla* and other ships for 'Exercise Eastaxe', before *Antrim* steamed round to Cardigan Bay to carry out missile firing. On 19 May, after a short period at Portland, *Antrim* sailed at the head of a group of nine ships which were to spend seven months on a Far East deployment. Flying his flag in *Antrim* was FOF1, Rear-Admiral D. C. Jenkin; the other ships in the group were *Coventry, Alacrity, Galatea, Naiad* and the RFAs *Blue Rover, Olwen, Resource* and *Stromness*. After leaving home waters the group called at Gibraltar before steaming into the Mediterranean, where they carried out a period of concentrated warfare training during which they settled into a routine of working together as an efficient fighting force. 'Opposition' was provided by the submarine *Dreadnought*, aircraft from the RAF and the French Navy. The Soviet Navy's presence in the area was much in evidence when the group encountered a powerful force of Soviet warships in the central Mediterranean. Soon after this encounter the group split up for several days, with *Antrim, Coventry* and *Naiad* visiting Istanbul while *Alacrity* and *Galatea* called at Cyprus. They came together again on 13 June off Port Said and next day they made their southbound transit of the Suez Canal. Once clear of the canal *Alacrity, Galatea* and *Blue Rover* were detached to Aquaba, with *Antrim* and the other ships continuing their passage through the Red Sea and the Gulf of Aden, where they took part in exercises with French warships, before steaming on into the Indian Ocean. On 23 June they slowed down for the Crossing the Line ceremony and that evening there was a night encounter exercise with the Kenyan Navy. During

HMS Antrim

the forenoon of 24 June *Antrim* led *Coventry* and *Naiad* into Kilindini Harbour, Mombasa.

After a break of six days the group re-formed in the Indian Ocean and headed north to exercise with the Sultan of Oman's Air Force and Navy, whose fast patrol boats made simulated attacks on the group. These manoeuvres were followed by 'Exercise Multiplex' with US Navy warships led by the aircraft carriers *Dwight D Eisenhower* and *Constellation*. After a visit to Karachi the group trained with Pakistani naval ships, including PNS *Taimus*, before rejoining the US Navy for the second phase of 'Exercise Multiplex'. On 21 July, with the group together once again, course was set for Singapore, with a brief pause off the Sembilan Islands in the Strait of Malacca, where there was time for relaxation in the form of banyans, before the group headed south to Singapore's Sembawang Dockyard.

The break at Singapore was brief and on 28 July they left Sembawang bound for Hong Kong, where *Antrim*, *Coventry* and *Galatea* arrived on 1 August to carry out an 18-day maintenance period. After leaving Hong Kong the group re-formed once again

HMS *Antrim* at speed. The limited confines of the flight deck and the hangar are evident in this view.
(Syd Goodman Collection)

County Class GMDs

HMS *Antrim* manoeuvring at speed. Note only two Exocet missiles have been embarked.
(Crown Copyright/MoD)

HMS Antrim

to exercise with the US Navy in the Subic Bay area, before visiting Manila and then setting course for Shanghai. On 2 September the group again split up, with *Galatea* and *Naiad* being detached, while the other ships continued on to the East China Sea.

In diplomatic circles in both Britain and China, the Royal Navy's visit to Shanghai was considered to be of great importance. It was the first such visit for 31 years, in fact since the Yangtse Incident, when China had used HMS *Amethyst* to signal to the West that they could no longer treat Chinese territory as their own. On this occasion, however, the welcome was unequivocally warm and it began at 0600 on 3 September when a Chinese warship met *Antrim*, *Alacrity* and *Coventry* off the Yangtse Estuary to escort them slowly upriver. All that day and into the night the four ships steamed up the mighty river, passing hundreds of junks and sampans. At one point the Chinese Air Force flew overhead in salute and at 0400 on 4 September the ships anchored for what was left of the night. At 0836 next forenoon they weighed anchor and as they turned into the Huangpu River on the final approaches to Shanghai, large crowds of inquisitive spectators were lining the banks of the river as *Alacrity* led the way. Finally, at 1213, *Antrim*, *Coventry* and *Alacrity* secured alongside where they were greeted by girls waving flags and banners proclaiming eternal friendship between the Chinese and British peoples.

Although Shanghai was no longer the cherished China Fleet run ashore, known and enjoyed by the Royal Navy only one generation before, the famous promenade along the river – The Bund – was still there, lined with grandiose European-style buildings which once housed the leading banks, trading houses and European consulates of the pre-war years. The old Shanghai Club, with its famous 'Long Bar' had miraculously survived, but as a cafe, which was open to all and not as the 'snobbiest' club in the Far East. The Chinese Navy had arranged a full programme of entertainment and visits, including a banquet for 400 officers and men on the first night.

During the forenoon of 8 September *Antrim*, *Coventry* and *Alacrity* slipped their moorings at the start of a three-day passage to Japanese waters, where the first two ships and RFA *Stromness* visited Tokyo. Their arrival was marked by a fireboat display, bands and a parade of beauty queens. Following the Tokyo visit the group dispersed for goodwill visits to six Japanese ports, with *Antrim* calling at Kagoshima. Before leaving Japanese waters they became the first Royal Navy ships to exercise with the Japanese Maritime Defence Force in a day-long series of manoeuvres code-named 'Exercise Fifi'. On leaving Japanese waters the group began the first stage, via Hong Kong and Singapore, of their passage home. On arrival at Sembawang Docks, however, there was a break as they carried out a 17-day maintenance period.

On 20 November, minus *Galatea* which was delayed in Hong Kong, the group left Singapore to make their way into the Indian Ocean for exercises with US warships and, in *Antrim's* case to make a four-day visit to Bombay. Following this *Antrim*, *Coventry* and *Naiad* set course for the Persian Gulf area to take their turn on the Armilla Patrol, which was intended to keep open the vital Strait of Hormuz during the Iraq-Iran War. *Antrim* remained on the patrol until 2 December when, having been relieved by *Avenger* and *Birmingham*, she and *Naiad* left the area and set course for Suez. On 9 December they steamed north through the Suez Canal and after a brief pause at Gibraltar, during the forenoon of 19 December *Antrim* secured alongside *Glamorgan* at Portsmouth's South Railway Jetty.

It was 12 February 1981 when *Antrim* put to sea again, this time to make a fast passage to Funchal, Madeira, where, on 17 February, she relieved *Norfolk* as flagship of NATO's Standing Naval Force Atlantic (Commodore D. Armytige), a force which also included HMS *Arrow* and USS *Claude V. Rickets*, as well as Dutch and German ships. During this period she took part in exercises in the Atlantic and in the North Sea, at the same time visiting Bordeaux, Bremerhaven and Zeebrugge. In April she joined *London* (flag C-in-C Fleet, Admiral Sir James Eberle), *Bristol*, *Ariadne*, *Euryalus*, *Minerva*, *Naiad*, *Rothesay*, *Bacchante*

HMS *Antrim* leaving Portsmouth for Portland and Devonport on 25 August 1981. *(Leo Van Ginderen)*

and *Achilles* for the 'Springtrain' programme of exercises from Gibraltar, and in May she visited Bremen. In June 1981, after taking part in Navy Days at Rosyth, she hoisted the flag of FOF1 to lead *London*, *Coventry*, RFA *Olmeda* and other ships for exercises off the Shetland Islands, which was followed by a visit to Oslo; on 1 July she returned to Portsmouth. In mid-August, while secured alongside Fountain Lake Jetty, *Antrim* was joined by the newly commissioned Argentine destroyer *Santissimo Trinidad*, which secured alongside her for a week. The Argentine ship was in Britain to carry out her sea trials and for training in the operation of Sea Dart missiles. Eight months later she would lead the Argentine amphibious force which invaded and captured the Falkland Islands. On 18 August Captain Brian G. Young RN relieved Parry in command of *Antrim* and on 1 September she put to sea for anti-submarine exercises off Portland, where she was joined by *Cardiff*, *Danae* and the submarine *Conqueror*.

At 0600 on 3 September *Antrim*, *Cardiff*, *Danae* and *Conqueror* rendezvoused in the Western Approaches with the Admiralty tugs *Typhoon* and *Roysterer*, which were towing the elderly Admiralty tank cleaning vessel *Switha* and the former frigate HMS *Rapid*. Soon after this they were joined by the submarine *Onyx* and the tugs slipped the two hulks, which were left for the warships to use as targets. During the afternoon *Antrim* and *Danae* fired Exocet missiles at *Rapid* and both scored direct hits to the superstructure, causing serious damage. Later in the day, at 1710, *Rapid's* bows were blown off by a torpedo from *Onyx* and a second torpedo hit her amidships on the port side, sending her quickly to the bottom. At 2010 *Conqueror* sank *Switha*, which, despite hits by *Antrim's* guns and Sea Slug missiles, had remained stubbornly afloat.

On 7 September *Antrim* left Portland to carry out her final exercise programme of the year and her last duties as part of the NATO Standing Naval Force Atlantic, namely 'Exercise Ocean Safari'. The other Royal Navy ships involved in the exercises included *Invincible*, *Bristol*, *Sheffield*, and a number of frigates and mine countermeasures vessels. Representing the US Navy were *Dwight D Eisenhower*, *Richmond*, *Comte de Grasse* and *Yellowstone*, and from France the aircraft carrier *Clemenceau*. The German vessel FGS *Bayern* and Dutch frigate *Kartenaer* were also present. The exercise was designed to provide convoy protection on the Atlantic trade routes and after a five-day breather at Lisbon the exercises moved from the Portuguese coast to the west of Ireland. On 26 October, however, with the exercise concluded, *Antrim* returned to Portsmouth to undergo a docking and maintenance period, which would take her into the fateful year of 1982.

For the Royal Navy the new year of 1982 was almost entirely dominated by the news of swingeing cuts to the fleet and the threat of over 500 redundancies. The newly commissioned *Invincible* was to be sold to the Australian Navy and both *Fearless* and *Intrepid* were to be withdrawn, as were *Antrim*, *Fife* and *Glamorgan*. However, one proposed cut which received little publicity outside the Navy was that of the ice patrol ship, HMS *Endurance*, which kept a tenuous link between Britain and the country's most isolated remnants of what had once been the British Empire, namely the Falkland Islands, and the even more remote South Atlantic island of South Georgia. There is no doubt that the withdrawal of *Endurance*, added to the apparent disinterest shown by the Foreign Secretary when negotiating with his Argentine counterpart, who had even considered handing sovereignty to Argentine and then leasing them back, encouraged the ruling military junta in Argentina to believe that although Britain may protest at any military invasion of the islands, they would not go as far as taking military action to recover them. The military junta in Argentina was deeply unpopular and in the past such unpopularity had been overcome by sabre-rattling about the Falkland Islands. At that time, however, as *Antrim* lay inboard of *Glamorgan* at Portsmouth's South Railway Jetty, the Falkland Islands, or indeed the South Atlantic generally, were not on anyone's minds.

At 1230 on 6 January 1982 *Antrim* slipped her moorings and sailed to begin post-refit trials in the Channel, before returning to Portsmouth where she secured alongside the redundant *Devonshire*. Throughout the latter half of January and into February the ship continued her training from Portsmouth and Portland, but during the forenoon of 17 March, wearing the flag of FOF1, Rear-Admiral J. F. Woodward, she sailed for Gibraltar. Accompanying her from Portsmouth for the annual 'Springtrain' exercises were *Coventry* and *Glamorgan*, and en route they were joined by *Ariadne*, *Broadsword*, *Battleaxe*, *Yarmouth* and other ships. However, on 19 March reports from the British Antarctic Survey personnel who were based on the island of South Georgia, indicated that a party of Argentine scrap metal workers had landed illegally and raised the Argentine flag. Not only had they landed illegally, but they had been brought to the island by an Argentine naval support ship *Bahia Buen Suceso*, which had also allowed its crew to go ashore. As this was the second such incident in the space of four months it was strongly suspected that the scrap metal workers were being supported by the Argentine government, but this latest was the most serious. In London it was agreed that HMS *Endurance* would be dispatched to evict the Argentines and at the same time there was a flurry of diplomatic activity. Matters soon took a turn for the worse when reports were received in London that Argentine warships were on their way to South Georgia to prevent *Endurance* evicting the men. By Saturday 27 March it was clear that there was also intensive naval activity at the Argentine bases at Mar del Plata and Puerto Belgrano, where the embarkation of large numbers of marines, equipment and vehicles was taking place. The next day the Argentine Foreign Minister made it clear that the Argentines on South Georgia would remain and that the blame for this situation lay with Britain for refusing to accept Argentine sovereignty. By 30 March, the C-in-C Fleet, Admiral Sir John Fieldhouse, who was at Gibraltar for the 'Springtrain' exercises, considered that the situation was serious enough for him to justify returning to

London. Before leaving Gibraltar, however, he ordered Woodward to, 'Prepare to detach a suitable group of ships to store, ammunition and to be ready to proceed to the South Atlantic if required.'

Meanwhile, having arrived at Gibraltar on 24 March, *Antrim* and the other ships were preparing for the exercises and at 0905 on Monday 29 March *Antrim* led 27 ships to sea for a high seas firing phase of the manoeuvres. On 31 March *Antrim* and *Glamorgan* fired some six Sea Slug missiles, four of them at pilotless drones, but two of them were used as targets for Sea Dart missiles. Lt-Cdr Ian Inskip from *Glamorgan* describes the firings: 'The Sea Slug missiles, weighing two tons apiece, leapt skywards. Once the four wrap-round boosters dropped off two miles down range, the sustainer motors took the missiles towards the Chukar targets, riding the radar beam, and both firings were successful.' Next day the force was operating in the Atlantic Ocean between Casablanca and Madeira. For *Antrim* the day had been routine, with the ship's Wessex helicopter 'Humphrey' engaged in target recovery for the high seas firings. During the afternoon an upturned yacht was found which, after a thorough examination by the ship's divers, was destroyed by a demolition team. That same evening down in the South Atlantic the destroyer *Santissimo Trinidad*, last encountered by *Antrim* at Portsmouth's Fountain Lake Jetty, was anchored off East Falkland and landing Argentine Marines of an elite amphibious commando company to attack the small, but now empty, Royal Marines Barracks at Moody Brook. Next morning at 0630 the main Argentine assault force landed just north of Stanley and despite a spirited resistance at Government House by the 80 Royal Marines, by the afternoon the Argentines were in control of the islands. In Britain the news caused an unprecedented sense of national shock and a political decision was made to dispatch a task force to the South Atlantic to retake the islands.

During the night of 1/2 April came the news that *Antrim*, together with most of the 'Springtrain' ships, was required to sail south with the initial destination being Ascension Island. At the same time three nuclear-powered submarines, *Conqueror*, *Spartan* and *Splendid* were ordered south to the area around the Falkland Islands, while at Portsmouth and at Devonport urgent preparations were under way to dispatch an amphibious task force to the South Atlantic. Suddenly the swingeing Defence cuts which had been proposed were seen to be short-sighted and wholly inappropriate.

On 3 April, as *Antrim* and her group steamed south, Argentine forces invaded and occupied the island of South Georgia, although the only people on the island were members of the British Antarctic Survey Team, together with a film crew. On 7 April the C-in-C Fleet, who assumed overall command of the operation to recover the occupied territory, was ordered to plan for the repossession of South Georgia. *Antrim's* CO was nominated as the Commander of the Task Group allocated to the task, the other ships being *Plymouth*, *Endurance* and RFA *Tidespring*, with *Brilliant* joining them later. Woodward transferred his flag to *Glamorgan* and work began to convert the Admiral's day cabin in *Antrim* to a military operations room. On Saturday 10 April, during the morning watch, Ascension Island was sighted on the horizon and two hours later, with *Plymouth* and *Tidespring*, she arrived off the island to begin an intensive period of embarking stores, ammunition and troops. Embarked in *Tidespring* was M Company, 42 Commando, Royal Marines, while in *Antrim* men of the SAS were embarked. *Antrim* remained in the vicinity of Ascension Island for two days taking on stores and equipment, before sailing to rendezvous with *Plymouth* and *Tidespring* for the onward passage south through increasingly inclement weather. On 13 April she transferred further stores and ammunition and additional special forces personnel from RFA *Fort Austin*. Next forenoon the force rendezvoused with HMS *Endurance*, which meant that the group assigned to the recapture of South Georgia was complete and the operation, code-named 'Paraquat', could go ahead.

As the group sailed south at 13 knots intelligence reports on Argentine forces occupying South Georgia indicated that there were probably some 50

HMS Antrim

A view looking down on the icy, inhospitable terrain of Fortuna Glacier, South Georgia, taken during the abortive SAS reconnaisance mission, which was intended to monitor Argentine activities in Leith Harbour, but was abandoned when severe gales and blinding snowstorms engulfed the glacier.

(*Imperial War Museum/FKD 133*)

to 60 marines at Grytviken, the main settlement, and up to 20 in Leith, as well as 15 scrap metal workers. It was recognised that further reinforcements may well have been landed. The reports suggested that South Georgia might be '...stiffly defended, but not "to the death" if confronted by superior force levels.' Another important factor to be taken into account was the weather, with the possibility of small boat and Gemini operations being impossible. It was apparent that helicopters would be vital for troop movements and as far as the ships were concerned there was also the likelihood of icebergs to the north and east of the island to be taken into account, but advice from *Endurance* indicated that an approach from that direction would be possible with caution. The operation was planned in three phases, the first being the landing of SAS and SBS reconnaissance parties by helicopter and, if possible, by small boats. The second phase would be the gathering of intelligence by these teams, and finally there was the main military landing and assault.

During the passage south, when weather conditions permitted, Gemini transfers were practised with 16 soldiers at a time being transferred between *Antrim* and *Plymouth*, while the ship's Wessex helicopter 'Humphrey', which had a general-purpose machine-gun installed in the starboard cabin window, undertook carried out intensive training as well as a large number of sorties transporting troops between the ships. On 20 April, during the latter stages of the approach to South Georgia, weather conditions began to deteriorate, with gale force winds, heavy seas, blinding snow blizzards and intense cold. Next day, the group arrived off South Georgia, still in very poor weather, but at first light, around 0930 as the ship was working in zulu time (Greenwich Mean Time), 'Humphrey' made an initial reconnaissance and despite driving rain and strong winds it was decided that the operation to land the reconnaissance parties could go ahead. The helicopter returned to pick up the troops, followed by *Tidepool's* two Wessex helicopters which had also embarked men from *Antrim's* flight deck. All three aircraft then flew across the bleak, inhospitable mountain ranges to Fortuna Glacier, itself an extremely dangerous and inhospitable frozen landscape, in order to land the troops who could then approach Grytviken from an unexpected direction. However, by the time the helicopters had reached Possession Bay, thick, low cloud was shrouding the area, together with driving rain and snowstorms, so the formation returned to their ships. By 1305, with weather conditions having improved, a second attempt was made to land the troops on the glacier and despite driving snow squalls, vast layers of blinding white snow which covered the area and sudden changes in the wind direction, all three helicopters landed on the glacier and successfully discharged their troops and equipment before returning to their ships.

That night, however, the barometer fell drastically and the ships spent the night riding out storm force winds, with gusts of up to 70 knots and mountainous seas. It was said that very few people on board *Antrim* slept that night as the ship rolled, pitched and juddered as waves hit her with tremendous force. It came as no surprise when, next day, the troops on Fortuna Glacier radioed to say that their position had become untenable and that they might not survive for more than another 12 hours. What had begun as a reconnaissance flight had now turned into a rescue mission and despite the fact that the weather was considerably worse than it had been for some days, the three Wessex helicopters were to attempt to evacuate the SAS troopers.

All three aircraft were launched at 1100, but with heavy, and at times blinding, snowstorms and gale force winds buffeting the area, they were unable to locate the party and they returned to their ships to refuel. At 1330 they were relaunched for a further attempt and this time, despite the strong winds and swirling low clouds interspersed with heavy snowstorms which were sweeping across the glacier, they located the SAS teams and managed to land. However, when it came to taking off again, the pilots of the two Wessex 5s from *Tidespring* had lost all points of reference and orientation in the 'white out' conditions, which resulted in them crashing, fortunately with no serious injuries. As there was no possibility of getting the aircraft airborne or recovering them, this left only *Antrim's* 'Humphrey' to evacuate both the helicopter crews and the SAS personnel. Given the appalling weather conditions the helicopter had to return to *Antrim* and wait for a break in the weather, which came later in the afternoon but with only a short period remaining before darkness fell. In the event 'Humphrey' was launched again at 1630 and Admiral Fieldhouse described the operation as, 'a remarkable feat of airmanship which succeeded in recovering the entire detachment and the crews of the crashed helicopters.' For readers who are interested in reading more of this extremely hazardous operation I recommend Chris Parry's book, *Down South – A Falklands War Diary*.

At 0215 the next morning, with the ship closed up at Action Stations and during a lull in snowstorms, *Antrim* steamed into Stromness Bay on the north side of the island where, after great difficulty starting the Gemini outboard motors, the SAS launched a second attempt to land reconnaissance parties on the island and by 0435 the ship had manoeuvred back out of the bay to patrol her area. However, the engine on one of the boats subsequently failed which meant 'Humphrey' had to be launched to search for it and eventually its occupants, having drifted some five miles from the drop point, were

A close-up of *Antrim's* twin 4.5-inch guns firing at Argentine positions on Brown mountain, South Georgia, on the day that the Royal Marines retook the island. The ship's Exocet missile launchers can be seen in the foreground.　　(*Imperial War Museum/FKD 55*)

rescued. That afternoon both *Antrim* and *Plymouth* detected an Argentine Hercules C130 reconnaissance aircraft overflying the area, but out of Sea Slug range. It was not thought that the aircraft had detected *Antrim's* group but at 1450 a signal was received that the Argentine submarine *Santa Fe* was in the area. It was vital that the RFA tankers were protected and this information changed the whole aspect of the South Georgia operation for not only was there enemy air surveillance, but the presence of a submarine posed a very real threat to the whole operation. That night Captain Young ordered *Plymouth*, *Brambleleaf* and *Tidespring* to remain north of the island while at first light on 24 April *Antrim* would land troops ashore at Leith. However, shortly before *Antrim* detached from the force to carry out this mission the group again came under surveillance by an Argentine Hercules. It was decided that the risk of *Antrim* being trapped by *Santa Fe* whilst carrying out the amphibious landing was too great and the operation was cancelled. However, another intelligence report indicated that *Santa Fe* would be attempting to land troop reinforcements on South Georgia and that she might enter Grytviken during the night of 24/25 April. As a result *Antrim* closed to within 50 miles of the island and at just after 0700 on 25 April the Wessex helicopter was launched to search for and, if possible, depth charge the submarine.

At just before 0900 the Wessex sighted *Santa Fe* on the surface some five miles north of Banff Point at the entrance to Cumberland Bay, on the island's north coast, and after carefully checking that the boat was definitely an Argentine Guppy-class submarine, the Wessex attacked with two MkII depth charges, which exploded close to the port casing. With oil streaming from its hull, and after some violent careering in the water, *Santa Fe* headed for Grytviken. *Plymouth* was immediately requested to launch her Wasp and *Brilliant*, which had recently joined the group, launched her Lynx. In addition to the machine-gun attacks by all three helicopters, *Endurance's* Wasp fired two AS12 missiles at the submarine which punched holes in the fin and exploded. By this time *Santa Fe*, with her bow low in the water, was no longer a threat and she eventually secured alongside the British Antarctic Pier at Grytviken.

As it was now obvious that the group's presence at South Georgia was known to the Argentine garrison, while the helicopters were in the area of Cumberland Bay the opportunity was taken to carry out reconnaissance to locate any military dispositions in the area; immediately following this preparations were put in hand for a landing at 1040 the same day. It was decided that the troops on board *Antrim* would be the first to land after a bombardment of the Grytviken area. This began at 1410 and was carried out by all three warships for 35 minutes, immediately after which an assorted force of Royal Marines, SAS and SBS was flown ashore. By 1730 the Argentine flag had been struck at Grytviken and next day, after a brief prevarication, the notorious Commander Alfredo Astiz signed a surrender document on board *Plymouth*. He was the leader of the small garrison of Argentine marines at Leith but was mistakenly credited with having commanded all Argentine forces in South Georgia.

Meanwhile, in atrocious weather again, with gale force winds and blinding snowstorms, *Antrim* anchored off King Edward Cove to unload stores for the troops ashore, while at the same time some 200 Argentine prisoners were distributed between *Antrim* and *Tidespring*. On 26 April, having carried out a survey of the damaged submarine *Santa Fe*, it was found that the boat was in a parlous state and to prevent it from fouling and blocking the only jetty at Grytviken, it was decided to shift the vessel across the bay to the old whaling station. Later that day Royal Navy personnel, assisted by a number of key Argentine ratings, began to move the submarine under its own power, but it rapidly began to lose buoyancy and an Argentine Chief Petty Officer moved swiftly to start the air pumps which would maintain flotation, an action which was misunderstood by his Royal Marine guard as an attempt to scuttle the boat and he was shot dead. The unfortunate man was later buried in Grytviken cemetery with full military honours.

During the early hours of 3 May, *Antrim* left the waters of South Georgia and soon afterwards her Argentine prisoners, including Astiz, the BAS personnel and two Antarctic Teal ducks (for onward passage to the UK) were transferred to *Antelope*, after which *Antrim* rendezvoused with the LSL group of amphibious ships, including *Sir Galahad*, *Sir Geraint*, *Sir Lancelot* and *Sir Percival*, to escort them south to the Falkland Islands. During the afternoon of 16 May, some 650 nautical miles ENE of Stanley, *Antrim* and her group rendezvoused with the main amphibious force led by *Fearless*, which also included the P&O liner *Canberra*. The whole convoy of 19 ships then steamed at an average speed of 11.5knots towards the Falkland Islands. Two days later, some 200 miles ENE of Stanley, they rendezvoused with *Hermes* and later in the forenoon with *Invincible*. That same day Argentina announced that her Air Force could muster well over 100 aircraft, with more than 70 Skyhawks, several squadrons of Mirage fighters and Super Entendards, with Exocet missiles, which had already demonstrated their deadly effectiveness against *Sheffield*. Next day the whole force went onto a war footing which, according to one officer, during the hours of darkness saw: 'Twenty-two darkened ships with no navigation lights charging around in the inky-black nights, which was highly dangerous and there was more than one close shave

HMS Antrim

HMS *Antrim* at South Georgia on 28 April 1982. She served as the flagship for 'Operation Paraquat', the recapture of South Georgia, before proceeding to the Falkland Islands ahead of 5 infantry Brigade in *Canberra*.
(*Imperial War Museum/FKD 344*)

as ships almost collided.' On 19 May there was a massive cross-decking of troops between *Canberra* and the other amphibious ships. Next day they were just 100 miles north-east of Stanley, heading west, with the task force and convoy taking station on *Sir Lancelot* and the escorts in an anti-aircraft formation. All round the amphibious ships were the screening destroyers and frigates, including *Antrim*, *Brilliant*, *Broadsword*, *Yarmouth*, *Ardent*, *Plymouth* and *Argonaut*, with *Invincible* in close company providing air cover. Ahead of the force were four anti-submarine helicopters on patrol and at 1100 the fleet began its fast transit of the Total Exclusion Zone.

At 2320 on 20 May, just before *Ardent* and *Antrim* led the invasion force into Falkland Sound, *Antrim's* Wessex was launched on the first of three missions to land a small group of SBS personnel and a naval officer to direct the naval gunfire support, onto the promontory of Fanning Head, which lay on the eastern side of the entrance to Falkland Sound. It was known that a section of an Argentine Infantry Regiment was defending the area of very hilly and uneven ground on that dark, moonless night, which made the missions extremely hazardous. By 0246 on 21 May the Wessex had successfully accomplished the three flights to land the troops. Just over 20 minutes later *Antrim* and

Ardent steamed into Falkland Sound to begin an extremely heavy and effective bombardment of the Argentine positions on Fanning Head, during which *Antrim* destroyed fuel and ammunition dumps. By 0520 large numbers of troops and their stores, equipment and ammunition had been landed, following which *Antrim* remained under way in the Sound, sheltered by the hills of Sussex Mountains. At 1245 the first Argentine planes were sighted, as Pucara light attack/reconnaissance aircraft attacked *Argonaut*. The twin-engined Pucara was the only aircraft the Argentine Air Force could base on the Falkland Islands themselves and its capabilities were very limited. However, a few minutes later the first Skyhawks appeared and soon afterwards the ships in Falkland Sound came under heavy air attack from them and Mirage aircraft which were being flown from the Argentine mainland. Being so far away from their bases meant these aircraft could spend only a relatively short time over the Falklands, which limited their effectiveness, but despite this handicap their attacks on the warships in Falkland Sound and San Carlos Water were fierce and they came at regular intervals throughout the day. During this period *Antrim* manoeuvred hard to avoid the attackers and with some success, but at 1325, in a heavy onslaught, Argentine aircraft strafed the ship with 30mm cannon, wounding three members of the ship's company, the most serious being CPO Terence Bullingham who was permanently blinded. In addition a 500lb bomb hit the ship, slamming through the port Sea Slug flash door situated behind the launcher, before punching its way through the pyrotechnic magazine and several bulkheads before coming to rest in the after heads (toilets), close to the Sea Slug magazine. Although it devastated the compartment, because it had been fused for high-level bombing, the low-level attack meant there had not been sufficient time for the bomb to be armed and it had not exploded. One officer who saw the missile descend described it as being olive green in colour, with an identification plate which showed it had been made in Derby.

Antrim continued to manoeuvre in order to avoid further air attacks and while awaiting the arrival of a bomb disposal team, damage control parties worked to clear away the debris, wedging the bomb to prevent movement and packing mattresses around it while awaiting the arrival of FCPO (Diver) Michael Fellows and his team. As it was impossible to determine whether or not the bomb was armed, the decision was taken to attempt to lift it from its position close to the Sea Slug magazine to the flight deck, from where it could be lowered into the water. However, this was to be a difficult and dangerous operation, made all the more so by the fact that throughout the operation the ship was under further air attack. This was the first unexploded bomb dealt with during the Falklands conflict but, despite the absence of precedent, Fellows led his team with complete disregard for personal safety. During the ten-hour period while oxy-acetylene cutting equipment was used to make holes in deckheads in order to lift the bomb onto the flight deck, smoke from the cutting and from burning materials forced personnel to wear cumbersome breathing apparatus. Eventually, however, with darkness having fallen, the ship's log records: '2345 - Let go the 500lb UXB over the starboard side in position 51°23.45S 059°05.5W.'

Friday 21 May had been a day of almost constant air raids which had seen *Ardent* sunk and both *Antrim* and *Argonaut* damaged by bombs which had failed to explode, but overall the landing of troops from *Canberra* and other ships of the amphibious force had been successful. That night *Canberra* left San Carlos Water and *Antrim* escorted her out to the open sea where they joined *Hermes* and *Invincible*. Four days later *Antrim* rendezvoused in the area which had been designated as the 'Tug and Repair Area' (TARA) with the oil rig support ship *Stena Seaspread*, which was carrying 160 personnel from the Fleet Maintenance Units and was equipped with lathes and other machinery. However, during the evening of 25 May, before the repairs could be completed, *Antrim* was ordered to steam to South Georgia to rendezvous with the Cunard cruise ship *QE2* and embark Major-General Jeremy Moore, the land forces commander, and his staff. Also on passage were *Canberra* and *Norland*, who were to embark 5 Brigade, made up of Scots and Welsh Guards and Gurkhas, from *QE2*. *Antrim* arrived at South Georgia during the afternoon and by 1535 she had embarked some 76 passengers and was heading back through heavy seas made all the more hazardous by the presence of icebergs, to the Falkland Islands. For most of the passage south, because of the lack of secure communications equipment, Moore had been incommunicado with London, so after boarding *Antrim* he had a great deal of catching up to do. During *Antrim's* return passage to the TEZ, Goose Green was captured, but at sea *Antelope*, *Coventry* and the merchantman *Atlantic Conveyor*, which had virtually taken on the role of an auxiliary aircraft carrier, had been lost. On board *Antrim* the damaged helicopter 'Humphrey' was repaired and after rendezvousing with *Fearless* during the evening of 28 May, Major-General Moore and his staff were transferred to the assault ship, while two Argentine POWs were embarked in *Antrim* before being transferred to *Hermes* the next day.

Antrim's stay in the TEZ was brief and on the last day of May she sailed for South Georgia once again. She had been designated as the Air Defence Ship for the island and during her time spent patrolling off the island news was received that *Glamorgan* had been hit by an Argentine Exocet missile, but had survived. While *Antrim* was under way, some 36 hours were spent changing the gun barrels of A turret and the new ones were then test-fired against an iceberg. That same day, 14 June, came the news of the surrender of the Argentine forces on the Falkland Islands and four days later ships of the Task Force began returning home. By 22 June *Antrim* was the last remaining ship from the original 'Springtrain' group left in the South Atlantic and two days later came the milestones of 100 days since leaving Portsmouth and her 88th day at sea. Finally, however, on Saturday 26 June, *Antrim* was ordered to rendezvous with the Task Force off the Falkland Islands and at 1345 she left

Small boats begin to gather around *Antrim* to welcome her home on 17 July 1982. *(Derek Fox)*

County Class GMDs

A Royal Marines Band, together with a good turnout of families, flocked to Portsmouth Dockyard's North West Wall to welcome *Antrim* back home after her service in the South Atlantic.
(Author's collection)

South Georgia to steam west, first to rendezvous with RFA *Resource* and then, during the forenoon of 28 June, to rendezvous with *Hermes* where instructions were received for the passage home. Finally, after a brief visit to Falkland Sound to collect a passenger, *Antrim* was homeward-bound.

The passage north was a relaxed affair, but initially the weather conditions were atrocious, with severe gales and heavy seas. During the forenoon of 3 July, *Antrim* rendezvoused with *Southampton*, *Birmingham*, *Apollo* and *Bacchante*, which were on their way south, and after a transfer of stores, ammunition and mail *Antrim* continued north at 22 knots, through what were now much calmer and warmer seas. During the evening of 6 July it was mild enough to hold a barbeque and 'Grand Falkland Draw' on the flight deck, the mood of which was summed up by one officer thus: 'It was all very good natured and the conversation and close engagement among all ranks reflected the intensity of shared danger, experience and success over the previous three months.' At 2145 on 7 July, Ascension Island was sighted and during the early hours of the following morning the personnel of the advanced leave party were flown ashore and the ship refuelled from the tanker MV *Alveda*. By midday the ship was once again steaming north, and during the early hours of 13 July she passed between the islands of Tenerife and Grand Canary. Later that day a medical case was flown ashore to Funchal, Madeira. At 0415 on 16 July Ushant was sighted and just over 13 hours later the C-in-C Fleet, Admiral Sir John Fieldhouse, landed on board to tour the ship and meet officers and men. At 2109 *Antrim* anchored at Spithead and next forenoon, having been away for 121 days, of which 110 had been spent at sea, she weighed anchor to steam up harbour to a rapturous welcome from a flotilla of small boats and crowds lining Southsea seafront. At 1115 she secured alongside and the last entry in the ship's log that day reads: 'Berthed starboard side to NWW (North West Wall) to a tremendous welcoming home.'

Following her return from the South Atlantic *Antrim* remained in dockyard hands for 81 days and it was Wednesday 6 October 1982 before she slipped her moorings from alongside the redundant HMS *Tiger* in Fareham Creek to begin her post-refit trials from Portland. After eight days of intensive training she visited the port of Larne, where she secured alongside the Tanker Jetty at Ballylumford for four days. *Antrim's* trials and work-up ended in late October with a passage into the North Sea to take part in an air defence exercise with RAF Phantom aircraft, before she returned to Portsmouth to give leave.

On 3 November *Antrim* hoisted the flag of FOF2, Rear-Admiral Robert Gerken, and five days later she left Portsmouth bound for the South Atlantic again. That same afternoon she was joined by *Liverpool*, *Ariadne*, *Charybdis* and RFA *Tidespring*, and after a short exercise with the submarine *Osiris*, the force set course. The four warships were to undertake guardship duties around the Falkland Islands and South Georgia where they would be joined by *Minerva*. The group arrived in the 'Protection Zone' on 27 November where they went to Defence Watches. *Antrim's* second tour of duty in the waters surrounding the Falkland Islands was much quieter than her first visit, with long patrols interspersed with exercises and manoeuvres with other ships of the group and the submarine *Warspite*. On 24 December she secured alongside *Stena Inspector* in Port William Sound where, at one hour's notice for sea, Christmas was celebrated. On 30 December, however, the ship's company were once again in Defence Watches as *Antrim* put to sea to continue her patrolling of the Falkland Islands Protection Zone. On 11 January 1983, as she lay alongside the oil tanker *British Forth* in San Carlos Water, the Prime Minister Margaret Thatcher made a two-hour visit to the ship and during the next patrol the destroyer exercised with *Liverpool* and *Minerva*. During the evening of 28 January she held a wreath-laying ceremony over the spot where, some eight months previously, HMS *Sheffield* had been sunk. On 27 February *Antrim* left San Carlos Bay and, in company with *Charybdis* and *Minerva*, she set course for home.

Pausing briefly at Ascension Island and for a

County Class GMDs

HMS Antrim

(Left) On 1 August 1983 *Antrim* returned to Portsmouth after a visit to the Danish port of Arhus. Note the lack of colour on the boats, masts and funnel tops. *(Crown Copyright/MoD 1983)*

weekend at Gibraltar, the three ships arrived in home waters on 24 March and during the early evening *Antrim* anchored at Spithead. Next day she steamed up harbour to secure alongside Portsmouth's North West Wall for a ten-week docking and maintenance period. On 15 April Captain Brian Young was relieved by Captain Jake D. L. Backus RN and on 31 May the ship put to sea to carry out her post-refit trials. During June, as part of her work-up she joined 'Exercise Ocean Safari' in the South West Approaches, during which she joined *Arethusa* in an 'attack' on a French carrier group and following this visited Cardiff. In July she joined *Fife* and *Glamorgan* for exercises in the North Sea, which included a weekend visit to Arhus. In August *Antrim* took part in a joint Families Day with *Glamorgan*, before returning to Portsmouth to give seasonal leave.

After taking part in Navy Days at the end of August, on 27 September *Antrim* sailed to Portland for weapons training prior to a 'Westlant' deployment which began two days later when, wearing the flag of FOF2 and accompanied by RFA *Pearleaf*, she sailed for Bermuda. Here, on 9 October, she rendezvoused with *Berwick* then the three ships steamed on to the US naval base at Florida's Key West. In mid-October *Antrim* was engaged in exercises off the Colombian coast and on 19 October she secured alongside at Cartagena's commercial dockyard.

Soon after *Antrim's* arrival in the Caribbean there were political problems on the island of Grenada, the most southerly of the Windward Islands, with an area of 133 square miles and a population of some 110,000. The island, which had been discovered by Columbus in 1498, was a British colony between 1783 and 1974 and following independence it had been politically stable. On 19 October 1983, however, a coup by hard-line Marxists led to the murder of the Prime Minister, Maurice Bishop, followed by civil unrest and disorder. The pro-Communist sympathies of the new regime worried the US President, Ronald Reagan, who was particularly concerned about the regime's contacts with Cuba. Whether or not Britain, as the former colonial power, was consulted by the USA regarding their intentions is a matter for some dispute, but during the early evening of 22 October *Antrim* was ordered to come to immediate notice for steam and prepare for an early 'sailing to Grenada due to troubles on the island.' However, it was not until the following morning that *Antrim* received the order to sail for Grenada and en route prepare for an 'opposed evacuation' of some 250 Britons, including 40 holidaymakers, who were known to be on the island. It was stressed that the ship would not interfere in the island's internal affairs. After leaving Cartagena at 0800 on 23 October *Antrim* rendezvoused with *Pearleaf* to refuel, before beginning a 24-knot passage to Grenada. Next day, at 2100, she passed south of a US Navy invasion fleet led by the aircraft carrier *Independence* and the assault ship *Guam*. At 0540 on 25 October, they landed a combined force of US marines and a contingent of troops from OECS States (Barbados, Jamaica, Dominica, St Lucia and St Vincent), with the island's airport as their first objective. That day *Antrim* remained in the area between Barbados and Grenada while preparations were made on board to accommodate the refugees. The Admiral's cabin was converted into a temporary wardroom, while the original wardroom was made ready to accommodate female evacuees. Five ratings' messdecks were prepared for male passengers, with the original occupants being dispersed around other messes, office spaces and the ship's hangar. In the event, however, although there was some resistance to the US-led invasion, order was quickly restored and *Antrim* was not required to evacuate British nationals, so after flying in supplies to the British High Commission, the destroyer patrolled off Grenada observing the movements of the US fleet. During the evening of 3 November, with the political situation in Grenada having stabilised, *Antrim* was stood down and, after a three-day break at Bridgetown, Barbados, she resumed her routine duties, which began with Sea Slug firings in the US Navy exercise areas off Roosevelt Roads. These were followed by visits to Savannah, West Palm Beach and finally St George's, Bermuda, from where *Antrim* set course for home, arriving in Portsmouth Harbour during the forenoon of 14 December.

During the first months of 1984 *Antrim* took part in a series of exercises and visits and for one major exercise in northern waters, which also involved *Illustrious*, *Andromeda*, *Arethusa*, the US assault ship *Nassau* and a powerful US carrier group, as well as French, Norwegian, German and Dutch warships, she flew the flag of FOF2, Rear-Admiral D. B. Bathurst. The manoeuvres took *Antrim* to stormy waters around Cape Wrath, the Faroes Gap, south of Iceland and the Lofoten Islands, ending on 30 March with enjoyable visits to Bordeaux and Lisbon. On 13 April she began a three-day farewell visit to her adopted county of Antrim when she arrived alongside at Larne. While she was there a number of Chilean Naval personnel joined the ship, for there had long been rumours that the destroyer was to be acquired by Chile. The ship's bell was promised to Antrim Council and the ship's company took part in a busy round of social engagements. Leaving Larne on 16 April, the next day was *Antrim's* last day at sea with the Royal Navy and during the forenoon of 18 April, flying her 664 ft-long paying-off pennant, she steamed up Portsmouth Harbour to secure alongside South Railway Jetty. That afternoon the main leave period began and most of her ship's company were dispersed. On 22 May, with the ship lying in D Lock, Captain Backus held a farewell lunch for *Antrim's* sponsor, Marjorie Mason, and seven days later a

A final view of *Almirante Cochrane* as she looked when serving with the Chilean Navy. She was finally sold for scrap in 2010. *(Armada de Chile)*

Chilean Navy steaming crew arrived on board.

It had been known since the summer of 1983 that preliminary negotiations with the Chilean Government for the sale of *Antrim* were under way, but these were not concluded until 1125 on 22 June 1984 when the handover ceremony took place in the forenoon with the ship having been renamed CNS *Almirante Cochrane*. By that time only a small party of Royal Navy personnel were left on board for liaison duties.

On 10 September 1984 *Almirante Cochrane* arrived at Valparaiso to begin a refit which lasted until April 1985, when she was recommissioned. In 1990 her Sea Slug missile system was removed and the flight deck extended so that she could operate Puma helicopters. Her Sea Cat missile system was replaced by the Barak 1 SAM system and in 1998 she took part in the first Chilean-Argentine naval exercises off the Chilean coast. Her career with the Chilean Navy lasted until December 2006 when she was decommissioned, but it was not until December 2010 that she was sold to China for scrap.

Commanding Officers:

Captain Hubert W. E. Hollins RN	18 March 1970
Captain David A. Loram RN	6 September 1971
Captain George A. F. Bower RN	23 May 1973
Captain Harry R. Keate RN	14 May 1974
Captain R. Michael Burgoyne RN	12 November 1975
Captain Gordon F. Walwyn CVO RN	3 October 1977
Captain Michael F. Parry RN	27 March 1979
Captain Brian G. Young RN	18 August 1981
Captain Jake D. L. Backus RN	15 April 1983

Battle Honours:

Falkland Islands 1982

Appendix One

APPENDIX ONE
SEA SLUG & HMS GIRDLE NESS

HMS *Girdle Ness* in September 1956, at around the time she began the first Sea Slug trials.
(Ken Kelly Collection)

The eight County-class destroyers were designed first and foremost to accommodate the Sea Slug missile system and its associated control equipment, with the magazine positioned amidships and the missiles being assembled in a central gallery forward of the magazine, from where they were passed aft to the launcher on the quarterdeck. The Sea Slug arrangements were designed for what was envisaged in the 1950s as a possible future nuclear war against Soviet-bloc countries, and apart from the launch itself all the handling of the missiles was carried out within the ships' airtight citadels. In 1954 the Director of Plans at the Admiralty described Sea Slug thus: 'Sea Slug will be to conventional AA gunnery as radical and revolutionary an advance in weapon development as rifles were to muskets – or even bows and arrows.'

The origins of Sea Slug can be traced back to the Second World War and a rocket test programme carried out by the Fairey Aviation Company known as 'Liquid Oxygen & Petrol Guided Anti-Aircraft Projectile' (LOPGAP). Most of the early tests and development trials were carried out at Woomera in Australia and at RAE Aberporth at the southern end of Cardigan Bay, which had been opened in 1939 as an artillery firing range and went on to serve as a rocket-firing range until, in 1948, is was designated as a 'Guided Projectile Establishment.' The first missiles fired from Aberporth in 1948 under the first stage of the Royal Navy's guided missile programme were early, wooden-winged versions of Sea Slug, which used a wraparound booster technique.

By the early 1950s the development of Sea Slug had reached the stage where the missile and all its systems needed to be taken to sea and tested in realistic conditions. Initially a number of options were considered, including fitting of Sea Slug to the cruiser *Swiftsure* and to a converted landing ship tank and using them in the role of guided missile trials ships. It was thought that the tank deck in the latter would provide plenty of space for the missile magazines and other equipment, but the poor seakeeping qualities of this type of vessel led to the idea being abandoned and in 1952 it was decided instead to convert the landing craft maintenance ship, HMS *Girdle Ness*, an unpretentious and ungainly looking vessel.

HMS *Girdle Ness* had been laid down in December 1944 by the Burrard Dry Dock Company at their Vancouver shipyard in Canada and she was just one of a number of Victory Ships ordered that year, with a view to employing them as maintenance ships in the Far East and Pacific for the final stages of the war against Japan. She was launched in March 1945, but by the time she had commissioned in September that year the Second World War was over. For some years she served as an accommodation ship at Rosyth, but in the summer of 1951 she was reduced to Reserve. In February 1953, having been chosen as the guided weapon trials ship, she was shifted to Devonport where she began a three-year conversion. During this period all her superstructure was stripped away, compartments were cleared out and much of the forward section of the ship was gutted. Her main boilers were replaced and additional generators were

Another view of *Girdle Ness* in 1956. She is much changed from her original appearance in the mid-1940s as a wartime Victory ship. *(Ken Kelly Collection)*

Appendix One

During Sea Slug trials in the Mediterranean in the late 1950s, missiles were transferred from RFAs to *Girdle Ness*. Here we see a missile packed in a cage being transferred from RFA *Retainer*. *(Ken Kelly Collection)*

installed. *Girdle Ness* was recommissioned for her new role on 24 July 1956 and next day *The Times*' naval correspondent, under the sub-heading 'Tangle of Masts' described the ship thus: 'In the past three years everything inside and above the hull has been transformed. The result is a vast, squared superstructure presided over by a tangle of radar masts and aerials which, in their number and variety are extraordinary even for modern ships. Forward, below the bridge, she shows her teeth; but the triple launcher for missiles is a surprisingly short affair which looks as if it consisted only of scaffolding. Below each of its ramps there is a flash-tight hatch from which the missiles will be raised by hydraulic power. They will come from their magazines on rails and will roll through flash-tight doors below decks to the launching site. The launcher can be trained and elevated and the weapons travel up it on tracks.'

In her trials role *Girdle Ness* had an overall length of 441ft 5in, a beam of 57ft 1in and a draught of 21ft 2in. She had a displacement tonnage of 9,107 tons and was a single-screw ship capable of steaming at a maximum speed of 9.5 knots. Forward of the bridge she was armed with a Mk 1 triple Sea Slug launcher and just in front of the forward mast was her octagonal Type 901 radar aerial. Such was the secrecy surrounding the guided weapons programme that *The Times* correspondent, on 25 July 1956, could only speculate thus: '...it is likely that the first weapon will be anti-aircraft, and it is assumed that it will be Sea Slug, the guided weapon which the Ministry of Supply have been developing for some years for the Navy. What the performance of the first missile will be is even more open to speculation.' On top of the mainmast was her Type 960 radar aerial and further aft were fitted Type 982 and 983 aerials. She carried a complement of 393 officers and men, as well as 50 civilians, of whom 20 were naval scientific officers. The officers' accommodation was mainly in the amidships superstructure, with senior officers' cabins and the wardroom mess in the after part of the superstructure. The civilian trials party were accommodated on No 2 deck forward and the ship's company were in broadside messdecks aft on No 2 and 3 decks.

In September 1956 *Girdle Ness* began her first trials in the area around Plymouth, in an area south of Eddystone, but as there was a great deal of Channel shipping in the area, subsequent firings were carried out in the Portland exercise areas B and C, in Lyme Bay, which proved to be suitable for short-range firings. In the Irish Sea, training in the handling of pilotless drones was undertaken. When the first missiles were launched the bridge and forward part of the ship were evacuated, but it soon became clear that this was unnecessary, as was the wearing of ear protection. The level of noise on the lower bridge during a launch was described by her commanding officer, Captain M. G. Greig, as being likened to '...that of a tube train emerging from a tunnel into an underground station.'

The first phase of the Sea Slug trials was carried out in home waters and in September 1957 came the first successful trials of the 901 beam rider. The missile used was a fully equipped prototype and at 5,000 yards after launch the radar beam had locked on and tracked the target until break-up at 21,000 yards. In early 1958 *Girdle Ness* steamed out to the Mediterranean, where the Sea Slug trials continued in the exercise areas around Malta. It was on 1 November 1961 that *Girdle Ness* fired her 209th and last Sea Slug missile, and in the following month, having returned to Devonport from Malta, she paid off. In 1962, together with HMS *Duncansby Head*, she was used as an accommodation ship at Rosyth under the name of *Cochrane*. Finally, in August 1970, she was towed to Faslane where she was scrapped.

The Sea Slug missile itself was designed by

Having completed her Sea Slug trials in December 1961 *Girdle Ness* left Malta to return home. For a time she was used as an accommodation ship at Rosyth before being scrapped in the summer of 1970.
(Ken Kelly Collection)

Appendix One

A Sea Slug missile being fired from a County-class destroyer. The missile is surrounded by four booster motors which detach in flight.
(Courtesy of John Simm)

Armstrong Whitworth as a surface-to-air missile, which was intended to engage high-flying nuclear-armed bombers. During the long trials period and, indeed, during much of its service it was dogged by controversy, mainly over cost, delays and the fact that the increasing pace of technological progress quickly rendered it obsolete. The missile was fitted with four wraparound booster motors which separated after its launch, when the main motor ignited to power the missile onto its target. The boosters were positioned in such a way as to generate acceleration and a gentle role to the missile after launching. Guidance of the Sea Slug was by radar beam-riding Type 901 X-band, fire-control radar, with its distinctive searchlight-shaped aerial. The main flight mode was known as 'Line of Sight, Beam-Riding' (LOSBR), during which the missile flew up a radar beam which was tracking the target. There was also a 'Constant Angle of Sight with Terminal Drive (CASWTD) flight method, where the missile climbed at a low angle, before diving onto a low-altitude target. Later, when the Mk 2 Sea Slug entered service, another flight method, 'Missile in Constant Altitude While Beam Riding' (MICAWBER), was introduced, which allowed for a terminal low-level glide phase so that the missile could be used against ships. However, this method was said to suffer from interference with light reflecting off the sea and disrupting the radar beam.

Throughout its development the overriding factor was the cost of Sea Slug. In 1958 the unit cost of a missile was shown as £20,000 and it was envisaged that each ship would have an outfit of 24 missiles, with reserves of 48, which was equal to two outfits. It was not long, however, before the unit cost had increased to £23,000 per missile and the Director of Gunnery could not give any unequivocal statement that the missile would not be obsolete by 1962, the date the first of the County-class ships was due to enter service. His report read: 'The missile possesses some capabilities for dealing with supersonic attack and should not therefore be obsolete, although potential enemy aircraft of supersonic speed are expected to be in operational service by 1965.' His report concluded: 'In view of the potential size of the (financial) commitment and the lack of any really reassuring report of Sea Slug's prospective capabilities, I have added the First Lord to the marking list.'

Although the Mk 2 Sea Slug did not enter service

until *Fife* was commissioned in 1966, it had first been test-fired some five years earlier so, as with the Mk 1, development was painfully slow. The Mk 2 Sea Slug had a better low-altitude performance, giving it a limited anti-ship capability. It also incorporated a homing guidance system which allowed for other targets to be illuminated while the first one was engaged. It was controlled by a modified Type 901 M radar, an improved proximity fuse and a continuous rod warhead.

By March 1982 Sea Slug was well and truly obsolete and during the annual 'Springtrain' exercises off Gibraltar the missile was given a new role, when *Glamorgan* fired two Sea Slugs as a target for the new Sea Dart missile as part of a tracking exercise for HM Ships *Coventry* and *Glasgow*. A few weeks later came the Falklands War when, some 20 years after it had entered operational service, Sea Slug was for the first and last time fired in anger. On 8 May, the day she was hit by a bomb which failed to explode, *Antrim* fired a Sea Slug at an approaching Argentine aircraft and a few weeks later *Glamorgan* fired two Sea Slug missiles at land targets around Port Stanley airfield. Lt Cdr Ian Inskip describes the occasion the first missile was fired at 0345 on 26 May: 'I piped "Glamorgan Airways announce the departure of their one-way flight to Stanley airfield!", and the first ever Sea Slug in the bombardment mode was launched. Firing at 17,000 yards allowed us immediately to engage with our 4.5-inch guns. Sea Slug landed in spectacular fashion. Whereas a shell burst flashes for a split second, the Sea Slug fireball, travelling at mach 2, held on for about two seconds, covering a wide area. Those on the airport would have had no warning, just a loud explosion and huge fireball.' However, the firing of Sea Slug was a distraction from the main business of the night as Ian Inskip goes on to describe: 'We then commenced the serious business of lobbing 150 shells in the wake of Sea Slug.' During the early hours of 30 May *Glamorgan* fired a second Sea Slug which Ian Inskip describes thus: 'When about 11 miles from the airport, we launched another Sea Slug. The arrival of the missile was announced by a brilliant flash as the fireball erupted across the airfield.' It was the last time Sea Slug was fired in anger and, once again, it was followed up by a 4.5-inch bombardment.

In August 1986, when *Glamorgan* was paid off for the last time, as far as the Royal Navy was concerned it was also the end of Sea Slug. The missile had been in operational service for some 23 years and in the following year the last of the County-class destroyers was sold, consigning the ships and their weapons into history.

Sea Slug Technical Data

Manufacturer:	Armstrong Whitworth/Hawker Siddley Group	
Length:	Mk 1: 19ft 8in (6m);	Mk 2: 20ft (6.1m)
Diameter:	Mk 1: 1ft 4in (0.42m);	Mk 2: 1ft 4in (0.42m)
Wingspan:	4ft 8in (1.44m)	
Weight:	Mk 1: 4,585lb (2,080kg);	Mk 2: 5,255lb 13oz (2,384kg)
Warhead:	Mk 1: 200lb (91kg) blast;	Mk 2: Continuous Rod
Engine:	Four, solid-fuel, jettisoned boosters and liquid fuel sustainer	
Operational Range:	Mk 1: 30,000 yards (27,000m);	Mk 2: 35,000 yards (32,000m)
Flight Ceiling:	Mk 1: 55,000ft (17,000m);	Mk 2: 65,000ft (20,000m)
Speed:	Mk 1: 685mph;	Mk 2: 1,370mph.

Appendix Two
Sea Cat

The Sea Cat GWS 21, short-range, surface-to-air missile was intended to replace the Bofors 40mm anti-aircraft gun. Developed by Short brothers of Belfast, it was tested in the early 1960s on board HMS *Decoy*. The first Royal Navy warship which was to have been fitted with the system was HMS *Falmouth* in 1961; however, there were a number of delays in production and it was not ready for *Falmouth* which, for the first seven years of her career, used the 40mm Bofors gun.

Sea Cat was a small, subsonic missile, powered by a two-stage solid fuel rocket motor. It was steered by four cruciformly swept wings and stabilised by four small tail fins. It was guided by a command-line-of-sight system, via a radio link, which meant that flight commands were transmitted by an operator who had both the missile and the target in sight.

The first four County-class destroyers were fitted with the Sea Cat GWS 21, with a modified 'Close-Range Blind-Fire Control Director' (CRBFD) with Type 262 radar. This system offered manual radar-assisted tracking and guidance as well as visual modes. In the later County-class vessels it was replaced by the GWS 22, which could operate in automatic radar-guided or visual-guided modes. It was the GWS 22 which saw active service in the Falklands War, but only one confirmed 'kill' was attributed to it when, on 25 May 1982, HMS *Yarmouth* shot down an Argentine Skyhawk.

The standard 6,600lb launcher carried four missiles and was a manually loaded, trainable launcher incorporating a radio aerial for the command link. At one time over 100 ships from a number of NATO countries were armed with the missile which, by the time of the Falklands War in 1982, was largely obsolete.

Sea Cat Technical Data

Manufacturer:	Short Brothers, Belfast.
Length:	4ft 10in (1.48m).
Diameter:	8¾in (0.22m).
Warhead:	40lb (18kg).
Detonation Mechanism:	Proximity to target.
Engine:	Two-stage, solid fuel, rocket motor.
Wingspan:	2ft 3½in (0.70m).
Range:	1,640ft to 16,404ft (500 to 5,000m)
Speed:	Mach 0.8 (608.96mph).

Appendix Three
Exocet MM38

This French-designed anti-ship missile which, in place of B-turret, was fitted to the second batch of County-class destroyers, earned a fearsome reputation during the Falklands War in 1982. Indeed, it was HMS *Glamorgan* which, thanks to the prompt action of her officers and men, survived an Exocet hit and, until May 1987, she was the only major warship to have done so.

Exocet was developed between 1967 and 1974 by Nord Aviation/Aérospatiale and it entered service soon afterwards. It can be launched from the air, sea, land or from submarines and it is initially guided inertially, until late in its flight when its own radar switches on to locate and hit its target. In order to counter air defences around the target it maintains a very low altitude, skimming at only three to six feet above the sea surface during its approach, thus increasing its chances of avoiding radar detection. With a speed of 1,030 feet per second (315 metres per second), a range of around 25 nautical miles (40 kilometres) and a 360lb (163.3kg) warhead, Exocet is a formidable weapon.

Exocet MM38 Technical Data

Length:	15ft 6in (4.724m)
Diameter:	1ft 2in (0.356m)
Wingspan:	3ft 7in (1.09m)
Weight:	1,500lb (670kg)
Warhead:	360lb (165kg)
Engine:	Solid propellant booster.
Range:	25nm (40 kilometres)
Speed:	1,030 feet per second (315 metres per second)

County Class GMDs

Appendix Four
County Class Technical Data

Programme

Designed in the 1950s this class of eight ships was built in two batches between 1959 and 1970. Batch 1: *Devonshire, Hampshire, Kent, London*: Batch 2: *Fife, Glamorgan, Norfolk, Antrim*, all carried names which had previously been given to cruisers. It was thought that during their initial development the design underwent over 60 changes. These handsome ships brought the Royal Navy into the age of the guided missile, being designed wholly around their main missile system, the controversial GWS1 Sea Slug SAM. Like cruisers which had gone before them these destroyers carried large complements, a high proportion of whom were skilled technicians, a factor which would play a part in their early demise. They were fully air-conditioned and were fitted with stabilisers. The on-board facilities included a fully equipped sickbay and operating theatre, a dental surgery, a 24-hour laundry, a NAAFI kiosk and a closed-circuit TV studio. The ship's company accommodation was of a high standard, with bunks replacing hammocks and a system of centralised general messing, with separate dining halls for senior and junior rates.

Technical Details

Displacement (Standard):	5,440 tons
Displacement (Full Load):	6,200 tons
Length Overall:	520ft – 6in (158.6m)
Beam:	54ft (16.5m)
Draught:	20ft (6m)
Armament:	Four Vickers 4.5-inch Mk VI guns in twin turrets (forward). Batch 2 ships had B turret removed and replaced with a quadruple Exocet MM38 surface-to-surface missile launcher. Two Sea Cat GWS 21/22 quadruple surface-to-air missile launchers. Two single mounted 20mm Oerlikon anti-aircraft guns. Post 1982, Batch 2 ships fitted with triple-barrelled STWS-1 324mm anti-submarine torpedoes. Corvus chaff mortars (post 1982 replaced by Super RBOC)

The County-class destroyers were the first Royal Navy ships to be armed with two different types of guided missile system.

Electronic Equipment:	Type 965 air search radar with AKE1 single 'bedstead' aerial (B1 ships), or AKE2 with double 'bedstead' aerial.

County Class GMDs

Type 901/901M X-band fire-control radar for Sea Slug, with 'searchlight' type aerial.
Type 262 (GWS 21) gunnery fire-control radar on Close-Range Blind-Fire Control Director (CRBFD) (B1 ships)
Type 903 (GWS 22) gunnery fire-control radar on Medium Range System director (B2 ships)
Type 277Q (B1 ships) or Type 278 (B2 ships) height-finding radar.
Type 992 S-band (B1 ships) or Type 992Q (B2 ships), later
Type 974 (later Type 978) X-band high definition navigation radar.
Type 667 Jammers operating in S/C and X-bands
Type 177 and 184 sonar.

Propulsion: Twin screw and twin rudders. COSAG (Combined Steam and Gas Turbines) Y102 plant, consisting of two Babcock & Wilcox, superheat, water-tube boilers, supplying steam to two sets of English Electric geared turbines, which generated 30,000shp. Also four Metrovick (Metropolitan Vickers) G6 gas turbines generating 30,000shp. Maximum speed 32.5 knots. Operational radius of 3,500 nautical miles at 28 knots.

Complement: Average number 471. Thirty-three officers and 438 ratings.

Disposal Details

Devonshire (D02): Laid up 1978. Proposed sale to Egypt failed. 17 July 1984 sunk as target in Western Approaches.

Hampshire (D06): Paid off March 1976. Arrived Briton Ferry 28 April 1979 to be scrapped by Thomas Ward & Co.

Kent (D12): Static training ship at Portsmouth. 14 November 1997 left under tow for scrapping at Alang, India.

London (D16): Sold to Pakistani Navy March 1982, renamed *Babur*. Scrapped 1995.

Fife (D20): Sold to Chilean Navy 12 August 1987, renamed *Blanco Encalada*. Sold for scrap November 2005.

Glamorgan (D19): Sold to Chile September 1986, renamed *Almirante Latorre*. 11 April 2005 sank at sea while under tow to scrapyard.

Norfolk (D21): Sold to Chile June 1984, renamed *Capitán Prat*. September 2008 scrapped in Mexico.

Antrim (D18): Sold to Chile June 1984, renamed *Almirante Cochrane*. December 2010 left Chile under tow for Chinese scrapyard.

ACKNOWLEDGEMENTS

I would like to thank the following for their kind help and assistance:- Terry Bolton, Berkhamsted: Dr Ian Buxton, World Ship Society, Tynemouth: Michael Cassar, Valletta, Malta: Philip Eastwood, Williamson Art Gallery & Museum, Birkenhead: Derek Fox, Portsmouth, Hampshire: Brian Hargreaves, World Ship Society, Tynemouth: Captain David Hart-Dyke CBE LVO ADC RN, Hambledon, Hampshire: Commander David Hobbs RN, Yeovil, Somerset: Commander Ian Inskip RN, Truro, Cornwall: Ossie Jones, Liverpool, Merseyside: John Lambert, Maulden, Bedfordshire: Michael Lennon, Waterlooville, Hampshire: Billy McArthur, Antrim, Northern Ireland: John Morris, Dalgety Bay, Fife: George Mortimore, Action Photos, Ryde, Isle of Wight: Dr Richard Osborne, World Ship Society, Nailsea, Bristol: Steve Parrott, Grimsby, Humberside: Rear-Admiral Christopher Parry, Portsmouth: Selim San, Izmir, Turkey: Don and Dave Smith, Selby, Yorkshire and Wormley, Hertfordshire, respectively: John Simm, Edinburgh, Scotland: Frank Stockton, Llay, Wrexham: Derek Taylor, Colchester, Essex: Adrian Vicary, Maritime Photo Library, Cromer, Norfolk: Jon Wise, World Ship Society.

I would also like to thank the staff at the following for their kind and efficient help, often above and beyond the call of duty:-

All the staff at Cheltenham Public Library, Clarence Street, Cheltenham GL50 3JT.
The Reading Room Staff and Special Production Team at the National Archives, Kew, Richmond TW9 4DU.
Mike Critchley and Steve Bush of Maritime Books, Liskeard, Cornwall, PL14 4EL, for their help, support and for their patience when deadlines were missed.
Finally, to my wife Freda, who spent many long arduous hours patiently line-editing and proof-reading, for her support and encouragement.

County Class GMDs

BIBLIOGRAPHY

Jane's Fighting Ships, all volumes 1960s to 1990s (Jane's Information Group)

The Falklands War, Sunday Times Insight Team (Sphere Books 1982)

Fight for the Falklands, John Laffin, (Sphere Books 1982)

Eyewitness Falklands, Robert Fox (Methuen 1982)

The Falklands Conflict, Christopher Dobson, John Miller, Ronald Payne (Coronet Books, 1982)

Canberra – The Great White Whale Goes to War, Lt Cdr J. L. Muxworthy RN (P&O S. N. Co, 1982)

The Winter War, Patrick Bishop & John Witherow (Quartet Books 1982)

Ships of the Royal Navy, J. J. Colledge & Lt Cdr Ben Warlow (Greenhill Books, 1982)

Our Falklands War, Geoffrey Underwood (Maritime Books 1983)

British Warships Since 1945 – Vol 5 Destroyers, Mike Critchley (Maritime Books, 1984)

No Picnic, Julian Thompson (Leo Cooper, 1985)

The Battle for the Falklands, Max Hastings & Simon Jenkins (Michael Joseph Ltd, 1983)

The Malta Grand Harbour and its Dockyard, Joseph Bonnici & Michael Cassar, 1994.

Conway's All The World's Fighting Ships 1947-1995, Robert Gardiner, Editorial Director, (Conway Maritime Press 1995)

Naval Institute Guide to World Naval Weapons Systems, Norman Friedman (US Naval Institute 1997)

SS Canberra 1957-1997, Neil McCart (Fan Publications 1998)

Ships for a Nation, John Brown & Co, Clydebank, Ian Johnston (West Dumbartonshire Libraries & Museums 2000)

Ordeal by Exocet, Commander Ian Inskip RN (Chatham Publishing 2002)

One Hundred Days, Admiral Sandy Woodward (Harper Collins 2003)

Official History of the Falklands Campaign – Vols 1 & 2, Sir Lawrence Freedman (Routledge, 2005)

There and Back, Admiral Sir Jeremy Black (Elliot & Thompson, 2005)

Bomb Alley – Falkland Islands 1982, David Yates (Pen & Sword Maritime, 2006)

Forgotten Voices of the Falklands, Hugh McManners (Ebury Press & Imperial War Museum, 2007)

Four Weeks in May, David Hart-Dyke (Atlantic Books, 2008)

Down South - A Falklands War Diary, Chris Parry (Viking, 2012)

Journals, Newspapers & Periodicals

All issues of *Navy News* between 1960 and 1987.

Various Commission Books for County-class destroyers.

The Times newspaper 1953 to 1997.

Daily Mirror newspaper.

The News Portsmouth newspaper.

The Herald Plymouth newspaper.

Marine News – Journal of the World Ship Society.

Warships - Journal of the World Ship Society.

Warship - Journal published by Conway Maritime Press.

Documents Consulted at the National Archives, Kew

ADM 1 & ADM 199 Series – Reports (various)

ADM 53 Series – Ships' Logs 1960 to 1984

County Class GMDs

County Class GMDs

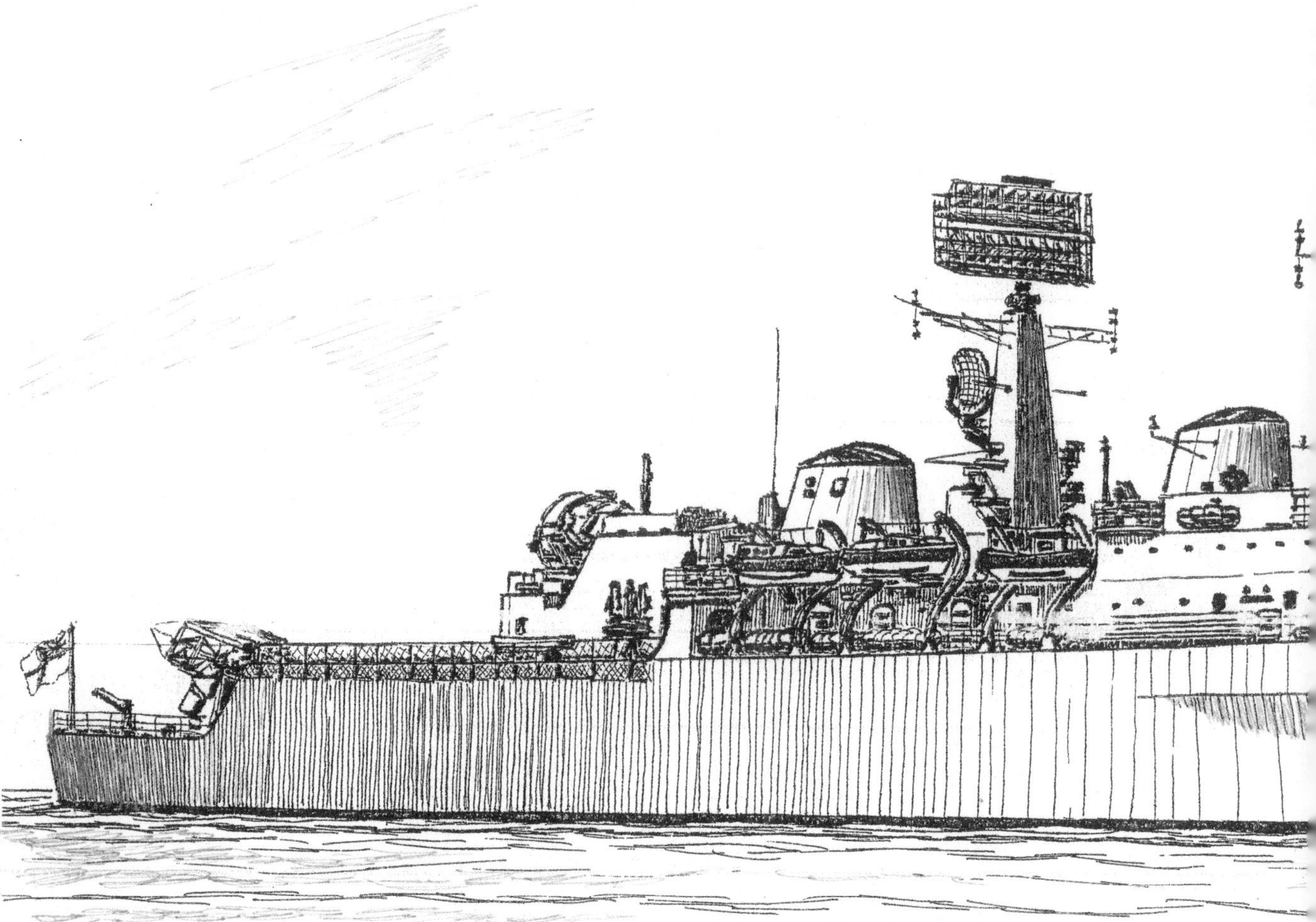

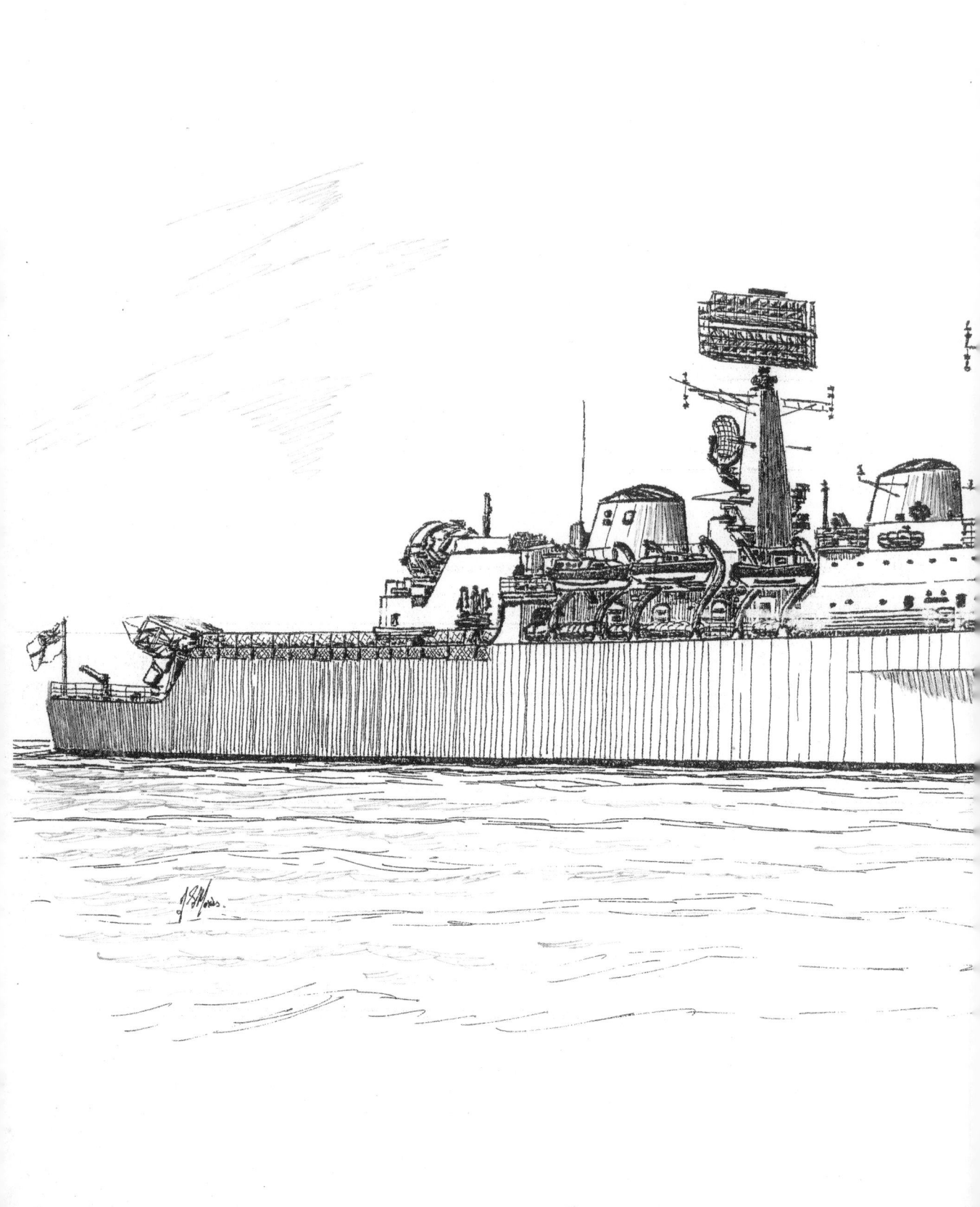